The Natural History of a Mountain Year

The
Natural History
of a
Mountain Year

Four Seasons in
the Wasatch Range

Claude T. Barnes

Foreword by Pamela M. Poulson

University of Utah Press
Salt Lake City

©1996 by the
University of
Utah Press

Printed on acid-
free paper

LIBRARY OF CONGRESS CATALOGING-IN-PUBLICATION DATA

Barnes, Claude T. (Claude Teancum), b. 1884.
    The natural history of a mountain year : four seasons
in the Wasatch range / Claude T. Barnes ; foreword by
Pamela M. Poulson.
        p.   cm.
    Originally published as four separate books.
    ISBN 0-87480-474-4 (alk. paper)
    1. Natural history—Wasatch Range (Utah and Idaho)
2. Natural History—Wasatch Range (Utah and Idaho)—
Outdoor books. 3. Seasons—Wasatch Range (Utah and
Idaho)   I. Title.
QH105.U8B27   1996
508.792'2—dc20   95-51399

To Louise Atkinson

Contents

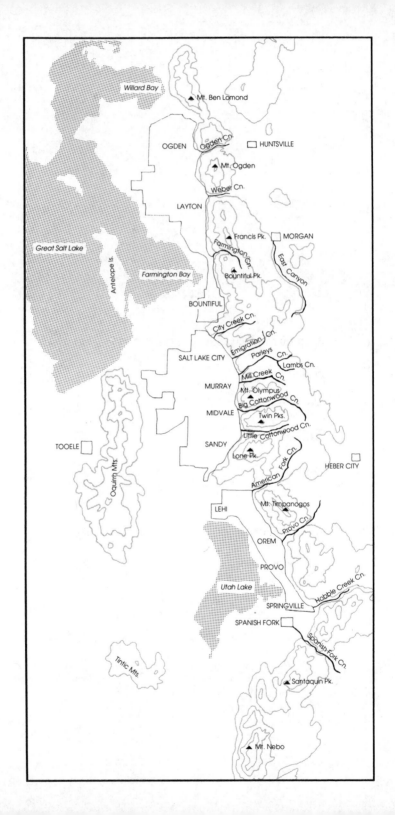

Foreword

"To love nature is to live—to live beyond the uncertain happiness bestowed by the trials and tribulations of man; to live in observation of the great mechanism that somehow pervades every form of life. Man is but one in a tremendous ensemble."

The Wasatch range is a steep-fronted set of mountains that form the north–south backbone of Utah. Rising from the remnants of an ancient sea floor now four thousand feet in elevation to ridges and peaks as high as twelve thousand feet, the range stretches for 150 miles from Logan Canyon at the top of the state to Payson Canyon in the south.

Those of us who live along the Wasatch Front have all had our personal experiences and memories of these mountains. A growing number of us document them in journals, diaries, or mileage logs. What was for a period of time considered a quaint habit, maintaining detailed travel records, has thankfully come into fashion again—though records may now be computer input or even videography. Records of our thoughts and observations will continue to be a treasure for future generations. Such are the writings of Utah naturalist Claude T. Barnes. The opportunity to experience the Wasatch Mountains as they once were is preserved in his diaries, journals, scientific collections, and photographs.

From the early 1920s to the late 1950s, Barnes ventured forth as often as he could from his "home on the foothills just four hundred yards east of the mouth of City Creek Canyon" (359 10th Avenue) into the "declivities" of the Wasatch. He felt that his home was ideally and centrally located for trips into the canyons along the length of the Wasatch. Being an avid bird watcher, Barnes and his associates also recorded many hours of observations at Farmington Bay on the Great Salt Lake.

In the early years Mr. Barnes walked or rode horseback into the Wasatch. In later years, as canyon roads improved, he drove his automobile. Most early excursions were made alone to collect birds and mammals. Later, he concentrated on observing of animal habits and habitats, making extensive documentary collections of plants and insects. Barnes was accompanied by noteworthy naturalists and botanists of the day, such as the astute Louise Atkinson and the peculiar Marcus E. Jones, who had collected and described most of the herbaceous plants of the Wasatch Mountains around the turn of the century.

Regardless of the weather, Barnes "went forth prepared to observe everything alive in the wildlands." He held a collecting permit for both flora and fauna, and carried a gun with him to aid in the collection of any new birds and mammals he encountered. As discovery of new species became more infrequent, he traded his gun for binoculars, a plant press, barometer, insect bottle, and camera.

Barnes carefully recorded not only what he saw but what he felt. In poetic narrative and the vernacular of a slower and more thoughtfully observant time, he wrote of "deserts forlorn," "pine fledged peaks seeped with lingered snow," and "pellucid creeks." He recorded colors, behaviors and "onomatopes"—the written approximation of a bird call or other sound maker. He was a true observer. Not one item of nature escaped his or his associates' notice. He documented every day—and some nights—of the years included in these pages. Herein is a broad accounting of plants, animals, birds, snakes, lizards, fish, insects, spiders, mollusks, fungi, snails, and amphibians, as well as views, sounds, smells, textures, and flavors. "The truth is, there is scarcely an animal, bird, flower, tree, reptile, insect, fungus, or snail that is without beauty when closely examined." Do we see so much on our own outings? "Can it be that such a thing of intricate beauty is unnoticed yet within our grasp at every wayside?"

Barnes selected the most exciting entry for each given date and published them in four volumes from 1956 through 1959 as *The Natural History of a Wasatch Winter, Spring,* and so on. Shortly thereafter he issued a limited edition that combined all four seasons under the title *The Natural History of a Wasatch Year.* Of his work he said, "The writing of this book . . . is but a token of love of a naturalist for the beauties and mysteries of the wildwoods."

In reading the descriptions republished here, we should be tolerant of the common language of the time. Archaic terms, spellings, and nicknames are found throughout the book. Not only did Mr. Barnes call raptors, "raptores," and muddy streams "roily," but senior citizens are referred to as "old codgers," western coneflowers are called "niggerheads," and Native Americans are called "Red Men." There are other examples of what we would today call politically incorrect.

Biologists may note that some of the scientific binomials have changed since Mr. Barnes recorded them. Box elder, which Barnes called water ash was then correctly documented as *Acer interium*. Of course today, several botanical congresses later, we record that common tree as *Acer negundo*. Although most bird and mammal nomenclature has remained the same in the intervening years, plant names in some cases have changed drastically, especially common names. A listing of plant synonymy is included at the end of this book.

Probably the best reason for republishing these journals is to remind us of what used to be. Though Mr. Barnes had more than we, what we still have now is well worth close observation. "Nature divulges its innermost secrets only to them who consistently tread its by-paths, ever alert to hear or see its undisturbed manifestations. . . . "

The Wasatch Mountains are now much different than they were, particularly the foothills. Some of Barnes's intimate sites have been obliterated by freeways, suburbs, and shopping malls. Certain birds, flowers, amphibians, and insects are gone. Barnes speaks familiarly of the duck hawks (peregrine falcons) that he sees every day clutching ducks from the mouth of the Jordan River or sparrows from his own yard. Today, we cherish the single nesting pair we see on the overhangs of Hotel Utah or above the North Salt Lake stone quarries. He speaks of flushing a turkey vulture off the carcass of a putrifying bear-killed sheep on the foothills of the Wasatch and of alfalfa mowers slashing snakes and game bird nests along the benches. Some conditions still remain: "Many boisterous canyon streams, some temporarily turbid with sand, are going to waste in the inland lake of brine. . . . "

Barnes admonishes us to partake of and enjoy the living world around us. His attitude was "constantly one of interest and wonderment, interest in the distribution and ecological factors affecting species and wonderment in the overwhelming development and congruity of it all. . . . "

What we have of the Wasatch Mountains now is all we will ever have. We should visit the Wasatch, observe its intricacies, learn its secrets, savor its beauties. We should preserve as much of it as we can for the future. "More and more we realize that the mountains should belong to all the people, not to one class or another, but equally to all for their recreation and enjoyment; and a great part of that enjoyment is knowledge of the varied forms of life in the wild woods."

Claude T. Barnes left us a snapshot of the Wasatch Mountains of the past, some natural treasures of which no longer exist. Every day, more and more of Barnes's beloved seasons of the Wasatch are disappearing. What will we leave for the future? One hopes we will leave more than just a record of intimate places and experiences that once were.

Pamela M. Poulson
Red Butte Garden and Arboretum
October, 1995

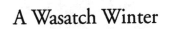

A Wasatch Winter

INTRODUCTION

Although this book has the chronology of a single season, in reality it brings together writings made at the various locales described during the course of over thirty years observations of the natural history of the Wasatch mountains. Seasons vary—there are early seasons and late seasons, wet years and dry years, autumns without frost and autumns with sleet and snow, winters so mild that violets bloom on New Year's Day, and winters so snowy and cold that bushes and valley fences are for weeks almost buried—, hence a canyonside of gorgeous coloring one year may on the corresponding day the following year be either yet green or blizzard-stricken and unattractive. The variation of nature's development, however, seldom exceeds a week either way from normal; and thus, for instance, year after year, the Audubon warbler arrives about the fourteenth of April. One thing is certain: each page herein was written on the actual date it bears, notwithstanding, perhaps, years before or after that of its adjoining page; but in some instances there may be a later addendum.

The Wasatch mountain range is the north-south geologic backbone of the state of Utah, the division line of drainage between the Colorado river system at the east and the desert, deprived of outlet, the Great Basin at the west. From the middle of the Wasatch, forming a great T, the Uintah mountains run eastward to the very base of the mighty Rockies of Colorado, being the only mountains in America with an east-west axis.

The lowest surface at the west of the Wasatch is occupied by the Great Salt Lake, which at an altitude of 4200 feet actually at places laves the foothills of the mountains. Excepting these foothills, which feed it with brooks of limpid purity, the lake is surrounded by the desert, which constitutes the well known "artemesian" biotic province of Dice and others. Sage brush (*Artemisia tridentata*), greasewoods and the atriplexes robe all but the very highest reaches of the mountains.

The loftiest peak of the Wasatch is Mount Timpanogos (11,957 feet); the greatest of the Uintas is King (13,498); and the highest point of the Colorado Rockies is Mount Elbert (14,420). Having studied the flora and fauna of all three mountains, we are convinced that Dice is correct in the inclusion of them in one Colorado biotic province. With few exceptions the birds are identical; but the Colorado Rockies

3

have the beautiful Abert squirrel (*Sciurus aberti concolor*) not found here; and the Utah white oak (*Quercus gambellii*), which grows all over the Wasatch, does not occur in Colorado at all. Some birds that breed on such high ground as Gray's Peak in Colorado descend to the Wasatch in winter; for example, the water pipit (*Anthus spinoletta alticola*) and Townsend's solitaire (*Myadestes townsendi townsendi*).

Nature divulges its innermost secrets only to them who consistently tread its by-paths, ever alert to hear or see its undisturbed manifestations; and thus, notwithstanding that this book is about a definite mountain range, your mountain wherever it may be has forms of life so similar that we likely have at once a common ground of inspiration and joy.

This book is the last of a series of which *The Natural History of a a Wasatch Spring, The Natural History of a Wasatch Summer,* and *The Natural History of a Wasatch Autumn* have already been published.

Knowing my interest in such matters, many people throughout the years have brought to me for identification a great number of uncommon birds, insects, reptiles and even mammals, some of them, such as the rubber boa, being rare; for all of which I am truly grateful. Sometimes the cooperation has had another phase; for instance, my friend, Elias L. Day, saw to it that I had a portion of a roast from the first moose ever legally taken in Utah, a fine bull killed by John E. Plattner of Sandy, Utah, in a willow park near the Whitney Ranger Station of the Bear River unit on the north slope of the Uinta mountains, on September 27, 1958.

It must be apparent to all who read these books, that, although the author has with meticulous care identified the species and subspecies of animal and botanical life that have won his attention, his attitude has been constantly one of interest and wonderment, interest in the distribution and ecological factors affecting species and wonderment in the overwhelming development and congruity of it all. There is an eventual mystery that he cannot solve, and, as a naturalist, he can only in humility await the development of greater knowledge.

May, 1959

CLAUDE T. BARNES

4

DECEMBER 22

It is in winter that fog sometimes enshrouds the valley and hoar frost enlaces all the trees, a condition of extreme cold that may endure for a week or more. At such a time objects a hundred yards away appear vague in outline, and at double that distance, invisible.

During such periods house sparrows congregate among the frosted branches of trees and leafless shrubs, such as lilacs, and venture forth only occasionally for a crumb or a lawn seed, while a robin may mope in a tall bare-limbed cottonwood and emit only a perfunctory call.

This frozen mist is more intense and brilliant in moonlight; in fact, in cold, foggy nights even barbed wires of field fences seem brittle enough to break by hand, and strong power-lines really do snap from the sharp whip of a falling limb. Young spruce branches, which in summer are tough and resilient, now, frosted and stiff, break off readily when bent with one's hand.

Hoar-frost, a mere assemblage of quadrangular prisms indiscriminately piled, is the lacy adornment of all nature in the freezing atmosphere of a heavy fog. In it the monticoline white-tailed jack rabbit seems to delight to sit on a knoll until every protruding hair of its pelage is as frost-laden as a twig.

Tabular hoar-frost crystals—those that occur in platelike aggregations, as distinguished from the columnar ones—are the more common forms in the foggy, zero weather of winter, just as the columnar are most prevalent during autumnal and spring frosts; nonetheless, the twig we hold as we write, brought quickly indoors, is covered with rime-crystals that stick up like quarter inch fingers of airy snow. So it goes! nature has infinite variety of beauty and form, whether of flower or snow, mountain contour or floating cloud. "Hoar" is from the old English word "har", meaning "old", "venerable", hence when we come upon a weed that is grey-headed with frost, the aptness of the term is at once apparent.

Pluck a feather from a barnyard fowl and you will discover it, also, to be a work of art. It consists of a stem or *scapus,* constituting its entire central axis, this being divided into the quill or *calamus,* the hollow basal portion, and the shaft or *rhachis,* the solid terminal part to which the fibres are attached. The webs or *pogonia* (from the Greek "beard") are the fibres implanted on the shaft, generally having barbules or hooks along the edges that interlock with each other. That is why the feathers of a bird lie more or less flat and do not show hoar frost, whereas the hair of a mammal like a horse bristles up considerably in zero weather and displays the frost as might a twig.

One need not be a student of morphology to perceive the infinite variety, complexity and beauty of nature's forms, and, if he desire more than the figures apparent to the ordinary eye, he has but to use the microscope to find a new world of configuration.

DECEMBER 23

Whenever in a sweeping blizzard of the foothills we examine those pretty rosy finches belonging to the genus *Leucosticte,* which is Greek for "white" plus "pricked", we are convinced that the name refers to the nasal plumules of the bird, which are not only so distinct as quite to cover the nostrils but also so bristly and firm as to suggest prickles.

At any rate there the birds are, swarming among the weeds protruding through drifted snow. All of the leucostictes have either pink or reddish on their flanks or silvery gray on their rectrices or tail quills, or on their remiges or wing quills. Unlike ordinary sparrows they are terrestrial in habit, finding enjoyment and food on the weeded snowbank rather than among the branches of trees.

The gray-crowned rosy finch or (*Leucosticte tephrocotis tephrocotis*) appears to us more plentiful than any other snow-birds of its kind, since it occurs here in huge flocks during all of autumn, winter and part of spring. It has a black forehead, grayish-white nasal tufts that give it its generic name, a general body shade of chestnut brown, but rump, flank, upper and lower tail coverts of pink.

The Hepburn rosy finch (*Leucosticte tephrocotis littoralis*), one of our winter visitors, could easily be mistaken for the gray-crowned, in that it merely shows more gray on the sides of its head. The finesse of ornithology! That word *tephrocotis* is from the Greek *tephros,* ash-colored, and *kotis,* the top and back of the head.

The black rosy finch (*L. strata*) is so like the gray-crowned that one would say it only replaces chestnut brown with brownish black. The word *atrata* is from the Latin *atratus,* black as in mourning. It is commoner here than the Hepburn; but the three varieties of rosy finches sometimes flock together on snow-drifted weedlands, and it is often difficult to estimate relative numbers.

Since the naturalist never desires to kill, except to supply food for his larder or specimens for his scientific collection, it is understandable that any act in violation of that rule causes repentant regret. It is little wonder that he should not forgive in himself or others any act that is thoughtless enough to be wanton.

Despite the falling snow, a dozen domestic sparrows have just engaged in an imbroglio on the stone parapet of my porch, with the center of attraction a female snapping viciously at her insistent suitors. I surmise that the little coquette has indicated a mating mood, for propagation among them at this time of year is dependent only upon a warm, snug nesting site, and ready access to food such as may be obtained in a manured corral or at a chicken feed-yard.

DECEMBER 24

It being a day of wintry fog and cold on Farmington bay, even a horse standing in a rusty field looks rimy and forlorn. Above it in a high tree a blackish object sitting on a down-bent limb arresting our attention, our seaman's glasses so clearly penetrate the mist that they reveal its identity—a golden eagle preening itself contentedly despite the dismal atmosphere. Solitary and frosted it may be but not unhappy and lonesome, notwithstanding that nowhere do we see its lifetime mate. What a self-reliant and magnificent bird!

We move on; salt grass, weeds, sunflower stalks are all dry and straw-color above the snow-whitened land; but docks are still maroon. Canals of sluggish water are unfrozen, but boys are skating on the ponds where a few weeks before we saw thousands of water birds feeding and swimming contentedly.

A fairly large hawk in the distance is pecking at some carcass on the dreary ice; and then to please us it flies directly over our heads but a few yards away, disclosing unmistakably that it is a female marsh hawk, a common inhabitant of these ponds whatever the season.

The north pond is rough with snow-frozen ridges like waves, which technically we should call "sastrugi"; but the pond at the south of it over the dyke for two hundred yards or more is a sheet of smooth clear ice, a demonstration for farmers of the protection of even a ten foot high windbreak.

A killdeer, a male marsh hawk, a few horned larks comprise the avian delights of the bay, notwithstanding a score of duck hunters are hopefully waiting.

To tell the truth, few sportsmen are out for the meat they might obtain; after all, the fascination of hunting on the marshes, when one is clothed with waterproof garments so warm as to resist near-zero blizzards, consists in the feeling of wild freedom and adventurous self-reliance, in the occasional cup of hot coffee from the vacuum bottle, the pat of the dog companion snuggling at one's feet, and in the exciting observation of the trend of a distant flock.

On our return the golden eagle has merely moved to another tree.

We betake ourselves into the winter-chilled mountains where old snow mounds the verdure of the hillsides as well as the brook-sung cloughs. There before us, running from a snow-weighed sage to the roots of a dwarf or mountain maple, is the trail of a white-footed mouse, with its tiny foot marks showing clearly, followed by a line-mark of the tail. It is in all likelihood that of the deer mouse (*Peromyscus maniculatus rufinus*) which is the member of its genus that we have taken here in summer. It is a wood brown mouse with dense, thick pelage and with a clearly bicolored tail. This little deer-mouse or wood-mouse, as it is sometimes called, stores some food for winter but ventures forth on the snow for seed. It is said to appropriate bird nests for its habitation in summer, but such we have never seen.

DECEMBER 25

Christmas has a charm for most men. Not that they all believe in Jesus as the Saviour of mankind; not, indeed, that all give credence to the New Testament or the Bible. All men, whatever their race or creed, do however enjoy the spirit of kindness, tolerance, neighborliness, friendship, unselfishness, charity, and love; men at some time or other ponder on the fleetingness of life and devote themselves to the emblem of goodwill, whatever that emblem may be.

Nature itself has no such perennial demonstrations of universal brotherhood; on the contrary, so far as we can see, it cares not for anything, not even the perpetuation of individual species, and, least of all, for the predominance of the individual within the species. Nature, in other words, permits the start of the seed, the germ, the ovum, fetus, embryo, on its course; and cares not how you win your way. The result is an endless conflict between mammals, birds, insects, fish, trees, and microbes of less noticeable existence. The truth is, that the bills of some raptorial birds and the teeth of some carnivorous mammals are so made that they would starve if they could not feed upon the flesh of other species.

Thus in this wide world of ours such antagonisms are so apparent that one cannot restrain the thought that man is superior only in his vanity and we are to the lesser kinds of existence, such as the mice and the shrews, but the elephants of their experience. Men come and go; ants breed, work and pass away; birds sing, die and new ones sing; and so *ad infinitum*. Nature does not say "fight"; rather, it is wholly indifferent to what you do.

We know, however, the characteristics of that expression of nature known as *Homo sapiens*—man—we know him and all his frailties; furthermore, we see in him the expression of some of nature's highest attainments. Nevertheless, as we inspect the intricate tunnels of the ant, we are not sure, not positive that man represents the acme of development.

Nature ignores the vanities of man or beast in its inexorable movements. This, however, it does recognize; a life of purity and sweetness, such as that of the great Christ, avoids many of the pitfalls that nature spreads before us all.

One cannot ever again be arrogant, bigoted, proud and supercilious, after prying into the secrets of biochemical cytology and discovering how unified are the origins of life, whether in the sea urchin or man, and how the ultimate particle must be practically the same in all.

Whether you be an eschatologist, who is certain of such final things as death, resurrection, immortality and judgment, or one, who like ourselves humbly does not claim to know, let use gather about yon sizzling pine-log and give adoration to the symbol of love, and at the same time say, as might a stranger among us, the highest joy must consist of "the right resolve, right word, right act, right life, right effort, right thinking and right meditation."

DECEMBER 26

One of the most pleasing diversions of a bright winter day is to visit different locales with eyes and ears eager to see and hear the birds that visit us usually only when the ground is wrought with snow. To commence, we drive to the mouth of the Jordan.

It is a mild winter, with sloughs thinly frozen in the night and thawed by the warmth of day, one of those times when a wide-eyed violet might peek at us from its sheltered nook beside the south wall, before we venture beyond the dripping eaves of our beloved home.

There they are, the birds of our expectation, shunning the snow, ignoring the cold, and apparently enjoying chill waters—a pied-billed grebe, a ring-billed gull, a wood duck, a lesser scaup duck, an American golden eye, some lesser snow geese, and a flock of whistling swan. (This time the observations of years are crowded into a single day).

Repairing to the oak-skeletoned hillside, we notice in the winterly sky a rough-legged hawk (*Buteo lagopus s. johannis*), which with the glasses we distinguish from the red-tail by its lack of red on the tail, from the Swainson by its white primaries, and from the ferruginous by its black belly. We have plenty of time to study it as it soars repeatedly over us; furthermore, at this time the Swainson and ferruginous are in the southlands.

We stop at a boxelder tree to watch a flock of western evening grosbeaks eating seeds; in an orchard we linger beneath a flock of Bohemian waxwings; and later see a northern shrike attack a winter-visiting tree sparrow (*Spizella arborea ochracea*), which latter we identify by its brown cap and black breast spot. Feeding largely on insects, mice and small birds, this shrike has a hooked bill that is a death-dealing weapon indeed. There is a question yet undetermined—whether it impales its victims on a thorn to hold them securely while it eats them (it has weak legs) or to store them for future use.

In the course of the day we see some gray-crowned leucostictes, Shufeldt's juncos, a water ouzel on a creek, and, as we enter the home yard, robins are fluttering about a cucumber vine, and a red-shafted flicker is interested in a Boston ivy. The knowing English sparrows still refuse the new feed-box because it resembles a trap and swings on the hook from which it is suspended.

The end of the year precedes a glorious reawakening in spring; the end of life forebodes the eternal darkness of the tomb. Would that in the despair of his heart man could see some spark of light in the unfathomable reality ahead!

If man be but an organism in the ensemble of existence, a unit so insignificant that in the billions of years to come he, like the dinosaurs, will have long passed from the scene, then he will have exemplified an astonishing degree of intelligence, nothing more; an intelligence shared to some degree by everything that creeps, crawls, swims, runs or flies. In not one whit does nature care for the destiny of man, for it is wholly indifferent whom or what it aids or harms.

DECEMBER 27

Nature strives for counter balance; the lion imprisoned in its cage grows a mane of length and beauty; the lion free in the wide, open veldt scratches his mane away beneath the thorny shrubs of the grassland. The cougar can climb high from danger, hence he is not favored with either the courage or the strength of the African lion. The rattlesnake has fangs filled with poison hence it cannot run so fast as the blue racer. The jack rabbit can jump and scamper away rapidly hence it cannot fight it out on the spot like a weasel. A skunk has a sickening odor but nature requites it with freedom from molestation; a porcupine bears a complicated burden of quills but only the fisher and sometimes the mountain lion attack it with impunity. The evening primrose depends upon the moths of night hence cannot afford to display its lively corollas in the day.

So it is, one thing after another; grasp too much and you give on the way; have no ambition and you endure the slothfulness of decadence. This truth always bear in mind: nature rewards use, whether it be muscle, tendril or brain; and it makes the sweetest flowers, the biggest trees, the finest bodies and the greatest intellects where demand is made upon it to produce them. It likes symmetry and equivalence, poise and equipose, requital and recompense, and it has a habit of rewarding them who try.

So multiform is the evidence of it that evolution is now seldom denied by intellectual honesty. The theory, that all organisms sprang from an original, simple type of life, and that it in turn arose somehow from inanimate nature, goes back to the ancient Greeks. Nowadays we have much to prove its truth—comparative anatomy, geological succession, geographic distribution, classification, embryology, serotology and genetics. Darwin's thesis that changes in species have come about through natural selection is to my thinking no longer regarded as the major cause; nevertheless, although much has been done in cytogenetics to prove that the genes and chromosomes are very important in the transmission of hereditary characteristics and in the creation of mutations, and, although there has been much study on the influence of climate, isolation and environmental factors, no one can yet say with certainty what causes species to change their form. In 1867, eight years after the appearance of Darwin's *Origin of Species,* one F. Jenkins gave such an overwhelming criticism of the Darwin theory, and let us say, of the modern claim of the importance of mutations caused by genes and chromosomes as well, that I at least have never seen it successfully answered. Jenkins' simple contention was this: no matter how favorable a variation chosen by natural selection might be, and, we might add, no matter how desirable a mutation produced by genes and chromosomes, it would be swamped and vanished in no time by the sheer numbers of regular breeding.

DECEMBER 28

Certain apt and truthful similies with respect to animals and birds have crept into the language. Thus; frugal as an ant, uncouth as a bear, industrious as a bee, sportive as a butterfly, deceitful as a wild cat, poetic as a cicada, faithful as a dog, harmless as a dove, majestic as an eagle, cunning as a fox, timid as a hare, innocent as a lamb, cheerful as a lark, vigilant as a lynx, garrulous as a magpie, wise as an owl, lascivious as a sparrow, wily as a spider, sunshiny as a swallow, graceful as a swan, rapacious as a vulture and cruel as a wolf—all have the merit of truthful comparison. Others are not so happy. Thus the bat should not symbolize blindness, for not only does it have remarkably good night-seeing eyes, but as far as we know, it is the only animal capable of avoiding objects in its flight when its eyes have been either sealed or entirely removed. Crows should not especially exemplify longevity for in this respect they fall far short of either the tortoise or the swan. A goose is not foolish; indeed the Canadian honker is in our opinion the wisest of all birds. A gull is not gullible nor easily duped; indeed the California gull of these mountains manifests intelligence of the highest order. We prefer to believe that "gull" comes from "stuff" and "cram", in other words from the Dutch *gullen* and the French *engouler,* meaning to devour voraciously. Of course it is a mere fable that the raven brings bad luck and forbodes death and infection; it is true it feeds upon or *ravens* dead bodies, perhaps not disdaining the corpses of the battlefield; but in doing so it prevents rather than brings infection. The word "raven" is from the Old French *raviner,* meaning to take by force, ravish, hence we derive the modern application, to devour ravenously. Maggots are used in wartime to eat dead flesh in which blood-poisoning has set; and the raven's work is similar. Serpents are not particularly wise, despite allegorical references.

We might suggest a hundred new but truthful similies. Thus: affectionate as a barn swallow, alert as a sharp-shinned hawk, angry as a cornered rattlesnake, apprehensive as an avocet, beautiful as a Bohemian waxwing, boisterous as a long-crested jay, bothersome as a woodrat, brilliant as a humming bird, busy as disturbed ants, changeable as the gorget of a humming bird, chaste as a bluebird, cheerful as a chickadee, clean as a wild cat, clear as the song of a meadowlark, coarse as the bellow of a bittern, courageous as a badger, courteous as a cedar waxwing, dainty as a fawn, delicate as a spider's web, dignified as a black-necked stilt, diligent as a kinglet, dull as a porcupine, content as a porcupine, dumb as a butterfly, early as a crossbill's nest, fierce as a weasel, gentle as a bluebird, graceful as a mountain lion, harsh as a night heron, haughty as an eagle, impetuous as a humming bird, inconspicuous as a hiding quail, indolent as a porcupine, keen as a dragon fly, lonely as a horned owl, nearsighted as a wolverine, obedient as a fawn, pure as the song of a hermit thrush, restless as a water ouzel, sad as a Say's phoebe, slow as a porcupine, sneaky as a cougar, stupid as a shrew, watchful as a magpie, bloodthirsty as a weasel, faithful as an eagle, and so on.

11

DECEMBER 29

The keeper of a marshy duck club, which we frequently visit, has turned muskrat-trapper, to occupy the idle hours of the closed hunting season; and if the number of reeded hovels in the icy slough be an indication he will have a hundred pelts by spring. It is surprising how this resourceful little muskrat manages to find for food the roots of such aquatic plants as sedges, and does not hesitate to devour a frozen carp hibernating in the mud. If the pond be covered with ice the rat is usually limited to under-surface foods, though one of them has been known to us to burrow into snow for succulent grasses.

In swimming beneath ice the muskrat is said by some to expel its breath against the icy ceiling and re-inhale the bubble when it becomes oxidized; by others, to rise only to take in bubbles already there. We have seldom come upon ice clear enough to reveal the facts, and certain it is that before the muskrat can eat its under-ice food, it must rise to the floor of home or go through some other vent to the outer air. By the way, it is surprising how big carp frozen as stiff as boards in the ice, revive and swim with the advent of spring. The nutria (*Myocastor coypus*), a South American brownish rodent like a muskrat, but two feet long in body length, having been released in these parts, seems to be surviving.

Rambling from slough to mountain, we notice that despite long-endured freezing weather tiny oyster-shell mushrooms grow with surprising freshness and profusion beneath the bark of old cottonwood trees. They are small and brownish, like little fingers, but vigorous and succulent. Throughout the sylvan year there is at all times somewhere something vernal in sturdy freshness and beauty; so every hour of life has some wee sparkle of hope and happiness.

None of those liquid woodnotes that delight the springtime ear now issues from the leafless branches of the canyon ravine; rather everything there is stark and drear, responsive only to the susurrant drift of wind-kissed snow. In the by-paths of life are frozen dells that need only the warmth of understanding to thaw them into beauty and promise. No matter how lonely your heart, someone, somewhere, is hoping you will come.

Very early the naturalist learns that the truth of reality is independent of his belief concerning it. High in the mountains he may be plodding through pathless snow in the belief that he is utterly alone and unobserved, only to discover that a mountain lion hidden in a big fir has been watching him all the time; he may be about to touch a pretty black-widow spider, only to be warned that her bite is deadly even to man. So it goes: on the pine-clustered mount he may gaze into the rich blueness of the sky, wonder at its deep ineffability, and then reverently picture a heaven there, only to realize later that he has no proof of the reality of his dream. Nature is a great leveler, for all the wealth, all the vanity of this world mean nothing to its impartial and inexorable laws.

DECEMBER 30

On the snow-covered foothills one would expect to see some living creatures, especially cottontails in sage-fledged gullies, but somber silence reigns. It is true that here and there in a cove or on an exposed knoll appear the tell-tale footprints of rabbit, weasel or bird, or the scooping furrows of a hawk-tail where it touched with a swoop upon the snow; but woodland denizens are both scarce and seclusive. Nevertheless, there is something for them to eat: tender maple buds in the intervales; alder catkins dangling brown over an ice-choked brook; crisp rust-colored oak leaves yet unfalling on the slopes and still harboring nuts and bugs; tall dry grass bunches and tender green shoots on bare sun-warmed southern exposures. It is deep snow, not cold, that sometimes makes subsistence a tragedy; nevertheless it is surprising how many animals in bad weather seek a snug hole and sleep, not hibernation, but sleep.

Suddenly a mountain hare (*Lepus townsendi townsendi*) bounds up a gulch to a ridge, looking like a frosted white lamb; and there in a thickly wooded clough is a huge deserted nest, the twig-built bushel-basket home of the magpie. This mountain hare or white-tailed jack rabbit, which is almost uniformly dark gray above in the summer, becomes white in winter, except for the blackish tips of its ears. It makes trails to the haystacks of the upper valleys, where on freezing moonlight nights farmers are accustomed to sink themselves to their shoulders in the hay, and thus kept warm, shoot the rabbits one by one as they leisurely approach to feed. These hares do much idle sitting on frosty nights, hence thousands of them each year are run down by automobiles whose approaching lights bewilder them. Magpies, ravens, hawks, and coyotes watch the highways for such easily obtained meals. In fact, compared with the black-tailed jack rabbits of the lowlands, these mountain hares seem mentally obtuse, slow and weak. Among the many that we have shot we can scarcely recall one that was not dead when we reached it; whereas the desert jack rabbit is so tenacious of life that nearly every other one of the hundreds we have killed had to be clubbed or kicked behind the ears before it succumbed. We are not proud of it now, yet wheat farmers must live. In the course of years we have noticed an equal dissimilarity of tenacity between gallinaceous birds, such as grouse, and raptorial birds, such as owls. Almost invariably an owl dies fighting, even after it is fatally shot, having in this respect the fortitude of a miniature grizzly bear.

It is difficult to understand what makes one animal so tenacious of life and brave, another so spiritless and timid, when physically there may be little difference in their powers. Generally, when we separate birds and mammals into their orders, such as *Falconiformes* (birds of prey), *Anseriformes* (geese, ducks, etc.), *Carnivora* (flesh-eating mammals), *Rodentia* (knawing mammals), we arrive at the conclusion that the animal that fights hardest to get its daily prey is the one that dies hardest before the gun.

DECEMBER 31

The end of the year is here, the end of a fascinating, wending year, and with it the end of many a joyous and arduous year in one ensemble of delightful notation and experience. We almost regret its coming to a close; for every day of it has been a sweet diversion, every day a new experience in the infinitude of nature; every night a dreamy but hopeful gaze towards an incomprehensibe eternity. How weak, how lonely, how inconsequential we are! We live, we die, and have the reward that the deeds of accomplishment and good really survive. The fitting of them into the plan of eternity is something we do not understand but, nevertheless, we do not deny.

Having surveyed tree, flower, and bug, reptile, worm and bird, we have come to this conclusion: all species of nature are somehow interrelated. How they come, whither they go, no one really knows.

The Wasatch mountains have a few distinctive forms of both animal and vegetable life, but not more distinctive than those of the Alps, the Andes, the Himalayas, and many other mountains of this terrestrial sphere. Wherever man may be, whether in the Arctic or the Equator, the jungles of India or the frosted upper reaches of the Rockies, he meets life in the wild, life of little variation of form and no variation of eventual purpose.

"Man is that he might have joy" is true throughout nature; every species is that it might have joy, mature—and pass away.

As we write these lines, at the end of the warmest December 31st ever so far recorded here (1942—58 degrees), we feel that we have merely wandered in a big circle and are back again to our starting point. It is like reaching the end of the dictionary—there is no more. In the group before the sputtering log someone wonders what is the last word in the English dictionary, and upon investigation, it turns out that save for the obsolete Kentish "zyxt", meaning "see", the last word is "zymurgy", the art of wine-making. One thing leads to another, and, as the embers flicker low and bells begin to sound, the host gets from the cellar a bottle of home-made raspberry wine.

Of this we may be certain at the end of the year: there will be another year. Whether it be for you or us individually seems little to concern nature; but another year will surely arrive; and our part in it is to dwell in the sweetness of hope.

Some day *a priori* reasoning, designating that form of knowledge which comes by conjecture alone and not through experience, hence that form which is presumptive, without examination, may persuade intelligent men, for in it are involved all supernatural claims; but for the present the naturalist can recognize only knowledge that is *a posteriori*, meaning that which is derived from the observation of facts and known only through experience. The naturalist denies nothing—he awaits with hope and humility the great answer.

JANUARY 1

Crisp and cold is the early winter-glazed morning, a morning fresh from the knells of a parted year, exultant with the paeans of a new. The year may have its calendar-made birthday, though why even a follower of Apollo and Artemis should rejoice over the passage of time is incongruous; nevertheless, nature is a constantly recurring ensemble of birthdays, a continual expression of life's infinite forms, all striving for subsistence, all working for survival and reproduction.

It is a wintry morning of zest and hope; to the naturalist one of joy, for to him is assigned the delightful undertaking of describing nature's appearances throughout one entire year in the Wasatch mountains. The purpose is to represent facts and ascertain truths concerning all forms of wild life there, for only in regions untrammeled by man does nature give the fullest expression of its meaning.

At the entrance to a canyon, where the atmosphere is cold and the sky drear, snow-dust is floating like infinitesimal particles from a flour mill, and settling upon trail, tree and boulder. Ephemeral powder seldom lingering in just that form, it is really snow-dust, which the Germans call *schneegestober*, for it is raised by a wind from the ground, and floated into the atmosphere horizontally, even under a clear blue sky.

Further upward, in a bank-walled cove, snow-maculated yet crusted with ankle-deep leaves, a brook guggles peacefully at the bottom of its channel where overhanging, rime-fringed birches, alders and willows adorn banks beneath stark maples and cottonwoods. Straight, strong and bare, the cottonwoods stand, as if with paternal care over the slender trunks and drooping limbs of their water-loving kindred below.

All nature appears to slumber, save where chinking juncos throng over the dried weeds of yonder hillside and long-tailed chickadees peck contentedly about maple-twigs. Signs of life are not plentiful, but they are there in the canyon, whether in bud or den, for day by day will come the variety, the mystery and the beauty of their unfolding.

As we look upon the snow-drifted mountains and think of the homes of the various mammals we have seen thereon, we involuntarily reflect upon the beavers on the other side—Beaver and Shingle Creek—, for their habitation is called a "lodge". We think of the inviolable wolves and the dutiful coyotes that live in rocky "dens". The elk and deer toward Black Mountain above us are dwelling in their "yards", snow-trodden nooks embowered within spruce and pine. We have never quite applied the word "lair" to the sanctuary of the mountain lion; but we have often spoken of the "aerie" of the golden eagle, well known in these hills.

Into each of our lives come moments of exquisite joy, moments when we know not only that we love but that we are loved in return. Money, avarice, distinction matter not—we have tasted the divine where such mundane things are unknown.

JANUARY 2

With a temperature range of from forty-two to sixty-one degrees Farenheit, the year 1943 was the warmest New Year's day recorded up to that time in this valley; and from that event we have been induced to scan our notes to ascertain what effect mid-winter warmth has upon the occurrence here of both rare and non-seasonal birds. A short stretch of either mild or extremely cold weather is apparently of little consequence, but record snows, like those of 1916-17, are disastrous indeed. In the season of 1948-49 there were 95 days with snow on the ground, and 74.5 inches of snow for the winter.

Townsend's solitaire (*Myadestes townsendi townsendi*), hardy breeder in mountains from Alaska to Wyoming, descends regularly in mid-winter from blizzard blown peak and ridge to lower slopes and even to our own playa flats and marsh-lands, where, much to our surprise, it sometimes gives an exquisite rendition of mountain music.

Along the sloughs at the mouths of the Jordan and the Bear rivers a few summer residents may linger throughout winter, even when thousands of their relatives have departed to southern climes. In this category come such birds as Wilson's snipe (*Capella gallinago delicata*), the cinnamon teal (*Anas cyanoptera septentrionalium*), black-crowned night heron (*Nycticorax nycticorax hoactli*), Treganza heron (*Ardea herodias treganzai*), and rarely the western grebe (*Aechmophorus occidentalis*). The records cover ordinary as well as mild winters.

In recent years there have been several notations of the occurrence here in winter of the herring gull (*Larus argentatus smithsonianus*), a bird not heretofore included in our avian fauna; but the records are not associated exclusively with either harsh or mild weather. Likewise the bald eagle (*Haliaeetus leucocephalus leucocephalus*) is so often seen in the winter marshlands that some ornithologists are tending to believe it to be the northern variety (*Alascanus*) on sojourn from Alaska. Only actual specimens can answer the query.

Barrow's golden eye (*Bucephala islandica*) visits our winter fens, as do whistling swans (*Olor columbianus*), the latter regularly and often in a flock of a thousand individuals. The pied-billed grebe (*Podilymbus podiceps podiceps*) occurs here in winter more than at any other time; but the marsh wren (*Telmatodytes palustris plesius*), like the horned lark, is always present.

The winter appearance of the snowy owl in these mountains is apparently determined by the periodic shortage of lemmings and hares in the far north. Sometimes, as in the winter of 1926-27, one or two are seen; then again none is taken for several years. It is all very interesting; but it is certain that besides weather many factors such as food and accident influence the occurrence of winter birds.

It has required many years to fill the gaps, but we now have a complete record of the occurrence of thunder and lightning in these mountains at some time or other every week of the year.

JANUARY 3

As we trudge down a snow-impeded canyon trail through a copse of bare, scrub-oak trees, our boots unexpectedly kick the snow covering from a cluster of the freshest, most colorful verdure one would see in many a day—the trailing barberry (*Berberis repens*), which often is gathered for Christmas wreaths. It is a revelation of pleasing, harmonious color: as we stoop to admire the leaves, we notice that most of them are dark green above and biscay green below; but among them are individual leaves of almost every shade and tint. One is a beautiful pansy purple; another, rose-red washed with capucine orange; but several others vary from spinach green to claret brown.

With its fresh, spiney-toothed, evergreen foliage nestling in vigor beneath the snow, it is a happy reminder of the permanent vitality of nature in this sole representative here of the barberry family. Over yonder on a slope, where the warm winter sun has seeped the snow away, there is in fact a whole patch of barberry, which in the distance appears maroon, like richly colored pebbles and stones about the sage bushes.

And there just ahead on the mountainside is the rambling track of a cottontail (*Sylvilagus nuttalli grangeri*), the timid mammal that like the barberry is one of the few indicators of life on the snow-drifted foothills. It feeds on dead grass, buds, and the bark of willows, never straying more than a few rods from its accustomed outskirts of home. Yet there above us flies a prairie falcon (*Falco mexicanus*), while goshawks and snowy owls likewise are sometimes scanning the hills for just such tender tidbits as the mild-eyed cottontail. The spiney edges of the leaves of the barberry and their rather leathery texture explain why the cottontail seldom if ever eats them. Nature's expression of vigorous, growing, evergreen health beneath the snow—such is the refreshing barberry.

In a sunny labyrinth near a home in the path of our return a flock of English sparrows is engaged in a fierce imbroglio, as if it were the mating season of April. This reminds us, that in sites much favored by warmth and sunshine, such as the straw-thickened roof of an open shed or stable, close to cattle well fed in their corral, English sparrows may nest here at any time after the first of the year.

While tediously going through Locke's famous essay on *Human Understanding*, I came upon a passage wherein he queries: how do we know that rocks and such inanimate things do not think? When we reflect that everything—stones and brains included—consists of the same atoms, which in turn have the same protons, neutrons and electrons, we are in no position to deny what capabilities yonder stone-faced cliff might possess. The harmless little cottontail over there breathes tremulously; who am I to assert categorically the limitations of a stone?

17

JANUARY 4

When our old friend, the famous botanist, unexpectedly rang the door bell and, having shaken the snow from his overcoat, sat down to enjoy the warm hearth, the conversation somehow turned to onomatopoetic names of some of the birds and animals of these mountains. An onomatopoetic word is, of course, one formed in imitation of a natural sound; hence, while he specializes in the depiction of silent life, the botanist ponders his wide experience and makes many helpful suggestions.

The word "chickadee" is undoubtedly an onomatope.

The "curlew" of our long billed curlew (*Numenius americanus americanus*) of the summer salt grass flats, is from the modern French *courlieu*, formed in imitation of the bird's cry; indeed, in the poetry from the fifteenth to the nineteenth centuries the stress appears to have been on the second syllable, and thus more echoic of the bird.

Our poor-will (*Phalaenoptilus nuttallii nuttalli*) is so named in resemblance to its disyllabic note, the first use of the word, so far as we know, being that of Dr. J. G. Cooper in 1870, who said the notes sounded like the words. Theodore Roosevelt in the Century Magazine of March, 1888, wrote: "At night fall the poor-wills begin to utter their boding call from the wooded ravines back in the hills; not 'whip-poor-will', as in the East, but with two syllables only".

We stir the logs, crack a nut or so, discuss momentarily the genus *Astragalus,* on which our friend is preparing a monograph and actually intending to do the printing in his own library, and then go on to the phoebe (*Sayornis saya saya*), which all agree must be named from its tender double-note of spring. Phoebe is the Greek goddess of the moon, hence the accommodation to her in spelling, but the reference is to sound. Thus Washington Irving, in 1839, wrote: "Another of our feathered visitors . . . is the Pe-wit, or Pe-wee or Phoebe bird, for he is called by each of these names, from a fancied resemblance to the sound of his monotonous note."

From this we admit that while the western wood pewee (*Contopus sordidulus veliei*) has but a single note *deer,* it takes its name because its Eastern relative really sings *pee-ah-wee.*

In the course of the conversation someone mentions "mag" as an onomatopoetic word used in naming the "magpie", and we all agree that while "mag", which is a funny shortening of Margaret, means chatterbox, it is also echoic of one of the usual notes of the bird. The European magpie *Pica caudata,* is known for its chatter, hence we learn that in 1605, they spoke of being "as merie as a magge pie", from all of which we conclude that "magpie" is a combination of both imitative sound and gossiping ability. This leads to a discussion of onomatopoesis in general, particularly the difficulty of expressing complicated songs of birds with written letters and syllables.

JANUARY 5

The bell rings, and as we open the door the botanist is outside in a blizzard of snow. He shakes his high galoshes and, shedding his snow-flecked muffler, enters. Eccentric man, with his grey beard, lonely habits, and abiding profundity; but his eyes gleam at the comfort of the welcoming hearth now aglow with coals roasting chestnuts. The conversation of course finally drifts to onomatopoesis for which he has brought commendable data; furthermore he is a Greek and Latin scholar.

The bobolink of our meadows in spring was originally called "Bob Lincoln" or "Bob o'Lincoln" in imitation of its call, though we must admit its song is far more complicated than those simple words. Thus Washington Irving, in 1796 wrote: "In the merry month of June . . . (when) the luxurious little boblincoln revels among the clover blossoms of the meadows".

The words "merry", "luxurious" and "revels" divert us to a discussion of the habitually buoyant spirit of Irving, who saw much joy in life and living; but "revels" inadequately describes the fantastic *capriccietto* of the bobolink, which is like a bursting of the notes above the fragrant alfalfa field.

Our cowbird (*Molothrus ater artemisiae*) not only likes to be around cows but, also, at least, according to Audubon: "From the resemblance of its notes to that word *cow, cow* this cuckoo is named cowbird in nearly every part of the Union".

There are several towhees in these mountains—the mountain (*Pipilo erythrophthalmus montanus*) is a rather common breeder, as is the green-tailed (*Chlorura chlorura*); and, while we divert upon the pleasant chat we had with Dr. Oberhosler when he called upon us, we conclude that "towhee' is an onomatop—"from one of its notes", as Newton says. Thus in 1893 the June number of Scribner's Magazine explained: "He utters his loud 'towhee' a note so characteristic that it became one of his names".

Our shrikes, both the winter visiting northern (*Lanius excubitor invictus*) and the breeding loggerhead (*L. ludovicianus gambeli*) get their names from the old English word *scric,* applied to any bird with a shrill cry. For instance, *shrike* and *shrike-cock* are dialectic names of the missel-thrush. We might compare the mating cry of the badger at rutting time. I have often enjoyed Wilson's description of the voice of the loggerhead shrike as resembling the "clear creaking of a sign board in windy weather".

We go to mammals, and conclude that "chipmunk" is an Indian word echoic in origin; that "chickaree", as applied to the Wasatch species (*Sciurus hudsonicus ventorum*), is an onomatopoetic word, Thoreau having mentioned, in 1849, "the larger red squirrel or chickaree" and others, in 1860, having said that "the chickaree winds up the clock".

JANUARY 6

It has been a day of ornithological good fortune, for we have at last taken a Rocky mountain water pipit (*Anthus spinolette altocola*). We say "at last" with emphasis, for in truth this bird, which selects Pikes Peak and lofty places of the Uinta mountains as its breeding home, has always heretofore eluded us in its winter visits to our comparative lowlands, although sharp eyes frequently discern it along highways cleared by snow.

While wading in the snow about the foothills of City Creek canyon, we noticed before us a bird of the general appearance of a horned lark, but it not only walked rather than hopped along but, also frequently bobbed its tail, as if it were a sandpiper. Furthermore, when it flushed, it zig-zagged up and down in flight in extraordinary fashion, and uttered a thin *tee teet*. To make identification sure we were compelled to take it and place it before us for study as we write.

It is a grayish brown bird nearly seven inches long, with a superciliary stripe and under parts of pinkish or creamy buff, and with its chest, sides and flanks streaked brown.

In appearance and mannerisms the pipit most nearly resembles the larks (*Alaudidae*), with whcih it is easily confused, although in the field it appears very much like a vesper sparrow.

Since it makes its summer home on lofty mountains above timber line east of here, the pippit necessarily nests on the ground, utilizing such mosses and dried grasses as are available, and laying eggs that are so profusely speckled with brown as to appear almost entirely of that color. It subsists chiefly on insects, small crustaceans and tiny weed seeds; but it dwells mostly in the higher Uinta and Rocky Mountains, being known to us only in its winter visitation.

Some birds, like our water ouzel, for instance, are peculiar to our western mountains; but we can claim no such exclusiveness with respect to the pipit, of which more than thirty species have been described throughout the world. In the west end of London, where we used to ramble in the fields of Shepherds Bush, the bird-catchers, whom we delighted to watch, called the "pit-pits" or tit larks. With a captured bird singing in a little cage, it is astonishing how wild birds are easily trapped. I have never seen a song-bird catcher in the Wasatch mountains or valleys, which proves to me that in thickly populated regions of the world, where there are more applicants than jobs, men are driven to all sorts of strange vocations to gain a livelihood.

As we watch a vicious wolf chained to a corral post we remark upon the incongruity of closely-related mammals in their tameability. You may tame a dog but not a wolf, a horse but seldom a zebra, a cow but not a bison, an Asiatic elephant but not an African, a llama but not a vicuna, although both are cameloids. Coyotes and foxes do not tame easily; but a mountain lion can be trained to be a veritable housecat.

JANUARY 7

When once the late Dr. E. W. Nelson called upon us to see a roseate spoonbill that we had recorded from the desert region west of these mountains, our conversation somehow drifted toward another rare but by no means accidental bird-visitor, the snowy owl; and we shall never forget the description by this famed naturalist of how, when in Alaska lemmings are abundant, the owls verily dot the drear landscape there as they feed upon this rodent prey.

The snowy owl, strong, graceful, self-reliant, a raptor equal to the fiercest in courage, visits our mountains usually only when its northern food is scarce, its natural habitat being the circum-polar tundra where it feeds upon lemmings and hares. For some yet unknown reason these mammals are both subject to periodic population fluctuations wherein they one year are so numerous as to be a plague and, six or seven years later, so scarce as to be nearly extinct. Our own deer and prong-horned antelopes are subject to similar but much longer population cycles, though in our observation game laws have been much more important control factors with respect to them.

When the snowy owl does visit our hills, it is eager to prey upon everything from a blue jay to a short-eared owl, from a hare to a rat, mouse or shrew; and in its ferocity it even attacks trapped mammals of fairly large size, and holds its ground against an unarmed man attempting to steal its food.

One reason why the snowy owl is seldom taken in the Wasatch is that, being accustomed to the treeless tundra of the polar north, it habitually sits on some high, winter-blasted rock in an open space and with natural wariness constantly surveys the entire countryside for both victims and enemies. Other owls are frequently flushed from trees within range of a gun, but not the shy snowy—it is ever alerted and forewarned at safe distances.

Although the snowy owl is a rare winter visitor here, the comings and goings of our other owls are not so clearly defined. The barn owl, being nocturnal and seclusive, is seldom seen at all, although there are indications that it is likely resident throughout the year. The screech owl (*Otus asio inyoensis*) dwells all winter among valley trees, and the flammulated owl (*Otus flammeolus flammeolus*), which nests in woodpecker holes, is inclined to go southward but does sometimes linger through the winter cold.

Our great horned owl (*Bubo virginianus occidentalis*) remains here all winter about trees and ledges; and both the short-eared owl and the long-eared owl stay over, as do the pygmy owl (*Glaucidium gnoma californicum*), and the saw-whet (*Aegolius acadicus acadicus*), the last named, chiefly among aspens and streamside conifers.

Although the habitat of a pair or so of burrowing owls — the mounded embankment above the borrow of a saleratus meadow ditch—his since boyhood days been under my observation season after season, I have never seen the birds there in winter time.

JANUARY 8

Like the chirm of a pack of sheep-chasing curs are the jargling yaps of a dolesome coyote, as he sits at evening on a dreary knoll within view of habitations and sniffs the savory odors that waft from kitchen to hill. It is scarcely believable that one animal can imitate ventriloqually the combined cries of many; yet, when darkness enshrouds his wily course, he may suddenly startle the countryside with barks, yaps and howls. Verily he is the bobolink of animaldom.

The word "coyote", which is from the Spanish *coyote* and the native Mexican *coyotl,* is in the Wasatch mountains almost always pronounced "ki-o'-te", with the "i" long and the accent on the middle syllable. Once in a while we hear a sheep herder or farmer pronounce it "ki'-ot" in two syllables with the accent on the first; but seldom indeed hereabout is the correct Spanish "ko-yo'-ta" spoken. Many Spanish words in common use in these mountains lose their softness and in some cases even almost their identity. The correct name, for instance, of those leather open-trousers worn by cowboys is "chaparajos", but hereabout few would understand the term, as the men invariably call them "shaps".

The coyote of the Wasatch is known as *Canis latrans lestes,* a richly colored animal of medium size, which lives principally on dusky grouse, snowshoe rabbits, cottontails, ground squirrels, fawns and lambs. Very often we see one lurking about a herd of milch cows; for, when some cows give birth to their calves and decline to go to a barn, they hide their calves in willow thickets. A sneaking coyote will wait all day long for a cow to leave her helpless calf for a moment; but in the night time several coyotes together may chase sheep and kill a score in a few minutes. Sneaking cur of the mountains, the coyote is nevertheless one of the wildest and wisest of our mountain mammals, second only to its big cousin, the howling wolf. We shall never forget how, having bowled a coyote over with a shotgun at twenty feet, we carried it on our shoulder for a mile when it suddenly revived and put up a real fight.

Many a night we have slept with one ear listening to the garbled barks of coyotes while we worried over the cooped chickens; but then we did not know that a barrier three feet high is insurmountable to a coyote. It would have been easy to remove the entrance plank to the chickens' dormitory.

The carnivores of the Wasatch appear in size from the black bear to the weasel, and, excepting bears, which eat anything that appeals to them, whether vegetable or animal, they are all exclusively flesheaters. Our largest mammal is the moose; our smallest, the shrew. Evidence is slowly accumulating in favor of the view that both coyotes and wolves mate for life.

JANUARY 9

When one traverses wind-swept by-paths, he often wonders what the Indians of this region used for clothing to withstand the rigors of winter. It is reported by old white people who knew them that the red men wore jackets made of deer skin, leggings of somewhat the same material, moccasins of buckskin, and blankets sewed from rabbit pelages. Caves and places where huge boulders abounded near water such as those in middle Weber canyon, were undoubtedly utilized in periods of severe snow and cold, and, since they well understood the art of making fire, they probably existed in a miserable, unsanitary, half-starved condition all winter, but with a little smoky warmth. Some even huddled beside a large sage on the flatlands. Buffalo robes were usually unavailable to the Wasatch Indians, hence their scale of living was perhaps the lowest of all the redmen of this continent. Daughters were frequently sold into slavery in exchange for food.

Nature, on the other hand, usually provides not only for resident animals and birds but for visiting ones as well; and this too when apparently there is naught but naked limb and drifted snow. Deer snip buds and sprouts from willow, sage and evergreen; cottontails feed on the single grass blades of their favorite slades; mountain sheep paw the snow down to grass-clumps beside rocks; mountain lions lurk the intervales for unsuspecting deer; the coyote marks a dotted trail after the huddled grouse, rabbit or quail; the wolf prowls the valley for the willow-sheltered steer; snowy owls on darksome hillsides pounce on venturing rabbits, mice and grouse; and other visiting birds feast on juniper berries, hackberries, wild currants, rose-hips, red osiers, snow-berries, or happily, as the Bohemian waxwing, on rotten apples frozen and lingered on the winter limb.

Most animals have places of refuge from blizzard and storm. Grouse find a haven beneath some spruce or under over-hanging willows within the gurgling sound of an icy rill; quail seek the thick cover of underbrush and endure near starvation; wolves retreat to rocky caverns; chickarees merely remain under the snow-burdened canopies made by balsam limbs; flickers claim sanctuary through some attic hole to warm brick chimneys; house sparows snuggle beneath some snowy roof made by thick honeysuckle vines; a bear sleeps in such places as the hollow of an old tree trunk, a cave, or the base of a cliff sheltered by thick fir limbs; and so on, each animal having a different retreat.

Even as we write we can see through the back window a pair of Shufeldt juncos (*Junco oreganus shufeldti*) in the midst of a stinging blizzard actually nipping contentedly at some weed seeds in a sheltered thawed spot not over two feet in diameter below the garden wall. Perhaps one may always find some nook of happiness in the storm of life, but if so it is one untroubled by vanity and inspired by the pursuit of truth.

JANUARY 10

Seldom now do we of these once untraveled mountains hear a wolf; indeed, not since 1919 have we seen the tracks of one. We remember one chained on a ranch at the mouth of the Jordan river — vicious, strong, uncompromising brute he was, the embodiment of hatred and untameability! Several times in the moonlight of a gloomed creek ravine we have studied the cruel, unblinking eyes of a pack of captured wolves separated from us only by wire, in a wooded setting so still and lonely as to incite all the natural enmities of these wise and aggressive animals; and never once have we seen aught but malignancy in their stare. Mountain lions, black bears, wildcats, learn really to like men, after the shock of capture abates, as numerous instances of their use as pets will attest; but not so a wolf. This is strange when we realize that the cousin of the wolf, the domestic dog, will pine away and die over the grave of its departed man. In February, 1941, an airdale named "Laddie", of Chanute, Kansas, languished because his master, Private Everett Scott, had been called to the front; and, though the broken-hearted dog was taken by airplane to Fort Ord, California, he was too far gone for even his "master's voice" to save him. Several hundred people attended the faithful animal's funeral, and many more grieved.

The wolf of our mountains is known as *Canis lupus youngi*. It is a comparatively light colored subspecies, with considerable buff overlaid with black on its upper parts, and in size larger than the wolf of Nebraska (*nubilus*), but smaller than that of the Liard river region of Mackenzie, Canada, or that of the northern Rocky mountain district.

A mountain lion prefers deer and colts to any other food; but a wolf chooses cattle, especially calves and yearlings. It is a big job for even several wolves to tear down an old bull. Wolves mate for life and are so tender of their young pups that they habitually disgorge chunks of meat they have swallowed so that the little ones may have the food in partly masticated form. Man might well look to the much-hated wolf for ideals of domestic fidelity and bliss. It has been painted well by Giotto, Sassetta, and Andreas da Firenze.

In very early days of pioneer life in Wasatch valleys as many as half a dozen big gray wolves were destroyed in a single night by impregnating the carcass of a cow with strychnine, but since the turn of the century the wolf has become so wary of poisoned meat that it has declined almost all food that it did not kill itself. Coyote is a Mexican word that in the history of the West was variously spelled "cuiota", "cayota", "kiote" and so on; and, since pioneers did not know the word, they called the coyote a "prairie wolf", a term by which it is known to this day in parts of Texas, to distinguish it from the big gray wolf.

Of course almost any trapped or cornered wild mammal will resist a threatening man; a few of them, like the migrating muskrat, for instance, will fight him if he appears in their path; but I have never heard of a wolf's attacking a man in the Wasatch mountains.

JANUARY 11

Whenever one sees in a snow-laden boxelder tree a bird of small robin size with a whitish bill so swollen that its mandible is as wide at the base as the length of its keel, and, in company with others of its kind, it is eating boxelder seeds, he may be convinced he is looking at a western evening grosbeak (*Hesperiphona vespertina brooksi*). If it has a bright yellow patch above the eye, black tail, black wings save for large white patches, it is a male; and the smoke gray bird at its side is a female. Though one of the *Fringillidae* or finches, it is much larger than a domestic sparrow.

During childhood days we watched these inoffensive, gentle birds busy themselves during all the winter day in our favorite kitchen-shading boxelder. We well remember how confiding they were, even when first we took one of them for identification, for after the sound of the .22 rifle two birds of the flock actually remained unfrightened in the tree.

In the winter of 1929 our friend, the late J. V. Crone, successfully enticed a flock of evening grosbeaks to eat from a window platform at his home. They were especially fond of nuts cracked for them, somewhat reluctant about wheat, and almost wholly indifferent to bread. They were up and about at dawn, chirped incessantly throughout the day, and always dominated the English sparrows, which sat like little jackals while lions fed.

When in 1825 Cooper gave the name *vespertina* to this species, he apparently was under the impression that they uttered sounds only in the evening, but they certainly chirp all day long.

Being acquainted with these birds only as regular winter visitors to these valleys, we have not yet chanced upon their nest, which is said to be placed high in a conifer or willow and to be made of roots and sticks. Robert G. Bee and John Hutchings reported a nest at Salem, Utah, on May 27, 1936, in an oak twelve feet above ground, well constructed of twigs, rootlets and asparagus fern. The green eggs are blotched with brown. Since they are birds of our high mountains they breed in lofty zones infrequently visited by even mountaineers.

It is from the sociability and kindly demeanour of the evening grosbeaks that we get our greatest delight, for, like the waxwings and pine siskins, they appear only in flocks and never fail to manifest sweet consideration for one another.

When in a valley a fog occurs so thick that one cannot see more than thirty feet away, a phenomenon so rare here as to happen only about once a year, it indicates, as today, that warm, clear upper air has homehow entrapped a blanket of air next to earth a thousand feet thick or more; and during it we note this peculiarity—upper mountain peaks are clear and warm, twenty degrees warmer than the valley; and it looks as though ridge after ridge were connected by a whitened floor below. The fog condenses and forms snow crystals on every twig.

JANUARY 12

Most destructive of all the accipiters, unexcelled by any other bird in fierceness and valor, the goshawk wins our admiration for its intrepidity at the very instant it provokes our enmity over its ruthless destruction. Only audacity of the highest order could induce a bird to steal a headless, flopping chicken from the very feet of the holder of the axe; only rashness could persuade a hawk to pursue a frightened hen inside a kitchen door; but ornithologists attest such bold actions of the goshawk.

Yonder torn rabbit, crimsoned on the snow, abandoned only when we entered this oak-branched gully, so interests us that we feel no more fitting place to mention this winter predator.

The goshawk (*Accipiter gentilis atricapillus*), a breeder in the Wasatch mountains, is a gray hawk nearly two feet long, with gray markings and mottles on its whitish undersides; but the female, like Penthesilea, the queen of the Amazons, is more resolute and vengeful than the ordinary male.

Many a farmer, many a fisherman can vouch for the daring and fortitude of this valiant raptor, which seems almost to go insane with fierceness when clutching its prey, or with fury when the region of its nest is intruded. Men have been constrained to fight it off with clubs or hold their coats as shields from its cutting talons.

Research indicates that at one time or another it feeds on woodchucks, rabbits, hares, muskrats, squirrels, chipmunks, kittens, weasels, shrews, mice, ducks, snipe, chickens, quails, grouse, pheasant, small hawks, and owls, pigeons, doves, woodpeckers, crows, kingfishers, blackbirds, robins, sparrows, grasshoppers, moths and beetles; so the wonder is, that anything of small size in either farm yard or forest is permitted to escape its sudden devastation. It is the one hawk uniformly hated by mankind, though, unfortunately, in their anger at it they often unwittingly kill large beneficial hawks such as the Swainson.

If spirit, courage and tenacity win the fight of life, the goshawk should long survive; and this, because whatever the season, whether of pleasant verdure or chilling snow, some victim to its taste creeps, crawls or flies in a hopeless attempt to escape its talons.

We ponder, as is our custom, on the meaning of it all. If perchance these words will be read a thousand years from now, that curious investigator of antique thought will know no more than we the mystic meaning of the words "God" and "soul". Is design but the average of the chance direction of individual particles?

JANUARY 13

In a snow-solemned clough of the canyon, where the brook frets through icy mantling, the thin, repeated "tchips" of chickadees sound while the birds pry over the branches of overhanging birch trees. Each pecks at a cone, which like a brown caterpillar suspends from a branch; and then works out the seeds with its bill against a limb. Again it pecks a catkin, once more working the little bill, hopping from twig to twig, uttering *tchip* and *tchip*. Rarely from the happy feeders comes the familiar call *chick a dee dee dee,* but as a result of their eager industry the snow below them is strewn with catkins, seeded and torn.

We have two chickadees in this mountain: the black-capped (*Parus atricapillus septentrionalis*) and the mountain (*Parus gambeli gambeli*). They may be readily distinguished in the field by the fact that the upper half of the head of the long-tailed or black-capped is solid black, while the black of the mountain chickadee is interrupted by a long white stripe over its eye. They sometimes congregate merrily together in flocks, since both of them breed in the high mountains and descend to the valleys mostly in winter; but the long-tailed habitually seeks a colder habitat than the mountain, its range extending even to Alaska and the Slave Lake district of the province of Mackenzie in Canada. Nests are usually old woodpecker holes, those that we have seen being in quaking aspen trunks within reach of the ground. The fledglings hiss like snakes at the intrusion of one's hand.

The family *Paridae* or Titmice, to which the chickadees belong, and the *Sittidae* or Nuthatches, include in these mountains such tiny, delightful residents as the common red-breasted nuthatch (*Sitta canadensis*), the black-eared nuthatch (*Sitta pygmaea melanotis*), the lead-colored bush tit (*Psaltriparus minimus plumbeus*), and the gray titmouse (*Parus inornatus ridgwayi*). All are wee, confiding birds with conodial bills much shorter than the heads, and with plumages never marked with spots, streaks or bars. Every one of them is extremely active, arboreal as well as omnivorous, and migratory only in the local sense of alpine forest to mountain valley. The blunt tongue is tipped with horny bristles, which doubtless serve as a tool in food-gathering.

Often we have marveled at the endurance and cheerfulness of chickadees. Little balls of fluffy black and white feathers, they hop from branch to branch in the coldest of weather and deepest of snow, ever searching into nook or cranny for some mite of seed or bug, often clinging upside down in their business of feeding, and ever trusting the presence of man.

We who love the joyful warmth, blossoming and promise of spring, the tranquil hours beside fretful brooks in the lazy afternoons of summer, the gorgeous coloration and fruition of autumn, can scarcely believe that any bird or mammal deliberately chooses winter.

JANUARY 14

Nature has many inconsistencies of character. A mountain lion has been known to bring down a horse and even a moose; a golden eagle, to slaughter a grown deer with its talons; yet neither the lion nor the eagle has ever, so far as we know, defended its young against the intrusion of man. The eaglets in their eyrie, the kittens in their lair, are deserted without resistance upon the approach of a human being and temporarily at least left to their fate.

The incident that has brought this thought to our attention is yonder buck deer, a three year old we would say, lying dead on this snow-robed slope, its back cruelly lacerated and the crimsoned story of its floundering spread all about the scene. A golden eagle flew from the carcass as we approached; and no other tracks appear in the dazzling snow. It must have been a struggle; but there it is—the grim story of the killing of a deer by an eagle.

Worthier by far to illustrate our national emblem than the timid, carrion-eating bald eagle, which, however, does belong only to America, the golden eagle wins our admiration in these mountains, not only in the summer but also in winter. It is an early spring-nester here, and sometimes, even when the snow covers its favorite crags, it may sally forth with its lifetime mate in courtship-sailings, swoopings, and intricate aerial maneuvers astonishing to the human eye.

Golden eagles kill and eat everything they can conquer, from deer to pocket gophers, calves to weasels, skunks and rabbits, great blue herons, turkeys, geese, quails, pigeons and meadowlarks; but most surprising of all is that they overcome rattlesnakes in fair fights. Many mammals and a few birds are agile and brave enough to tease a rattlesnake into striking and then to grasp its head before it can recoil, and a mule deer will cut one to shreds by jumping on the reptile with all four hoofs held together. Eagles, however, meet their fate when they tackle a porcupine—the end thereof is sometimes starvation and death.

The swiftest bird in flight hereabout is very likely the duck hawk (*Falco peregrinus anatum*); but a pair of golden eagles that we watched at the mouth of the Jordan flew over the marshes from a grove of cottonwood trees with such marvelous speed and dexterity that we stood in astonishment.

We once saw a pair of golden eagles in a cage with a great horned owl; and at all times the master of the situation was—the owl, obviously even against the two of them! The eagle is only in fiction king of birds.

Many great artists have delighted in painting the golden eagle, among them being Raphael, Mantegna, Basaiti, Tura, Cosimo, Titian, Correggio, Francia, Pisanello, and Jacob Bellini; but the bald eagle does not occur in Europe.

JANUARY 15

Even on a mild winter's day such as this one would not expect to hear western meadowlarks (*Sturnella neglecta neglecta*) singing atip the fenceposts of yonder alkaline field; nevertheless there they are. Song-gifted, beneficial birds, they make delightful the pasturage when ice covers the stagnant pools and all the landscape is drear. Hereabout such a winter-lingering is not rare, as some of them spend the frozen months as far north as the Canadian line; but usually they sojourn during snow-burdened times in that thawing region just beyond the southern tip of the Wasatch mountains.

Ever searching for grasshoppers, beetles, crickets and other insects that pest the valley-fields, the meadowlark is, to our notion at least, one of the most beneficial birds of all these mountains, equalling the burrowing owl, or his companion of the meadowings, the marsh hawk. The grain that it takes is more than compensated by the weed seed it consumes. By the way, "meadow" is not an apt name for this lark in these regions, because we see it as often on the scrub-oak hillsides adjacent to grainlands as lower in the valleys in the grassy fields; but not, however, in winter.

Varied, strong and clear, its song is easier for a good whistler to imitate than for a penman to describe; however, the syllables, "Oh, here's a PRETTY place" with an accented, drawnout "here's" and an accented "pret", fervently whistled, will illustrate the usual song. This six-noted carol may in the ecstacy of spring become a capriccio of extended beauty. One today sang *"Tre tre TRE la la"*.

Flying slowly, straight away, the meadowlark is an easy target; moreover, it is not so wary as the swift-darting dove or the wild-crying killdeer. Relative of the bobolink, the blackbirds and the orioles, it is more important in sturdy melody than any of them if for no other reason than that it enraptures the seclusion of the wide-open fieldlands.

We know of no other bird more endeared to our heart, for not only did it delight our boyhood gunning afield but it enchanted us as we wearily piled the new-mown hay. It has always pleased our later visits not only to meadow and field but also to dry uplands of scrub oak and sage, home of the lazuli bunting and the Lewis woodpecker, for it clearly prefers the site of native verdure rather than the furrowed field. While the songs of most birds that please us greatly, such as that of the lazuli bunting, the house finch, the hermit thrush and the warblers, are distinctly audible for a distance of about two hundred feet, that of the meadowlark sounds clearly over the fields for nearly a quarter of a mile; furthermore, even though it be the snow-melting days of very early spring or the bare limbed noontides of a frost-bitten November, the sweet bravura of this delightful bird may ring clearly over the fieldlands.

JANUARY 16

We are in the lane of a valley meadow, where willows are so frosted as to appear white in the mist, and flakes of rime fall occasionally from them as if snow. It is the first time we have observed such a phenomenon—the crystalled lacery of trees breaking off with its own weight and fluttering like tinsel to the ground-snow below. We can explain this only on the theory that for the past two weeks there has been almost constant zero weather with fog, and rime has accumulated beyond the strength of its fragile threads.

Be that as it may, it is a day full of unexpected interest to the naturalist. Horses in the snow-robed fields are pawing down to salt grass, and the hair of their sides and faces is so thick and stiff as to make their heads and bodies appear big, grisly and fluffy; inside the barbed wire fence is a trail in the snow where the animals have trod wistfully in the hope of some escape from their dreary imprisonment. A red-tailed hawk flushes from a black willow and soars by.

Seven ravens (*Corvus corax sinatus*) are sitting on the posts of a marsh-bordering fence, the first birds of their race that we have seen in this particular locality. They caw frequently, and once two of them course together in the air as if courting, sometimes actually tumbling over as they touch, but eventually descending to the posts to rest in tranquility side by side. It is a silly pagan superstition that ravens portend evil. They devour some eggs, corn and even an occasional young bird; but they are eaters of carrion, true scavengers, much apprecited in regions like Alaska.

These ravens are as large as marsh hawks, as they sit on their icy perches, but the moment they take the air they flap constantly. While we are observing them a female marsh hawk actually flies over them, disclosing the unmistakable white rump patch, and sailing with wings held above the horizontal. We never mistake a marsh hawk even though it hunt the meadows a quarter of a mile away.

During the hour that we watch the ravens a red-shafted flicker clucks its call from the gurgling brook's willows, a meadowlark indulges in a perfunctory if incomplete song from a power-line wire, a score of male redwings talk matters over among the dry reeds of the lane's borrow, and two large ducks, probably mallards, sail down from the sky to settle among the rushes of a spring-fed meadow-hole. Perhaps it is upon them that the marsh hawk feeds, for no where that we can see is the soft covering of snow broken by the footprints of either jack rabbit or mouse; only the dry stalks of sunflowers and card teasels obtrude above the white of meadow and field.

No weather hereabout could give the test of longer cold, no ground be more deeply blanketed with snow, that what we endure and see today; yet a meadowlark sings and red-wings converse. We come to one conclusion: whatever the weather, whatever the time of year, to learn the secrets of nature one must go to the wild places.

JANUARY 17

In their marriage relations birds and mammals are either (a) promiscuous, (b) polygamous with small harems, (c) monogamous for the present brood only, (d) monogamous for the season, or (e) monogamous for life. In utter promiscuity could be placed our prong-horned antelope and the European ruff (*Philomachus pugnax*), a bird related to our sandpiper, while among those mating for life we might list our wolf, raven, eagle, and most hawks. Pheasants maintain harems, while many of the monogamous birds are faithful for one season only, or, like the wrens, for a single brood.

Darwin found no evidence of polygamy among the *Cheiroptera*, *Edentata* or *Insectivora*, and, except for the common rat, he included the *Rodentia* as well; nevertheless, Vernon Bailey asserted that "like all rodents" the kangaroo rat is polygamous. It is a subject needing much careful observation.

Most birds are monogamous either for the present brood or the season, and some, like the ravens, loons, hawks, and the eagles, for longer periods, or even life. Some birds, like the ducks, guinea fowls and canary birds, are monogamous when wild and polygamous when tame. Animals that are monogamous for life include the wolves, coyotes and foxes, and those for lesser periods, muskrats, wolverines and skunks.

Among polygamous animals may be mentioned gorillas, baboons, deer, cattle, sheep, antelopes, wild horses, wild boars, rats, African lions, mountain lions, mountain goats, mountain sheep, seals, sea lions, sea bears, caribou, wapiti, mink, marmots and porcupines; and among polygamous birds, widow birds, redwings, humming birds, peacocks, bustards, pheasants, ruffs and domestic ducks.

Mammals whose marriage relationship is too little known to determine in which category to place them include lemming mice, voles, shrews, pikas, gophers, beavers, badgers, meadow mice, bats and weasels. Seton placed the badger among the monogamous animals, but Bailey disputed this; and so it goes, the status of even the bird of Paradise being undetermined. Men should not make positive assertions unless they know.

Darwin, who seemed to have had little definite information on the subject, concluded that when the male of any species is much stronger and more beautiful than the female, he is apt to be polygamous, and, if he is somber like the female, he is usually monogamous; yet we know that male and female mountain lions are very much alike in appearance and that the male seeks a new mate after about two weeks attention to one female.

One of the most interesting of all polygamists is the sage hen. A master cock seeks a breeding spot where he mates with a score or more females as they come to him, while a rival cock and several lesser males watch and not very often have the courage to interfere, at least until their master is rendered indifferent by satiety.

JANUARY 18

Dust laden are the country roads and wayside trees; soot-begrimed is every habitation within the smoky gloom of the city; yet through it all the sun shines with vernal warmth and cheer. No songster, however, disports himself in the genial atmosphere—there is naught awing but the common, much ignored *Passer domesticus domesticus,* an intimate sparrow who lives where he is indifferently condemned. This English importation looks as if he had not bathed for months; but he catches with alert eyes the tender blades of grass that peep from beneath fences, and for the moment is happy. These astonishing birds have erotic battles even in midwinter.

Sometimes, thought not often, January has the radiant mildness, the langurous atmosphere of middle May; yet, notwithstanding the dusty roads, the clear cerulean sky and the murmur of brooks, no green leaves, no bird's rapturous song, no incessant humming of bees, no stridulation of insects, fill the air with joyousness. Nature being skeletonized, few humans are deceived by several weeks sunshine into the belief that January is not January still.

At the summit of the mountains, on the morningside, the rounded north-sloping hills are sprinkled with snow, save where they are fleckered with groves of spruce and fir. These trees are solemn, still, and as dark as Tyrolean green. Grounded in winter immobility, the concourses of evergreens appear as though some vast, incomprehensible spirit were pervading them, as if in the apparent silence of the tomb they were in determined unity planning for the promise of springtime, indeed, pondering in a way we know not about the group-life of eternity. These grave old senators are mooding the ways of pinedom.

The mountainsides themselves elsewhere are colorless, except for seedless weeds and bushes of grayish brown; and dingy aspen groves, white and naked, below the forest of spruces and firs.

True montivagants, like ourselves, roamers of the lofty mountains even in winter, see many more phases of nature than do the canyon dwellers therein, for a hillman is usually much localized in his outlook. He eventually knows a few mammals and birds so intimately that they become pets in his cabin dooryard, whereas the montivagant rambles up one canyon and down another, seeing this snowbank, that spring, this water ouzel and that crossbill, this deer and that nutcracker, each day adding to the rich vista of his experience. To the naturalist all live things everywhere are the attractions constituting his happiness; but arduous are the climbs, and, sometimes, dismal the day.

The naturalist cannot hope for any reward beyond the joyfulness of his knowledge, for in a world gauged to hysterical and pubescent tempos, riveted to mechanical entertainments, and swayed by the inanities of social contacts, there is little room for the man who desires to think undisturbed and to try to fathom the great mysteries of life.

JANUARY 19

In a letter today from the well-known ornithologist, Mr. G. Willett, this sentence occurs: "Truly, those of us who love the outdoors and its continuously unfolding beauties are the most fortunate of humans, particularly in times like the present when so many carefully erected artificialities are trembling."

In our correspondence throughout the years with ornithologists, mammalogists, and other naturalists, we have always noted this sweet simplicity, this abiding belief, that there is a greater happiness in a love of nature than in anything money or transient glory can bestow. The pursuit of truth and fact in all living things is the perennial fascination that makes "three score and ten" years all too short a time to live; for multitudinous the variety, endless the road of research. To some indeed in this troubled world money is not a god and selfishness not a trial.

We should like to see someone take the trouble to ascertain if longevity characterizes naturalists, for love of the wildwoods together with tranquility of spirit should lengthen one's years. Merely to name some of the sciences dear to the naturalist will prove why to him there can never be an idle moment; thus: silvicology (a word of our own coinage referring to the study of the forest); phenology (study of the periodic phenomena of animal and plant life, as migration); bryology (mosses); conchology (shells); ecology (environment); helminthology (worms); herepetology (reptiles); ichthyology (fishes); microbiology (microscopic organisms); morphology (forms of organisms); mycology (fungi); entomology (insects); ornithology (birds); limnology (lake and pond life); selenology (moon); nephelology (clouds); potamology (rivers); speleology (caves); orismology (definition of terms); taxonomy (classification); arachnology (spiders); dendrology (trees); botany; mammalogy, and so on.

Man is compelled to live upon other forms of life, whether it be the seed, the fruit, the fish, bird or the mammal; hence endless the joy, infinite the value, of ascertaining the ways of living things. The hope of the naturalist is that some day he will understand; but in entertaining that view he knows that he must rely on facts, be they of the living or the dead. The naturalist bows his head before the infinitude of it all. At the moment, favored with the electron microscope, biochemical cytology is coming closest to solving the mystery of life; nevertheless, although the constituents of cells and even atoms may all be found, it is doubtful that man will ever discover the guiding principle or factor of nature, if such there be. Fortuity is not quite convincing and satisfactory.

JANUARY 20

Despiteful, alert, and as furious as a demon when actually cornered, but at times as gentle and warm-hearted as a giraffe—such is the wild cat (*Lynx rufus pallescens*) according to circumstances and mood. The fine specimen stretched on the crimsoned snow before us has been no exception to the rule, a fiend of claw and fangs to the very last in the face of peril.

Look at the house cat when it lies serenely before the hearth—it purrs affably with an almost angelic sweetness in its big round eyes. Watch it when a strange dog appears—it assumes a diabolical aspect, spits, growls, and emits bitter enmity from every hair. You have seen a diminutive lynx or wild cat. When undisturbed its benign features are so pleasing and mild that we readily understand why Pisanello loved to paint them.

There are two members of the lynx genus in the Wasatch mountains: *Lynx rufus pallescens,* with a yellowish gray coat in winter, which becomes lighter in summer; and the larger gray *Lynx canadensis canadensis,* with crested cheeks, large feet, tasseled ears, short tail and long legs. The pale lynx has a black half ring on the end of its tail; and the Canada, a tail tip black all round.

The Canada lynx prefers the high forests where in winter with its large feet it bounds like a ghost over the snow in pursuit of rabbits; but the other prowls about the foothills in search of birds, squirrels, mice, grouse, cottontails, and, in fact, any small game, not excepting snakes, frogs and insects. An old prospector informs us that the pale lynx habitually lurks about sheep-herds, killing both lambs and adults. In overcoming a sheep the lynx jumps upon the victim's back, scratching until it falls, and then bites into the sheep's jugular vein. It then sucks the blood and, if the victim is a ewe, proceeds next to eat the udder and milk. Then it devours the eyes, and the soft flesh along the nose, and finally, drags the remaining carcass away and covers it over. If disturbed while eating, it emits a low humming sound, smoother and softer than the growl of a dog, yet fiercely defiant and uncanny.

The home of the wild cat is usually in a hollow stump, or in a thick tangled coppice between the interlocking branches of a fallen tree. Here on a soft bed of moss and dry grass, the ill-tempered kittens, usually three, are born, though one of them may be devoured at once by the incomprehensible mother. In two or three months the kittens are weaned and taught to hunt, soon themselves becoming ready alone to face the chill winds and scanty food of winter. Snarling cats of the winter sageland, they now and again are the prizes of our jack rabbit hunts.

JANUARY 21

It is a dark misty night, twenty degrees below zero; but in our love of adventure we care not for the bitter cold. We have fitted our coupe with a big movable spotlight; we wear mackinaws, felted boots, stocking caps and hair-lined gloves; for we are on our way over nearly two hundred miles of hunting course—the night-shooting of the white-tailed hare (*Lepus towsendii towsendii*). It is the gelid trail of the Lincoln highway, snow-plowed and passable, from the western side of the Wasatch, up through Parley's canyon, over Parley's park, down Silver Creek, up Echo canyon to the Wyoming line and return.

It is seven o'clock at night as we start, and though the frost-scintillating snow is mounded and banked several feet high at the roadsides on the way up Parley's canyon, we see nothing wild in the misty rime floating over all. The summit is clouded, hoary and intensely cold, yet not until we reach the frozen mounds of Parley's Park does our spotlight reveal some shining eyes on the arctic hillside. There they are—three white hares, ghosted by the frost and bewildered into immobility by the brilliant rays of the search light. One of us holds the spotlight while the other uses the blister-cold shotgun; and in a moment a white, bleeding rime-covered rabbit lies on the snow.

We chuck it into the car and proceed onward. The bitter cold! Through village and town; and then as the road skirts the high cliffs of Echo canyon the fun once more begins. There is a rabbit by a clump of frosted sage in a rocky gully; and its eyes gleam until the very instant of the shot. We dare not touch the frigid metal with our bare fingers lest the skin stick and tear away.

Higher and higher we go along the bleak canyon. One hare bounds through a fence, but we bring it down on the deep, glistening snow; and as we climb through the hoary strands of barbed wire it seems that we could snap them in two, they are so brittle, frosted and cold. Every twig is pruinose with frost crystals. On we go, clear to the Wyoming line, alternating at the icy wheel and the gun, lest we freeze. Even to guide the search light through an open window quickly numbs the gloved hand. But we are satisfied—we have sixteen white-tailed jack rabbits, now white all over save for the black tips of their ears. One of our friends hunts this hare at moonlight by burying himself to his shoulders on top of a haystack and shooting them as one at a time they lope in to feed; but we prefer our way, despite the frigid weather.

The return ride seems endless and frightfully cold; but at last we arrive home at seven A.M. But dear me, in an hour my little left finger seems numb and white. It is frozen; and to this day it shows the effect of a midnight hunt of the mountain hare. Should we have known, as Jonson wrote: "A witch is a kind of hare", and that it is held sacred at least by the Hindus, who perceive its outline in the moon. Nevertheless to our dying day that left little finger will be inefficient and crooked.

JANUARY 22

There it is in the snow among the boulders at the foot of a cliff, the unmistakable loping trail of a weasel (*Mustela frenata nevadensis*), where it proceeded, stopping here and there to peer with its snakelike head, but ever relentlessly following the mufflike treads of a rabbit. We know that the little cut-throat takes its time; we know that the timid rabbit has perhaps sought its burrow in mortal dread of the determined assassin. The footmarks being very fresh, we whistle and hurry, knowing that a weasel's curiosity is great. There its head arises over yonder boulder, looking wonderingly at us. We fire; and a medium-sized weasel in its winter coat of pure white save for the black tail-tip is our reward.

Revelling always in scenes of the most heinous butchery, sinking its long white teeth deep into the throat of every victim its dauntless courage will permit it to tackle, and passing like a flash in search of more blood and more devilish killing, the mountain weasel is truly the most murderous animal for its size that wanders through these hills and valley. An eagle, mink, coyote or wolf will usually cease its killing when hunger has been appeased, or at least gormandize for days on the victims of a one-night slaughter, but not so the weasel; like thugs of India, who murdered everyone they could as a religious practice, it glories in its fiendish work of destruction. It is probably the wickedest and most unloved fur-bearer in America. What fury in a handful of fur, muscle and teeth weighing less than half a pound!

Weasels groan, snarl, hiss, puff and make reiterated sharp barks; they chatter when angry, coo or chuckle to their young, and bark at puzzling objects. Though they mate in March the male cares not a whiff for the half dozen young weasels that might occupy the nest; and for that matter he is ready to fight both male and female weasels most of the year. The dying squeak, the final spasmodic quiver, the hot gushing blood—these are the delights of the weasel, which is ever active, ever courageous and bloodthirsty.

Ground squirrels are fortunately its principal food, though it tackles practically all rodents and fowls; furthermore, it can enter any hole down which you can push a hen's egg lengthwise. Climbing very well, it sometimes chases a chipmunk to its doom; swimming equally well, it chases the rat to a watery grave; but unless very hungry it takes only the blood of its victims. Despite this craving for hot gushing blood it does once in awhile drag several bodies, such as rats, into a pile, as if intending to eat them; and then—leaves them to spoil. It is the graceful, slender bodied vampire of the night that steals with the silence of a bat upon the sleeping chickens and leaves them dead, strewn upon the floor; nevertheless, it should never be forgotten, in spite of its ferocity, that in its destruction of mice, rats and other rodents, a weasel may actually be a valuable friend about the farmyard.

JANUARY 23

A stiff south wind today has rapidly melted the snow and ice lying over the gently-sloping foothills, revealing a pleasing carpet of alfilaria (*Erodium cicutarium*). Locally it is called "clocks", "storksbill", "pinkets", or "May flower", in truth, its generic name *Erodium* is Greek for "heron", from the resemblance of its fruit to the beak and bill of that bird.

It now gives the fields a garnet hue; but on inspection each plant appears as a close rosette flat upon the ground, with the petals of its flowers pink purple with darker veins. The rosettes grow taller and more straggling as the season advances. The ovary is beaked by the united styles, the beak, when the seeds ripen, separating into five long tails which twist when dry and untwist again when moistened. "Filaree" is from the Spanish "alfiler", a pin.

This interesting member of the geranium family is a common weed in Europe, as well as in most parts of the United States; but in these mountains, where it blooms from January to January, it is highly regarded for forage, especially on spring lambing grounds. It is tender and succulent when even blades of grass are scarce on the hillsides; furthermore, it seems actually to prefer the waste places.

Another geranium (*G. fremontii*) with distinctly emarginate petals of pink, and one with white petals adorned by roseate veins (*G. richardsonii*) appear more often in the aspen and spruce belts of the Wasatch mountains than below, and more frequently in moist shady places than on dry hillsides.

Our hat goes off, however, to the Erodium, for, having been introduced here from Europe, it has not only climbed to the aspen groves but has also given a beautiful maroon to the mountainsides when all else, save the gum plant (*Grindelia squarrosa*) has yet failed to attempt a bloom.

Many is the time in winter that we have idled with gun in hand upon a lower "bench" of the Wasatch and gazed with delight upon fields and declivities clothed with the maroon-colored alfilaria. It is perhaps only for us that such sights bring joy, as if we alone were transported into the region of foresight in the realms of nature. Do others care—or for what do they care in this strange world? Never make the mistake of thinking that the thing you like to do, whether in the field of literature, art, music, science or recreation, is necessarily the thing dearest to the other fellow's heart.

The East Canyon reservoir is ice-covered and drear. We recall that once on a twenty-fifth of September, at four o'clock in the afternoon, when approaching this artificial lakelet from the east, we beheld its entire surface to be scintillating and dancing as if adorned with a million moving diamonds. It was easy to understand: we were at the exact angle to catch the reflection of the sun upon the innumerable faucets or tiny mirrors of the rippled water.

JANUARY 24

What a wondrous pre-sunrise cloud hovers over the eastern mountains—it is one vast panorama of flame scarlet, almost grenadine red, so red that one of us likens it to blood, the reddist cloud we have ever beheld!

Preferring to observe rather than to kill, not often do we shoot either bird or mammal except for positive identification; therefore today, when on a cliff above a scrub-oak hillside a falcon appeared, we now have the sturdy raptor in hand; and well we might, for it is a female prairie falcon (*Falco mexicanus*), a rare but notorious western killer.

It is a rather large raptor with pointed wings, in fact, it is almost a foot and a half from tip of bill to tip of tail, clay brown in color but streaked and blotched on its light undersides. She is, however, dirty and sooty, with talons covered with dry blood, proving that although the overhanging smoke of the city nearby may have dulled her plumage, she still has pursued her murderous career. Close kin of the duck hawk, she perhaps provokes our enmity for that affinity; nevertheless, many a grouse, meadow lark and quail, many a blackbird, horned lark and Say phoebe has known the death-throe caused by those gruesome claws. Perhaps we should not thus condemn her; for, after all, she slaughters harmful ground squirrels, pocket gophers, shrikes and lizards as well as beneficial ring-necked pheasants and doves. Unlike the Cooper hawks and the sharp-shinned, whose depredations readily condemn them, she retains a fifty-fifty vote in economic ornithology. She even makes the marsh hawk drop its captured mouse, and takes the prey as it plummets in mid-air.

Such is the prowess of this agile bird that even a jack rabbit twice her weight squirms and squeals in helplessness before her onslaughts.

Below the cliff, from which we took her, cottontail footprints lead about the brush of the gullies and beneath sage and scrub oak. Here and there, where the snow is melted, rabbit resting places appear; and, as we walk, a bunny scampers from our pathway. Plump little body of rich sayal brown has the cottontail, hence no wonder the great falcon watches for the moment when it hops into an open space.

The prairie falcon nests in these mountains as early as March 3, placing her eggs on the bare ground on the shelves of rocky ledges; nevertheless, like several other raptors, this falcon has each year become harder to find in the mountain scene.

What a display of superiority and rivalry we have hereabout: the prairie falcon makes the marsh hawk release its captured mouse in mid-air; and then, later, as the falcon arises with a struggling meadow lark in the grasp of its talons, a golden eagle dashes down toward it, causing the falcon to drop the lark, which the eagle in turn clutches for its own prey. We have elsewhere seen a bald eagle likewise in mid-air cause an osprey to release the fish it had hoped to consume. There is much internecine warfare over Farmington Bay.

JANUARY 25

It is a bitterly cold day with snow mounded high along every valley roadway; but out there in a white meadow six hardy ring-necked pheasants are picking seeds from weeds that protrude through the snow. It is so foggy and gelid that even the field posts are rimy. A lonely valley quail (*Lophortyx californicus californicus*), which from his black crest we know to be a male, is treading hungrily along the very roadway itself, in the hope of picking up some kernel of wheat, some leaf of hay, dropped by passing wagons.

After more than a month of sub-freezing weather and much checkered snow, animals as well as birds are sorely tried to survive, for not cold but food—that is the problem.

We can remember when neither quail nor pheasant could be seen in these valleys, for they are both importations; and, if we observe correctly, only the pheasant could long endure the penerating cold and deep snows of some of our winters. Many pheasants have been introduced into the United States, but only the ring-necked has established itself generally.

Our Wasatch quail are not migratory, as they should be when the rigors of our climate are considered. Thousands of European quail (*Coturnix communis*) are, for instance, netted as they fly southward each autumn over the Mediterranean.

Except where they are semi-domesticated and accorded the freedom of the barnyards and thick shrubbery about homes, quail are year by year scarcely increasing in number, and that too in the very field-breaks where pheasants thrive by their own resourcefulness. In the early days of their importation it was the custom to feed quail during the winter months, the roosting places of great covies in certain oak ravines and bushy tanglewoods being well known, but since that custom ceased they have steadily declined.

So well do the ring-necked pheasants thrive in regions of winter snow that they have become the most important upland game birds of the Wasatch mountains. They eat harmful insects, mice, weed seeds and crustaceans, but, on the other hand, destroy much sprouting wheat, corn and peas, and peck ripe tomatoes of our own fields. We cast our vote for them, for few things delight the hunter more than the beautiful plumes and delightsome flesh of a pheasant.

Recently introduced chukar partridges (*Alectoris graeca*) seem able to survive in the dreary cliff region of the southern Wasatch plateau; and we believe that the red-legged partridge (*Alectoris rufa*) of Europe might withstand an ordinary Wasatch winter. Our climate is not warm enough for such birds as the seesee partridge of Turkey, the black-necked pheasant of the Caspian Sea region, the black Francolin of Cyprus, the gray Francolin of Iran, or the black-bellied sand grouse of Spain. The gray or Hungarian partridge (*Perdix perdix perdix*), known well in Ireland, Scotland and Norway, appears, however, to survive introduction here.

JANUARY 26

Under a thawing afternoon, roofs loaded with snow are dripping copiously, and the pathless old home orchard, too long unvisited by us, is inviting once again. Like eaglets from their aerie, youths seek new homes, and in the course of years perhaps return. There is reminiscental joy in it, for in this very orchard is the memory of our first Bohemian waxwings, chickadees, purple finches, evening grosbeaks and others that came with the unfallen, rotted apple, and the lingering snow.

The trees are changed, replaced, for where is that limb from which we sprawling fell, where is that big trunked tree whose apples always seemed small and sour? Yet we are not disappointed, for there, pecking about the bark of a very old apple tree, is a woodpecker with a white back, black and white wings and tail, white underparts and a scarlet nape. We are excited indeed, for the only woodpeckers here with white lines down their backs are the Batchelder's downy woodpecker (*Dendrocopos pubescens leucurus*) and the Rocky mountain hairy woodpecker (*Dendrocopos villosus monticola*); and the hairy is not common. Though both birds are marked the same, the hairy is much larger, two inches or more longer; and, sure enough, our glasses disclose it to be a Rocky mountain hairy, the only one we have seen in the past five years. The scarlet nape indicates it is a male. It is called "hairy" because its nostrils and chin are covered by a tuft of bristle-tipped, hairlike prefrontal feathers that are antrorse, that is, directed forward, a characteristic not quite so conspicuous in the downy.

There it climbs, sometimes hiding from us on the far side of the seeping trunk, often walking upside down, and occasionally uttering a clear *eek* sound. In its restless endeavors it clings on limb after limb, trunk after trunk; and then, with several sharp pecks with its chiseled bill on a likely spot, it protrudes its long speared tongue and pulls out a larva for its reward. Whether it smells or listens no one knows, but it seldom fails. By the way, its tongue is so long that when at rest it coils back almost completely around the right eye socket.

Since the greater portion of its food consists of larvae of harmful beetles, ants and wood-boring caterpillars, and only a small ration of seeds and wild fruits, it is one of our most useful birds. Though the food of the downy is much the same, it is not given to the bark boring habit so much as the hairy, apparently preferring to pick up ants, caterpillars and weevils, when convenient, without digging in for larvae.

But there he goes, restless sprite of the old apple tree, favoring one locale for only a few minutes with his beneficial attention, but altogether too busy to notice or care that he is a solitary bird among dampened trunks and snow-drooped limbs.

It is only in Europe, when thousands of miles away from home for a long period, that we have suffered nostalgia, although there, despite the multitudes of people and the loveliness of such haunts as Kew Gardens, Hampton Court and Epping Forest, homesickness was at times poignant and almost unendurable. Mere people mean little.

JANUARY 27

Once in awhile during a very severe winter someone brings to our attention a snowy owl taken in these Wasatch mountains. While this spectral bird may be considered rare, its occurrence is neither casual nor accidental; but there are birds whose visitation to Utah has been so unusual as to make the records thereof conspicuous in ornithological literature. To review some of them is an interesting diversion.

For instance, the Blackburnian warbler (*Dendroica fusca*) was taken at Ogden, Utah, by Dr. Allen in September, 1871, a record that, so far as we know, has never been duplicated; for this bird seldom appears West of Nebraska.

In similar manner Ridgway collected a red-headed woodpecker (*Melanerpes erythrocephalus caurinus*) at Salt Lake City in June, 1874, a record that stood until Cecil S. Williams shot another at the mouth of the Bear river on August 26, 1941. It seems to be drifting now into the Salt Lake valley.

On July 2, 1919, the author of this book recorded the taking of the roseate spoonbill (*Ajaia ajaja*) at Wendover, Utah; and this beautiful pink member of the ibis family has, we believe, never reappeared. He has also recorded the brown pelican (*Pelecanus occidentalis*) at Farmington Bay, May 27, 1944. One cannot tell which brown in even a studied sight record.

Henshaw once saw the great condor (*Gymnogyps californianus*) in southern Utah, but this mighty bird has now become limited to a few individuals in an isolated valley of California.

The dunlin (*Erolia alpnia pacifica*) is a casual migrant, as also is the semipalmated plover (*Charadrius semipalmatus*) and the mountain plover (*Eupoda montana*).

A brown thrasher (*Toxostoma rufum longicaudum*) was taken by Henry Grantham December 9, 1935, who also collected a golden crowned sparrow (*Zonotrichia atricapilla*) in the summer of 1935 in the vicinity of Zion National Park. Both birds are now there in the museum.

A ruddy turnstone (*Arenaria interpres morinella*) was collected by Archie V. Hull at the mouth of the Bear river in August, 1930; and a purple gallinule (*Porphyrula martinica*) was taken at Haynes Lake, Salt Lake County, November 23, 1924, by John W. Sugden.

Vasco M. Tanner took a dwarf cowbird (*Molothrus ater obscurus*) at St. George in July 1927; A. O. Treganza on June 3, 1916, found an alpine three-toed woodpecker (*Picoides tridactylus dorsalis*) nesting in Salt Lake County. The wood ibis (*Mycteria americana*) occasionally passes through the state after breeding, although some of them do breed at the northern end of the state.

The author once took a chimney swift (*Chaetura pelagia*) at Kaysville, Utah, and found the calliope humming bird (*Stellula calliope*) nesting in Provo canyon on July 10, 1926.

JANUARY 28

Along the fences and ditch embankments of snow-drifted fields flocks of meadowlarks are gathered about the brown and drooping weeds; not "flocks", to be sure, in the sense of a hundred ducks flying high overhead, but an assemblage of a score of birds scattered for a hundred yards or more, never flushing all together but always flying about the same neighborhood as if they fain would linger within sight of one another until sweet mating time. They prefer grassy stretches beside steaming embankments exposed below the blanket of glistening snow. They are sturdy birds thus to enjoy themselves while rime still lingers on the frosted creek-grown willows.

In chinking, isolated flocks on the weeded snow near the meadow larks are even hardier birds, the flitting juncos whom no blizzard can discourage nor cold weather keep from their feasts on weed-seed. Several species of juncos winter in Wasatch valleys, the commonest, perhaps, being the Montana (*Junco organus montanus*) and the gray-headed (*Junco caniceps caniceps*), which latter is likely the only one that breeds in these mountains. The slate-colored junco (*Junco hyemalis hyemalis*) is not so frequently seen here as in the Rockies at the East. The pink sided (*Junco oreganus mearnsi*) often appears in flocks about Christmas time, and the Shufeldt is not uncommon during the winter.

One of the most extraordinary bird experiences that ever befell us occurred in the winter of 1910-11 on the exact spot where the Veterans' Hospital of Salt Lake City now stands. In the search for specimens we came upon an enormous flock of small birds that fed at weeds and then arose in a veritable cloud. Approaching them, I fired twice with my shotgun, just as they swarmed into the air. We picked up ninety-seven dead and bleeding bodies! They were rosy finches or gray-crowned leucostictes (*Leucosticte tephrocotis tephrocotis*), with stouter bills than those of the juncos. To this day we still feel the ensuing sadness and regret of that moment of appalling slaughter. We had wanted to be sure of one or two for identification!

Repeated cold rain is perhaps a greater menace than snow to the brooding junco. One summer, when encamped in a high mountain during a period of daily thunder showers, we saw a junco's nest in a weed become wet, soggy and cold, and the fledglings die in spite of every effort of the mother to save them.

As we examine the complicated structure of an ordinary feather or behold the eye of a wild mammal, we wonder if after all there can be knowledge beyond factual experience, whether our insistence upon the *a posteriori* methodology of science be too rigid? Does hypothesis sometimes replace demonstrated truth, especially in metraphysical fields, and how greaatly may we rely upon it? Must we look to conjecture for explanation of that feathered design? Can beauty be fortuitous? There are many lacunae in our empirical knowledge, yet to guess is to dream and finally to indulge in the idyllic phantoms of complete delusion. *Semper dissero.*

JANUARY 29

All will perhaps agree that the words "diurnal owl" are paradoxical, yet, in so short a phrase, we know not better how to describe that elfin of the coniferous woods, the Rocky Mountain pygmy owl (*Glaucidium gnoma californicum*). Here is one now, grasped alive by hand as he sat in drowsiness on the sered extremity of a canyon limb—a drowsiness and fluffiness caused perhaps by the zero-cold. Nevertheless his sluggishness could have been only a siesta, for beneath his perch are the fresh feathered remains of several juncos.

Gnome, indeed! Just as Phocylides and Theognis in ancient Greece were known as the gnomic poets because they uttered maxims of much strength, so in this small owl is the valiant spirit of a bird thrice its size. It is a real pygmy, shorter than my outstretched hand and fingers, a miniature of owldom and hawkdom. "Hawkdom," we say, because though an owl, it acts like a hawk, hunting in the daytime.

Uncommon resident of these mountains, this little owl inhabits the forests that fledge the upper canyons and ridges, and spends its time either sitting sleepily against the protective coloration of a pine-trunk or flying into the open sunshine after some small bird, mammal or insect. Like a bantam rooster it is extraordinarily fierce and courageous, sometimes in summer overcoming a ground squirrel double its own weight, and, on very rare occasions, so fixing its claws into a victim that it cannot extricate them.

About the first of June the pygmy owl lays its three or four white eggs in a deserted woodpecker hole, and, the duties of incubation over, enjoys its alpine forest land alone, living the summer through on such tid bits as grasshoppers and mice. In winter it naturally drifts to the valleys where sparrows abound; but on the whole it is a beneficial species. How different this elf from the great horned owl!

Strange to say this goggle-eyed hermit of the woods may be decoyed by the easy imitation of its hollow-sounding, somewhat dove-like notes or call.

My friend, J. K. Reese, told me that, once in chilly weather while working on a power-line in Bear river country at the north end of the Wasatch mountains, he and his companion chanced to see a great horned owl asleep on a cross-board beneath a man-high wagon bridge. Since Reese wore not only a thick coat and gloves but also heavy rawhide forearm gauntlets, they decided he should try to grab the bird with his hands; accordingly, while his friend made considerable noise, causing the owl to face him, Reese slowly approached from the other side, and did clutch the bird by the body. Immediately the owl sank its claws clear through the leather gauntlets, but not quite through the coat sleeves as well. Reese firmly held the wings. After inspecting the vicious bird for a few minutes, they let it go; but to this day Reese has never ceased to marvel at claws that could penetrate the heavy leather of his gauntlets.

JANUARY 30

We are cabined in a snow-drooped spruce grove near the top of a canyon; and, after a day of skiing and snowshoeing followed by bounteous food, we are assembled before a hearth burning log. The weird scream of a great horned owl skimming the whitened hills in the moonlight, probably to clutch a rimy white-tailed hare, turns the conversation to the cries of animals and their expression in the English language.

One insists that last fall he heard an elk "bugle" and a deer "bell", while one who had been in India informed us that a tiger "growls" like a bear. The first went on to the effect that a grizzly bear, however, gives a *woof woof* in warning, an *aw aw aw* sound when fighting, an *err-wow-ooo-oof* call in distress, and that grizzly cubs *row row* to their mother.

Someone pokes the log, and then we learn that wolves "howl", elephants "trumpet" and "rumble" (at least Alice the elephant does), baboons "bark" and "roar", monkeys "gibber" and "chatter", donkeys "bray", dogs "bark", "bay", "howl" and "yelp" as do foxes, horses "neigh" and "whinny", hyenas "laugh", pigs "grunt" and "squeal", sheep "baa" and "bleat" and guinea pigs "squeak".

The naturalist volunteers that a porcupine "grunts" and "groans' like an old man, and that a female lion in the mating season gives a long piercing *ow-w-w-w,* and that the alleged blood-curdling scream of the mountain lion is no longer in doubt among informed mammalogists, some of whom once claimed it to be the misinterpreted cry of the great horned owl.

Guests begin to roast chestnuts or popcorn, as the topic drifts to birds, concerning which many accurate observations are made.

Sparrows "chirp" and "peep", swallows "twitter", bitterns "boom", grouse "drum", blackbirds "whistle" an *okadee,* ravens "croak", peacocks "scream", magpies "chatter", chickens "pip", swans "cry", "whistle" or "bugle", canaries "sing" or "quaver", owls "hoot" or "screech", cocks "crow" and crows "caw".

The naturalist says that in England he heard the nightingale "pipe" or "warble" and another claims he heard a gorilla in a circus "shriek" and "scream" and an orangutang "whine", "shriek", "bellow", and "roar".

Again the conversation drifts to birds. Jays "chatter", doves "coo", ducks "quack", geese "cackle" and "hiss", eagles "scream", hens "cackle" and "cluck", and red-shafted flickers *tuck tuck tuck tuck* in the spring.

As we put on a new log, the conversation broadens to other forms of life.

Bees "hum", beetles "drone", bulls "bellow" and cats "mew", "purr", "swear", "caterwaul"; crickets "stridulate" and "sing"; cows "moo", "low" and "bellow"; flies "buzz"; frogs "croak"; grasshoppers "chirp" and "pitter"; mice "squeak" and "squeal"; snakes "hiss", alligators "roar" and "bellow".

JANUARY 31

Half frozen, hungry and weary, we toss our last jack rabbits, which we have lugged for several hundred yards, into the express car, and board the train awaiting us at Promontory on the North end of the Great Salt Lake. What a day when among three hundred hunters we are accounted high man! But that is not our real joy—we have just seen a flock of over five hundred sage hens (*Centrocercus urophasianus urophasianus*) feeding on the thick stunted sage, unmindful of the driving snow. Protected by law, they were unmolested by us, though we should rather have possessed one of them than the several thousand "jacks" in the railway car. "Sage flavored meat" some would complain; but there is a neat trick about that—the moment such a bird is shot the experienced hunter slits its abdomen, grasps its wings and feet together, and with one quick swing and jerk casts its sage-filled entrails to the ground.

Never again do we expect to see so many of these desirable birds, largest of American grouse, for protection has perhaps been almost too tardy to save them. We have shot them in many frequented vales of the Wasatch, their favorite habitat being some isolated gully where sage brush grows tall and a spring trickles not over a mile away. Flushing with thunderous notes of agitated wings, they alternately flap and sail, being an easy mark for the gunner; and we have never seen them alight upon trees. A mature cock may weigh up to eight pounds, but the average hen is less than half that size.

There is no doubt that this large game bird should be called "sage grouse", as it was by Coues in 1884. In 1859 the ornithologist S. F. Baird was as much in error in designating it "sage cock" as sportsmen from 1861 onward were in naming it 'sage hen', doubtless because its cluck reminded them of the barnyard fowl.

Though subsisting principally on the leaves of the sage, which few other birds or mammals deign to eat, the sage grouse like many other birds gorges itself on insects in the summer.

In spring the sage grouse have a veritable breeding pen or open space, possessed by the champion cock of them all, and margined by bushes and hopeful males. One by one the females come to be served by the avian king; and when satiety weakens him he drifts away, thus allowing lesser males to take his place.

Some gastronomists claim that the finest tasting game bird in the world is the Scotch grouse, which feeds entirely upon the tender shoots of heather. At any rate you may have your ducks, pheasants or quail, your venison or trout, but give to us the breast of a sage grouse cooked over a balsam fire. By the way, here is a gastronomic secret: the jack rabbits or hares are distinguished from ordinary rabbits by their dented lip, which characteristic is very apparent in the young jack. Roast the young jack; put the old one into the soup kettle.

FEBRUARY 1

As it snowed softly last night, the atmosphere this early morning is rich in color and serene; all outdoors is a gorgeous polychrome; and, strange to say, the most beautiful tints are on the western side of the valley. The mountains there are pale mazarine blue, while those of the east are gray and white, sharply defined against a sky of burn blue. The clouds of the west are pale rhodonite pink, beautiful indeed alongside the brighter pinkish peaks of the mountains just blushed by the rays of a rising sun.

Overhead the sky is light columbia blue, a blue transpicuous and ineffable, and the moon is a crescent of whitish silver; smoke over the city is a blanket of mouse grey, in striking contrast with the purity of the upper atmosphere.

There is an old saying: "Red in the morning, sailors take warning; red at night sailors' delight", which has much meteorological truth, even in these mountains. When the morning sky is red it is an indication that it is laden with moisture, which before long is likely to precipitate; and, while the sunset of evening is often red for the same reason, there is usually the chance that the coldness of night will take away some of it in the form of dew.

Jesus said to the Pharisees: "When it is evening, ye say, It will be fair weather; for the sky is red. And in the morning, It will be foul weather today; for the sky is red and lowring".

The Wasatch sunsets are ordinarily beautiful at any time of the year; in fact, as one reaches the land of the painted hills at the southern extremity of the Wasatch mountains, sunset tints and glows often intermingle with the natural pinks and reds of bluffs and mounts so as to form vistas of gorgeous coloration.

It is said, that in winter a ring around the sun or the moon is an indication of storm, since the phenomenon is caused by light shining through vast expanses of extremely fine ice crystals ready to descend when encouraging conditions arise.

We once knew a farmer who claimed that for fifty years following 1860 he kept weather records, using an old iron kettle in which to measure rainfall. We ourselves saw this well known kettle. A long cloud along the ridge of the Wasacth mountains between Weber canyon and City Creek meant to him the approach of a terrifying "East Wind", and dark lowering clouds over "Mack's gap" southwest of the Great Salt Lake indicated storm. Often in winter he was called to the stove-warmed circle of a country store to furnish a weather date or make a prediction. This was before the time of weather-bureau forecastings, and his advice was seldom ignored.

Today we see a thousand house sparrows and a hundred Brewer blackbirds enjoying life with a flock of sheep at a feeding ground in a snow field. Here and there a blackbird is perched on a sheep's back picking up bits of food flipped upon the wool.

FEBRUARY 2

Much confusion exists here concerning what is a "ground hog"; some think it to be the "pot gut" or ground squirrel (*Citellus armatus*) of the Wasatch hillsides; others, the white-tailed prairie dog of the Uintas, (*Cynomys leucurus*) to which indeed it is closely related; but many do not recognize it as the golden mantled marmot (*Marmota flaviventris nosophora*) an animal in size nearer to a badger than to the ordinary squirrel, and one that they have seldom if ever seen alive in the wildlands. The *flaviventris* refers to its golden color, and *nasophora* is from two Greek words "nosis", disease, and "phora", carrying in reference to its ability to carry Rocky mountain fever.

The truth is, since early American days the ground hog has been known variously as "siffleur", "moonack", "marmot", "rockchuck", "woodchuck", "wuchak", or "otchock". Marmot is the proper scientific designation, from the Latin words *murem montis,* mountain mouse, the term "marmot" having been used as early as 1607 by Topsell to designate an Alpine animal of the genus *Arctomys* "about the bigness of a badger". The French word is "marmotte", the Italian "marmotta" and the Spanish "marmota".

In America the animal was first known (T. Glover, 1676) as a "monack' or "moonack" (Latin, *monax*); but in New England in 1689 they began to use the word "woodchuck", from the Cree Indian name "wuchak" or "otchock". In 1703 Baron LoHontan called it "siffleur", a name existent among French Canadians even today.

In 1789 in Maryland there was mention of a "monack or ground hog", but the word "ground hog" gradually became the common designation in the Southern states, especially among the negroes, who held it in superstitious awe on account of its ability to dig, and who started the absurd legend about ground hog day. "He gwine to die; he seed the moonack", is how Schele de Vere described their fear. Zoomancy, that is, divination by observing the action of animals, is an unreliable art, although many dwellers in the wilds are real zoomantists in that they claim that the actions of various animals indicate a hard or a mild winter.

Imagine an animal four or five times as big as the ordinary squirrel, but really a squirrel, in fact the largest of the family *Sciuridae*; a rodent that lives on the grass, tender leaves and stems of rocky mountain hillsides; a tremendous squirrel that in the fall becomes so fat it can hardly waddle, that stores no food, but sleeps most of the winter.

One of these brown-eyed marmots, captured in June on the slopes of Ensign peak near our home, was eating sego lilies. Though weighing about eight pounds, she was rather helpless when suspended by her tail, and when confined to a barrel she hissed, ground her teeth and chirrped, at intrusion, especially from a dog. She would eat radishes and potatoes, but rejected meat. Becoming too vicious to keep, she was released finally at her old homesite.

FEBRUARY 3

As we travel a snow-banked road northward towards the mouth of Weber canyon the ridges of the mountains are cloaked in mist and the white lower slopes and canyons are fledged with dark junipers, stalky oaks and maples. The landscape is still white, cloudy and cold.

As our eyes are attracted towards a solitary bird sitting in fluffy quiet on the tip of a snow-glazed scrub oak at the very roadside, we slowly stop in order not to disturb it, and then we bring it so close with the glasses that we can even detect the occasional winking of its eye. It is a bluebird, and from the fact that its breast is rust color, an unfailing mark, we instantly know it to be a chestnut-backed bluebird (*Sialia mexicana occidentalis*)! Though this mild member of the thrush family winters just south of these mountains, this is the earliest date of its arrival we remember, especially as hereabout this winter we have had almost constant snow and cold since Christmas. It utters a soft *pew* as we gaze; and then from the dark gully below it a hoary ruffed grouse (*Bonasa umbellus incana*), apparently unable to bear the uncertainty of our presence further, flushes and with burring wings goes sailing down over the hill tops, but not too quickly for us to catch its gray brown color and black-banded tail tip. This is another surprise, for this grouse is becoming very scarce. During the winter it subsists largely on buds, seeds and dried berries, and to find a covey we usually have to walk up a sylvan side canyon that is trickled by a spring. It is a hardy, resourceful bird, able to resist most everything but the encroachment of man.

When we reach the Weber river we go westerly to the valley, noting the pink coloration of male willows along the way. Here and there about a farm yard stand skeletonized boxelder trees, which reveal many last year's birds' nests, especially those of Bullock orioles and Arkansas flycatchers, sometimes a half dozen nests to a tree.

We tarry in a fieldside lane for a cup of coffee; when lo! there flies before us, not over thirty feet above the snow-covered ground, a marsh hawk (*Circus cyaneus hudsonius*), readily distinguished by its white rump and pale coloration. Living chiefly on meadow mice and other small harmful rodents, as well as reptiles and insects, this hawk is an economic benefit, despite its occasional foray into the barnyard and not infrequent destruction of water birds.

The pure in heart may readily find peace and joy in the higher wild woods: in winter there is snow, white, mounded, untrodden by man or beast, a covering undefiled and sheltered by solemn heaven-pointing firs; in spring there is gradual transformation and awakening, as if some great hand were directing the way to joy; in summer limpid runnels chatter through groves of pine, deer graze contented in flowered glades and birds unafraid direct their songs towards the flush of dawn and crimsoned clouds of eventide.

FSBRUARY 4

Loveliest of birds, the Bohemian waxwings (*Bombycilla garrula pallidiceps*) are here again. Standing beneath them as they feed on the rotted fruit of a big apple tree, watching them as they chat incessantly and show kindest courtesies towards one another, we are delighted that birds so beautiful and mild-mannered as they should flock to the snow-laden orchards of our February valleys. "Beautiful", yes, to us at least, the most beautiful of all the birds of this region.

They belong to a family (*Bombycillidae*) all of their own, with cedar waxwings the only other representatives, unless such silky fly-catchers as the phainopepla (*Phainopepla nitens lapida*) be included, though this southern Utah bird might as well belong to the thrushes as to the waxwings.

The Bohemian sexes are alike, and, as we notice their blended crests, soft fawn colors of vinaceous grayish brown, velvety black throats, yellowish abdomens, and wing secondaries adorning their shafts with tear-shaped spots of the color of glossy red sealing wax, we not only catch the imports of their name but also stare in admiration of their silken blended beauty, far beyond the ability of either pen or brush adequately to describe.

Year after year we have heard the *zeeing* of these delightful vistors when they arrived in flocks of a hundred or more and settled to their garrulity on the upper limbs of lofty locust trees; winter after winter we have followed them from one apple orchard to another, standing often so close that we might have touched some of them with a stick, ever enjoying their sweet comrady ways, ever regarding them as the gentlest living things we knew. Sometimes there are so many of them that when they alight on a˙Lombardy poplar they bend the tree top.

Concerning their nests and eggs we know only what others say, for their nidification belongs to the far north region of Hudson Bay. When with us, they subsist on frozen orchard fruits, lingered on the limb, or on such dried mountain berries as those of the ash and juniper, and such house-yard favorites as the pyracanthus.

Whatever be their ways of migration, whatever be the secrets of their home, this we realize, that to them we owe our very incentive to pursue the diverting paths of ornithology.

We believe that few men could watch these beautiful, gentle and polite birds at a distance of five or six feet without ever afterward feeling a conscientious scruple at the killing of *any* bird.

Delightful are the jingling notes of the snow birds (*Junco oreganus montanus*), as they flit from tree to tree, for it is very cold and snowy and they generally appear when all other birds are silent in the grim business of obtaining food. Somehow the sound always reminds us of marbles being hit together. Whenever we see juncos in the back yard, we involuntarily inquire, are there plenty of dry hearth-logs in the cellar? These and the waxwings come when it is snowy and cold and when one thinks of companions at the warm fireside.

FEBRUARY 5

A sooty red-shafted flicker (*Colaptes cafer collaris*) is just now standing against yonder housewall, with its feet clinging to a Boston ivy limb and its tail acting as a prop against the brick; and, thus sitting at ease, it is eating the ivy fruit at will, while robins, likewise partaking from the vine, do considerable fluttering and nipping before securing their berries. Since the rectrices of the flicker's tail are abruptly acuminate at the end, they sufficiently stick into the infinitesimal holes of almost any perpendicular surface to support the weight of the bird. So much for its weight; but, as its body nearly always learns backward when it is probing for food, it must clutch some rough surface with its feet to keep from falling, in this instance either a seam between bricks or a branch of the ivy itself. It is like a man on a perpendicular ladder —his weight may be on his feet but he still must have some sort of hold with his hand.

Every member of the woodpecker tribe (*Picidae*) has a tongue so long as to coil around the back of the inner skull, as if on a spool, sometimes even forward again to the very base of the bill; but the barbed tongue of the flicker is pointed at the tip, not chisel-shaped like that of its downy relatives. The flicker on the wall before us does not extend its tongue, as it would if probing a hole for an insect, but nips off the ivy berries with its mandibles as does the robin. Having a clear side view with the glasses at twenty feet, we can see each berry roll into its throat without assistance from the tongue.

Nearly every day in the year we observe flickers about home (on the foothills of the Wasatch at an altitude of 4665 feet); we see them in the midst of winter-blizzards feeding on the old ivy's berries; hear them in March tatooing roofs with their strong bills and uttering their loud *if if if if if if* of verbal exuberance, as if a barnyard hen had raised her voice an octave higher than its wont and increased its penetration triplefold; and notice them in summer, voicing merely the dispirited clucks of molting time. We once sawed a woodland juniper trunk punctured with an old woodpecker den, brought it to our gardenyard, and watched our neighborhood flickers adopt it as their own, raising for several seasons nearly a dozen youngsters each year. We have often hoped to see the parents regurgitate food to the tender newborn, but we have caught them only placing insects in crevices for the fledglings to peck out in imitation of mature practice. Foolishly, we finally replaced the old trunk with a new-fangled purchased box affair supposed to be able to entice any woodpecker; but our flickers disdained it and have nested there no more.

Ants, a thousand at a meal, are the flicker's food, though crickets, grasshoppers, spiders, larvae, seeds and berries enter into its fare, and it even catches beetles and locusts *a la moucherolle,* on the wing.

We delight to hear these strong-billed birds hammer tin roofs; for without hope of drilling a hole, they nevertheless enjoy the clang.

FEBRUARY 6

Snow-choked and cold, City Creek canyon along its narrowed but gurgling brook has a bleak and dull appearance; except for an isolated oak-clump here and there, and for an occasional maple, the trees and shrubs are bare of leaves; and only the skeleton of nature appears, in shapes, sizes and strengths undiscernable in summer.

Were it not for the birches and maples there would be little striking color; in fact, the birch trees (*Betula fontinalis*), a sub-species peculiar to this very stream, adorn the bank-sides with patches of madder brown, which on closer inspection of the bark, shows tints of vandyke and acjou red.

The big-toothed maples (*Acer grandidentatum*), however, display the most delightful bits of color in the canyon; they are numerous in the shady declivities near the stream, and some of their dry leaves are almost as thick as in autumn. Most of the leaf-bunches are cinnamon-buff; but here and there are groups of surprising coloration; some are light coral; some coral red; others brick red or brick red shaded along the veins with hessian brown. Another species, the ash-leaved maple or boxelder (*Acer interius*), a tree nearly eighty feet high, has scarcely a leaf left on it.

Russian thistles (*Salsola pestifer*) rolled to the roadside, are a deep natural gray; but close inspection reveals that the plants are dead except their seeds, which remain inclosed in paperlike perianths and held in place loosely by numerous twisted hairs. In biting one of the twigs we find it to be salty, hence, readily understand its generic name *Salsola,* a diminutive of the Latin word *salsus,* salty. The tumbleweeds (*Amaranthus graecizans*) beside it show more color, and are so stiff they readily roll over the snow. The bare yellow tall sticks of white sweet clover (*Melitotus alba*) are abundant everywhere, and the dead sunflower stalks yet lingering in the snow are cinnamon brown.

As we emerge from the canyon we listen *arrectis auribus* to the song of a meadowlark!

If, as some will claim, in the three or four billion years of the earth's existence, a million animal species have risen and sunk into extinction; if more than a million different species exist today, each struggling to prove that its way of life best assures survival; and, if as certainly as we breathe, thousands of living species are doomed to pass into oblivion, among them possibly being man himself, we are driven to great humility before it all; for, bear this in mind, only in his ability to form concepts does man excel among the mammals of the world. Physically, outside of his brain, he is far down the list in capabilities; but in his growing knowledge, especially of how to conquer disease, he may in some measure prolong, if not determine, his fate. Man has the unique ability to *store* knowledge—in books, tape recordings, disc records, and the like—and to pass it on from generation to generation, thus giving him a tremendous advantage.

FEBRUARY 7

Wherever in winter along the foothills we enter a snow-drifted arroya that is marked by stumpy caverns at a brookside and thickly grown with scrub oak and tall sage, we know even before we discover its tracks that a cottontail is likely to bound suddenly from our tread. We are standing now where precisely this has occurred, in a brookless ravine, however, of northern slope; and the incident recalls how once for several months we imprisoned a rabbit in a barn where its only hope of moisture was from the dry hay on which it fed.

This little cottontail (*Sylvilagus nuttallii grangeri*) which by the way, is a *bonne-bouche* on any man's table, especially if guests do not suspect the identity of the savory dish, is called the Granger and is accounted the only cottontail of the Wasatch. It is a race of buff color, frosted on its head with gray and washed on its back with black.

Meek and timid in nature, the cottontail is nevertheless one of the most interesting mammals of the lower ravines. Rabbits in general vary little among themselves, but sharply from other species of the gnawing tribe: the soles of a rabbit's feet, for instance, are not bare like those of rodents, but covered with hair, a fact which accounts for the lack of sharp definition in their footprints; furthermore, behind the two big front teeth of a rabbit's upper jaw are another pair of small teeth, which do not reach far enough down to be of any use. These inservient molars indicate that the ancestral rabbits of prehistoric days had four large front teeth instead of two. These and other peculiarities are such that rabbits are no longer classified in the *Rodentia* (rodents) but are placed in an Order of their own, the *Lagomorpha,* from the Greek *lagos,* hare, and *morphe,* shape.

A rabbit's front legs are so constructed that they cannot be turned inwards and used as hands in feeding. Thus a rabbit may reach high to nibble some tid bit, but its feet hang helpless during the process; in fact it does not use its front feet for much of anything except running, standing and stamping in anger.

Briar-grown berry patches, sage grown ravines, isolated clumps of bushes, whether on the roadside or the mountain slope—these are the haunts of the cottontail. Creek embankments and places of impenetrable foliage suit it to a nicety; winter and summer it thrives in a woodland only a few rods square; although I see it more often in arroyos, dry but verdurous, than at brooksides.

The food of the cottontail is more varied than that of most other mammals, as it includes in summer fruit, grasses, vegetables, and almost any herbaceous bit it fancies, and in winter, dead grass, buds, the bark of poplar, and leaves of juniper or spruce; and always it is a pleasing denizen of the uncultivated places.

It has been so mild today that we have trimmed the garden roses; a half hour ago it thundered; and now in late afternoon has begun to snow furiously.

FEBRUARY 8

Diverting our path for the hour to the snow-molded trails of a nearby canyon, we chance to break a twig from an antelope bush (*Purshia tridentata*), that delightful member of the rose family which in April wafts an apple-blossom perfume; and find to our surprise that its pithy brown marrow is even now pervading the air with the spiciest redolence we have ever sniffed in the wilds. We recall that the rabbit brush of autumn was graveolent, but this odor is not only strong but pleasing. A twig must be broken to reveal the subtle redolence of the antelope bush, for evidently it is the precursor of its blossom's far-reaching fragrance of spring. The bark is gray, flecked with a paler color, and the small flower-buds are brown, dotted with maroon. What delights of life are frequently unnoticed at our very door!

This interesting discovery persuades us to snip the branch of a scrub oak, which though gay and sturdy despite its galls, has no scent; but its small buds are the color of cedarwood. We break one of the tiny bud-cones away, finding it to be not only as firm as a nut but also a light pea green tint inside.

A twig of the birch has bark the color of a Burmese ruby, thickly specked with white lenticels. It has no sweet smell; its pistillate catkins are dried away, but its staminate catkins are little greenish maroon cylinders nearly an inch long. A birch's solitary pistillate inforescence distinguishes it from the clustered formation of the alder.

We stroll along the ice-margined creek to a narrow-leaved cottonwood (*Populus angustifolia*) where a broken limb gives no perceptible odor. Its bark is oyster gray, but its pointed, scaly, resinous buds are softer than the oak buds but tinted the same light green.

When next we break a branch, this time from a big-toothed maple, we find its interior dry and scentless, its bark dark gray and its small buds a Spanish raisin shade.

We break off the young branch of a boxelder and notice, much to our delight, that its bark is prune color frosted with a white bloom. The buds encircle the stems in threes or appear at the branch tips in a cluster of five; and they seem even more frosted than the stem, indeed even pubescent or covered with downy hairs. We are delighted to find a true "bud sport", the buds encircling the stems in threes, which is unusual.

Thus ends an hour's meander in the snow-choked canyon, where a purl-endeared brook sings as merrily as in summer; but that hour is enough to show the variety of nature's ways. Nevertheless, we proceed along an open highway, ever upward toward the ridge, where at last we gaze upon the infinitude of the firmament.

> The sky above is deep and hyaline,
> Ineffable and mystic in its blue;
> It clearly leads to thoughts of things divine,
> Yet gives no final meaning to the view.

FEBRUARY 9

Though the day be cold and drear and all vegetation drooped with snow, in the fields about the Jordan river flocks of desert horned larks (*Eremophila alpestris utahensis*) feed on the seeds of the pigweed, salt bush, ragweed, amaranth and other noxious weeds, which here and there protrude through the white blanket.

It is not difficult to distinguish these birds in the field, since, being larger than a sparrow, they have two hornlike tufts of feathers, one on each side of the head; but the most characteristic feature of the *Alaudidae,* the famous family to which they belong, is the scutellation of the tarsus of their legs, the scales being so arranged that the rear of the leg is as blunt as the forward part and there is a scale-meeting groove along the inner part of the leg. We say "famous" family because to it belongs the skylark (*Alauda arvensis*), which we have frequently heard in England, the same skylark of which immortal poets in ecstacy sang. Though recent studies have greatly increased the number of the horned races the principal breeding race of this renowned family in the Wasatch is the one designated above; indeed, so far as we know, the sweet-singing skylark of the old world has not been successfully introduced into America excepting in Vancouver Island.

But there they are before us, the desert horned larks, with us winter and summer, never singing much more than a twittered tinkle, or uttering a drearsome call *tee-tee ti.*

Like the meadowlarks, when overcome by the exuberance of spring, they do indeed soar high with ebullient song, lingering sometimes on outstretched wings for some thrilling expression of their passion, a capriccietto of love.

Their nests, made of delicate bits of dried grass, we shall expect to find later on the ground; but for the present we are delighted with their ever dependable companionship, for no matter what the weather or the day they lend their sweet charm to the sagelands.

As we return from the saline flats, geese vee overhead on their northward way. Half a dozen female marsh hawks are soaring, and looking straight downward with their flat head-tops pointed forward.

Somehow, from the valley, the mountainside canyons look uninhabitable, snow-drowned and cold.

The word "canyon", frequently used in these books, is from the Spanish "canon", meaning tube, ravine, gorge, quill. It has been variously spelled "canon", "kanyon", "kenyan" and "canyon", all of them, of course, phonetic; but apparently the first use of "canyon" in English was by O. Russell in his *Journal* in 1842: "This stream ran through a mountain in a deep, narrow canyon of rocks". The word in the West now refers to any narrow mountain valley that is large enough to have a perpetual stream and that has high steep sides, usually wooded. A minor slash without brook is called a gully, ravine, or even, again, the Spanish arroyo.

FEBRUARY 10

Draped along the back yard fence is a dried vine called the wild cucumber or wild balsam apple (*Echinocystis lobata*) with prickly brown fruits, crisp and egg-shaped, dangling from its branches. What attracts our attention to it this cold, blizzardy morning is, that fourteen western robins are feeding avidly upon it in a novel manner: each flies to a pod, hovers *a la colibri* before it, and pecks vigorously until the seeds begin to run, whereupon the hungry bird flutters down and picks the scattered seeds from the snow. Whether the ability of a robin to hover in the air, as if suspended on humming bird wings, is limited, or determined by the resistance of each pod, it is difficult to ascertain, save that the average duration of the suspended flutterings we timed was four and a half seconds.

Ordinarily one does not see the western robin (*Turdus migratorius propinquus*) in flocks, nor, for that matter, eating seeds alone; but on snowy mornings one must expect all birds to take such food as is available. As one sits beside a canyon stream at eventide, when the tips of the pines are being given a farewell kiss by a departing sun, he may in summer readily believe the robins are giving their twilight songs in flocks, but such periods of sweet rejoicing are due to accidental association in a congenial environment, not to the sense of flocking.

The naturalist never knows when some extraordinary incident is going to occur. How often must have been the thrills of Audubon, Wilson and Macgillvray, of Baird, Brewer and Ridgway, of Lewis, Coues and other early ornithologists and mammalogists in the virgin fields of America when birds entirely new to science were discovered by them! Now new species appear only among the smaller bits of life—the spiders, the insects, the worms and the snails—but their description usually remains in the highly technical tome.

The snow is a foot deep outside, and house sparrows are eager at the window feed box. There beside them just now is a Shufeldt's junco, which is readily distinguished from them by its pinkish bill, black head, rusty back, and by the fact that as it flits away its outer tail feathers show white. They sit with amicable tolerance, however, in the same tree, and it takes its turn at the feed box. Thus far, there having been no conflict of authority, mastership is undetermined.

To be a house sparrow is to live in a state of constant daytime apprehension. Even when perching in what one would believe to be a secure place, such as a niche in a wall, the little fellow is so wrought with fear that he moves his head and eyes every second or so in order to catch the slightest movement or what might be danger in his environs. If a robin approach on wing he merely squats, not in dread, to let the larger bird go by; but if a shrike or a sparrow hawk come toward him in somewhat the same appearance of size he immediately goes into a panic in an attempt to escape. The alertness and reflexes of the bird, his spontaneous movements and rapid motor response to stimulation, are astonishing.

55

FEBRUARY 11

It has been an arduous climb through deep snow and up difficult rocky slopes, but here we are on the 8,000 foot summit above City Creek canyon, nevertheless at the verge of a grove of gloomy-clustered spruces and pines, a spot filled with the memory of summer romance and beauty. We relax in the sweet enjoyment of the clear mountain air: but ours is not a skiing party, since we have plodded to this great height over wind-swept ridges with but one thought in mind—the crossbills. Here they are, a flock of them, males dull red, females olive, some of them flying with swift undulations from tree to tree, uttering their call notes *tic tic tic* as they fly. They are fairly large crossbills, the race known as *Loxia curvirostra bendirei*.

The genus *Loxia,* comprising those finches known as crossbills, is noted for the fact, that in all its members the mandible and the falcate maxilla are crossed at the tips, that is, in the adult birds, for the juveniles have no such bill-tip misalignment. This special contrivance of nature is an adaptation to the gathering of their favorite food, the seeds of the *coniferae;* and it leads us anew to an appreciation of Lamarck, who believed in the inheritance of acquired characteristics, and who in the *long run* of evolution may not be far wrong.

Notwithstandings our close approach the crossbills disregard our presence. They are constantly busy in parrotlike movements, frequently hanging upside down, holding a seed with one leg, clinging to twigs with the bill, and walking downward on the trunks of the spruces.

What pleases us most, however, is a female nesting on a spruce limb high above our heads. By the aid of the steep hillside further up we are able to get a fairly good view of her through the glasses; the nest is rather flattened and composed of twigs and bark. It is extraordinary, that incubation should be going on at this time of the year; but there she is, a determined little guardian against the bitter cold.

One may never be sure of seeing the crossbills; for unless it be a good nut-year they do not appear at all. As we look at them we marvel at nature's ability to provide one bird with a means of livelihood where others would starve. The finches, however, are a hardy lot; for among this great family are included such storm-resisting birds as: the evening grosbeak, the pine grosbeak, the cassin purple finch, the house finch, the leucostictes, the pine siskin, the Gambel sparrow, the white throated sparrow, the western tree sparrow, the juncos, the mountain song sparrow, and so on. Merely to list some of them indicates how much the snow-choked forests are indebted to the family *Fringillidae.* Our common introduced house sparrow (*Passer domesticus*) is really a weaver finch, and belongs to the *Ploceidae,* a different family entirely.

We believe that the reason such birds as crossbills and Bohemian waxwings are tame in the presence of man is, that in the cold regions where they breed they see only such large mammals as deer and bears, which give little heed to mere birds.

FEBRUARY 12

We are wading through the snow on the dykes of Farmington Bay, and delighting in the reward of our venture, for there on a roadside-mound ahead of us sits a Utah water pipit (*Anthus spinoletta alticola*), a slender billed, sparrowlike bird with buffy, streaked underparts. As we watch it, it constantly bobs its tail up and down, a movement, as far as we recall just now, that is duplicated only by the water ouzel; but the ouzel bobs not with its tail but with its entire body, by a genuflexion of the legs. Constantly the pipit's tail rises and falls; nevertheless, this winsome member of the *Motacillidae* or wagtail family entertains us with an occasional *pee pee,* thin and clear, higher on the scale than the notes of the horned lark, which we are accustomed to see on this identical locale.

We flounder on, encouraged by the sight of a hundred pintails; and then to our gratified vision sixty two whistling swans disport for an hour two hundrred yards off shore. Old and young (we know the young by their grayish plumages) engage our attention, proudly swimming with heads held high and necks arched, softly calling their throaty trumpets or whistles. As the older birds flap their wings we notice no black except on legs and bills. Their note is not a whistle but a soft *ho hoo,* closely resembling the call of a girl to a friend. As a bird flushes from us it patters and flaps along the water for several yards, making considerable noise, but when it at last masters the air it flies easily with its long neck held straight ahead and its black legs tucked against its body.

On our return we notice a robin-sized grayish bird with a black bill and a black stripe through its eye sitting at the very top of a poplar tree. It is a northwestern shrike (*Lanius excubitor invictus*); and as it flushes each time before us it drops almost straight down before rising again. It is alone, and apparently not interested in anything except the scenery from the treetops.

We have noticed a hundred scattered, solitary red wings, a score or more singing meadowlarks, a Treganza heron, a flock of horned larks, a score of female marsh hawks and a few mallards.

In the dreary alkali-mud flat in the northeast part of Farmington Bay we come upon a deep hole or pit five yards across, filled to about ten feet below the land surface with what looks like watered blood! Ugh! We promise that we will some day later in this year return with a bucket and rope to ascertain what it is; but in the meantime it is our *pit of blood.* There are only a few extraordinary natural objects in the Wasatch region—the Great Salt Lake, one fourth salt in which one can lie on his back and read a newspaper at the same time; the Devils Slide in Weber canyon, rocky escarpments in long parallel formation; a cave with beautiful stalactites and stalagmites, in American Fork canyon; and nothing more except several delightful hot springs.

FEBRUARY 13

Although it is a warm sunny noontide at the summit of Parley's canyon, where the snow is three feet deep, the atmosphere is filled with infinitesimal ice crystals, some of which float with a tiny sparkle within a few inches of one's eyes. The ever-pleasing groves of evergreens on the mountainside at the southeast are blackish green save where their limb-tips are drooped with snow. We know many forests in these pleasing mountains but none that excels this vista of shaded tranquility and charm, of assembled pines, formal, straight and round, ambrosial and serene.

Descending the canyon, we see few tracks: two hungry deer have trailed a ridge here; a nervous rabbit has hopped along this arroyo; a white-footed mouse has left its nocturnal tracks in the scrub oak patch at our side. Only a magpie is awing.

A few yards below the reservoir an alder (*Alnus tenuifolia*) has staminate catkins so plentiful and drooping as to resemble inch-long pendants of dull brown hung like jewels all about the tree. The branches are gray, and, when we examine one closely, we find that every few inches along it a quarter-inch maroon colored leaf-bud grows on a little stem of its own. At the tip of most twigs are four staminate catkins cylindrical in shape, more than an inch long, garnet colored and spotted with brackish slate.

Further down the canyon a hawthorn (*Crataegus rivularis*) has branches of coral red flecked with gray. Its inch-long thorns are gray, black-pointed, sharp and strong; but its buds are mere pin-heads of waxy garnet.

A choke cherry (*Prunus melanocarpa*) has bark of raisin color spotted with gray; its pin sharp buds are yellowish brown, a quarter of an inch long, each on an individual stem.

We trudge through snow-limbed labyrinths after these interesting things, noticing, however, that the mountain sides are dappled gray where noonday suns have thawed the open hills. Here and there willows are orange or greenish gold; and young cottonwoods are ghostly white along the creek.

We watch some deer browsing contentedly on a shrub-stalked knoll, and then ourselves trudge homeward with the realization that vigorous, intricate, varied life does exist in the bleak and snowy hills.

One of the most wondrous sights of the Wasatch appears about a mile west of the divide between East and Emigration canyons on the old Mormon trail: there to the south is not one ridge of mountains, not two, not three but four, one above another, as if colossal alligators stood side by side to form the landscape. To see one mountain in the distance is usually very interesting, but to look upon four, rising from the foremost to the highest one in the distant background, is inspiring indeed.

FEBRUARY 14

The following true grizzly bear story was related to me many years ago by the late John E. Godfrey of Clarkston, Utah:

In February, 1863, a famed bear hunter named Graham went with his son-in-law, Andrew Shumway, for wood on the Logan river at the West side of Cache valley in the northern Wasatch mountains. Having stood his gun against some willows, Graham started to cut hawthorn limbs for pitchfork handles when without warning he was attacked by a she-grizzly whose den he had disturbed. She knocked him down, one of her claws tearing into his right eye and puncturing the roof of his mouth; then severed his head with one bite so that it hung only by neck-shreds; and finally bit every part of his body that quivered.

Young Shumway fled to the sleigh and clung on as the panic-stricken horses ran home. A party of twenty five armed horsemen was assembled from Wellsville and Clarkston, headed by one of Graham's friends, a bear hunter named Hill.

Arriving at the scene, they saw by tracks in the snow that the grizzly with her two cubs had ambled down the stream, and, soon finding her, they sent dogs into the willows after her. Two of the dogs sprawled out with broken backs, so this method of attack was abandoned.

Finally Hill dismounted, and with gun in readiness approached the bear copse alone. He, having reached its verge, she rushed out at him, arising on her hind legs the better to strike him. Hill aimed steadily, pulled the trigger, but the gun only snapped! Thrusting the gun barrel into her throat, the intrepid man held it there as she chewed and pawed it, and then actually turned his head around and exclaimed: "Boys, it's the first time it has refused to go off"!

Worried about her cubs, the bear unexpectedly whirled and ran into the brush to them. Hill deliberately squatted on the snow, calmly reloaded with his powder horn, and was just putting on a new cap when the infuriated bear charged him again.

Suddenly, among the men his son, James Hill, shouted: "Pa, sit still and I'll fetch her", and an instant later shot over his father's head, knocking the bear down. Old man Hill instantly sprang up, and then emptied his six-shooter into the butt of her ear.

Many shots were then taken at the cubs as they swam the river, one of them being killed on the spot, and the other being found dead a few days later with sixteen bullets in its body.

Some ten years after I published the foregoing account in a local magazine, Mrs. Cora Sales called upon me to assure me that it was true in every detail. She was a great, great grand daughter of the Graham mentioned, whose full name was Thomas Bedford Graham, and had heard the story many times from her grandfather. During several decades of careful watchfulness I have authenticated a score or more extraordinary adventures with wild mammals with proofs that satisfied me both as a lawyer and as a scientist; but a natural history is not the proper place in which to recount them.

FEBRUARY 15

It has long been a matter of doubt with us, whether the badger (*Taxidea taxus taxus*) really hibernates in these mountains, for we have records of its occurrence above ground during every month of the year. it seems more likely that, instead of resting in a state of almost rigid torpidity as do the spermophiles upon which it feeds, it sleeps naturally in the winter between meals, relying upon its abundant fat to tide it over. We arrive at this conclusion because it issues from its burrow whenever there is a winter thaw, and, though it does not like to trail along the snow, it manifests an activity incited by hunger. No one knows how extensively it follows the burrows of hibernating ground squirrels beneath the snow, and how like the shrew it feeds though there be a blanket of snow outside, for it is a fossorial mustelid that spends most of its time beneath the surface of the ground.

A badger is noted for the fact that its lower jaw is locked into a long hole of its cranium, and thus it is able to hold its bite with great tenacity. Mr. J. R. Stringham of Holden, Utah, has informed us that in sixteen inches of snow he followed a badger to the place where it had encountered two coyotes; but with frequent lickings of their wounds they had withdrawn and the badger, unbleeding, had taken refuge in its burrow two miles away.

Ground squirrels are the badger's principal food, and its chief victims hereabout, especially along the flatlands of lower foothills where we frequently see the larger animal's burrows. So difficult is digging in the higher mountains, where sometimes the soil is but a few inches deep, that the badger seeks those places only in summer, at which time its fare may be varied even by grasshoppers, lizards, horned lizards and some carrion. Its burrows are much commoner on the flat sagelands of the valleys than in the mountains, even than along the foothills. This is the main reason why there is some prejudice against it, since many a saddle horse has broken its leg in a badger-burrow; nevertheless it is doubtful that the habits of any other mammal hereabout are as beneficial to man as those of the badger. Governmental coyote- poisoners should have some sense of shame—they are the ones who are exterminating the useful badger.

The cruel European sport of badger baiting—setting dogs upon a badger holed in a barrel—is unknown in the Wasatch mountains. In this connection etymology has an interesting story: "badger" likely comes from "badge" plus "ard" in reference to the animal's white forehead spot or badge; but to "badger" one is to annoy, tease or worry him, in reference to the so-called sports with dogs.

Although we have heard that an occasional tender lamb will fall headfirst into a badger hole, and helplessly die, we have never seen an example of it; the truth is, that a fairly large round hole beside a sage, for instance, may be a danger to several species of mammals, who thoughtlessly leap into it.

FEBRUARY 16

Whether the high mountains be snow-drifted or flower-bloomed we seldom traverse them without seeing a magpie (*Pica pica hudsonia*), and having thus noticed it in all kinds of weather, we believe that in mountainous hardiness, resourcefulness and self-reliance it is equalled by few other birds except eagles, hawks and owls. Often when a secluded gully is swept by a zeroed blizzard and nothing but oak trunks protrude above the snow, a magpie will flush as from nowhere at our approach; and, as we plod the choked trails, it is apparent that stricken rabbits are soon pecked clean by the ever-watchful "mags".

Pica is Latin for "pie", "magpie"; but *"Cleptes"*, the generic name given by Gambel to his bird in 1847, being Greek for "thief", is a reminder of a pet magpie of ours, which stole everything from spoons to hairbrushes.

Besides its rare black and white coloration, a magpie's most conspicuous field-mark is its surprisingly long tail, which is actually more than half of its total length, and, furthermore, so graduated that the middle rectrices are more than twice as long as the lateral ones. Though at a distance a magpie appears entirely black and white, when taken in hand it is very beautiful: its crown is bronzy greenish, its back bluish green, its wing coverts metallic steel blue glossed with greenish bronze, and its tail is bronzy green. This bird is a relative of such other members of the *Corvidae* family as the jays, the Clark nutcracker, ravens and crows.

Frequently seen in the vicinity of isolated slaughter houses and about dead animals of the wastelands, the magpie in this locality is not always credited with subsisting mostly on crickets, grasshoppers and larvae, as well as berries and leaves; nevertheless, it has been known to peck at the back-sores of cattles and horses, and devour young birds and eggs. Few birds decline some insects in their fare, a truth that leads us to doubt the advisability of destroying any bird. Even the Cooper, sharp-shinned and goshawks take some destructive rodents in their murderous stride.

We never pass the huge lattice work-nests of the magpies in the scrub oaks without admiring these energetic birds, especially when we realize that they are intelligent enough to post sentinels and otherwise manifest characteristics that are really admirable.

In considering a bird like a magpie, which in our judgment will eat any flesh that it can obtain—from carrion to helpless fledglings in a nest—we must bear in mind that it likes open spaces, such as deserted corrals in either the sagelands or the scrub oak districts. For instance, we never see magpies in the swamps and meadows of Farmington bay, where thousands of water birds raise their young, and seldom along canyon streams or in high mountain glades. I should be most surprised to observe a magpie enter a creekside willowed labyrinth to rob the nest of an Audubon hermit thrush. The very habitat of the bird limits its destructiveness.

FEBRUARY 17

Most mammals and birds make no provision either for winter or the morrow, preferring to depend upon the foods that regular seasonal changes bestow. Migration is to a degree a substitute for storage, indeed, in some instances, as with the hummingbirds, which must have flowers, it is a necessity; but food is no explanation for the long migration of the Arctic tern (*Sterna paradisaea*) from the north Arctic regions where it breeds to those of the Antarctic on the South where it winters! Migration being perhaps a custom developed in the Ice Age, each bird likely has inherited a sense of direction to make it possible. Certain it is that some of our Wasatch birds, such as the Forster tern (*Sterna forsteri*), breed here in June, and then in winter go south to another 'June" climate, but do not breed there. Thus there is a general breeding in the cold north and a migration south, but little counter movement northward.

The pika has its hay stacks, the beaver its submerged branches, the squirrels their acorns and seeds, the wood rats their piles of edible bits, and so on; but of the birds only the Lewis woodpecker as far as we recall makes any attempt at storage, which by the way it accomplishes by thrusting acorns into cracks of stumps and poles. A mountain lion may kill two or three deer in a week, taking a meal from each in turn and then burying the carcass in the snow; but this is only a desultory and temporary storage, instinctive and selfish in nature, for it will likewise bury victims under leaves in summer when food exists in certain plentitude. It is more what we might call a next-meal storage than a permanent one for the uncertainties of winter.

Human beings differ as widely as the birds and wild mammals: some make due provision for future contingencies, others take no thought of the morrow, indeed they follow literally the sermon:

"Take no thought for your life, what ye shall eat, or what ye shall drink; nor yet for your body, what ye shall put on . . . Behold the fowls of the air: for they sow not, neither do they reap, nor gather into barns".

Such a philosophy might be practical where in winter a valley of the Jordan is comparatively warm (ice is mentioned only twice in the Bible, and then in a figurative sense); but it would not be the course of wisdom in this valley of the new world Jordan, which is verged with ice and snow.

No two trees, no two flowers, no two mammals are exactly alike. Perhaps what we have called design in nature is not design at all but the manifestation of a strange capability and purposiveness on the part of the individual cell, which changes its direction in accordance with the obstacles, environment and nurture it receives. It is self-willed, and, if for instance its purpose is to form an ear, it will form some kind of an ear even if grafted upon the back, sometimes of another animal entirely.

FEBRUARY 18

A friend has just come in with an interesting story. Being duty-bound to visit one of his mining camps, even in the blizzard of a week ago (1942), he himself would have floundered and become lost save for deer tracks leading, as he hoped, to a spring he knew; and when he did arrive, he found his miners had just rescued a white man and an Indian from a mountain haystack in which they had buried themselves from the storm. The Indian was in good condition, but the white man's legs were frozen from the knees down. When our friend entered the cabin the rescuers were rubbing the man's legs with snow, and the poor fellow himself was moaning with pain.

Looking on, the Indian finally grunted: "Huh—legs no good no more", and thereupon left the cabin with an axe in his hand. In but a few minutes he returned with a portion of the trunk of a pine (we think it a *Pinus monophylla*), which he immediately proceeded to cut into two foot lengths and split them in two. He then mortised out the wood so that only about a quarter of an inch of it still adhered to the bark. Thereupon holding these half cylinders of bark in the oven long enough to warm them through, and then placing them against the bare flesh of the frozen legs, he wrapped each bark-covered limb with burlap, and placed the stricken man in bed. All of the others pondered over the strange Indian remedy, and waited. The next morning, when the bark-casts were removed, the flesh was as red as if spanked and the white man, being not even lame, arose and went to work. No ill effects have since befallen him. Such is the way of an Indian.

Grateful to our friend for this information, we somehow found the conversation drifting into the realm of Indian words, especially their names for that winter prowler, the mountain lion, the tracks of which he had seen on his way to the cabin. With the assistance of data by Julian H. Steward this was the conclusion: The Indian names hereabout for the mountain lion are as follows: *takovitc* (Ft. Hall Shoshoni); *toyuduko,* (Lemhi Shoshoni); *tukw* (Utah Lake Ute); *piaduk* (Pahvant Uta); *tukumunts* (Las Vegas Paiute); *toyaduko* (Gosute, Skull Valley and Promontory Shoshoni); *tukumuts* (Little Lake Shoshoni); *tukumuns* (Lida Shoshoni); *toyadoku* (Lower Snake river); *tukumuts* (Little Lake Shoshoni); and *tukuwits* (Morey Shoshoni).

It is reported to us that once when a man was bitten on the ankle by a rattlesnake, a Mexican friend pinned the writhing reptile's head down with a rock, slowly cut its body into chunks and bandaged them upon the wound. The snake's flesh turned green, but the man's leg was not even sore next morning.

When it is backed by physical prowess nature respects domineering arrogance: the pride of the master sage cock; the haughtiness of the he-grizzly; the overbearing disdain of the bull wapiti; the lordly courage of the bull moose; and the chisel-ripping thrusts of the male muskrat.

FEBRUARY 19

In a snow-wrought pasturage, where several rime-coated horses stand asleep at noon, our attention is diverted to the two hawks, almost as large as eagles, sitting atop some willows. The glasses reveal them to be too grayish for golden eagles; and, when we walk to within one hundred yards of them, one flies and thus reveals a black belly, black tail-tip and black bends of its wings with the rest of its under plumage white and gray. They remain so long under close observation that identification is sure. They are American rough legged hawks (*Buteo lagopus s. johannis*), tremendous birds only six inches shorter than golden eagles and of all the hawks the most beneficial to man. They have a wing spread of nearly five feet. They are the birds that the Paiute Indians call *assutte queh nah;* the Washoe Indians, *ma-hoo-ehk;* and the Shoshones, *peahguen-nah.*

For over an hour we watch them; for they like to perch on the top of an electric power line tower and sally down occasionally for easy flights a few feet above a meadow ditch, alternately flapping and sailing as they go. The truth is, they are hunting for field mice and other rodents, for despite their great size and power no other hawk so seldom attacks a bird. To us they seem very mild and inoffensive, having none of the swift daring of the goshawk, sharp-shinned and Cooper tribe.

Leaving the frozen snow-drowned meadows, where only the rough-legs win our attention, we return along a lane lined by Lombardy poplars. On top of one is sitting a bird so large and dark as to make the roughlegs inferior in size, and fortunately we are able to approach it close enough to see the movements of its eyelids. It seems to be eating something; and, when it becomes so apprehensive of us that it flies, we notice that underneath it is entirely black execpt for some whitish at the base of its tail. It is a golden eagle (*Aquila chrysaetos canadensis*), the great raptore that the Shoshone Indians call *guehnah,* the Paiutes *quehnah* and the Washoes *pohtahlingehk,* a bird with a wing spread of six and a half feet.

To see American rough legs and a golden eagle in one afternoon is one of those pleasing experiences that make rambles in the lowlands memorable.

When in 1955 in his *The Duration of Mind* this writer stated that some of us are coming to believe that "all matter, all life, all mind, are in the last analysis one and the same thing—either electricity or chemical processes under the stimulus of electricity", the statement was challenged as without justification. Now, however, such particle-physicists as Oppenheimer are able to demonstrate that matter consists of impermanent objects; that the atom, with its thirty particles, consists of the electron, the proton and the neutron and their electrically opposite counterparts or antiparticles. Additionally we know of nine other groups. Three are weightless—the light quanta of Einstein, and the neutrinos and antineutrinos of Enrico Fermi.

FEBRUARY 20

In the valley meadows of Farmington creek the pussy willows are in bloom. We stop to admire them; and then, near the willow trees (*Salix lasiandra*) further on, our attention is arrested by the fluty chirm of a hundred red-wing blackbirds (*Agelaius phoeniceus fortis*). They are all males, and, as they chatter contentedly on the limbs, only whitish yellow margins of the red wing patches are visible, giving one the impression of a black bird with a whitish blotch on its wing. It has been our experience that the red of the lesser wing coverts becomes more conspicuous as spring approaches.

The redwings are paludicoline members of the *Icteridae*, with semiterrestrial habits; in other words, though manifesting a preference for damp meadows, they are apparently contented on the willows above a pond or near an alfalfa field. Being close relatives of the meadow-lark, they like somewhat the same habitats, indeed, as we look at that flock of a hundred expectant males conversing in the willows there now, two meadowlarks are with them in the same tree. There is this difference: blackbirds are always near water; meadowlarks may be far away.

Many redwings remain in these valleys all winter, depending on cattle-feeding corrals and the like when their favorite swamps are frozen over; at any rate, very early each year the males appear in flocks and sing their fluty *o ka DEES* until the arrival of the streaked brown females later on. They are not so hardy as the Brewers, which scorn the winter if food be obtainable.

Many a time we have mowed a meadow in June and seen with what vociferous remonstrance the blackbirds objected to our intrusion. The nests, neat grassy affairs attached to timothy stems and adorned with from three to five pale bluish eggs marked with black gray or brown, were such objects of solicitude that often we have been almost but not actually pecked by furious males.

Since they feed on insects and seeds with not too harmful forays into the grainfields, it has never been our disposition to destroy them; in fact, their aesthetic value is great, for the males are handsome in their glossy plumage and scarlet epaulettes; they have sweet flutelike songs, and they inhabit wet places not ordinarily attractive.

To us the Brewer blackbird (*Euphagus cyanocephalus*), which is a larger bird, all black except that the female shows some brownish gray on her head, neck and underparts, is not so attractive as the redwing. Its voice is harsh, its damage to grainfields more extensive, and its mannerisms hardly winsome. More Brewers than redwings winter here; but somehow they have always lacked what the redwing possesses to a marked degree—paludal charm.

If you have never waded through the reeds of a slough in search of a blackbird's nest, smelled the musty odor of the ponds, felt the warm brown-flecked water on your bare feet and the tickling of new grass and warm mud between your toes, you have been denied one of the sweetest joys of meadowland.

FEBRUARY 21

House finches are singing again with sweet and irrepressible melody; indeed, every year at this time we expect to hear their exquisite ariettas from the house tops, aye even from the skyscraper parapets, for through the din of voices and horns their trills come down to the pavement as clear as tinkling bells.

Our house finch (*Carpodacus mexicanus frontalis*), like all members of its genus, differs in its coloration of male and female, the male having a forehead and rump of rose pink, the female, one of grayish brown; but both are more or less streaked, and at a distance easily confused with the house sparrow.

All year round house finches are about us, never becoming pestiferous like the lascivious, nook-stuffing domestic sparrows; and, on the contrary, they occasionally delight with rapturous songs superior to that of the caged pet indoor. Bird-catching as we have seen it practiced in the meadows along the Thames river in England is unknown here; ornithologists secure specimens either to band or skin, so house finches do not become house pets. The domesticated canary (*Serinus canarius*), a native of the Canary islands, is, however, a real finch, not a warbler, as many might suppose, and thus is not related to our summer canary or warbler (*Dendroica aestiva morcomi*), which commonly lilts about our brookside willows.

There are many pleasing songsters in these mountains, belonging to widely different families. Some that occur to us at the moment are: Bullock's orioles, meadowlarks and bobolinks of the family *Sturnidae;* desert horned larks of the *Alaudidae;* pale gold finches, western vesper sparrows, western lark sparrows, white-crowned sparrows, mountain song sparrows, and lazuli buntings of the *Fringillidae;* the various wood warblers of the *Mniotiltidae;* the water ouzel of the *Cinclidae;* rock wrens and canyon wrens of the *Troglodytiaae;* the catbirds and the sage thrashers of the *Mimidae;* ruby crowned kinglets of the *Sylvidae;* and Townsend solitaires, Wilson thrushes, olive backed thrushes and Audubon hermit thrushes of the *Turdidae.*

It is thus apparent that our song birds are passerine and mostly arboreal in habit. Water birds as a rule have either harsh or shrill voices without melody, although the *syrinx* or voice-box of a canvasback differs little in structure from that of our favorite, the luzuli bunting. We say "favorite" for we have heard a male sing half an hour at a time with apparently no thought of anything but the sheer joy of chippering a sweet chansonette in a fragrant canyon-air.

Far back in the age of the *Dinosauria* there was perhaps no song in swamp, meadowland or plain. The only sound we ever heard a reptile make was a hiss.

FEBRUARY 22

Snow falls gently for a long time, and then, as if angered by our tranquility, sweeps with blizzard-intensity by the firs and over the maple stalks into our cabined sanctum. We delight in the uncertainty of this particular period; one day the sun is so mild in its warm effulgence that we expect any moment to see a ground squirrel peeping from its hole or a ferruginous roughleg soaring over the hillcrest after it; the next, the bitter rushes of ice-flakes are so stinging that we feel it must be Christmas again, and eagerly hurry to shelter and warmth. We know that such early plants as the Indian parsnip (*Aulosperum longpipes*) and the squirrel corn (*Dicentra uniflora*) are about to rise, even beside the snow; we realize that, in the garden, croci, tulips, chionodoxa and hyacinths are vigorously protruding their stems; but somehow we feel these February storms are thrusting us back into the holidays of Thanksgiving, Christmas and New Year's. It is a transition period when the naturalist may be favored with the sight of winter species or astonished by the appearance of summer visitors.

He may for instance on some balmy day see a pied-billed grebe, a loon, a herring gull, a Sabine gull, a wood duck, a scaup duck, a golden eye, a pygmy owl, a Lapland longspur, (*Calcarius capponicus alascensis*), or a northwestern shrike; or, to his surprise, come upon a killdeer, a sharp-shinned hawk, osprey, scoter, hooded merganser, red head or golden eye. No one can quite predict the unseasonal occurrences of this particular period.

Nature has its schedule; and, though there be blizzards in June and apricot blossoms in January, there nevertheless is an average about it all that year by year is reassuring. In our diary for February 22, 1917, we find this: "Snow! snow!! The winter of 1916-17 will long be remembered for its unprecedented snow. All bird and animal life has suffered, deer having sought the haystacks of the valley, and thousands of birds, ordinarily wild, having shivered near the habitations of man. Blue jays and Clark nutcrackers have come to the door; and the list of dead includes many quail". That, indeed, *was* a winter, when valley people walked over their fence rails and the squeak of the pathway was the sound of the morning.

How can we forget winters of tremendous depth of snow, when many roofs sagged and some caved beyond repair? In the winter of 1916-17 we walked on snow over the tops of fences; in 1948-49, when the total snow fall was 93.1 inches, hungry deer stood against my neighbor's housewall to grasp the leaves of a Boston ivy; but on March 25, 1952, we could record the greatest total fall of snow ever known during the winter in this valley—117.3 inches for the season! At such a time it is highly important to wild life that the snows are intermittent with intervening periods of thaw.

FEBRUARY 23

Pompey the Great once asserted that the rising sun is more worshipped than the setting sun; however, a winter sunset, seen from a valley edge on the western declivity of the Wasatch mountains, is sometimes a panorama of wondrous beauty, especially to him who observes the various changes of tint and hue from fading daylight to starlit darkness.

In late afternoon the sun shines bright from a sky of light squill blue; the cloud stream over the mountains at the east is pale neutral gray, while that above the southern horizon is pallid purplish gray. Just before sunset the sun rests beyond the western mountains, a fulgid ball of molten gold; the clouds of the heavens to the south become lilac gray, and both the east and west mountains themselves fade into lavender gray.

Immediately following sunset the afterglow is fulgent salmon buff with bittersweet pink at each side; then slowly the bright segment loses its dazzling brilliancy and tints into a light salmon-orange, soft and glorious.

A little later the place of sunset has become grenadine pink: the clouds of the south firmament have changed to safrano pink, with a narrow strip of the same tint extending throughout the antitwilight arch of the east.

Gradually in the clouds of the western mountains a mere patch of splendor remains; and even it has darkened to a strawberry pink. As we look, this remnant is losing its deep redness and fading; soon only the faintest trace of pinkish remains. The stars shine brightly; darkness overshadows all. Shortly afterward a full, white moon rises over the ridge of the Wasatch to gleam upon the silent night.

> Behold the lurid colors of the sun,
> As clouds of fire it glows above the rim;
> The day is ending yet anew begun
> To them who greet a glowing morning dim.

About a valley pond, which is marged by the dead stalks of reeds, a flock consisting of one or two thousand redwing blackbird males (*Agelaius phoeniceus fortis*), is assembled. Sometimes the birds grub over the muddy meadow; again they fly in a vast concourse half a mile long; and then once more they all alight on the bare limbs of tall black willow trees, where among them only one bird or another now and again gives vent to the well known song. The birds are drab with scarcely noticeable spatulas of red; furthermore, they are not voicing that incessant chirm, which in a week or so is bound to mark their activity.

If there be no vital principle in nature whence comes the widespread appearance of continuity and seeming design; if there be a vital force whence arises the fortuity of individuals as if by mere chance directed and controlled?

FEBRUARY 24

When capital and labor disagree they should both go into the hills and see how the lichen manufactures soil from the rocks; for the lichen is two plants with but a single name, an alga and a fungus working in perfect harmony with full knowledge that if one shirk both must die. Even as it snows we cannot resist the impulse to scrape some lichens from yonder moulding canyon stone, and take them home for examination under the microscope.

The fungus not only holds water, as if it were a sponge, but also dissolves the hardest rock with its acid branches, while the alga, being able to take food from the air, adds these to the water being held by the fungus and the minerals dissolved by it, and works them up into starch and sugar after the manner of the higher plants. Thus the algae and the fungi, working together symbiotically as Fungus Alga Company get along without quarrels or strikes, gathering such dust as floats to them, entering their threads into the crevices of winter ice, making mold as their bodies die, and thus furnishing that essential thing to the life of the world—soil.

Mosses come, then ferns, then spruces, junipers, pines, maples, and other trees that can exist on shallow ground; indeed, in the Wasatch mountains, we have a member of the saxifrage family known as an alum-root (*Heuchera rubescens*) that actually forms mats in rocks-crevices on vertical cliffs, and subsists as well as any other plant on the soil made by the lichen.

The higher one goes in the Wasatch the finer the lichens appear, often in varying colors of orange and gray, and sometimes with five or six different species on a large rock exposure. When broken away, they have clinging to them a layer of the partly dissolved rock as if it were made of sand.

The soil makers are the crustaceous lichens, but there are other kinds; the foliaceous lichens, which resemble small crumpled and folded mallow leaves; the fruticose lichens, which look like small shrubbery stems; the beard lichens, which often hang from the bark of old trees; and the gelatinous lichens, which resemble black lumps of wrinkled or wavy jelly.

It is not often I hear the loud, penetrating *te! te! te! te! te! te! te! te! te!* of the red-shafted flicker (*Colaptes cafer collaris*) so early in the year; but there it is, firm and clear, coming from the roof of a neighboring house. We have had two weeks of springlike weather, causing roses to bud early and box elders to show their catkins. The song of the flicker is difficult to express onomatopoetically: sometimes I catch a metallic quality in it; at other times, a sibilant base. It is too rasping to be ringing, but it is uniform in tone with every note accented, usually enduring for about a score of notes, and without undulation ending as strong as it was in the beginning. It is audible a quarter of a mile away.

FEBRUARY 25

Most gregarious of birds is the pine siskin or pine finch (*Spinus pinus pinus*). Before us a flock of one hundred fifty of the sociable little fellows is swarmed with chatty contentment on a bare tree not over twenty feet above a Wasatch boulevard, where scores of cars are passing beneath them. Unafraid, apparently oblivious to anything but their own consolation, they literally dot the tree's branches everywhere, and they are chatting the syllables *sweer, sweer, sweer,* as incessantly as if they were a swarm of bees about their queen. In mock fear of a passing automobile there they fly into the air, only to circle and settle back upon the same tree; yet, as they do so, a solitary individual left behind utters two *chirp chirp* notes in the manner of an English sparrow. What pleasing examplars of companionship, jollity and trustfulness!

Our records show the faith and good fellowship of these companionable birds; thus on one March 29th: "Took two specimens of this tiny bird as a flock of them were pecking about some peach tree buds. They were tamer than even the chickadee, alighting with the utmost confidence within two feet of me! I stood still and motionless, and one flitted within a few inches of me as if to alight on my head."

Close relative of the gold finches and the house sparrow, the pine siskin nests in the coniferous trees of the Wasatch and winters in the valleys. "Siskin" is apparently an onomatopoetic word; for, if one were to sound at once the word "siskin" as it has appeared in the various languages, he would get a fair impression of a flock of the birds singing together in a tree. Thus he would have "sisschen" or "zeischen" (Greek), "sijsken" or "cijsken" (Dutch), "sisgen" (Danish), "sisik" (Norwegian), "siska" (Swedish), "czyzik" (Polish), and "chizhek" (Russian).

When we first became acquainted with the pine siskin it was called a "pine goldfinch"; but when resting it looked like a small striped sparrow more than a goldfinch, which has strongly contrasting yellow and black plumage. However, when the little fellow spread its wings and showed yellow clearly, the close relationship to the gold finches, with which it sometimes flocks, was revealed. The goldfinches build their nests in small trees or bushes, but the nests of siskins occur almost exclusively on the limbs of pines and other conifers. Both birds are placed in the genus *Spinus*.

The security and dependability of pines lead one to wonder why the mammals and birds that inhabit them are not extraordinarily numerous. Nevertheless even such comparatively large species as Clark nutcrackers and long crested jays cannot always escape from golden eagles and great horned owls, nor can the frisky chickaree forever dodge the agile fisher. Probably there is no place in the world, on land or sea, where a bird or mammal, including man, may say, here I have no enemy.

FEBRUARY 26

There they are! It is the realization of many a year of hope—wild elk or, wapiti (*Cervus canadensis nelsoni*) in Parley's canyon! In 1910 perhaps only seven native elk survived in the state of Utah, these in the Uinta division of the Wasatch national forest; but from 1912 to 1916 inclusive 181 head were transplanted from Jackson Hole, Wyoming, thus instilling hope that eventually they would appear in all the mountains. Now several hundred are shot each year, the breeding herds containing an estimated 2263 individuals; and at last (1942) they are in Parleys, one of the busiest of the Wasatch canyons. Four of them are standing before us, majestic and aglare, on the mountainside above the reservoir.

The word "elk" is properly applied only to either the extinct Irish elk (*Cervus megaceros*) or the northern Europe elk (*Alces malchis*), of which the American moose (*Alces americanus*) is but a variety. It was in 1758 that Linnaeus gave the name *Cervus alces* to the northern Europe elk, the animal referred to by Goldsmith (1774): "It is known in Europe by the name of elk, and in America by that of Moose-deer".

Wapiti, the correct name for the animal above us in Parley's, means literally "white deer", from the Cree Indian name "wapitik", or the Shawnee "wahpetee". Probably the earliest use of the word as descriptive of *Cervus canadensis* was in Thomas Thomson's "Annals of Philosophy" (1817) as follows: "At the same meeting (of the Linnaean Society) was read a description, by Dr. Leach, of the Wapiti deer, a species of animal from the banks of the Missouri", though in 1829 Sir J. Richardson wrote: "The trivial name of wapiti has been only recently adopted in scientific works".

It often happens that correctness says one thing, popular usage another, but when *Cervus alces* is commonly taken to mean Wyoming wapiti it is not ungracious to indicate otherwise. In recent years some have prefixed "American" to "elk"; but in similar fashion to say "American lion" would not make the cougar a close relative of the African lion, which is a non-climbing, larger, and more dignified animal.

At any rate they are there—wild wapiti in Parley's canyon.

Since deer and elk meat is usually somewhat dry and tough when fresh, it is the custom among some hunters to hang it up in an airy cool place for several days before cooking and eating it. That practice works very well if the days and nights of autumn are close to freezing; but sometimes they are so warm that meat spoils rapidly. After our regular rabbit hunts of years ago we used to give an English family three or four of the jacks, and, it being winter, they hung them in a cold shed for a week, claiming that it made the meat tender and delicious.

FEBRUARY 27

It is one of those pre-spring days, with the memory of blizzards a week ago, a day when all the roadways are seeping and the sunny atmosphere is cold but not quite freezing. We seek the meadows east of the mouth of the Jordan where springs and artesian wells assure open patches of water.

Along the sluggish wayside, borrow-pits and ditches, card teasels six feet high stand thick as rushes, with dry, spiney flower heads brown and conspicuous. As we stop to examine them, we see a thousand dark birds standing at the edge of a depression three hundred yards away. The glasses disclose them to be ducks sitting on a muddy interspace; and, as we approach them, treading from snow patch to snow patch to avoid the meadowed seeps, they take to the air a hundred or a score at a time as if for respite from their moping idleness.

They are lesser scaup ducks (*Aythya affinis*), constituting the largest flock of water birds we have seen for many a day. Though dried grass is upon the alkaline mud-humps for their taking, few of them are doing aught but sitting with their faces towards the warm afternoon sun. We know them to be lesser scaups because they appear no larger than teals, and the broad white stripe at the hind edge of the wing extends only about half way to the wing tip. With good field glasses one may detect minute markings at a distance of a hundred yards.

These lesser scaup ducks winter usually in the southern half of North America, and breed mostly in Canada; but in their migrations they appear in all kinds of weather. Some of them have been taken in these very marshes at Christmas time. They seem to know when the melting snow will leave open meadows where even in freezing weather they may feed like a flock of blackbirds; for they prefer fresh water ponds and streams to the ocean waves where the greater scaup is more frequently found.

The food of the lesser scaup consists of snails, worms, crawfish, larvae, water insects, small mollusks, as well as seeds of grasses.

Most mammals and birds are much more sociable in winter than in spring, summer and autumn, a trait due largely to the wane of breeding activities. The male redwings that fought in the spring in the selection of mates, and, in the summer, in protection of their respective territories, now chirm together in a cavalier chorus; the male mule deer that battled, often to death, in the piny glades of autumn now concourse with females and other males in happy assemblages. Nature subdues the ardor of the buck deer by shedding his antlers and requiring him to go about with an inflamed and tenderized head while growing new ones. The process is apparently not painful unless the swollen part be touched by a flipping branch, hence pregnant does readily free themselves from annoyance by seeking a willowed or brushy labyrinth.

FEBRUARY 28

Fascinated yesterday by the sight of an estimated thousand lesser scaup ducks, we again seek the Jordan meadows. The scaup ducks are still there, and several pintails (*Anas acuta*), a very hardy duck.

Suddenly our ears are attracted skyward by the soft honks of a flock of lesser snow geese (*Chen hyperborea hyperborea*), which in seven loosely connected Vs performs in an aerial circus miles in circumference, as if solely for the benefit of us spectators below. Not northward bound but circular bound as in play, the estimated five hundred of them veer and glint in the sun, each flashing with its white body the reflected light, then turning and showing its black-wing tips like specks in the sky. If leaders they have, the leadership is not of the stern dignity of that of the Canada geese; for unlike them these birds sometimes break line, and constantly reform their Vs. Canadian honkers wedge northward in one great V with several supplemental Vs forming from its side wings; but the snow geese appear in a mile-long line consisting of several leaders equally at the front.

Many ornithologists have described the calls of the snow geese as "falsetto"—we do not know who started it, but, as we listen now in the distance the honks are infrequent, soft and mellow, like the distant voices of dogs beneath a treed cougar.

Geese are models of fidelity, wisdom, communal sociability, mutual helpfulness and self reliance. They are noble, independent birds; yet for centuries such epithets as "gabbling", "haranguing", "noisy", "screaming", "waddling", "hobbling", "affected", "empty", "vain", "proud", have been applied to them. Nevertheless, such is their watchfulness that they are said to have warned Rome of the Gauls sneaking upon it, and in both ancient Egyptian hieroglyps and Greek mythology are evidences of the esteem in which they have been held. In India today they are the very symbols of ceaseless vigilance, yet the "goose-step" elsewhere is an absurd conception of their vanity.

Geese differ from the ducks in that the sexes are alike in appearance and the male is a faithful assistant in the process of incubation.

We cannot watch them there in the sky without admiration and respect, especially when we realize that they survive our cold winters, subsisting on tuffy grasses, tasty culms and bulbous roots, meeting every hardship with good spirit, avoiding their gunner enemies, and then seek far away the chill swamps of Siberia to rear their young. Man does not practice all the ways of happiness.

Male robins now display beautiful intensity of plumage-coloration; and, even in the midst of falling snow, there is considerable activity among both sexes, consisting of restless flying about and some chasing. The only notes I hear among them consist of a short *chuck!, chuck!* uttered as one is about to take wing. It is very odd that in nature some animals have colors as conspicuous ,and others, as inconspicuous as possible.

FEBRUARY 29

As we sit contented before the pine-glowing hearth and our wistful memories turn towards verdant fields, warbling birds, and wayside flowers, someone casually inquires what is our favorite odor, not perfume, but scent from common and natural things. A fair and delightful question on a snowy day; so we ponder.

More outspoken than the rest, E. immediately names gardenias, apples, burning logs, pines, and gasoline at a service station! J. soon follows with: the ocean, an apple orchard in bloom, a well smoked pipe, roast beef cooking, good wine, an oil field and sage brush. And while we smile at his oil field, L. comes forward with her list as follows: a fresh cigar smoke on a cold morning (ah, perchance I smoked it), new-mown hay, fresh coffee, gardenias (yes, again), a new baby's breath (of all things!), clean laundry dried over green grass, sage, rain on a dusty day, logs on a fireplace (unless they be pine, this must be sentimental), a kitchen when pickles are being canned, new-baked bread, whisky, pines and popcorn (freshly popped).

Not to be outdone by such novel bouquets K. then votes for: clean linen, new clothes (methinks there's the wearing not the redolence there!) toilet soap (brand undesginated, though I know she means non-carbolic), burning pines (must they be burned), cooking coffee, frying bacon, fish and chips, baking potatoes, cheese, furs, witch hazel, pears, cantelopes and the ocean.

Finally C. admits that he likes the fragrance of: new-mown hay, balsams, freshly ground coffee, apples, freshly cut mint, burning tar, cigar smoke on a frosty morning, uncooked tea, Worchestershire sauce, frying bacon, a cow's breath, apricot blossoms, cooking finnan haddie, and the sweet smell of the bitter brush (*Purshia tridentata*) that in the spring scents a nook of the canyon nearby. The argument begins. What joys before a winter-hearth!

To vary the discussion someone ventures the query: what kind of a stream do you like best for trout-fishing? The general opinion seems to be that the rocks of the upper Provo river are too sleek and mossy for safe wading; that the upper Weber is too boisterous; and that East canyon is too thickly margined with willows to make it enjoyable. There are several beautiful creeks in the northern third of the Wasatch; but they are too narrow and tumbling for the expert fly fisherman. It was concluded that the ideal for the long caster is the upper Snake river between Big Springs and the Rapids, a sand-bottom stream a hundred yards wide with grassy embankments before a background of forested pines; a stream so fed by the mighty springs that it is always of the same depth, rockless, placid and beautiful, always so mild that hundreds of times we have waded it to within an inch or two of our chest high boots without peril.

MARCH 1

Winter or summer one is always sure to see an avian population of water birds in those interesting marsh lands, alkaline sloughs and meadows about the mouth of the Jordan river, a place of interest to the ornithologist rarely excelled in the world. Though its meadows be fledged with snow, its pasture-springs nearly iced over, its reed patches dried and stricken down, its landscape bleak, leafless and bare, we visit it again in the hope of once more hearing the chutter of the snipe and the clarion cry of the curlew; but we are too early for some of them, almost too late for others already following the northward verge of snow.

A meadowlark sings sweet hosannas to the melting day; but our attention is attracted to a large flock of ring-billed gulls (*Larus delawarensis*) in close and agreeable association with lesser scaup ducks in a meadow. They are smaller than the California gulls (*Larus californicus*) with a lighter, more graceful flight, which resembles somewhat that of the Forster tern. They fly in groups of scattered individuals, as if enjoying the warm air and the bright sun, and then settle back with the ducks again.

Except for its egg-eating habit, the ring-billed is probably the most useful of gulls; it pounces upon field mice and other small rodents as if it were a hawk; and, in season, catches grasshoppers on the wing with all the alertness and dexterity of an Arkansas flycatcher. As we watch them they appear milder and more tolerant than their larger relatives, the California gulls, with whom they are here most frequently in company.

Unlike the California gulls, which breed in colonies on the islands of Great Salt Lake and the dykes of Farmington bay, the ring-billed nest mostly in the wilds of Canada, but they are the commoner gull of the Wasatch winter.

While we are watching these gentle gulls, four members of the California tribe fly over us, strong in body, sturdy in manner, disdainful of any association with other bird species, true resourceful and independent spirits in this land of cold.

There are some who believe in meliorism, the doctrine that the world tends to become better and that man may aid in its betterment. The truth is, although there may have been some shiftings of climate, nature is practically the same as it was a million years ago, no better, no worse for man; and, while man has learned how to store and transmit knowledge, he has made no progress towards physical perfection in the past several thousands of years, nor mastered laziness, avarice and crime. In one or more of the five senses—hearing, sight, touch, smell and taste—man is excelled by almost any wild mammal or bird that one might name. Man's thinking tends to eliminate the necessity of his own physical effort; and disuse inevitably leads to retrogression and decay.

MARCH 2

With diverting expectancy we have been waiting for the snow to seep from the lawn so that the croci might bloom, and at last here they are, brilliant dwarfs of yellow, purple and white, cultivated eye-openers of spring. Would that they were as common here as we have seen them in the pastures of England; would that they grew wild as they do in Greece; for here they bloom while yet the sward is brown, while tree limbs are leafless and soiled and snow lingers unthawed on the shaded slopes of habitations. It has been suggested that where the Bible says, "the desert shall rejoice, and blossom as the rose" (Isa. 31:1), the reference is to the autumn crocus. If so, it would there be the fall species *C. sativus,* which yields saffron. Crocus is derived from the Greek word *krokos,* saffron. Be that as it may we are hard put to discover anything in the Wastach that blooms earlier, unless of course it be the snowdrop. There were never native roses in Palestine, although a wild species does exist in Labanon.

We have a few plants that blossom the entire year around, snow or no snow, ice or no ice, but always subject more or less to location. In this category we would place: shepherd's purse (*Capsella bursa-pastoris*), a familiar wasteland weed, and the alfilaree, a weed whose pink-purple petals open at all times until noon, even when a momentary sun melts their covering of snow.

Competitors for ever-blooming honors, however, are the arnica or gum plant which may fail only in December to show its yellow blossoms, and that introduced member of the mint family called the henbit or dead nettle (*Lamium amplexicaule*), whose purple, red or white flowers appear on the waste places from February to October.

There it is, as we hoped it would be when we ventured into this canyon—the Dutchman's breeches, squirrel corn, bleeding heart, or steer's head (*Dicentra uniflora*), as it is variously called, an inch-high member of the fumitory family, bitter-juiced, a tiny herb springing from the grain-like summit of its fleshy roots, bearing a single flesh or lavender heart-shaped flower, blooming for only a few days at the very edge of the seeping snow. Even the sweet flower seems to have tried to hide from us beneath the crusted leaves of the autumn before. We admire, we wonder, and give it the prize, as the earliest attractive bloom of the year.

Human beings rapidly languish and die unless in their minds they look forward to another spring of joyful activity and promise. The greatest form of eternity is work uncompleted, work that urges one onward, ever onward, in the vast realm of accomplishment and acquision of knowledge. Other mammals have come and gone—for instance, the mastadon and the great *Elephas imperator,* which stood $13\frac{1}{2}$ feet high—; hence it is for man to live for health and knowledge so that in the eons of future time he too will not pass from the living picture.

MARCH 3

Brown are the meadows, darkened and soiled the wayside trees; yet, hold, behind those pinkish willows yonder is a field sparsely grown with rabbit brush (*Chrysothamnus graveolens*) of a pea green tint, the only real green thus far along our rambling way.

We are in the valley west of Timpanogos, that lofty snow-sculptured mount which in the clear atmosphere of this March day shows with awesome certainty its coffined woman veiled in white. The ridge provides her contours, the highest peak giving the profile of her face, the lesser crest and valleys to the north outlining her robed body and feet. Sometimes she seems more definite and serene as I gaze westward at her when coming down the Provo river. Varied indeed are the stonefaces of the Wasatch, but none of them has the magnitude, mystery and sublimity of this prostrate figure immaculately shrouded there on high.

A marsh hawk flying downward with wings tilting quickly at every new glimpse of a creeping rodent; a solitary redwing clinging lonesomely to a dry reed; some Brewer blackbirds foraging unafraid near a farmyard—these are the movements afield on our way up Provo river, which, winter or summer, is a place of singular interest, beauty and charm.

At the mouth of the canyon we flush a veritable swarm of pine siskins, which circle briefly and then alight on a bare hillside twenty yards away to feed busily on the seeds and mites obtainable there among the weeds.

At the Upper Falls we begin to see long-crested jays (*Cyanocitta stelleri macrolopha*), not as solitary individuals, as we usually find them, but in twos, apparently pairs; furthermore, they are flying about the willows of a river pond and not among the conifers as is their wont.

We go onward to our newly found *Crataegus,* discovering that some of its long thorns have dropped with the leaves, but new thorns, now a half inch long, are growing on it as if they were buds. Dried red berries linger here and there. We must come again to our *Crataegus.*

Like human beings plants grow from cells; some quickly perish; some linger in frailty for awhile; others strive and flower year after year until even they finally pass away. The healthy ones usually leave progeny to carry on; but the others, save for moulding skeletons in the soil, are gone forever. In the summer and early autumn the stricken ones are often hidden by the thick leafage of their neighbors; in the winter the bare branches of the departed and the living are equally laden with snow—; but in the springtime the stems and branches of the dead—dry, brittle and yellow—stand out stark and drear beside the budding vigor of the living. Only among the conifers of the evergreen forests does the grim pallor of death in winter mark its victims. Death—great, impartial, indifferent death!

MARCH 4

Here we are in Provo canyon at an altitude of exactly one mile, where the open river is running clear and peacefully, where a half score robins sit motionless and fluffed, with wings spread on the bare branches of embankment hawthorns, and where deep encrusted snow obtrudes upon our rambling way. But the venture is not in vain, for there, scampering over the deep snow of the hillside, is a Utah rock squirrel (*Citellus variegatus utah*), one of the few that we have seen thus enjoying the bright sunshine of winter.

This rock squirrel, locally differentiated from the Uinta or armed spermophile by the name "long-tailed gray squirrel", has a pinkish buff head, white eye rings, grayish white shoulders, brown back, gray-white undersides, and a tail of buff and black; furthermore, it climbs so well that once we spent half an hour trying to shake one from maple trees, only to see it jump from limb to limb, tree to tree to avoid us in the manner somewhat of a flying squirrel. Being distributed throughout these mountains, it is a pleasing divertissement of nearly all of our excursions.

True to its tree-climbing ability, the rock squirrel may, indeed, make its permanent home in a hollow tree a rod above ground; but it usually burrows a nest beneath a boulder or under some brookside labyrinth. Unlike the armed spermophile (*Citellus armatus*), which spends so much time in aestivation and hibernation that it sees the upper ground but five months of the year, the rock squirrel possibly does not hibernate at all, depending rather in winter upon the vast storage it has accumulated, and venturing occasionally, as this one today, out upon the snow of a winter sunshine for dried berries and other edibles.

Acorns are apparently its principal subsistence hereabout, though we have known at least two individuals to make their homes in the vicinity of apricot trees and to feed habitually on the dropped stones.

Sometimes when one is taken we find that its cheek pouches contain service berries and wild currants; for doubtless it gathers any edible seed or dried fruit of its environs.

But to see one running on the snow—that makes the day worth while.

Observing a house sparrow eating from a crust of bread about an inch and a half in diameter on the flat surface of a stone parapet, I was surprised that the only tool it used was its bill. It would peck until a tiny bit came loose, which it would immediately swallow or, at times, grasping the entire crust with its bill, give it a jerk or two until a crumb or two fell out. Not once did it hold the crust down with a foot as it pecked; not once did it indicate that its feet had any use except to stand on. We must admit that although the stone afforded a broad firm floor the bird was incapable of a concept that would call a leg and a foot to its assistance.

MARCH 5

So joyous is the recollection of many moonlight hours spent on the meadows at the mouth of the Jordan as to make every visit there, whatever the season and the weather or the time of day, an incident of both delightful reminiscence and interested expectations, yet, among all the quawks, whistles and songs that linger in our memory, none is more deeply entrenched than the mystic chuttering of the Wilson snipe (*Capella gallinago delicata*) in the semi-darkness of moon-favored evenings. When one is constrained to be away from it nostalgia develops from the ensemble of such simple things.

There it is, flying to the spring of our favorite field, but alighting with its bill turned upward as if it were still intent on rising, a characteristic attitude of this diverting shorebird. Not yet is it "winnowing", that peculiar chuttering sound produced in downward flight in its throat, for this performance is mostly an exultation of breeding time; in truth it is merely reconnoitering its wonted locale. Some of these birds, really most of them, winter somewhat south of the Wasatch; but many refuse to desert their warm favorite springs hereabout even in the coldest winter. Subsisting as they do mostly on earth worms, larvae and marsh-seeds, and habitually probing their bills into the mud of the actual shore line, where water meets edge, and either sucking or nipping the succulent mites that meet their fancy, they are fully entitled to the designation "shorebirds". In summer they do not decline an occasional meal of grasshoppers, insects by the way that enter more or less into the fare of nearly all birds, be they seed or flesh eaters.

Though breeding as far north as Alaska, Wilson snipe nest in our meadows, sometimes during May and June, though at times as late as the twenty fourth of July; nevertheless, we do not recall ever having been about the damp pasturage, spring, summer or fall, without hearing their peculiar "winnow", especially on days and nights when storm was imminent.

On the Jordan and Bear river sloughs night sounds are heard at every season of the year except winter, but, aside from an occasional coyote's medley, they are the cries of water birds, especially the Wilson snipe, which likes to chutter in the moonlit sky. On the mountains throughout the year one usually at night hears only the babble of a cascading brook, for except the ridges there are few places beyond earshot of such halcyon purling.

We may say here, once and for all, that, contrary to the accepted view of other ornithologists, we ourselves have on actual observation only a few yards away, determined that the "winnow" of the Wilson snipe is not the sound of wind upon either its tail or wing, but actually a voice-intonation, produced as we have seen it with ripples of its emission down and out the throat.

MARCH 6

Melting snow leaves boulders exposed, and odd stretches of ground blotched a dull gray or brown. Nature's skeleton is being unrobed; for so capricious is March that the blizzard of morning may be a quickly thawing, sun-warmed tranquil scene of afternoon. Everywhere appears the sheer beauty of unsoftened outline—naked trunks and limbs of tree and shrub, revealing the secret runs of the brookside covert; rugged and broken angles of rocks; and the traceries of hilltops and canyon crests against an uncertain sky.

We tarry at the entrance to Mill Creek canyon (how many streams of the Wasatch bear that name!); the northern exposures are snow-wrought; the southern, bare brownish and drab; oak trees are grayish with a faint purplish tinge; sage bushes, greenish gray; willows along the indifferent creek, a vivid rust.

Fields are maculated, snow being alternated with rich dark loam; but dry sunflower stalks stick up as reminders of last year. In a straw-berry patch the ground is matted with dead leaves; but green ones are showing.

On the foothill, where the afternoon sun is especially warm, in the midst of dry grasses, we chance upon a sluggish grasshopper, jaded and parched in appearance, lively enough to crawl, but too stiff and numb to hop over our obtruding hand.

Meadowlarks, robins, redwings, these seem the real venturers, the real fore-runners of spring, unless, as we suspect, they have been here all winter and come forth only between storms. In desultory fashion, however, a red-shafted flicker momentarily tatooes a cabin roof for our delight, but not yet does it give forth its harsh but exuberant *ca ca ca ca ca,* a love-call of joyful spring.

We linger a moment at what to us was a favorite summer glade, if only to anticipate its bowered retreat for the summer picnic; but there, flying from tree to tree in drowsy fashion, is a butterfly, a mourn-ing cloak (*Vanessa antiopa*), which has hibernated in the imago or undeveloped state and now is the first to take wing in the air of another year. Its caterpillars feed on willows, cottonwoods and quaking aspens, where eggs in clusters have been laid. "Mourning" in color but not in spirit and hardiness, it is always to us a beautiful and self reliant insect of the mountains.

As we look forward to spring it is interesting to note that all of the sweet songsters of the wildlands are small birds—from robinsize down. Although they all belong to the *Passeriformes,* birds of perching habits, that great order, which comprises about half of all birds, includes some that are not singers, i.e., tyrant flycatchers (*Tyrannidae*), jays, magpies and crows (*Corvidae*), shrikes (*Laniidae*) and starlings (*Sturnidae*). In our mountains that thumb-sized morsel of birddom, the ruby crowned kinglet (*Regulus calendula cineraceus*) can fill a piny glade with exquisite song.

MARCH 7

Walking homeward from the mountains at midnight, we are delighted to hear the sharp calls of three killdeers flying overhead. It is not that we infer that these first of the shorebirds to come and go do not often endure the cold winter through, but rather that while stragglers sojourn with us the vast throng of migration is now beginning to appear. Few sounds are more penetrating than the excited calls of the killdeer, flying in the wild winds of March; few birds incite more quickly our recollection of swampy but pleasant fieldland, pastured pond, and apprehensive bird.

Not many people mistake the killdeer (*Charadrius vociferus vociferus*), for it shrills its remonstrance from every reservoir and pond, every mere and sump, every wayside plash and slab. Being palustrine by nature, it is fond of the meadowlands where graze unobtrusive cows; wherever it may be, however, it may lay its eggs as if intending them to be tramped by wandering hoof, although invariably water is somewhere near, still or running, saline or fresh, from the edge of which it worms its living.

Sometimes in the early days of March one may hear the wild killdeer crying constantly with penetrating clarity, as for an hour at a time it courses back and forth over the lea. It acts as if the ecstasy of the approaching nesting time had driven it into a sort of delight and anticipation.

To us the killdeer is a nervous and tricky bird; it flies jerkily, swiftly; and always leads us to believe its wing is broken, always persuades us by various manoeuvres to withdraw from its nesting locale.

"Killdeer" is, of course, an onomatopoetic word, and, if the accent be placed strongly on the second syllable, the imitation of sound if uttered with shrill emphasis is excellent. If its voice be insufficient to identify it, its straw-colored legs, buffy upper tail coverts and rump, together with its two black breast bars, add to its marks of individuality. It runs swiftly along a bare shore; waits, runs again, often being almost indistinguishable from mud, stone, weed, or clod; and then, unable to bear intrusion longer, flushes high into the air with wild and piercing objection. Feeding principally on grasshoppers, ants, bugs, spiders, ticks, earthworms, weevils, crickets, wireworms, and the like, with occasional meals of weed seeds, it is one of man's best friends.

Times may come; times may go; but the ensemble of experiences in the wildlands is a fountain of sweet memories from which one may drink at will. It is the extraordinary event that is repeatedly quaffed— the surprised bear so quickly decamping from its wallow that willows flip back upon our astonished face; the flying fish line that had caught an ouzel by the toe; the uncanny, almost human sounds of a porcupine beneath a cabin floor; the bull that held us in a wide, open field; and the footprints of a mountain lion obviously following us in the snow. Merely to recollect is to relive; and to lay one's head upon the pillow at night is to breathe the memories of it all.

MARCH 8

On our way to the Jordan marshes today we have in the course of an hour seen approximately fifty flocks of snow geese, containing in all about five hundred birds. Flocks have consisted of from twenty to several hundred individuals, all moving northward in the very middle of a sunny day; and then, to reverse all ideas of the general trend, an enormous flock of several thousand overhead is just now flying—southward! Our impression is that these beautiful white denizens of the sky play about the neighborhood of retreating snow, and when they make up their minds, advance northward a hundred miles or more a day.

Reaching a vast shallow slough, which in places is ice-covered, in others, marked by stretches of brown salt grass, we tarry for an hour to enjoy the proximity of several hundred ducks there feeding and drowsing in the contentment of a warm, bright day. Some of them are standing in obvious slumber on the ice; many more are ducking their heads into the inches-deep water to probe therefrom the succulent root or worm.

In the order of their abundance we identify them; pintails; blue-winged teals (*Anas discors discors*); red-heads (*Aythya americana*); and baldpates or American widgeons (*Mareca americana*), As they sit there, the male pintail, which has a long pointed tail, puts his head up on a long slender neck higher than do the other ducks; but his streaked brown consort does not have the blue on the fore wing edge and white crescent before the eye. The male redhead, as its name indicates, is easily identified by its red-brown head and blue bill, and though it is not unlike a canvas back it is not nearly so whitish. The female is more brownish, with wing stripes of gray.

The baldpate is well named; for as we look at the male bird we can easily detect its white shining crown.

All of them seem to be enjoying themselves; and, while there is little to indicate sexual interest and excitement, the blue-winged teals are obviously paired.

Just as we leave the slough, five mallards (*Anas platyrhynchos platyrhynchos*) draw out attention to some deeper water; and then like a post on the ice appears another bird that we must reserve for the morrow; and in the meantime we go home to ponder on ultimate meanings.

As we try to digest some of the latest findings of biochemical cytology and its techniques, we are lead to hope that the very basis of life will someday be discovered. The methods, embodied in such technical and constantly improving sciences as ultraviolet microscopy, microcolorimetry, microspectrophotometry, microfluorometry, microtitrimetry, microdilatometry, and microchromatography, astonish us. For instance, with a microrespirometer one may measure the oxygen consumption of a single frog egg! How can nature's vital secret elude such capable investigation?

MARCH 9

Yes, just as we are leaving the Jordan slough, there out on the ice-sheet-verge is a post, a stump, a motionless thing—but a bird, a solitary Treganza heron (*Ardea herodias treganzai*). (What memories that name Treganza brings—of the hours we spent with him, of the charm of his wife, Antwonet, an equally good ornithologist who rode tandem style *a la motorcyle* with her husband to mountain and swamp for bird nests. An architect by profession, he finally left the Wasatch for California. To differentiate a pallid subspecies of the Great blue heron occupying the plains and semi-arid regions of the West, this bird was named in his honor by Edward J. Court in 1908).

There it stands on the ice, a motionless, black-crested contemplative thing of pale blue with whiter frills about its head and neck, a bird four feet high with long pointed bill, and next to the sand hill crane, the largest wader of these valley sloughs. No wonder he is here, for this is his feeding ground; but Bird Island and Hat Island thirty miles or more westward in the Great Salt Lake are his nesting homes. In a week or so throngs of them will gather there; females will give their soft, coaxing calls; males will battle thrust for thrust, bill for bill, parry for parry, with all the skill of fencers using rapiers, but causing little mortality; mates will be selected and atop rock or sage five foot nests raised for many a year will be reoccupied with but a few new sticks to indicate another incubation. The four young birds will be fed at first by soft food regurgitated through a parent bird's bill, but later by fish gathered too often, let us admit, from crystal runs of trout breeders, but more frequently from the reed-covered sloughs where now we stand in admiration. Not only fish such as carp, suckers, minnows, but also frogs, tadpoles, salamanders, lizards, meadow mice, and grasshoppers enter the fare.

Few American artists have taken advantage of the opportunity to paint the lovely blue colors of the great blue heron or depict the statliness of the patient bird as it stands its favorite slough. Pisanello and Francesco del Cocca alone among the Italian artists seemed to appreciate the heron in Italy, though Gozzoli, Pinturicchio, Marco Bello and Pietro Lorenzetti faithfully painted the wild duck. Yet now many a competent brush is painting the beauties of the Wasatch mountains.

There is not only beauty in the Wasatch mountains but comparative safety as well—wild beasts may be perilous in Africa and India, but not here.

The authors that I have read over and over again, always with one at my bedside, are: Plutarch, Milton and Ruskin; the books that I have most often consulted throughout the years are: Roget's Thesaurus and that incomparable Oxford English Dictionary of thirteen volumes. These have been my mental playmates; and, if I were cast upon a lonely island to dwell as did Crusoe, I should crave little else except the physical comforts of life.

MARCH 10

During many years' observations it has been our experience to see mallards in the reeded sloughs of these valleys during every month of the year; for even in the severest winter there is always some warm open spring in which migration's stragglers may find refuge. Days of driven snow are succeeded by thaws. Mallards care not for the cold—all they ask is some place of open water, preferably secluded even though small.

Just now the males display their finest iridescent plumage, for the breeding season is nigh; but their fine feathers are destined to leave them later for the unattractive eclipse plumes of summer.

It is not generally known that the mallard sometimes lays its eggs in the nest of other birds, nor that, although it feeds principally upon grasses, water weeds, and berries, it eats the larvae of mosquitoes whenever it comes upon them.

Never shall we forget the thousands of dead and sick mallards we saw along the shores of Great Salt Lake in 1910; but sick ones that we placed in fresh water recovered within a few days. Later extensive study of the mortality convinced Dr. Alexander Wetmore that the birds were suffering from alkalai-poisoning, though some individuals with shot-pellets in their gizzards showed indication of lead-poisoning.

All of the surface feeding ducks (*Anatinae*) have two well known characteristics: without diving they dip their heads for food, and when flushed they rise straight up out of the water. Among them are such birds as the mallard, the black duck, the gadwall, baldpate, pintail, the teals, the shoveller and the wood duck.

The diving ducks (*Aythyinae*) on the other hand dive for their food, usually in more open and deeper waters, and when flushed, skim along the surface for some distance before conquering the air. Among them are the redhead, canvasback, the scaup ducks, the golden eyes, buffle head and harlequin.

As we are leaving the slough we come upon five female marsh hawks feeding on a dead pintail. There are no signs of a struggle, from which we conclude that probably being sick, it had crawled on shore to die. There are no doctors, no nurses, no hospitals in wild life—the stricken individual usually trudges to protective seclusion there to languish alone until better or dead.

We never cease to marvel at the exquisite beauty of nature, especially as seen under either the hand glass or the microscope, whether it be the feather of a bird, the throat of a flower or the back of an insect. There is such multiformity of design that the pattern-makers of the world should more and more seek the geometric intricacies therein displayed; and, as far as color is concerned, one discovers such variegation, iridiscence and maculation as to make him wonder at the gorgeousness of it all.

MARCH 11

On our way to Emigration canyon, rillets are trickling down the faces of open cuts where the remnants of valley snow are gradually thawing; but the mountains even to the foothills are snow sculptured except on the warmest exposures. The grass, mostly beaten into clumps of brown and gray, is beginning to show a newly sprouted green.

One mile up the canyon a flock of about one hundred sparrow-sized birds is feeding on the weed seeds of a grassy flat below a snow bank; their heads are black and gray, their bodies brown, their wings pink with black tips, their rumps pink and their tails black—from all of which we know them to be leucostictes. From the fact that the gray spot on the back of the head extends only to the eye we determine them to be gray-crowned leucostictes or rosy finches. It is often difficult in the field to distinguish these birds from the Hepburn leucosticte and the black rosy finch, both of which visit us in the winter; but in their flushes, sallies and return, these birds at their closest are only twenty feet away. Once in awhile the whole flock takes to wing, making a circle a hundred yards in diameter before it comes back again; but stragglers ignore the imagined danger and remain either in trees or on the feeding ground. Since flocking is a means of mutual protection, it is not strange that it is most used by migrants in unfamiliar terrains.

We press onward to the divide on the way to Parley's, where just below the ridge we are persuaded by the beauty of the scene to stop and ponder: the pale blue sky is marked by majestic cumulus clouds; the snow molded mountains at the south are huge, clean cut and white as wedding cake, with scarce a tree relieving the immaculate wave of ridge and ravine; the mountainsides at the west sink in gentle slopes below us, patches of blackish scrub oak alone maculating the white, a white glistening in the clear afternoon sun as if ice, mingled with water, trickled and seeped upon it. So transpicuous is the atmosphere, so definite the snowy outline of ridge against sky, that for the moment we have the impression of being in a dreamworld of mountains of snow.

But no—we turn to the north; and there on the open grass strewn hillside is one of our favorite shrubs, the partridge berry (*Symphoricarpos rotundifolius*), whose older bark is grayish but its younger branches deep brownish vinaceous in tint, and shining.

We pluck the branch of a sage (*Artemisia tridentata*) and all the way home enjoy its pungent odor.

We must be fond of sage, as we use it constantly on roasts, in soups, and in turkey dressing; in truth we pluck the leaves from our little herb garden, dry them and preserve them in bottles for winter use. We do the same with parsley and chives, By the way, we want some sage cheese, made by the cheddar cheese process, with a green mottled curd caused by adding of the green sage leaves before the curd is hooped; and, if some one can, please bring a pound of that soft English flower cheese containing the petals of roses and marigolds.

MARCH 12

Two hawks in undulating flight having attracted our attention, we watch them with the glasses until they come quite near, when their broad rounded wings and the rufous-red of the upper sides of their short wide tails indicate unmistakeably that they are western red-tails (*Buteo jamaicensis calurus*), very likely in courtship manoeuver. We had not expected to see these hawks for a week or more, at least in any great number; but hardy individuals never leave the Wasatch at all.

Nest-making or nest-rejuvenation as we might call it (these birds return to the same nest year after year) is taking place now, the site usually being some lofty tree of the wilder woods. Since they apparently mate for life, both the male and the female assist in home duties, one or the other carrying to the nest a fresh green bough every day to act as a parasol over the fledglings—what sweet romance in the wild woods!

The red-tail does more good than harm, for its principal food consists of mice, rats, spermophiles, squirrels, shrews, rabbits and frogs, crickets, beetles, caterpillars, grubs and earthworms, though occasionally it does take such birds as quail, poultry, doves, woodpeckers, king-fishers, robins and sparrows. It is like the boy who is good six days a week but raises Cain on Sunday—his good qualities greatly outweigh the bad.

Being constantly fearful of men, the red-tail inhabits preferably the sparsely settled portions of the Wasatch, at least we seldom observe it so near man and his workings as the places where the Swainson habitually sails.

Our *Buteos* or buzzard hawks have so many color phases that it is sometimes very difficult to distinguish the birds as they fly overhead. The red-tail shows the red of its tail only when seen from above or when it veers in flight; but its wings are broader, its tail and body wider than those of the ferruginous rough-leg or the Swainson. The feathers of the legs of a ferruginous rough-leg are usually so light as to show clearly from below; and a Swainson has more sharply pointed wings than those of the red tail. After considerable experience one learns to distinguish these three hawks by their shape alone, and always locale and season are great aids to determination. For instance, if in July I am sitting in a dry sageland of the valley and a large hawk is soaring in circles overhead, I know almost without looking that it is a Swainson.

It is very interesting to think that someday the wolf will "dwell with the lamb", the hawk with the mouse; the leopard "lie down with the kid"; the young lion with the calf; and the cow with the bear; but when they do some of them will go hungry, unless "the lion shall eat straw like the ox", a food his teeth are not made to masticate and consume. Thus the hawk is by nature made to prey upon flesh.

MARCH 13

Walking along the muddy bank of this clear but reedy valley-brook, we are startled by the heavy rise of a bird resembling a loon, which flies somewhat like a mallard but with head and body held horizontally. It is a large duck, black and white above, with green head and white underparts—a male American Merganser (*Mergus merganser americanus*). We should not have been surprised, since many a time we have seen this sheldrake or fish duck here in the winter months, but one not only respects any bird that is able to cope with ice and snow but also welcomes the merganser as a true harbinger of spring. Like the redwings the male birds are the advance guards of migration, the females following them two weeks or more later.

Since it breeds usually further north the sheldrake is chiefly a winter or migration visitor; even then it is not common and is more apt to appear along such streams as the Sevier, Bear, Provo and Weber than in the still marshes which harbor great flocks of the duck tribes. Its flesh being fishy, it is very seldom sought by the hunter.

The merganser has an anatomical characteristic that distinguishes it from all other ducks: its slender cylindrical bill is armed with sharp recurving teeth, whereas other ducks have bills with a cutting edge and a series of lamellae. The teeth of the hooded merganser (*Lophodytes cucullatus*) do not recurve.

The reason for this armament is the habit of the merganser: it lives almost exclusively on fish, to capture which it dives under water and pursues them in their own haunt, clasping them with its serrated bill. Sometimes several mergansers work together in cornering fish and grasping them one by one.

So long as the diving power of the merganser been recognized that, in giving a name to the bird, Willughby in 1676 chose the word "merganser", from the Latin *merg-us*, diver, and *anser*, goose; and, as early as 1759, B. Stillingfl wrote: "In the autumn, when the fishes hide themselves in deep places, the merganser . . . supplies the gull with food".

The word "sheldrake" should not be used to describe this bird, as it properly refers to a duck of the genus *Tadorna* of Europe, which, resembling a goose, is allied to the tree duck, and nests in a burrow. It is, however, black and white.

The whistling swan are departing, and California gulls are congregating on their breeding ground.

In life there is much of sweetness, much of pain; a lot of brightness, a lot of cloud; but through it all nature ever looks forward with hope, ever working towards perpetuation. In our limited way we do not comprehend all, nor are we certain of destiny; but somehow, the quiescence of nature followed by its resurgance, gives us the thought that a rhythm so omnipresent and comprehensive must have eventuality, not oblivion. Our insignificant minds cannot prove, but in humility they perforce deny. *Quis me manet exitus?*

MARCH 14

Much of the charm of our pellucid canyon streams is due to the water ouzel and the belted kingfisher (*Megaceryle alcyon caurina*), the former an always dependable resident, the latter, except in deeply frozen winter, an equally constant inhabitant. We are for the hour on the bank of the Provo river whose deep shaded pools and clear waters are ever delightful to the fisherman, be he man or bird; and there the bird is a kingfisher, rattling like a New Year's Eve noise-maker, hovering momentarily upon its favorite rock at the river's border. From the fact that he appears to have only one breast band, we know him to be a male; for the female would more likely show two. It is impossible to tell whether he is a migrant or has been a resident hereabout all winter; for a mild winter and a warm brook often win against migration's urge.

So frequently have we seen a kingfisher perched upon a willow-sheltered rock, which had spattered evidence of its habitual visitation, we have concluded that it sometimes prefers a boulder to a limb from which to plunge for fish. It likes the larger mountain streams that here and there form deep bends or pools of unbubbled hyaline water in which fish lazily resist the slow current. We admit that having often come upon this bird while we ourselves were fishing for trout, we have felt that despite its attractive wings and a pretty scientific name it was destructive of our prey; but our correspondent and friend, the late famous A. C. Bent, who considered many bits of evidence, concluded that the greater part "or nearly all" of its food consists of suckers and other harmful or neutral fish. When a kingfisher catches a small fish, by a plunge from a perch or a dive from the air, it immediately pounds the victims's head against a rock until insensibility occurs, tosses the fish into the air, and swallows it as it descends. Digestion takes place rapidly, making it difficult sometimes to identify fish that have been eaten; in fact a kingfisher has been known to swallow a fish so large that the victim's tail protruded outside of the bird's bill until digestion made room for it.

When a kingfisher burrows its nest one would think it had turned into a rock squirrel or rough-winged swallow. Selecting a perpendicular cut or embankment that towers thirty feet above a bend of its favorite transpicuous mountain stream, it pecks a hole with its strong bill, scratches out the debris with its feet, and with its mate works until the burrow runs four or five feet inward. Here in an enlarged chamber it rears its six or seven young fishers, feeding them at first with a fishy smelling vomit, but later with tiny fishes themselves.

When young birds later emerge from their dungeon, they must be taught to plunge for their own food; and to do this the parent forces them to dive for dead fish killed for the purpose; but, the knack of it having been learned, off the little ones are driven to crackle their way alone.

MARCH 15

An assassin that clutches its prey and often begins to eat the breast before the victim's screams have ended—such is the Cooper hawk (*Accipiter cooperii*), the real "chicken hawk", worst of the murderous trio that includes the goshawk and the sharp-shinned. One of them has just stricken a sweet-singing meadowlark and before our surprised and indigant eyes carried the fluttering victim away. We are in the mood therefore to reprobate this hawk in no uncertain terms.

By observing certain rules one may at sight distinguish the *Accipiters*, the genus to which the three villians belong, from the fine large *Buteos*, such as the rough-leg, Swainson and red-tail, and the pleasing *Falcos*, such as the sparrow hawk. In the air both the *Accipiters* and the *Buteos* appear to have fingered extensions to their wing tips; but the falcons have long single pointed wings, the wings of the *Buteos* are broad, those of the *Accipiters* rounded; those of the falcons, long, narrow and pointed. The tail of a *Buteo* is broad; that of an *Accipiter* long and narrow; that of a *Falco*, long. Whenever therefore, one sees in the sky a hawk with *fingered wing tips and a long narrow tail*, he may presume it to be one of the destructive *Accipiters;* if it is larger than a crow it will likely be a goshawk, if smaller than a crow, a Cooper, and, if smaller still, then a sharp-shinned. The only bird that might be mistaken under this rule is the marsh hawk, but it flies about thirty feet over the open meadow whereas the three killers hunt about trees.

We go thus into detail, because first our enmity is aroused and, secondly, too often the farmer in his anger shoots hawks that are really his best friends. The harmful hawks are sudden, quick, unexpected in their movements, jerky in flight with only brief sailings; whereas the beneficial hawks usually soar. This again is to the disadvantage of welcome species, for under ill-considered antipathy towards all hawks they are the first to succumb.

The Arkansas flycatcher and the kingbird in fair combat drive the Cooper hawk away, but in return for the affront, the raptor destroys chickens (as many as a dozen in one afternoon, if unmolested in its foray), ducks, shore birds, grouse, quail, doves, sparrows, flickers, robins and song birds of many kinds. The few squirrels, rats and mice it takes little atone for all this depredation.

We pick up an earthworm, and take it home for examination, dissection and observation under the glass. It is incredible—the mouth and the anus ends look alike; and that swollen portion near the center is the clitellum, a glandular expression. We open the little fellow, finding a tiny brain, a pharynx, heart, esophagus, crop, gizzard, intestine, besides a sort of nerve cord running along the ventral side. We marvel: if ever our interest in ornithology, mammalogy, and botany, should subside, we can easily drift to the *Annelida* (segmented worms) and the *Anthropoda* (joint footed animals). For that matter the puddle in the back yard has *protozoa* worth a life time of study.

MARCH 16

Flocks of mountain bluebirds (*Sialia currucoides*), having appeared, it is interesting to see them hover over a snow-topped telephone wire, which so bothers them that they decline to alight upon it until one of their number chances to jar off the snow.

The mountain bluebird is light purplish blue above and pale blue below. The mountain, as its name indicates, prefers the high canyon parks and meadows for its home; and many years' records convince us that its usual time of arrival is the middle of March, though we have recorded stray individuals in February.

Being close relatives of the thrushes, robin and Townsend solitaire, the mountain bluebird's young have chest feathers edged with brown but such as to give a squamatic or streaked appearance instead of the spotty design of young robins and thrushes. Our bluebirds nest in old woodpecker holes, or suitable niches about houses; but the finest lot of mountain bluebirds we ever saw were nesting in chalk boxes nailed by a school teacher on the posts of his home in a mountain sage-clad valley. All of the score of boxes were occupied, apparently being exactly to the birds' liking.

The voice of the western bluebird (*Sialia mexicanus occidentalis*) is but a short tender *nu*, but the moutain bluebird has a sweeter warble than its valley cousin.

During the hundreds of times we have watched both of these birds feeding their young we have never observed anything but insects in their mouths; but they are known to take various wild berries in the fall.

The western demands an open expanse of ground before its nesting box. It will nest in a box placed on a house or stump, but the year another house obstructs its open field, that year it moves on and outward to the fringes of human habitations. Mild mannered, soft-voiced birds of heavenly color, they are as refreshing in spring as the buttercups of grassy knolls.

We listen for sounds in the wildlands after nightfall: In the Wasatch there are only a few disturbing nocturnal cries. The uncanny shriek of a great-horned owl is not to be despised as a frightful sound; it may be the "scream" attributed by many a woodsman to a mountain lion. The howling jabber of a coyote is hair-raising to the inexperienced, especially if heard nearby. The howl of a wolf is usually forlorn and mournful, like the reboation of a distant bull; but this animal is so close to extermination here that the mere hearing of it again would be music to our ears. The zee of a rattlesnake is the most ominous sound of these valleys, but for the moment we do not recall the biting of a human being by a rattlesnake at night. This reptile is diurnal in habit; nevertheless in early days the author's mother once shrieked in horror at the presence of a rattlesnake that without her knowledge had during the night sought refuge from the cold and shared her cabined bed.

MARCH 17

An old codger hereabouts tells us that to make carp edible compel them to live in fresh water for several days after catching them. We doubt not that the experiment could be easily tried, for sometimes we have seen carp still manifestng signs of life several hours after having been thrown upon the wet grass, hence they would long survive immersion in a tub.

Many years ago it was reported to us that the European carp (*Cyprinus carpio*) was planted in the trout-blessed waters of Utah lake by the game department as a contribution towards the sport of this region; now, alas, the trout have well night disappeared and carp and catfish occupy this beautiful body of water. The catfish are three kinds: the channel (*Ictalurus punctaus*), the horned pout or small catfish (*Ameiurus nebulosus*) and the blue or mud catfish (*Ameiurus melas*). Both the large-mouthed bass (*Huro floridana*) and the small-mouthed black bass (*Micropterus dolomieu*) have likewise been introduced to the waters of Wasatch lakes and ponds; but these have found it as difficult as trout to endure carp.

Besides many species of trout several other varieties of fish have been imported to these mountain waters, such, for instance, as yellow perch (*Perca flavescens*), blut spotted sunfish (*Apomotis cyanellus*), bream (*Lepomis auritus*), crappie (*Pomoxis annularis*), the Tench (*Tinca tinca*) and mosquito fish (*Gambusia patruelis*), but only the last named are well known to us. Each spring officials visit our garden fish pond to deposit therein a score or more mosquito fish; and we must admit that while they apparently sometimes devour the spawn of the gold fish confined with them they do make mosquitoes unnoticeable where once they were pestiferous indeed.

In our *Summer* book of this series, under date of August 30, we have detailed the extraordinary occurrence of a black tarantula (*Eurypelma*) spider as big as a boy's hand clicking its way along the hardwood floor of the living room, into which it had entered as the front door was ajar, and how we feared it little, as its bite was reputed to be no more annoying than that of a red ant or possibly a honey bee. It has just come to our attention that, while it is capable of causing only temporary pain and injury to human beings, its bite is deadly to a cold blooded animal such as a reptile. We have, at least in the Salt Lake valley of the Wasatch, a beautiful and harmless reptile known as the Arizona king snake (*Lampropeltis pyromelana*), which kills by constriction, and, being immune to the venom of a rattlesnake, actually overcomes and swallows the fearsome rattler. One would think the king would crush the tarantula to death in seconds; but no! —I have seen a moving picture of a fight to the death between the two; and the tarantula, apparently unharmed, emerged the victor, as the king slowly died from the poison the spider had injected into it. Some things in nature are almost incredible.

MARCH 18

It has been a memorable day, for at the mouth of the Jordan we have seen stately sandhill cranes (*Grus canadensis tabida*) seventy five strong. It is many a year since we heard their mile-distant bugles from these very salt grass lowlands; hence to have heard and seen again revives a sweet memory. Tall as men, proud as peacocks, wary as geese, telescopic in vision, they stalked the marsh like visiting Senators; yet even with the glasses we admired their protective coloration, which is so like the scant vegetation that obviously the great birds depend upon it.

These astonishing paludal inhabitants—they are four feet long from tip of bill to tip of tail, with legs that extend further backward as they fly—winter in Texas and Mexico, migrate northward in March, breed in that region between Utah and Canada, and fly southward in October and November, living on frogs, lizards, mice, snakes, grasshoppers, worms, insects, succulent roots, and, in the fall, berries and grain.

These big cranes fly with their long necks horizontally ahead, their feet straight behind; but herons, somewhat like them, fold their necks backward in flight. The bugled call of the sandhill crane, a sort of repeated *Gar-oo-oo-oo* is so loud as to be heard miles further than the voice of any other bird we know. With ponderous bodies and large wings they appear burdened and slow, but they sail on and on, easily making remarkable progress in the sky.

Their nests, ordinarily located somewhat north of the Wasatch, are constructed of dead rushes placed on tiny islands in ponds; and two eggs are the usual annual contribution towards survival of the race.

Early inhabitants of these inland valleys were so accustomed to the sandhill crane that every farmer boy knew its cry; perhaps the bird nested here; but the days of plenitude have disappeared with the drainage of wet lowlands.

Male redwings in a flock are singing the chorus of the cavaliers; but no red on their wings shows. As they sit in the willows there is only a yellowish crescent where the red should be; but, when they fly, the red is bright, conspicuous and beautiful. They do much clucking with their singing.

The sandhill crane, being provided with legs long enough to be stilts, which raise its height to nearly that of a man, seems to enjoy walking even more than flying, for on occasion it will with deliberate long steps and constant far-distant viewing of the surroundings, walk a mile or more for a drink of fresh water.

In the kaleidoscope of memory there is this: (a) of people, an endless variety, some sweet, some liars, some thieves, some hypocrites, many pretenders, many upright men, many loving women and a few criminals at heart; (b) in nature, an endles variety, all independent, all mystic, all energetic, all fruitful, all industrious, all constantly struggling, all with but one aim, the perpetuation of the species.

MARCH 19

We have just spent half an hour watching three lesser yellow legs (*Totanus flavipes*) on a half submerged meadow. Accustomed to the wild alarm cries of these birds in summer, we were surprised at their tameness, silence and tranquility, for during the entire time we were observing them at a distance of about a hundred feet they uttered not a single sound.

It is so difficult afield to distinguish the lesser yellow legs from the greater yellow legs (*Totanus melanoleucus*) that one may never be quite sure, especially when they are silent, unless there be comparative objects; but today these lesser yellow legs were within a few feet of some killdeers, which they only slightly exceeded in size.

The plumages of the greater and the lesser yellow legs are very much alike; upper parts mottled with gray black and white; white upper tail coverts; gray throat; white underparts spotted, however, on the chest. Their yellow legs are a quick mark of identification among all the shorebirds.

The meadow was checkered with grass clumps and patches of water a foot or so in diameter; and in this inch deep water each bird waded, gracefully and slowly taking a step, then thrusting the bill into the water an inch or so, and picking up something we could see it swallow. There was nothing hurried about the movements; and though a stiff breeze was blowing it seemed not to disturb their serenity.

The food of this interesting bird consists of larvae, snails, worms, grasshoppers and other insects.

Both yellow legs winter south of the United States and breed in Canada. Our record today may be considered a fairly early migration date, for a month from now many of them will likely appear.

Yellowlegs, greater and lesser, belong to the order *Charadriiformes,* which includes the gulls as well as the shorebirds. Their closest relatives hereabout are the willets, the godwits and the sandpipers. On Farmington bay one sees many shorebirds, but each has some characteristic pose, shape or color that readily discloses its identity to the trained observer. Unless you know what you are looking at your comments in ornithology are worthless.

You may read this and read that—some of it moss-enshrouded with the leaves of antiquity, some of it boldly assertive as if it knew far beyond the ken of ordinary man—; but, when all is spoken, all is read, despite our humility and willingness to learn, the great problems of life, diety and immortality remain the mysteries they were when as babes we entered a million and a half years ago into to the great realm of thinking beings.

MARCH 20

With forsythia, croci and violets in bloom about home, we decide to stroll up City Creek canyon to see what is flowering there, our companion for the day being the noted botanist, M. E. Jones.

The only plant at all common is the Indian parsnip, a low perennial of the parsely family with yellow flowers. It appears somewhat like a mat, as we almost tread upon it. Another species (*Cymopterus ibapense*) with white or cream flowers inhabits the gravely soil of higher elevations—it was named and described by our companion. The Indian parsnip of our trail today studs the ground here and there with flowers of gold, mostly on the dry, sunny slopes, but at least up to the limit of our climb, approximately one mile above sea level.

Children on the road are carrying bouquets of that pretty yellow member of the lily family known locally as buttercup (*Fritillaria pudica*) though properly as yellow bell, lily bell, or orange fritillaria. This sweet flower, a true butter-colored cup if there ever was one, growing on a stem three to eight inches high, blooms in May and June,

In a dense oak copse we unexpecetdly come upon a bed of Easter bells, yellow dog tooth violets, adder's tongues or trout lilies as they are variously called (*Erythronium grandiflorum parviflorum*), another member of the lily family. Up the mountain they will bloom for us to the very highest glades and until the warm sun of July makes verdant all those sweet sub-Alpine trails.

We look for the pussy willows and find them.

Many years of observation in nature's wildwoods have convinced us that the aim of all species of animals, whether bug or bear, spider, bird or cougar, is security, meaning plenitude of food, freedom from enemies, and climatic conditions favorable to reproduction and contentment. Those three desiderata result in the astonishing multiformity that is everywhere apparent.

One species selects the desert on account of the scarcity of enemies but struggles for food; another chooses the swamplands where food is plentiful notwithstanding an increased number of enemies. In the great struggle species develop fangs, claws and stings of diverse shapes. Some learn to endure intense heat, others extreme cold; and, doubtless, there are thousands of species yet unknown. But bacteria are not everywhere as some have claimed. In conversation with Dr. R. G. Frazier, eminent explorer with Byrd, I learned that in the Antarctic men do not catch cold or have influenza—the viruses cannot endure the low temperatures.

If the *Lingula,* a genus of the marine lamp shell (*Phyolum Brachiopoda*) is the one living animal who could trace its unchanged physical ancestry back four hundred million years, indeed, to the Ordovician geologic age, then man in his ancestry of only one and a half million years has much to think about, much to contemplate in the ways of survival.

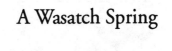

A Wasatch Spring

INTRODUCTION

At one time during several years the author, under permit as a scientific collector, made repeated journeys with a gun in hand to the valleys and canyons of the Wasatch mountains, in an effort to determine just what species of birds and mammals resided in, or visited this attractive region of many life-zones, ranging, as it does, from deserts forlorn to pine-fledged peaks seeped with lingered snow. Then, as the appearance of an unrecorded species became a rarity and need for further specimens waned, the gun was supplanted by field glasses, and the interest diverted chiefly to habits, with on-the-spot descriptions written on handy note books; often with onomatops, that is lettered imitations of voice and song. Those were solitary but delightful hours. Sometimes however a companion was the late Marcus E. Jones, an eminent botanist.

Then, as roads improved and it became possible to study almost any Wasatch canyon or valley in the course of a day's journey, the author had the assistance of the late Louise Atkinson in the gathering of floral specimens and their preservation in a botanical press; indeed, as the paraphernalia included not only field glasses and a botanical press but also barometer, camera and insect-bottle, we went forth prepared to observe everything alive in the wildlands. My companion, a real botanist, had not only remarkably discerning eyes, but also the ability to capture and hold almost any insect that attracted our attention, a knack she had retained from bare-foot wading days about the pastures and sloughs of her childhood home near the mouth of the Jordan river.

Throughout the years the rough field notes were invariably written into final form at the end of the day in which they were made, and, now that they are assembled here, we have the surprising result that the page of any particular day may have been written one year, aye even twenty years or more before or after a page adjoining it. It could not have been otherwise, when most of the journeys were taken on either week ends or holidays, as respites from the activities of a legal profession and business. This will account for differences in weather in adjoining pages, for one Spring may be cold and drear, another mild and lovely; nevertheless, as we all know, nature seldom varies more than a few days in its annual appearances.

97

Since this book is one of a contemplated series of which *The Natural History of a Wasatch Summer* has already been published, it is hoped that the ones on Autumn and Winter will be forthcoming in due time.

More and more we realize that the mountains should belong to all the people, not to one class or another, but equally to all for their recreation and enjoyment; and a great part of that enjoyment is knowledge of the varied forms of life in the wild woods.

Again the author is indebted to R. A. Hart, eminent consulting engineer, for critical perusal of the manuscript and valuable suggestions.

Claude T. Barnes

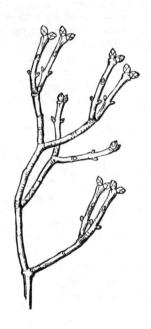

MARCH 21

Sweet are the songs of spring, but none more endearing to us than the tristful call "Re-T-E-A-R-" now being uttered by a lonely Say phoebe (*Sayornis saya saya*) from the top of a wayside pole. It is a call much sadder than the weaker but similar voice of the chickadee, and, furthermore, more clearly accented on the second syllable. Year after year we listen to its far-reaching dulcet notes; year after year we expect it within a day or so of the calendared advent of spring.

This plaintive bird is one of the great family of flycatchers (*Tyrannidae*), which includes such well known representatives as the kingbird; but it is much milder both in action and call than that skreeky belligerent. This phoebe wins our affection; the Arkansas flycatcher, and the kingbird, our admiration for their domineering courage; they screech about our homes, while the tender phoebe catches its insects without strident vociferous demonstration.

We have noted the arrival of the Say phoebe in these mountains as early as February 21st, but, ordinarily it comes in the middle of March. Its olive gray upper parts and rusty abdomen are unassuming in color, hence the bird is often difficult to find even when its voice is heard; but the pale rusty under side is a good field mark.

Its nests that we have found have invariably been placed on the crossbeams beneath bridges, usually those used by gravel-wagons on their way to the pits of the foothills; and they have always been neat round affairs made of many materials such as grass, hair, feathers, wool and moss. All of our efforts to persuade phoebes to nest in suitable house niches have been in vain, though usually such crannies were examined as if they were being considered.

Altogether it is an inoffensive bird of unquestioned benefit to man; nevertheless, it is somewhat incongruous to open our account of joyful spring with the saddest note of the year.

In most regions of the globe the advent of spring is more or less uniform in its effect upon the wild life of the terrain; but that is not so in a place of valleys and mountains like the Wasatch, where altitudes vary from the forty-one hundred feet of the valley low to the twelve thousand feet of the highest peaks. Here spring is creeping in its influence, causing many a species of flowers to bloom a month earlier in the lowlands than in the higher canyons. It is not so noticeable with respect to the activities of mammals and birds, although non-resident birds that breed in the glades of spruce and pine do approach their nesting homes slowly. The vast throngs of waterfowl usually appear on schedule as they seek the rivers, pools and sloughs of the valleys that constitute the great avenues of migration.

MARCH 22

We are pleased with an afternoon on Farmington Bay, the dyke inclosed bird-refuge that is one of the world's greatest points of interest to the ornithologist. With the vacuum bottle filled with hot coffee, and sandwiches in the basket, we are prepared to stroll, rest and gaze as birds appear.

They do arrive, but not in such numbers as a week ago, leading us to believe that there are two kinds of migrants—those like the snow geese that edge the receding ice, and those that follow with permanent residence in view.

The first thing we notice is that the coots (*Fulica americana americana*) are here. Five of them are walking in the mud or muck, as one might well call the slough with its inch-deep water; and very often they nip some tidbit. In walking, their webbed feet show clearly; and when they run they waddle in the manner of ducks. One of them, having reached deep water, dives half-way into it, whereupon its companion circles it twice as if in play. As they fly they paddle their feet vigorously, skim the pond for a considerable distance, and take off like hydro-aeroplanes. This habit has invoked many to call them "spatters", a very descriptive word.

Being practically omnivorous, coots eat reed seeds and seeds of other aquatic plants, leaves, fronds, wild celery, foxtail grass, minnows, tadpoles, worms, snails, eggs of crustaceans, and even bits of carrion; but today it is impossible to tell what they are picking up in the water. Sometimes as they walk about they resemble large valley quails, then guinea fowl; but wherever they go—in mud or water—their lobed feet do good service. They are much tamer than the avocets about them, but not nearly so dainty and attractive. Somehow we have never liked the croaking, grunting coots; for, although they associate agreeably with ducks, they are often uncouth and even murderous with each other. That they are smart no one can deny, especially when they splash together in such a watery ferment as to confuse the attacking eagle, but they are coarse and unattractive.

A pair of avocets (*Recurvirostra americana*) work so close that we watch for half an hour how they feed; usually it is a sweeping motion of the bill from right to left on the surface of the water, then again a head-ducking as if the birds were upturned boats.

Before leaving we see some ruddy ducks (*Oxyura jamaicensis rubida*), acting like grebes, and some handsome black and white greater scaup ducks (*Anthya marila nearctica*), these latter being rather uncommon sights in our many-yeared peregrinations.

MARCH 23

Having just spent an hour's time observing several pairs of ruddy ducks in nuptial plumage, we are delighted with the male, for with his rich brown back, white cheeks, black crown, blue bill and while-silver under parts, he is not only as beautiful but also as proud as a peacock. And he rides the ripples with his tail perked up in wrenlike fashion, his white cheek patch, ruddy back and white under tail coverts show conspicuously; but his mate is a grayish little body, with even her cheek spots lacking the immaculate clearness of the male.

This beautiful duck nests in the Jordan river reeds in June, often utilizing old nests of red-heads or western grebes, and the ten eggs more or less are so large than the first finder of them (W. H. Collins) is said to have mistaken them for brant eggs, until his astonished eyes proved their real ownership.

One must see the ruddy duck in the spring to watch it at its best, for, unlike some ducks, it has a distinct nuptial plumage, which becomes a drab and inconspicuous garb in the fall and winter.

The ruddy is a chunky, quick little duck, much given to hiding under water from danger, for, being able to dive as expertly as a grebe, it is aided by its strong, wide paddles to elude many a pursuer. Being a diving duck, it subsists on succulent roots, and the seeds of water plants, though readily taking such larvae, slugs, snails, minnows and worms as come within its grasp. Ruddy, of course, means "reddish", in reference to the brown back.

Four greater scaup ducks again win our approval, for with their black heads and tails and white bodies they look very prim and clean on the water. They are alert, wary and restless; and when they fly they show very clearly the white margin at the back edge of the wing.

Mallards and Canadian geese appear in pairs about the swamps; but pintails are in great flocks. The huge pond is dotted by hundreds of gulls and avocets, the latter showing much more cinnamon color then they did a year ago. Four whistling swans yet remain.

No man can become intimately acquainted with nature without the conviction that, whatever the destiny of man may be, all of the possessors of lesser brains—the sparrow, the duck, the eagle, the wild mammal—will likewise individually enter into the great plan of sempiternity, for if such a plan there be, it cannot ignore the gradients of intellectuality.

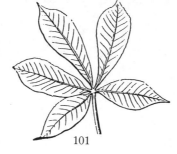

101

MARCH 24

The female red-wings are here! For several days we have noticed that the males were tending to break up their wifeless flocks and disperse over the meadows; and now thirty drab little females have arrived together, each, let us say, expectant, hopeful, but not betrothed. They stare curiously about the fen but as yet manifest little interest in the males. The males are likewise apparently indifferent, for one perched on a post beside the female flock gives but casual heed to them, and male after male flies about the pasturage alone.

Frogs are croaking for the first time this year; slate-colored juncos still chinkle their marble-struck notes along the field creeks and willows where meadowlarks are singing rapturously.

At Farmington Bay we watch six Treganza herons, and, flushing them, we are able to drive their pace at thirty miles an hour. Observers in automobiles and airplanes are gradually adding to the reliable records of the speeds of animals and birds, and we are ever alert to make our contribution. These herons flap their great wings slowly, but fly very evenly in the sky; and just before each alights on the mud it throws its head backward and its feet forward, reaching the ground without any shock. We see a pair of stately Canadian geese but when they alight on the bay they hit the water with a loud and very noticeable plunge.

A small flock of snow geese is circling about; and the bay is swarming with lesser scaup ducks, which are not so handsome as the greater scaups of yesterday.

The avocets of today are ducking their heads into the deep water; and for the first time we hear their tingling "chuck a tee, chuck a tee, chuck chuck".

A marsh hawk so white as to resemble a gull hunts from a few yards above the meadow, and from its pale gray color we know it to be a male.

On the way home we discover six hawks (Buteos) soaring over a canyon; but they appear so nearly black when seen from far below that we cannot determine the species. At any rate it is a pleasing sight again to see half a dozen hawks hunting together.

Our representatives of the great genus *Buteo,* including in summer such big, fine hawks as the western red-tailed, the Swainson and ferruginous rough-leg, and, in winter, the American rough-leg, have this interesting characteristic: their tails are shorter than their wings, and from three to five of the outer primaries of the wing are incised or cut on their inner webs, thus giving the wing that fingered tip appearance when they soar over one's head. In the serene atmosphere of a cloudless spring day, such as often occurs, there is something confident and untroubled in the soaring of a large hawk, as if nature had thrust one of its species above the cares and dangers of life below.

MARCH 25

Sometimes a persistent winter is so continuously cold that the end of March displays little to indicate that spring has arrived. Trees are leafless and brown, not even the apricot yet opening in bloom; birds are reluctant to come north, not even Say's phoebe being heard and no chestnut backed bluebirds being seen; spermophiles are late in emerging from their sleep; hawks are scarce and few if any flowers adorn the barren trail. Fields are yet vestured with winter-stricken grass; no cattle graze the bare meadows; and all vegetation is weatherbeaten and soiled. With such evidence it were useless to contend that wild flowers, wild animals and birds always appear on schedule in these mountains.

Gulls nevertheless are swarming about the early ploughman. Before us today a flock of two hundred of them are sitting, not on the cold water, but on a dyke roadway, contentedly enjoying the dry warm earth, sunning themselves and talking things over generally. They are resting with their bodies on the ground, as if they were a lot of toy-boats in dry dock rather than birds with sturdy wings; and when one flies it patters along the hard surface for several feet before gaining the air. Examining them carefully from a distance of ten yards, we discern not a one with a complete ring around its bill, hence conclude that they are all *californicus*.

Many years of almost sacrosanct gratitude and respect of local people have made the gulls tame; yet two Canadian honkers in this sanctuary are almost equally unafraid of our presence. Indeed, such is the quick response of wild things to protection and friendliness that almost every month a loitering deer is accidentally killed on the highways of these mountains, especially where there is much reserved area, and in spite of signs reading "deer-crossing."

Before we reach home a snow storm turns to rain, putting a crystal garniture of ice on the earth. All nature glitters and glistens like spun glass; and towards a brief sun behind a tree, every hue of the sky is revealed in the translucent prisms. Soon the glassy covering melts away, and the sheets of thin ice crack and slip on the frozen ground.

MARCH 26

On account of the many reeded marshes, alkaline ponds and spring-fed meadows in these valleys and parks, the *Limicolae* or shore birds comprise one of our most interesting sub-orders; furthermore, they so habituate themselves to their favorite locales that one may be practically certain of finding any regularly visiting species in season. None of these birds is over twenty six inches long; none has feet completely webbed; all of them are limicoline (mud-dwelling) or cursorial (adapted to running); all are long-winged and most of them long-legged.

Of the shore birds the family *Charadriidae* or plovers are coursing birds with pigeonlike bills and tarsi with hexagonal scales. They include hereabout such common summer residents as the killdeer, the pretty snowy plover (*Charadrius alexandrinus nivosus*), the rather uncommon black-bellied plover (*Squatarola squatarola*), the rare American golden plover (*Pluvialia dominica dominica*) and the casual semipalmated plover (*Charadrius hiaticula semipalmatus*).

The family *Scolopacifae,* including snipes and sandpipers, are shorebirds in which the tarsus is covered with transverse scutellae, except in the long-billed curlew in which the planta tarsi are marked with hexagonal scales. In the Wasatch they include the night-winnowing Wilson snipe, the western willet (*Catoptrophorus semipalmatus inornatus*), the common spotted sandpiper (*Actitis macularia*) and the long-billed curlew, all of which breed here, and such migrants as the long-billed dowitcher (*Limnodromus griseus scolopaceus*), the uncommon western solitary sandpiper (*Tringa solitaria cinnamonea*), Baird's sandpiper (*Erolia bairdii*), the least sandpiper (*Erolia minutilla*), the common western sandpiper (*Ereunetes mauri*), the rare sanderling (*Crocethia alba*), the marbled godwit (*Limosa fedoa*), the greater yellow legs and the lesser yellow legs.

The family *Phalaropodiae* comprises small shorebirds with compressed tarsi, membraned toes and dense gull-like plumage. Of them the Wilson phalarope (*Steganopus tricolor*) breeds in the Wasatch, and the Northern phalarope (*Lobipes lobatus*) is but a transient.

We mention the shorebirds here because few places in the world excel the Wasatch lakes and valleys for observation of them, and the migrants must be seen either now or in the fall, if at all.

MARCH 27

The entrance to Parley's canyon is a scene of exceptional interest and beauty, due not to any striking verdure but to the pleasing conformations of the geologic past; hence, while waiting for the reappearance of a cottontail that has crossed our path, we cannot help admiring the landscape. We notice that on the north side Jurassic limestone overlies a rippled sandstone and red shale, and on the south side the same basal Nugget sandstone overlies a Triassic red shale.

We pause in order more closely to ascertain the display of colors in the horseshoe of the entrance to the canyon. The upstanding stratum comprising the first cliff at the north is brownish vinaceous mingled with livid brown, while the remainder of that mountain side is old gold or buckhorn brown, save at the bottom where a cut has exposed a russet vinaceous tone.

Directly up the canyon, the south canyonside is marked by an almost perpendicular narrow escarpment of ocher red, running like a jagged knife blade down the entire hill.

The ridge of the south hill is pale brownish drab, but below it is a rounded monticule of vinaceous drab, which has at its base a well defined cliff of palid mouse gray overreaching the highway. This latter is joined at the west by a smaller bluff of pecan brown varying to Japan rose. Finally the south side of the horseshoe ends in a rounded ridge of pale olive buff.

We wait in vain for the shy little cottontail, so continuing our way up the canyon, which thence for three miles or more opens between hills of argillaceous limestone capped by shaly limestone and shale, we come to the upper side of the Mountain Dell reservoir, and there see in the first hill at the east a basal conglomerate that is said by eminent geologists to mark the westerly point of the once great Cretaceous sea. We owe much to the researches of such men as Gilbert, King, Emmons, Boutwell, Blackwelder, Mathews and Schultz, and feel that it is fitting that some of their names are immortalized in the great peaks of the Uinta range whose axis protrudes even into the Cottonwood district of the Wasatch.

We pause again at the summit of Parley's to examine the maroon shale and sandstone thereabout, and to view the andesite ridge at the north.

And then as we gaze southward on the forests of evergreen clustered there we are reminded that once at this spot in winter we wrote in our *The Wending Year,*

> The silvery spires of yonder teeming trees
> In canyon deep where blizzards seldom blow,
> Enfrost their limbs and rimy needled leaves
> And stand with feet enrobed in depths of snow.

MARCH 28

Another idyllic afternoon on Farmington Bay! Our companion, seeing a flock of seven birds flying straight and low over the water a few rods away, has just exclaimed "Long black crows!" They are to all appearances as black as ink, flying like herons but with more rapid motion of the wings and greater speed—much to our delight, they are white faced glossy ibises (*Plegadis mexicana*) just arrived. Medium sized herons with long decurved bills, they look black, but on closer inspection they show a white band about the base of the bill, hence the name "white-faced" though "white faced black ibis" would be more descriptive than "glossy". No wonder they are alert and active; for they have arrived at their breeding ground, where they nest in agreeable company with the Treganza heron, black-crowned night heron, snowy egret and other inhabitants of these attractive marshes. They have been southward, even some as far as Argentine, since early last October. Sometimes at migration time we have seen two hundred or more white-faced glossy ibises occupying a pond of not more than an acre's extent; and often in summer they probe the newly irrigated fields of the farm that we manage.

The nests of these birds, made usually in May or June, are built on bent down tules three or four feet above the water; and in each from three to seven eggs are laid, varying in color from green to pale blue. Their food consists of earth worms, crawfish, larvae, insects, leeches, frogs, and so on, to obtain which they probe or nip with their strong long bills.

As we watch the ibis feeding, they utter at times a "zwack" note, and we have heard them "ka-honk" several times as well.

While we are enjoying the sight of these birds we glance across the water towards some white objects moving about the marsh two miles away; they look as large as horses; and even with the glasses we are unable to tell whether they are whistling swans or pelicans. We drive five or six miles to get nearer to them; and then at last we approach them not over a quarter of a mile away. They are twenty eight white pelicans (*Pelicanus erythrorhynchos*), like small sailing ships on the water, a magnificent flock of these enormous birds. As they fly they soar easily and alight with remarkable grace and ease. The only note we have heard them give is a low, whining, coughing "grunt".

Today the gnats pester us in swarms, and, as we capture some of them, we notice that half of them are in a state of copulation. Such is the exuberance of spring! As we are leaving, a herring gull (*Larus argentatus*) flies close by, alternately flapping its wings and soaring, a rare sight indeed.

In the spring faunal species are seldom calm and quiet, as in the halcyon days of summer, for there is too much to do in the ardor of breeding and the duties of nesting to repose in sweet tranquility. Nature at times encourages activity, and such it gets in the spring.

MARCH 29

Unmindful of our presence, a robin and an English sparrow sit in a boxelder tree preening themselves persistently. Each uses the same method to rid itself of soiled winter-feathers—much turning and pecking with the bill, frequent flips, spreads and twitches of the tail, and occasional shaking of the entire body, as if it had just emerged from water and were flouncing itself dry. Their plumages lack luster, but the constant itching of their bodies (caused after all perhaps by blood thirsty creatures as annoying as inaccessible) does not quell their obvious good spirits. Sparrows and robins tolerate each other's presence with confidence and equanimity.

People are house cleaning, trimming their shrubs, raking debris from their yards, and painting soiled woodwork everywhere. Nature laves with fresh rains but depends upon new growths and flowers for its freshness of spring. Dry weeds, dead sticks and old leaves it clears away with winds, tears out with floods, and, failing that, rots back to mother-mold. Indeed, it will not long bear with the unsightly, whether of vegetation, mammal or bird, for, like the human stomach, it quickly breaks down the fallen things that come its way and transforms them into new protoplasm, new blood for new bodies.

When Alexander was about to undertake his war against the Persians he gave so much of the royal property to his friends—a farm here, a village to one, the revenue of some hamlet to another, and so on —that Perdiccas inquired of him what he was leaving for himself, whereupon he replied that he had his hopes. It is so with Nature: no matter how bounteous the harvest, leaving itself stripped of fruit and seed, it returns each spring with renewed hopes and provides as plenteously as before.

We forgot to mention yesterday, that what attracted our attention to the herring gull was its extraordinary size—exceeded only by the great black-backed and burgo-master gulls, which, of course do not inhabit this region—and by its habit in flight of flapipng its wings for a few strokes, then soaring, then flapping again and so on, while the California and ringbilled gulls very seldom soar at all. The herring gull is the scavenger of harbors and the follower of ships at sea; but it does at time rob nests and even devour its own young. It is a strong bird: but certainly an uncommon one in these parts.

MARCH 30

Soarer over the meadowing, what an interesting raptore is the marsh hawk, which is now preparing its nest in the fens of the valleys! In the ardor of his courtship the male repeats nose-dive after nose-dive and utters loud screams to enrapture his apparently indifferent mouse-searching mate. The depression-nest, lined with scattered straws and sticks, may be in a more or less open field, drier than the pasturage; but despite belligerent terns, which chase them, marsh hawks prefer the green timothy fields and the damp, grassy lowlands close to the plashy haunts of yellow-headed blackbirds, avocets, and black-necked stilts. Ever close to them is the clarion cry of the long-billed curlew on the alkaline flats adjacent to the meadows. It is a whistled, penetrating "ka hee".

As the female sits on her eggs, the male marsh hawk from time to time calls her forth to drop a mouse for her to clutch in midair, a method of feeding practiced later on the young hawks themselves. Notwithstanding such connubial tenderness, the marsh hawk habitually indulges in cruelty—the eating of the breast of a duck or other bird while yet the terror-sticken victim twitches and quivers with pain. It is said that the jaws of an African lion benumb their living prey, as hunters once attacked themselves attest; and one wonders if throughout nature some plan dulls the torments of the devoured. Certain it is that the sudden wounds of accident and war are at the moment more or less painless.

Any living thing that it is able to conquer is apparently satisfying food to this hawk of the meadow-land; its list of eatables might include meadow mice, small rabbits, pocket gophers, squirrels, frogs, snakes, lizards, grasshoppers, and young skunks, as well as birds. To name the birds that it attacks and devours would be to point out most of the smaller ducks, shorebirds and waders along the Jordan river, including not only doves, meadowlarks, blackbirds and flickers, to say nothing of sparrow hawks and screech owls, but also such larger fliers as bitterns and ring-necked pheasants. Since, however, its preference is for the mice of the meadows, wisdom would say keep the gun earth-pointed as it soars but a few feet overhead on its ever-hunting way. For some reason throughout the year we see ten times as many female marsh hawks as males.

We are deceived today in the meadows: two male redwings occupy field posts with a brownish bird on a post between them; but the brownish one proves to be a western lark sparrow (*Chondestes grammacus strigatus*), readily identifiable with the field glasses but to the naked eyes confused with the female redwing.

MARCH 31

Being engaged in the pleasant diversion of re-reading Plutarch for the nth time, and coming upon such passages as that where Alexander found five thousand talents worth of Hermionian purple, which, despite its nearly two centuries age, was fresh because it had originally been made in combination with honey, and other references to honey as a preservative, we stroll into the garden where eager bees about the flowers are heavy laden with pollen, and marvel anew at this food called "honey". We once knew a "honey man", as he was pleased to call himself, who claimed that honey can cure anything—from stomach ulcers to asthma, from scratches to burns. It is true that almost any bacteria die within a few hours after being treated with honey, a fact due perhaps to the dehydration caused by its nearly fifty percentum levulose content; hence we are not surprised when in Plutarch we read: "The followers of Agesilaus, for want of honey, inclosed his body in wax, and so conveyed him to Lacedaemon".

Though Palestine is, as the Bible says, "the land flowing with milk and honey", a land where many poor people make their living by gathering wild honey, and though in the Teesta valley of India bees' nests are so large that they may often be seen at a mile's distance, wild bees are so scarce in the Wasatch mountains that we do not recall ever having seen honey taken from them nor an account of such a happy circumstance by hungry pioneers. We do of course see wild bees.

It is said that honey gathered by bees from Wasatch valley alfalfa fields is so high in dextrose that it crystallizes quite rapidly when placed in contact with water, and that honey taken from the mountain mahogany tree is distasteful. We do not have any poisonous honey like that gathered by the Brazilian wasp (*Nectarina Lecheguana*) or that made from the rhododendron flowers of East Nepal. Certainly the malic acid content of honey is such that it creates a warming sensation in the throat, hence perhaps the old honey man knew what he was talking about.

Sweet smelling flowers do not necessarily produce the nectar that bees seek; indeed some odorless blooms secrete it more profusely and some fragrant ones are sterile fields for the bees. Thus, although we cultivate two or three hundred varieties of roses, bees seem not partial to them; but in the wildwoods nearly every native flower seems to be attractive to bees. The honey bee is however not a native of these parts; and the reason that we do not notice the nest of the bumble bee (*Bemus occidentalis*) is that it is not in a tree but in the ground, often the deserted burrow of a chipmunk or other rodent. Always in nature strange things appear.

APRIL 1

As we sit watching the wonderful aerial evolutions of a duck hawk (*Falco peregrinus anatum*) before and above yonder cliff, we are impressed by the fact that it is a male and, strange to relate, far more fond of the homesite than is its less constant mate. The truth is, such a male year after year will cling with deep affection to the home cliff, and, come not the female, will remain in stubborn celibacy there all summer.

Probably swiftest of all birds, the duck hawk and close relatives were used in falconry. Because the male is smaller than the female, they called him a "tercel", that is, as Goldsmith wrote, "a tierce or third less than the other". Even now, in ornithological literature, a male falcon or male goshawk is sometimes called a "tercel" or "tiercel", though the word to our notion is properly applicable to the male of any hawk, for among eagles as well, the females are larger than the males.

No aviator exhibiting figure-eights, tail-spins, nose-dives and other breath-taking curves of flight could equal the gyrations and plunges of the tercel as it lures its mate to a cliff; and no fighting plane could match the quick directness of its flight upon a frantic victim. To see one dash from its mountain home to the duck-favored swamps at the mouth of the Jordan river, clutch with mighty claws a frenzied water bird and return with the bleeding body is a sight of daring indeed. Every non-raptor that flies before it, from the tiny warblers and nuthatches to the heavy mallards and gulls, is apparently regarded by this marauder of the air as. legitimate plunder, though its choice is doubtless the bird of intermediate size, such as the jay of the mountains and the dove, meadowlark, flicker and pigeon of the valleys. Few indeed are the birds that can escape such marvelous speed and agility.

Hereabout the duck hawk nests near the first of April, and, although in following the wildfowl it is more or less migratory, some of its representatives remain all winter. The only note that we have heard it utter is a squealing "mi-e-e".

One thing about it worthy of comment is the infrequency with which we see it. We stroll for hours among the ducks and other water birds, day after day, without catching sight of this raptorial streak of lightning; hence we conclude that, since the very rapidity of its flight and food-gathering are but the work of a moment, much of the day among the waterfowl is usually tranquil. We often wonder how it would feel to be a bird, with every second beset with apprehension; for in watching hundreds of them we always note their almost constant watchfulness. Even the domestic sparrow upon the garden gate repeatedly scans back and forth with worried vigilance. No wonder—we once saw a northern shrike pick up a screaming sparrow from our very dooryard.

A WASATCH SPRING

APRIL 2

We hear once more the tinkling whistle of the Uinta ground squirrel or armed spermophile. Every year this species (*Citellus armatus*) emerges from hibernation soon after the disappearance of snow from the foothills. Being the commonest of Wasatch squirrels, it enters frequently into our records of observation; for in summer it appears in snow-seeped parks as well as in the scorched flats of the oak-grown foothills.

The Uinta ground squirrel, as it is called by some mammalogists, is a short-tailed mammal with cinnamon-colored head, face and ears, gray neck, cartridge-buff eye ring, buffy cinnamon front legs, sayal brown upper parts, black tail mixed with buffy white, and pinkish buff underparts. There is considerable variation in the color of individuals, and a molt occurs in June.

These squirrels prefer flat sedimentary ground near either a mountain stream or a high wet meadow. They like to keep their feet and burrows dry but to have water available. Wherever these little fellows occur there is some depth of ungraveled soil, hence they prefer more or less flat places of hillside or canyon.

Their burrows are complicated, interopening tunnels dug at less than a foot below the surface. One day we attempted to uncover the burrows of a colony at the mouth of Emigration Canyon, but after completing about two hundred feet of trench work, give up the undertaking.

These spermophiles are the champion sleepers among us; they emerge from their winter dens about the first of April, go to sleep again about the middle of August (estivation), come to the surface again briefly in the fall, and then spend the winter in hibernation, thus enjoying the open air for only about five months of each year. In winter their bodies are as immobile and apparently lifeless as chunks of wood.

We have seen these "pot-guts", as the boys call them, climb over bushes but never up trees. The only note we have ever heard them utter is a short, jingling whistle, a very penetrating alarm which is heeded by the entire colony. They are easily trapped, and the stomachs of those we have taken have always contained grasses or seeds, which, however, they do not store.

Since they occupy hillsides away from farmlands, they do little damage except along the borders of upper fields. They like soft dry loam, such as a flatland between mountain brooks or grassy embankments of larger streams. In the summer they often eat bread crumbs about our feet beneath camp tables, at which times their fear is apparently only of hawks; yet in this strange world all wild animals fear something. An elephant fears a mouse, and even the African lion is said to step aside for the ratel or honey badger (*Mellivora capensis*), which in combat goes for the testicles of its opponent.

111

APRIL 3

Thrilled each day with renewed expectancy, we revisit interesting Farmington Bay to greet the spring arrivals at this much favored avian sanctuary; and now, even before we see it, we hear in the distance the long-billed curlew whose clamorous voice is always our wildnote companion of the summer lea.

Yes, there it is; for no one could mistake a short bird with a bill eight and a half inches long. We are looking at one of the world's declining birds, doomed ere long to inhabit only that avian Elysium of the auk and the passenger pigeon; yet hereabouts this curlew is still fairly abundant. No longer in the East may they say with Scott: "Screamed o'er the moss the sacret curlew", unless they refer to the Hudsonian curlew (*Numenius hudsonicus*), for there the once common Eskimo curlew (*Numenius borealis*) has apparently disappeared forever, and a live long-billed curlew East of the Mississippi would be a sensation worthy of detailed report.

The long-billed curlews arrive on our saline flats about the first of April and depart early in October, nesting usually in April and May. It being their habit to remonstrate against intruders a half mile away on the open sage and salt grass lands, and to set up a loud series of cries such as, "cur leh', cur leh', cur leh' ", it is difficult to observe them courting. Being an onomatopoeic word, "curlew", whistled wildly and distressfully, is a good imitation of the cries of the birds.

We watch them closely a few yards away, and write:

> The curlews tread in pairs about the meads,
> And probe their lengthened bills within the sod.
> Their rounded eyes are black as eboned beads,
> And rusty shows their plumage as they prod.

The male is clamorous but the female determined as she sits on the nest; for she will not flush until one's hand is about to touch her. Since the four eggs are laid in the lonely haunts of the coyote that predator changes from jack rabbit to young curlews as often as opportunity affords.

Intelligent gunners do not fire upon these rare birds. Twenty pairs are before us, many individuals quite ruddy. Each bird is walking along meadowed grassland and every three or four steps probing its long bill three inches into the sod for worms. Their eyes are as conspicuous as black beads.

Being so near extinction, the long-billed curlew deserves detailed description: it is a pinkish cinnamon bird with head, neck and chest streaked with grayish brown, and its back is barred with dusky grayish brown. its legs are grayish; its iris, dark brown, as we have seen; but the extraordinary thing about it is its bill. Imagine a long-legged hen with a bill eight and a half inches in length. There is nothing else like it in local birddom, though the long-billed dowtcher is a close second in bill length.

APRIL 4

The conchologist in the Wasatch has to forget the beautifullly colored abalones, tritons, and other magnificent shells of the sea coast, for our molluscan fauna consists only of unattractive terrestrial snails (*Gastropoda*) and equally drab bivalves (*Pelecypoda*).

Our bivalve molluska—oysterlike shells shaped like an oval box with two concave valves that open like a book—are much less common than the spiral winding univalves; and in this region Utah lake is the best place to find them. Those that are over two inches in length include: *Anodonta oregonensis,* found at Utah lake; *Anodonta nuttalliana,* fairly common in the streams about Salt Lake City; *Anodonta wahlamentensis,* at both Bear and Utah lakes; and *Margaritana margaritifera,* a large one found in the streams of Salt Lake City and East Canyon.

The other bivalved shells we see here are much less than one inch in length. They include: *Sphaerium striatinum* of Utah Lake; *S. pilsbryanum* of Utah and Bear Lakes; *S. dentatum* of Utah Lake; *Pisidium abditum* of City Creek; *P. compressum* of Utah Lake; and *P. variabile* of both Utah and Bear Lakes.

Thus all of the bivalved mullusca of these mountains are thin-shelled species, not suitable for the manufacture of pearl buttons, which are made from their relatives of the Mississippi valley at such places as Muscatine, Iowa.

All of the fresh water mussels of the family *Unionidae* have a peculiar method of hatching their eggs and bringing forth their young. In the parent clam is a brood pouch in which the eggs are hatched and the young for sometime thereafter retained. For six months the young mussel is submerged in a mucus of the outer gill; and when this mucus is absorbed the young is cast out of the pouch. It then lies on its back in the water until a fish or other creature comes in contact with its byssal cord floating upward. It grasps the fish and sticks to its side until it gets enough nutriment to develop its internal organs. Having passed this test it sinks to the bottom where it grows by eating microscopic organisms. Verily its life has hung by a thread, verily it would have died but for a passing fish.

Somehow we are always happy when during a stroll from our camp fire we chance to rumple some dead leaves and expose a snail. We shall be condemned for having on several occasions heated a shell with a lighted cigar the better to observe the inhabitant thus compelled to expose itself.

The red-shafted flicker so persistently clacks his iterated roulade these happy April mornings that, as it sounds over the housetops, many times we try to make an onomatop of it. At last we conclude with this: "tic! tic! tic! tic! tic! tic! tic! tic! tic! tic!", rapid, high, shrill, rasping, penetrating, somewhat metallic, slightly ringing, loud notes, audible a quarter of a mile in the halcyon air of fragrant spring.

APRIL 5

With bill upturned the rigid bittern stands,
A pointed stake within the marshes lined,
Then slowly wades about the grassy lands
With head and neck in movement serpentined.

Before us in a fen of busy Farmington Bay stands a solitary American bittern (*Botaurus lentiginosus*), the first one of the year.

Its back being toward us, from our distance of fifty feet its neck seems about one and a half times as high as its body, the lower neck being as thick again as the upper. It holds its pointed bill constantly at a high angle in the manner of a cormorant, as if impelled by instinct to imitate a slanting reed. Slowly it turns its head from side to side without moving either body or neck; and we see its eye, a wild eye with a coal black pupil and a light yellow iris. An airplane goes over, whereupon the bittern stares with interest at the artificial bird.

It squats so that its body touches the water, then begins to wade forward, never more than a step in two seconds, sometimes much slower, lifting its big-toed foot from the slough as each step is taken. As it walks, the pointed bill is held horizontally; but the attitude of the uncanny bird is catlike, sneaking, almost reptilian, as the striped neck searches carefully forward. It is like a western grebe secluded on land. It enters the brown grass, ever pointing its bill skyward. We flush it, whereupon it tucks its bright legs behind and with heavy flapping flies away, uttering a soft grunt as it goes. So this is the bird that utters that deep hollow "a ka OOMP" of the marshes!

We have seen the uncanny bittern whose booming and hollow-sounded bellowing have always made us wonder concerning his actions in undisturbed loneliness.

Onward we go; and there in the main pond at last is a pair of blacknecked stilts (*Himantopus himantopus mexicanus*). They preen themselves; and, though for half an hour we observe coots, avocets, and lesser yellow legs, when we return the stilts still contently preen. Their long rose-pink legs, black bills and black and white coats are attractive, especially in the breeding season when their plumage seems to have a creamy pink cast and their eyes with the fire of nuptial combat are more carmine red than ordinary.

April is the vernal period of bird life, when flocks disperse, individuals pair, and territorial home-rights are established.

APRIL 6

Save for the tireless gurgle of the violet-scented brook and the occasional jingle of a spermophile, there is little sound now in the lower canyons; it is true that a gentle sough often sways the leafless branches, but it does so almost noiselessly, as if the resistance were not worth the effort. There is, nevertheless, multiformity in the scene: stones of white, lead and brown along the brook's verge, with here and there some moss-fledged; rust-colored pebbles and rocks beneath the pellucid, shimmering water; horse tails (*Equisetum hiemale*) upstanding beside clumps of bank-grass; reddish, dried leaves beneath a yet skeletonized birch whose limbs are banded in places where the bark has been peeled; a stalwart, rough-barked cottonwood with four trunks from one massive root, which overgrows the edge of the stream; a trailing barberry, green and hopeful in its shaded nest by the gnarled roots of the birch; a brick-red butterfly so small as to resemble a fluttering new penny (we could only guess that it is one of the hair-streaks, a *Thecla chalcis* perhaps, as it flies away); a dozen firs, green and healthy, clustered nearby on the damp, shaded hillside; distant vistas of greening north-sunny slopes patched with oak brush, dull and gray; maple trees, straight, gray, leafless and still. Bare is this scene of early April; yet, withal, interesting during the idle hour.

But that Hair-streak butterfly, tender little *Thecla!* In our mountains there are several of these delightful ones—the Colorado Hair-streak (*Thecla crysalus*) of purple wings margined with black; the Texas Hair-streak (*Thecla autolycus*) a brown butterfly with reddish spots broadening on its wings; the Bronze Hair-streak (*Thecla chalcis*) mentioned above, which is uniformly brown; the Hedge-row Hair-streak (*Thecla saepium*), slightly redder than the Bronze; and the Behr's Hair-streak (*Thecla behri*), yellow with each wing margined with brown. Lovely little butterflies!

Orchard apricot trees, covered with bloom, look in the distance like a snow storm coming in, as we ride by them to the duck sloughs. There on the road ahead in the marshes are what look like twenty narrow trees made of dark smoke; but, upon approaching them, we discover that each is a swarm of gnats like a whirlwind of dust fastened to one spot. Who knows the meaning of such frenzied ardor?

It is one of our delights to hunt mushrooms in the sheep-trodden sagelands about Great Salt Lake, but it is only recently that we learned that the worms in the mushrooms come from eggs laid by a fungous gnat, likely *Mycomya punctata*.

We catch a new song of a meadowlark—"twa twa twa twata twata twata", the first two syllables clear and ordinary, the last three husky, guttural and to us most unusual.

115

APRIL 7

Below the retreating, seeping snow-line of a canyon, at an altitude of between seven and eight thousand feet, there is even now much beauty, the beauty of awakening promise and budding joy. As we approach the spot and are stopped by stones winter-strewn from above, and by a snow-laden roadway, the jingle-alarm cry of a spermophile (*C. armatus*) is heard as the slow little mammal crawls with badger-like awkwardness up to its hole in a drying embankment; and a Utah rock squirrel, long-tailed and frisky, is seen to bound ahead of us down into the labryinths of the creekside. Perforce we linger to enjoy the scene.

Here and there in a side-ravine stand fir trees (*Abies concolor*) with their new needles appearing almost pea-green in color and themselves richly greened pyramids on the mountain slopes. Snow-patches are everywhere, often in the form of crusted slabs over the dead prostrate branches of winter stricken willows, with mountain hedge (*Pachystima myrsinites*) showing green and vigorous beneath the burdened covering.

Leafless dogwood (*Cornus stolonifera*) branches stand smooth and red at the creekside where a boxelder tree, still bare, has beneath it a carpet of papery ashen dead leaves. Here and there at the roadside a slender willow tree (*Salix caudata*) appears with hairy gray catkins, some of them densely flowered.

Away from the brook up the hillside a yard or so, a few pale-barked aspen trees (*Populus tremuloides*) stand like skeletons; and, as we break off a branch of one of them and hold it in hand, we notice that the unburst buds are brown, scaly, conical and waxy, but the opened ones bear little muffs of gray fur like the tails of imaginary thumb-sized rabbits. Elfin rabbits donate their tails to the aspen trees! Some twigs have two, some twenty of these round, gray rabbit-tails; and not yet are there any signs of those leaves that later will ceaselessly tremble on their flattened stems, tremble because the flat surfaces of the stems will be at right angles to the flat surfaces of the leaves.

A black fly, of all things a black fly! alights on the twig we hold. No birds sing, but what joy there is in just peeking the secrets of the hills!

By way of contrast we spend this afternoon on bird-thronged Farmington Bay where to our delight thirty eight Brewster's snowy egrets (*Leucophoyx thula brewsteri*) are scattered over the meadow, the first of their kind to arrive. As each walks with shoulders humped close to the head, the black bill is conspicuous, and there is just the beginning of nuptial plumage on the head and tail. Occasionally one utters a hoarse "cuk". In flying, each shows very clearly its black legs and yellow feet, the colored moccasins that are an unfailing mark of this pleasing subspecies. More of this bird later in season, for it is one of the glories of the marsh-bordered lea.

APRIL 8

Pick now a twig of a boxelder tree (*Acer interium*) if you would see a thing of tasselled beauty. The stem itself is dull green with a purplish hue, but crown on crown, tassel on tassel, along it appear the bunches of seasonal flowers. Flowers they are to be sure, from mixed axillary buds, greenish flowers like tender leaves, staminate flowers in umbels in one tree and pistillate flowers hanging in drooping racemes in another tree. And the anthers are reddish, giving one the impression that tiny red beads are dangling on pale green threads. Can it be that such a thing of intricate beauty is unnoticed yet within our grasp at almost every wayside? Over one hundred species of maples are known, yet this alone is sometimes called the "water ash".

And then, as we enter a canyon, we notice that the slender birch trees have a pinkish tinge, as they appear along the creekside, and that their catkins are erect, while the alders growing beside them have a greenish-gray bark somewhat like that of the cottonwoods, and their catkins are not erect but long and drooping. Members of the same family, they both like their feet near the flowing stream, yet the alders are not quite so slender and graceful as their cousins.

There beside them are red dogwoods and the still leafless maples and scrub oaks (*Quercus gambellii*). A magpie (*Pica pica hudsonia*) flushes from the willows as we approach; alert, resident bird, it withstands every wintry blast and scans the horizons in ceaseless vigilance against enemies. No song ever passes his raucous throat, for, being a member of the *Corvidae*, which family includes the crows and jays, he necessarily manifests their unattractive characteristics.

> 'Tis not the magpie's province sweet to sing,
> Nor yet the duty of the raucous crow;
> But many birds with joys of springtime ring,
> And only nature fathoms why 'tis so.

Those lovely hued birds, the black-headed jays are, however, ever-charming bits of blue in the piniferous forests, where they dwell almost constantly in sombrous tranquility.

We just heard of a gun accident down the canyon. Never play with a gun. In boyhood days we knew two men, who, being close friends, were playing cards prior to their expected departure for a sheep-camp next day. As each had a special winning, it was his custom to pick up an empty revolver lying between them, point it at the other, snap it and say, "I got you that time." When one went outside for a few minutes, the other thoughtlessly loaded the revolver. The friend returned, and, being unaware that the revolver was loaded, picked it up at his next winning and shot the one who had loaded it through the left eye. It emerged by his ear, not killing him, but maiming him for life.

APRIL 9

It is another fascinating afternoon on Farmington Bay. This time at the turn between the meadow lane and the marsh a score of yellow headed blackbirds (*Xanthocephalus xanthocephalus*) are perched on the fence railings before us. The yellow of their heads is fairly conspicuous but not so bright as we have seen it at later periods in the year. The females are not only smaller but also browner than the males; and all seem to be having a good time. There are no grown reeds for them to alight upon; but they emit their catlike meows and occasionally indulge in a low coarse note which, as we listen to it, we liken to the sound of a thin, distant circular saw. We record one's song as "Chul chul chul zawaaaa". The air is alive with millions of gnats in great swarms, and, as we watch the blackbirds, one of them resting on the fence snaps an insect without moving its wings. We shall record more of these pleasing reed-loving blackbirds as the season progresses.

Delighted with this new arrival we go onward, by flocks of female redwings still alone, by avocets, black-necked stilts, meadowlarks, mallards, lesser scaups, coots, Treganza herons, Brewster's egrets, and long-billed curlews; and there, wading in the shallow water, is another arrival, one we are especially delighted to see—the marbled godwit, a large brown shorebird almost as big as the long-billed curlew, with a bill fully half as long but turned slightly upward, not down. There are only two of them, but busier birds we have seldom seen. The lesser yellow legs near them continually wade about, nod their heads and peck at the water; the avocets wade about and emit many penetrating cries; but the godwits probe their bills assiduously in the water for minutes at a time, as if their lives depended on this meal. They move about very slowly; but keep their heads down so much that they look headless most of the time. Perhaps they really are hungry after a long flight.

On the mountainside on our way back we find the wild sweet pea (*Astragalus cibarius*), and the whitlow grass (*Draba raptans micrantha*) with its tiny white flower in bloom. The sweet smelling phlox (*Phlox longifolia*) is in leaf.

To love nature is to live—to live beyond the uncertain happiness bestowed by the trials and tribulations of man; to live in observation of the great mechanism that somehow pervades every form of life. Man is but one in a tremendous ensemble.

APRIL 10

If April is not the most beautiful it is likely the most welcome month of the year. Arriving after deep snows and enduring ice as well as chill blizzards, it is the first to prove that recurrent balmy days are possible. It has always been a beloved month, even in olden times when they spelled it: "Averil", "Averel", "Averylle", "Avryrylle", "Aprille", "Apryll", "Apprile", "Apprille", "Apryle", "Apryelle", or "Aprill".

Shakespeare wrote of "The uncertaine glory of an Aprill day" and "The Aprill's in her eyes, it is Love's spring"; Lytton: "The bloom, the flush, the April of the heart"; and Tennyson: "Half opening buds of April". Many such occur; for April marks the beginning of courtship with many mammals and birds.

In April all wild mammals hereabout are above ground; reptiles and amphibians are again active; insects daily become more numerous; trees begin to unfold their leaves; flowers start to show their lovely blooms.

Streams are roily, wild and full, for even upper snows are fast melting away. Violets peep beside the garden gate; daffodils are in full bloom; pansies open wide their eyes and on the grassy hills *Cymopterus longpipes* everywhere shows its flat but golden flowers.

Delightfully fresh, invigorating and promising is the April morning. From afar comes the plaintive call of the lonely Say phoebe; yet robin after robin carols in rhapsody as if awakening the neighborhood to a realization of the budding season. Some sweet-throated house finch trills gleefully from a Carolina poplar near at hand, as if conscious that his canzonet is essential to the ensemble of vernal delights and sounds.

Everyday now we are expecting the arrival of the willet, loon, eared grebe, black-crowned night heron, Sora rail, Wilson phalarope, semi-palmated plover, Swainson hawk, burrowing owl, and Audubon warbler. To greet all of the homeward bound migrants one would each day ramble from mountain park through greening valley to marshy lowlands, and not only discern every flit of wing but also recognize each rapturous song. Such can be accomplished only in the wildwood experiences of years and the joyful even if philosophic contemplation of the final resume. Trees are ever in place for revisitation; flowers are less dependable; but birds are so diverted by wind and storm that even the most vigilant may miss them as they pass by.

Today near the head of Emigration canyon at the edge of a snow bank we find a bright yellow, five petalled buttercup (*Ranunculus jovis*) in bloom, its starlike flower being an inch across, though the entire plant is only two inches high. The freshness of a golden willow is strikingly beautiful along a swollen stream.

APRIL 11

Upon our arrival at Farmington Bay this afternoon a pair of mottled gray birds with black bills two and a half inches long and dark legs are wading in a meadowed lagoon in company with long-billed curlews, avocets, black-necked stilts, white faced glossy ibises, and Brewster herons. With no color-pattern either above or below, except that one of them is a lighter gray than the other, they are among the most unattractive birds we have ever seen. Once in a while as they walk about we catch sight of a thin black line divided by white along the lower edge of the wing; and instantly know them to be Western willets (*Catoptrophorus semipalmatus inornatus*). The *inornatus*, meaning "unadorned", proves that William Brewster knew what he was doing when in 1887 he described this bird; but we have a surprise—they flush, and (one almost literally with its beak touching the tail of the other) actually course about us for a total distance of approximately five miles, the swiftest and handsomest birds awing we have seen in many a day. As they race, their backs are light olive and a white band extends across their black underwings. While we follow them with the glasses in their mile-circle, they are now over us, now a quarter of a mile away, flying with the swiftness and even the wing movements of doves; and every hundred yards the male appears as if trying to tread his mate in mid air, since he actually touches her tail. How two birds flying with the speed of teal can keep that close together, high in air, down almost to the surface of the lagoon, swerving this way, swerving that way, without mishap or interference, is an aerial demonstration that must be seen to be appreciated. Furthermore, we marvel that two slowly wading contented birds of drab color could so suddenly win our admiration for their beauty and their wing power. When the racing is about to end the foremost bird merely goes into a soar, the other instantly following suit; and they both alight within our view as if the five minute coursing were a regular part of the afternoon's entertainment. We naturally conclude it to be a courtship flight, for, once when a third bird appears, its intrusion is resented by the belligerent male. From tranquility, contented preening and feeding, to the wild ardor of nuptial flight, all in a few minutes time, is a transition as unexpected as the plumage of the bird awing is handsome compared with that of its wading somberness.

As these willets were prodding for food within a few yards of us, the male raised his wings as if courting the female, and at the same time uttered "Tuck a a a a , tuck a a a a, tuck a a a a." This is not the loud, shrill, whistled "pill-will, will-et" that they utter as they fly, but a conversational expression.

We are happy that we were able to observe these birds so closely, and, especially, to make two onomatops therefrom. Since the birds of Farmington Bay are accustomed to the keeper's truck, an automobile there makes an excellent blind, especially when the approach is very slow and there is no sudden movement, such as the quick opening of doors.

A WASATCH SPRING

APRIL 12

All the signs indicate a warm sunny April afternoon: farmers are busy, plowing, harrowing, raking and planting; valley trees are beginning to unfold their delicate green leaves; squirrels are frisking through brookside labyrinths; gulls and robins are calling noisily; meadowlarks are singing; and only the upper half of the mountains is showing snow.

As we ramble along the oak-grown foothills in the vicinity of the mouth of Big Cottonwood canyon, a pretty rusty tailed falcon, scarcely larger than a robin, hovers momentarily in the air and then alights at the very tip of a scrub-oak tree; it is a sparrow hawk (*Falco sparverius sparverius*), so named perhaps because it does feed habitually in winter on domestic sparrows, but more aptly called, if we adhere to the truth of its stomach records, "grasshopper hawk", for on these insects it usually makes its meal. When it kills a small bird, however, it does a neat job of it, striking the victim down with a beak-blow that penetrates to the brain, decapitates the stricken bird adroitly, and quickly flies off with the bleeding body. So seldom does this little raptor take a song bird that it may be classified as beneficial to man. We are always interested in it, for its wing-movements, when it is not hunting, are gentle and hovering; but in fierce action it is dashing and swift. We seldom hear it make any sound except a shrill "kil-e" when surprised.

In the canyon only a solitary clump of yellow dog tooth violets attracts our eyes; but these are striking indeed. Trees are bare, the choke cherries alone showing signs of leafage; the canyon side ravines are snow-choked; and the creek is boisterous and muddy.

Further along the Bonneville shore line a mountain blue bird is perched in an orchard tree beside half a dozen incessantly singing pine siskins. There is perhaps no lovelier sight in woods or fields than the mountain blue bird, unless we prefer that bit of blue in a pine, a long-crested jay, or that bit of flame in a wood, the Louisiana tanager.

We drift to a valley slough where for an hour we watch the diving tactics of two remarkable birds—a western grebe and a double crested cormorant (*Phalacrocorax auritus auritus*). The long neck and sharp head of the grebe, which it nervously turns from side to side constantly when above water, so resemble a snake as to be almost uncanny. The cormorant, on the other hand, holds its head at an upward angle without much apprehensive motion; it redives after but a second or so on the surface and remains under water longer than the grebe. A hoarse "croke" is about the limit of the cormorant's "song". Which is a water bird that sings?—we ponder momentarily in vain. Why have the passerine birds, those of the perching habit, been so highly favored with song over the water birds? Love is not the answer, for doubtless to the cormorant its "croke" is at times an expression of affection.

APRIL 13

So tame are some of the birds of Farmington Bay that extraordinary opportunities to observe them frequently occur. This afternoon, for instance, notwithstanding a bothersome breeze, thirty four white-faced glossy ibises stand like a flock of small turkeys about forty yards away, showing the dark chestnut of their shoulders and the iridescent purplish and greenish hues of their crowns and wings, the very shades that look black in the sky. The bill is so nearly the color of the whitish face that the narrow rim comprised within the words "white-faced" is scarcely discernible even at favorable distance. This bird is a relative of the black and white sacred ibis of Europe (*Ibis religiosa*).

We drift onward along the roadway at the side of which runs a deep slow fresh-water stream; and there twenty five feet away a pair of western willets feed contentedly, unafraid of us during the half hour we watch them. Their mild round eyes are coal black. Each is seeking edible morsels in the mud, to get which it bores down with its bill with the motion of an air-compressor drill breaking up pavement, with however only a fraction of such rapidity. Many times we count the drilling process; and the up and down movements of head and bill vary from four to ten, in accordance with the hardness of the soil and the depth of the worm. As its bill becomes too laden with mud at the tip after several drillings, the bird steps a few inches over into the water and swishes its bill back and forth to clean it. Very often it also stands on one leg and stretches the other leg as far behind as possible, lifting the wings at the same time. Then it frequently preens its breast with its long bill. One bird is also swashing its mud-covered foot in the water to clean it; and we think the edible tidbits they obtain must be tasty indeed to counteract the nuisance of so much mud.

We stir a little, whereupon they both eye us curiously, and one utters a soft but rather harsh "chup chup chup chup", opening its bill widely at each "chup". Still unafraid, they go about their business; and then, as a ten foot stretch of salt grass grows to the water's edge, they walk towards us on the dry ground and around it. The white lower edge of the wing on one bird shows on one of its sides and not on the other side. We reluctantly leave them, for, except for the phalaropes, they have afforded us opportunity for the closest observation we have experienced in many a day.

A thousand ducks being far out in the lakelet, we are constrained to open the telescope, with the aid of which we recognize pintails, a few ruddy ducks, and many others with black heads, white breasts and white marks ahead of the tails. We wait patiently until at last a pair fly towards us and alight within a hundred yards. We thought so— they are shovelers (*Spatula clypeata*), a handsome black and white male with his brownish mate.

As we return we notice that this very day the female redwing flock has dispersed; and each female seems now to have selected her mate. The red of the male's wing is now brilliant and shows constantly.

A WASATCH SPRING

APRIL 14

As we linger for an hour in one of the nearby canyons at an altitude of 6,000 feet, we are impressed in the beginning by the noise of a roily, turbulent stream, by the general lack of leaves, and by the presence of snow only a rod or so up the canyon sides. The buds of the maples are just beginning to burst, as likewise are those of the birches; but a forest of the latter gives a hazel tone to a lovely glade.

Over there on the gravelly hillside, however, a little patch of violets (*Viola venosa*) is in full bloom. What pretty flowers they are—the outside of the petals purplish or reddish, the inner side yellow! The fact is, as we trudge the lower mountain streams at this time of the year, we are most accustomed to seeing the purple or white swamp violet (*Viola palustris*) or the very small blue one (*Viola adunca*) which grows even in the loftiest alpine meadows. Later, perhaps a month hence, we shall see up here the big blue violet (*Viola nephrophylla*) of the springs of the valley.

And there, by the root of a maple is that tiny quaint member of the parsley family known as turkey peas (*Oregonia linearfolia*). The whole plant rests in the palm of one's hand, showing its smooth leaves with their narrow, long leaflets; its red papery sheath; and its cluster of minute white flowers, each looking like elfin-kittens' paws.

No birds sing; but on the ground beneath some maple limbs, recently cut by a woodsman and piled, there is a broken wasp's nest, a papery affair consisting of a comb formed of hexagonal cells. Strange to say some dead wasps half protrude from a cell here and there; other cells are entirely sealed. Nevertheless the most remarkable of all is that along the limbs are crawling immature wasps from a quarter of an inch to a full inch in length, all weakly winged, the smaller ones black with white bands across their abdomens, the larger ones black but with striking yellow bands. We touch the larger ones and they buzz in brief flight then crawl away. They resemble somewhat the mature wasp (*Vespula consobrina*), yet identification is not positive. Such is the multiformity of life even at the verge of the yet snow-barricaded upper canyon.

As we emerge from the mountains a meadow lark sings joyously. During many years we have observed that in April this bird reaches the acme of song, for then we have sometimes even heard it at midnight and often as it flew in the air. One song we have recorded as "che la CHEE! cha cha la a" with the third syllable high and much accented. Another has been: "Tra la la TRAKEEK", the terminal "trakeek" being a jumble of emphatic sounds. Still another in our notes is: "Twa twa TWEE' two ta tum". One bird chattered as it alighted; and so on with much variegation to our delight.

APRIL 15

Many are the ponderings we indulge as we wait, look and listen this April afternoon on a roadway dyke of Farmington Bay, haven of water birds. We wait for the possible sight of a newly arrived migrant; we look at the querulous avocet out there on the shallow pond among coots and shovelers; we listen to the deep-throated "konks" of Canadian geese and the lesser calls of glossy ibises and black necked stilts. In the distance we behold thirty white pelicans flying with little wing effort gracefully in the sky, showing even at a mile's distance the beauty of their black and white plumage.

We observe willets, yellow headed black birds, marbled godwits, ruddy ducks, pintails, mallards, bitterns, great blue herons, Brewster egrets, redwings, meadowlarks, California gulls, long-billed curlews, lark sparrows, lesser yellow legs—yet hope to see more!

We are surrounded by alkaline fresh water ponds, reeded sloughs, marshes and meadowed fens, sagelands and grasslands. Mountain brooks traverse the wooded cultivated uplands, and flow along their willowed lanes to all these lowlands of salt grass, reeds, mud, and to the eventual resting place, a body of water one fourth salt. Verily two miles walk east or west from where we sit and ponder would take us to orchard, garden and field or to quagmire, saleratus and utter desolation. From flower to bareness, loam to alkaline clay, sweet water to brackish—such is the prospect with all our fens, meadows, ponds and marshes in between. It is little wonder that the duck hawks nest on the crags of yonder hillside and sally forth with uncanny speed to the surprised victims of the marsh, for such is this interval, this interplace between the beauties of the mountain and the hopelessness of the brine.

As we are about to leave we catch sight of an eared grebe (*Colymbus nigricollis californicus*) the facial tufts of which are as bright as gold. We easily identify it by its black neck and its black crown-feathers which stand up in a distinct crest. It dives and redives for our entertainment, and is always a handsome perky bird, very smart and alert in action; but, though it seems to avoid the neighborhood of other water inhabitants such as coots and gadwalls, nevertheless it seldom goes over fifty yards from shore.

We build in our dreams a cabin in the midst of all this avian activity, a cabin where leisure and field glasses would give us intimate observation of all that wades and flies. Oh for the empathy to understand what goes on in their minds! Of all animals man in his uniqueness alone can form concepts, but the brains of some of the higher mammals now and then indicate a twilight of thinking.

APRIL 16

Most of the mullusks of these hills and valleys are of the terrestrial type in which a conical tube is spirally wound to the right, the closed end being the apex and the open end the body whorl. When the little animal withdraws into its shell it closes the aperture with a horny door, called the operculum. In order to identify some of these interesting animals it is necessary to dissect the soft body and examine the proboscis, tentacles, foot, siphon, mantle, osphradium, gills, oesophagus, heart, intestines, reproductive glands, and so on; but most of the species may be recognized by their shells alone.

Most of our mollusks are of the genus *Oreohelix*, land snails over half an inch in diameter, first described by Dr. Pilsbury in 1902 and quite thoroughly revised by Henderson, Cockerel, Walker and others. We have very often found *Oreohelix strigosa depressa carnea* in City Creek canyon at the base of lime cliffs beneath streamside decaying maple leaves, and *O. haydeni oquirrhensis* in the brooks of the valley below. Other species occur elsewhere; *O. cooperi* on Mt. Nebo and in Weber canyon; *O. rugosa* in Cache valley; *O. peripherica* on the Bear river; *O. peripherica newcombi* and *O. P. wasatchensis* in Ogden canyon; *O. haydeni corrugata* north of Logan; and *O. h. hybrida* at Logan and Devils Slide. Other members of the family *Helicidae* found here include *Vallonia gracilicosta* from Logan and Weber canyons and *V. cyclophorella* from the lower Bear river, as well as *Thysanophora ingersolli* from several places in the northern Wasatch.

All of these helices have well developed spiral shells and they are terrestrial air-breathers; but so often is there variable coloration in the same species that resort to the dissecting room for examination of internal anatomy is often imperative. Once the shell itself was enough for identification; then the jaw; now all of the soft parts, especially the genitalia.

Of the family *Pupillidae*, having cylindrical, many whorled shells we have *Pupilla muscorum* of American Fork canyon; *P. blandi* of Mt. Nebo; *Vertigo modesta corpulenta* and *V. M. parrietalis* of Ogden canyon, and *Columella alticola* of other parts of the Wasatch. A glassy shelled snail (*Vitrina alaskana*) occurs throughout these mountains and *Polita whitneyi* and *P. identata* at Salt Lake City.

We have seen some slugs, such as *Agriolisnax agrestis* that creep about after rains, resembling horned worms and others, such as the amber snails (*Succinidae*) that have almost superfluous shells. We have several of the sharp-pointed *Lymnaeidae*, which breathe above water but feed below, several of the rather square-mouthed *Planorbidas;* a few of the bladder snails (*Physa*) as well as species of *Amnicolidae* and *Valvatidae*.

If one be alert it is seldom that the day's ramble in the mountain fails to discover an interesting shell.

APRIL 17

Today we experience what amounts to an interesting coincidence; on this oak-covered hillside we have just flushed a turkey vulture (*Cathartes aura teter*) from the carcass of a sheep so putrid as to have tainted our approach for a hundred yards.

Not so intelligent as ordinary raptores, our high-soaring buzzards nevertheless have such keen senses of sight and smell that they detect carrion from lofty distances, probably by both sight and smell, although they apparently refuse to alight until they can actually *see* a dead animal, despite the odor. Any rotting flesh seems to suit their strange appetites, with dead snakes likely preferred; but since they feed their fledglings by disgorging the reeky mess directly into the infants' throats the nests are not usually noisome.

Being birds over two feet long, with wing-spreads of about six feet, the turkey buzzards with their bare crimson heads, powerful but not hawk-shaped bills, and toes with long curved talons, cannot be mistaken for any of the other birds of prey hereabout. In our boyhood days they were a common sight in the high, clear heavens of summer; but in recent years they have likely eaten so many poisoned rodents and coyotes that they have become seriously depleted in numbers.

We do not recall ever having seen them about these hills in winter, hence we must conclude that they are accustomed to a limited annual migration. In this climate they nest usually during the latter part of April, laying their two eggs on the bare ground of some inaccessible cavern or ledge. The young buzzards are fed for an exceptional period for birds, the design apparently being to have the youngsters in strong and full plumage before permitting them to vie with the sun in sustained altitude above the surface of the earth. Beneficial, loathsome birds they nevertheless possess some traits of commendable nobility and resourcefuless.

Since we have never seen this vulture attack a live animal, we examine the head and feet of a stuffed specimen to ascertain why. If the word "prey" refers to an animal being seized to be devoured, this vulture is not a "bird of prey" at all; in fact it is not built to prey. Its long, middle front toe (which in a falcon is a murderous weapon) has no claw whatever! Its hallux, or hind toe, is small and set so high that it is usless for grasping. The maxilla or upper jaw of the bill is too long for killing in the manner of a hawk, and although the tip is down-pointed, it seems adapted to hooking and pulling flesh. The mandible or lower jaw is not suitable for clasping a victim. This voiceless and repulsive vulture should be called a bird of carrion, not a bird of prey, and placed in a new order called *Vulturiformes*.

APRIL 18

Sitting on a dyke in Farmington bay this afternoon, we watch fifty three white pelicans deploy in the sky. Seven birds a hundred yards or more ahead of the rest keep in a rather definite V with an unchanging leader, but the remaining forty six follow in a loose line of two or three V's, then in one long line extending across the sky behind the others. Never in migration do they fly single file. Each bird soars easily for several seconds, then slowly flaps its wings to catch up again, but no squadron of aviators could give a more pleasing manoeuvre of majesty, grace and ease than do these great white and black birds.

The surprise of the day, however, is some twenty pairs of cinnamon teals (*Anas cyanoptera cyanoptera*) scattered among white-faced glossy ibises, Brewster herons, long-billed curlews, willets, mallards, avocets and black-necked stilts in the lagoons of the meadowed fens. Almost instantly each day upon our arrival we can detect a new migrant, for on that particular day its kind seems all over the place. Such was the case when the long-billed curlews, the Brewster herons, the avocets, the willets and so on returned to this avian refuge; but a few days afterward each large assemblage had dispersed, or like the marbled godwits, disappeared altogether. They come and they go, and leave only the breeders behind, is a good rule to remember hereabouts. The male cinnamon teal is a handsome duck, attentive to his mate; they are both very tame, and doubtless have come to nest. Most of the cinnamons perhaps went north early in March, but these are the first we have noticed.

On April 13th a tremendously large flock of ducks was so far out in the lake that even with the telescope we could not be sure what they were. From the flock two flew to us, which we identified as spoonbills. Today the same flock is out there, but more scattered; and we have the great pleasure of studying four of them only a hundred yards away. They are gadwalls (*Anas streperus*), and no wonder the flock looks black in the distance. They are dark ducks, the male gray and the female browner; but the white spot at the back of the wing is a sure field mark. A pair of them go to sleep within a stone's throw; even our shouting does not disturb them, for they are early and late feeders and mid-day nappers.

Just as we are leaving, a dozen tree swallows with white bellies skim over the water about the ducks, darting here and there for insects. One needs but eyes and ears to enjoy the April lea.

As we cannot hope to get a song out of these ducks or any other water bird, we content ourselves with recording the voice of the male gadwall as a shrill, reedlike "kac".

APRIL 19

To observe bird awakenings we arrive at Farmington bay in the darkness before dawn; and then in the gray crepuscle of advancing light undiscernible gulls scream overhead and unseen meadowlarks engage in rapturous song. The anti-twilight arch appears over the eastern mountains, and in the dimness scores of coots sleeping motionless show like black balls resting on the meadowed grass. A bright segment lights the eastern sky, and a dark segment sinks further and further in the west; but even in these crepuscular rays a flock of a hundred white faced glossy ibises moves across above us. In the twilight of morning, killdeers, redwings, egrets, willets, avocets and stilts begin to move about in their accustomed places; and we realize how difficult it is to identify birds by their colors in the dusky light. It being almost daylight, it is evident that most of the ducks are drowsing far out in the lake. At last there is the green-blue flash of the rising sun; and all about us is bird activity with its calls and sounds—another day is here.

After a time we catch sight of a bird swimming in a deep borrow pit, in fact, alternating swimming and diving. Its actions are like those of a grebe, but its bill suggests a small duck. Its bill is brown, the top of its head very dark brown, its back dark brown, its chin, throat and chest whitish—it is after all a pied-billed grebe still in its winter plumage. The breeding plumage with its whitish bill crossed by black, and the black chin and throat, must be acquired just prior to actual breeding, for this bird, which is solitary, does not show these marks yet. We go our way, and later when the sun gets very warm, return only to find our grebe sunning itself on the bank among dry grasses. Believing it to be a nesting bird, we almost step on it before it moves and we realize it is a grebe. For an hour we watch it at close hand. When it dives it does not make the lightning like descent of the eared grebe, but kicks its feet several times above water before getting under. Nor is it so perk and neat as the eared kind. As it swims it snaps at the swarms of gnats about it; in fact all the birds today of all varieties are feeding on these insects, even yellow headed blackbirds frequently flying from their perches a few feet into the air to catch these apparently tasty bits of food. The only sound the grebe utters is a low, cuckoolike "cow, cow, cow, cow". Where is there music among the water birds? Hold, come to think of it, what could be more musical, sweeter, softer and pleasing than the distant throaty song of the whistling swan (*Cygnus columbianus*) over these waters? It is a cooing, somewhat laughing "woo— hoo— oo — oo — oo — hoo".

APRIL 20

Following a week of rain and snow, the meadowlands quickly revive with bloom and song, under the warming rays of an April sun. A solitary Brewster's heron flushes from a laneway brook as we approach; and we notice as it flies that while its feet are yellow and its legs black its plumage is pure white.

In the same creek scores of tall, dry stalks of card-teasels stand with conspicuous black heads like the nigger heads (*Rudebeckia occidentalis*) of autumn canyons. This particular brook meanders from artesian wells, and encourages tender water cress (*Radicula Nasturtium-Aquaticum*) too tempting for us not to gather for a spring salad.

Male redwings fly from fence to fence; Brewer blackbirds sit languidly in leafless willows; meadowlarks sing; a pair of marsh hawks hunt over a field, soaring listlessly not over thirty feet above the meadow; and California gulls scream across the sky. A Rocky Mountain bee plant or stinkweed (*Cleome serrulata*) is already showing its pink flowers where cows are grazing in yonder field.

Suddenly from the sky ahead of us a bird shoots downward as if a bullet and, when but a few feet from the roadway, turns almost at right angles and alights in a hawthorn tree. From its size, color and especially its powerful notched, black bill we know it to be a shrike, likely a northwestern, but it darts away before complete identification is possible.

We proceed upward, past fields blooming with dandelions (*Taraxacum officinale*) and finally reach the mouth of Mill Creek, where lingering snow covers the foot hills. On the sandy roadside the golden blooms of the Indian parsnip form tiny mats on the ground.

The sagebrush (*Artemisia gnaphalodes*) hereabout has white-tomentose stems, unarmed, and its tender achenes are like glabrous gray marbles among the toothed leaves. We find miners' lettuce (*Montia perfoliata*) with its strange rounded leaves and white, wee flowers; and, a little further down among the oak trees, lady slippers or milk vetch (*Astragalus cibarius*) already showing its whitish purple bloom.

It is a sweet aubade, the musical announcement of an April dawn, for in the minutes of transition from darkness to light robins carol vociferously, as if filled with joy in the crepuscular hour. In my mind I call it "the rapture of twilight", for no other bird that I know greets with equal vigor the aurora of daybreak, or lingers with equal song as sunset, then gloaming suffuses over all the decline of day. Except in its song the western robin is not vespertime, but it does sing at its best in the first blush of the morning and before the bright segment of a descended sun. Even in the daytime, however, the light of a pine forest is crepusculine; and that is why even a robin in the gloom of a pine-fledged canyon sings from graying dawn to darksome eve.

APRIL 21

As an experiment in floral observation we decide to ascend from the Bonneville shoreline of the mountainsides upward into one of the canyons.

On a warm, dry, gravelly southern exposure of the shoreline near the mouth of City Creek canyon we find the wild Sweet William (*Phlox longifolia*) in bloom, its white to dark-pink flowers appearing abundantly, even if somewhat earlier than usual. At its side are dusty white coxcombs with tiny yellow center, an introduced puccoon known as the Corn Gromwell (*Lithospermum arvense*) with a rather disagreeable odor. Our usual puccoon (*L. angustifolium*) has yellowish flowers. There, however, on the same south-sloping hillsides is blooming one of the most beautiful flowers in Utah, the sheep-pod, lady slipper or wild sweet pea (*Astragalus utahensis*). Plucking one, we discover that the flowers are a "phlox purple"; and to think it adorns the dry, sage-flecked hillside!

As the house finches sing we proceed along the "shore-line" seeing patches of arrow-leaved balsams root or "big sunflowers" (*Balsamorrhiza sagittata*) with their long silvery green leaves and bright yellow flowers adorning the hillsides. Then, just as we enter Big Cottonwood canyon, we discover the pale lilac buds and light blue corrollas of the bluebells (*Mertensia foliosa*) studding the right roadside embankment.

In the canyon at 5500 feet altitude we find the alders, willows and maples half-leaved, as also are the cottonwoods and the elder berries (*Sambucus glauca*). The quaking aspens, and scrub oaks are only beginning to leaf. The gray, prickled thistle (*Cirsium undulatum*) is in full leaf but only six inches high, and beside it in full bloom are dandelions, yellow violets, trailing barberry, and filaree (*Erodium cicutarium*) with its tiny, pink-purple, dark-veined petals. On the bank of the stream are little balls of hairy, purplish bloom, the water-leaf (*Hydrophyllum capitatum*), the hairs being very conspicuous in the bud; and there, beneath the maples are the yellow flowers of the rag-wort or squaw-weed (*Senecio integerrimus*).

Further up, cottonwoods are showing only their brown catkins, and the boxelders, only small leaves such as those on the alders and birches. Above 7500 feet all the trees except the evergreens are leafless, and melting snow gives a rushing streamlet from every ravine into the boisterous creek of the canyon.

In a comparison of man, birds and mammals, we should say that in the naked body state birds are more favored than either of the other two. All are, of course, warm-blooded, but birds can take wing and migrate to joyful lands of eternal spring. Furthermore, birds almost daily express aesthetic qualities of delightful meaning—they sing, and sing pleasantly from morning until dusk, without stimulus, sometimes of sex, and never with thought of material wealth and aggrandisement. Perhaps to be a bird, a passerine bird, would not, after all, be too great a strain on happiness.

APRIL 22

Ducks like water but they dislike rain. Such is our impression when, having purposely visited Farmington bay in a rainstorm to observe the water-fowl, we find them scattered all about the meadowed grass. Each one of them occasionally raises its head to survey the surroundings, and disliking the pelting it receives, withdraws it to the protection of weeded cover.

The mallards for the most part are hiding along the grassy creeks in company with coots, Brewster egrets, and willets. They flush readily, however, and some of them are flying about voluntarily.

Male redwings endure the downpour by standing firmly on their favorite twigs, and to prove their nonchalance most of them through it all are singing their "O-k-lees". Coots seem most discommoded of all the birds, and high flying gulls the least disturbed. The black-necked stilts are hiding in puddles between clumps of grass; but four avocets are the most surprising and interesting of all. They stand at the verge of an open lagoon, fully exposed to the heavy rain and stiff breeze, side by side a foot apart with their cinnamon heads towards the storm. In the ten minutes we watch them they do not move, except that one reaches momentarily to preen; and they might as well be four china ornaments set in a meadow as four avocets full of life.

We see only two white-faced glossy ibises where ordinarily a flock of a hundred makes its stand; they are standing on a meadow of light green, occasionally shaking the rain from their plumage, and actually feeding.

Thunder, lightning and rain becoming more violent, we linger just long enough to look in vain for the yellow headed blackbirds, but find only killdeers at their regular haunts; so along the greening highways we wander homeward again. Within two hours the rain becomes snow, and everything is covered once again with the white mantle of winter.

Eight inches of snow this time in April is indeed a surprise. Stricken are the daffodils and tulips, heavily laden and smothered the blooms of orchard trees; yet, when it melts many shrubs and plants seem the better for its unseasonable visitation. It is not the snow that does the damage but the frost at night when all is settled, cold and clear.

Many mammals, insects, birds and amphibians that virtually live in water must come to the surface now and again to breathe; hence it seems somewhat paradoxical that they should find themselves uncomfortable in drenching rain. There is a passerine bird, however, that might be called an exception—the water ouzel (*Cinclus mexicanus unicolor*) of our mountain streams. This bird lives within the spray and rain of waterfalls and dashing water; its compact plumage is soft and underlaid with down; and, although I have watched one by the hour, I have never seen it shake the water from its feathers. It must enjoy a continual drenching.

APRIL 23

On the hillside at the mouth of a canyon, a flower half hidden in the fresh snow catches our eyes. By its woolly white, tomentose, rounded leaflets and other characteristics, we know it to be the lady's slipper known as *Astragalus utahensis*. Since there are at least seventy varieties of this genus in Utah, it is always interesting to take one of them in hand, even though we are not likely to find more than half a score of them in these mountains. This one is distinctive because its phlox-purple petals fade first to an aconite violet and finally to a bluish lavender; indeed these colors often appear in the living flower in the field.

From a snow-flecked apricot tree we pluck a blossomed branch to see how it endures an April blizzard. Its delicate leaves only a quarter grown are lettuce-green, while its flowers have faded to an acajou red or deep hellebore, depending on the light in which they are seen. The dried stamens are like knobbed hairs of gold. Opening one of the flowers we discover a green apricot a quarter of an inch long, and inside of this again, a white soft miniature of the future stone. The bark of the twig is dark corinthian purple, and we marvel at the varieties of beauty, the many tints and hues displayed by nature, if one inspect closely to discover them.

Wild Sweet Williams adorn the foothills with their pink flowers but *Hedysarum pabulare* is not yet in bloom. Nevertheless, a pretty plant, a foot tall with long green leaves and very small flowers, is blooming below the cross roads of City Creek canyon; it is a hairy puccoon or stoneseed (*Lithospermum ruderale*), which would be much more attractive if the leaves did not overcrowd the blossoms. Each tiny bloom is light chalcedony yellow, scarcely discernible among the sharp, harsh dark green leaves; but there is a fragrance about the plant that is penetrating and delightful.

To ascertain the exact tint of the corolla of a wild Sweet William or phlox (*Phlox longifolia*) we pick one, and find that some colorists would call it a cameo pink, others a light pinkish lilac. It is little to one's surprise to discover time and time again that literally hundreds of clearly differing tints and hues are not only unnamed but also apparently incomparable with any definite objects that would accurately convey them to the reader's mind. One has but to look straight overhead at a clear sky and then towards the horizon to discover the graduation of tint there is, for instance, in the term "sky blue".

There is an ebulliency about spring. The word, of course, from its Latin *ebullient-em* means to boil, and for us, it suggests a readiness to bubble forth or overflow. Every twig we examine, every avian song we hear, every verdant landscape, seems about to boil over with the enthusiasm, the joy, the urge, the great developmental process of the vernal season.

APRIL 24

On the slopes of the lower City Creek canyon today our attention is drawn to a member of the carrot or parsley family, growing nearly two feet high with smooth round hollow stems, adorned at the bottom with purple lines, ternate leaves finely cut or two or three times compounded in threes, and greenish flowers in an umbel like a dozen half-inch pin-cushion balls stuck together on pins at the end of a long stem. Each ball is deep chrysolite green, and looks like crochet work. The plant, known as sweet cicely (*Osmorhiza occidentalis*) has the rather pleasing delicate scent of vegetables. There are two or three species of these sweet roots in the Wasatch mountains, all inhabitants of the aspen and spruce belts; *Osmorhiza divaricata,* for instance, having white flowers, likes the verdured shade of streams; but it is quite difficult to identify the various forms without the fruits actually in hand.

Growing a few feet from the above mentioned flower, but nearer the creek, the holly grape or trailing barberry (*Berberis repens*) is in bloom. The flowers, which at first look like a cluster of citron yellow round berries an eighth of an inch in diameter, open into pretty blossoms of a bright wax yellow or a strontian yellow, each with six petals. As we pick at them to see how the pollen is discharged through the anther-valves, we are surprised at the heavy fragrance of this beautifully colored evergreen. No wonder the Oregon form (*Berberis aquifolium*) is the state flower of Oregon; and in Utah in winter what other plant can equal the beauty of its colored and fresh leaves beneath the snow? In the spring its yellow flowers are odd in form and pretty in color; in the fall its blue or purple berries are attractive in their bloom; but always the leaves are variegated and strong, as constant as those of the spruce and the pine in canyon color glory.

We drift to wayside trails where the effusion of spring makes us want to do something worthwhile, something that will make men understand and esteem the great lessons of nature, which, bereft of the motive of avarice and gold, strives ever to produce something permanent and beautiful. Is it a song?

Almost as varied as the voices of man is the language of a bird, ready as it usually is, upon a moment's notice, to express apprehension, alarm, surprise, defiance, greeting, caution, comradeship, affection and encouragement. Its song is an ebullient expression of well-being; and often the exultant songster cares not whether a female be listening to his rhapsody.

APRIL 25

At the southeast corner of Farmington bay there are grassy low-lands watered by a limpid mountain stream entering through a willowed lane. Having reached this delightful lane-end, where willows, Carolina poplars and flooded stumps make it the paradise of the redwing black-bird, we are diverted by some two score violet green swallows (*Tachy-cineta thalassina lepida*) coursing over and along the wide-spreading brook. With their green heads, purple collars, green backs, violet tails, and white rump patches almost meeting above, the males are handsome birds, especially in certain lights; and then, as they turn and swerve, exposing their immaculate underparts, one is constrained to remark the beauty of white as a contrast with color. Half a dozen females, drab and unattractive in comparison with the lustrous males, bead a fence wire, as if spectators of the aerial performances; but often one of them sallies forth in flight a few feet above the water. None of the males, so far as we can see, is resting; on the contrary all of them are flying across and along, seldom over ten feet above the water, never more than a hundred yards away over the adjoining meadow, darting this way, swerving that, between trees, over stumps and around bends. Some-times a male gives a female a fleeting love-tap in the air, a moment of exultation; for apparently there are yet neither mates nor mating. The only sound they make is a simple "tseet", repeated as they fly. For an hour we watch them, noticing that their under white almost encircles the eye—a good marker—; and then later upon our return from the bay not a swallow is there.

We wait, observing that the eye of a Brewer blackbird is a light yellow with a black center, and listen to the sweet song of a newly arrived Audubon warbler; but it is in vain—the swallows have gone their way. We are however satisfied, for on the watered mud of the bay we have actually counted eight hundred four marbled godwits! The flesh colored bills with their black tips, together with the cinnamon plumage, make identification easy; and they stand idle or probe their long bills into the mud, as we count them!

Listening to a pair of willets flying swiftly overhead and uttering their penetrating whistle "pill-will-willet", we conclude that the bird's name is onomatapoetic only with respect to the last two syllables of its song.

APRIL 26

Meandering along the willowed creek and verdant fields at the mouth of Parley's canyon, where peach trees and choke cherries are in blossom, we observe many interesting birds. Gambel sparrows (*Zonotrichia leucophrys gambelii*), which even in the field may be identified by the long white eye stripes extending from the bill to the back of the head, are singing their variable songs. This pleasing bird not only breeds in these mountains but also frequently winters along their valley streams. The white-crowned sparrow (*Z. leucophrys oriantha*), in which the white stripe extends back only from the eye, winters further south and thus is not so common hereabout; it does, however, have a melodious song, somewhat like "dear-e-e-e-whe-e".

In some boxelder trees a mountain song sparrow (*Melospiza melodia montana*) with its multi-streaked breast is likewise singing a sweet chansonnette, which has the introductory notes "twee twee twee"; and once we watched in a cottonwood a bird much like it, but with finer breast lines and the additional marks of a buffy breast band and a thin eye ring, from which we identify it as a Lincoln sparrow (*Melospiza lincolni altocola*), a bird whose gurgling song has always seemed more melodious than that of the song sparrow. Listening to a Lincoln, we get this onomatop: "twe a tu twa, twee, twee, twa, twa, twa, twr-r-r-". It is sweet, soft, somewhat robinlike in certain notes, like a little robin in the introductory notes. It ends with a twittering roll; and the whole song lasts eighteen seconds.

Scratching about the oak brush are several spurred towhees, birds easily distinguished in the field from a robin by their smaller size and the many white markings on wings and backs. They are members of the Fringillidae, the great family that includes finches, grosbeaks and sparrows, and thus are not related to the *Turdidae* to which the robin belongs. Spurred towhees are permanent residents of the oak-clothed hills, where they mew somewhat like a catbird.

We are pleased when we see a less common towhee, the green-tailed, (*Oberholseria chlorura*) whose rufous cap and olive green back readily distinguish it. It mews like a towhee but sings with a melodious voice as well. It has been taken here at Christmas time; but, as we have never seen it in the lower valleys, it must migrate from hill to hill along the mountains.

135

APRIL 27

In traversing the foothills from the mouth of City Creek canyon eastward, we notice that in the late afternoon sunshine the scrub oak patches show the hue of light vinaceous purple; indeed, at first glance upon an isolated copsewood on the side of a distant gully, we exclaim "dogwoods". Upon examining a twig, we discover that both the broken bud-sheaths and parts of the tender leaf-sprouts are vinaceous-lilac in color, the remaining parts of the bursting leaves being light grape green. The twigs themselves are light purplish gray; and thus we understand the soft, purplish hue of the oak thickets of springtime, aye leafing time; it is a color transition confined to the period between the opened bud and the developed leaf.

On the dry hillside we find in full bloom not only the wild sweet William with its pink to whitish corollas, and the arrow-leaved balsam root or big sunflower (*Balsamorrhiza sagittata*) but also those odd little white coxcombs known as puccoons or corn gromwell (*Lithospermum arvense*). The loose spikes of these flowers are remiform, that is, like an oar with the paddle end upward and the handle stuck into the base of the plant. There are several oars or coxcombs on each plant, and each flower has a yellow center.

As the sun descends our eyes catch an inflorescence of white and rose nestling beside a rock on the graveled sageland. It is an evening primrose (*Oenothera caespitosa*), a plant not over seven inches high, with three white flowers in full bloom, one of livid pink shrunken and withered, its duty done, and twelve pointed salmon-colored buds awaiting their turn to bloom. The narrow, long, sinuate-dentate leaves all spring from the root-base and are leathery and smooth to the finger touch.

We examine one of the bell-shaped white flowers, finding that it has four cleft white petals, eight stamens, and a pistil split into a four branched stigma. The stamens and pistil are pale dull green yellow, but the anthers are straw-yellow. The pollen is strewn as if it were a spider's web.

The evening primrose opens at night to give the moths a kiss, then withers and dies. Thus the flowers bloom one at a time so that the precious moment of ecstacy be not denied it when the joyful visitor comes. Such is the romance of a flower, seeking to entice its lover by a fragrance delightful and far-reaching—the wide-eyed primrose of a starry night.

APRIL 28

In our rambles we linger at the top of the hill on the roadway leading into Mueller Park, where the altitude is 5500 feet and a stream roars a hundred yards below us in a verdured gully.

The upper third of the high mountains before us are partially snow-laden, but not only are there brown patches of unleafed quaking aspens here and there about them but also pyramidal pins of spruces and firs stuck in the snowy places.

But trees are leafy about us; and the scrub oaks vesturing the sandy slopes are not only in half leaf but also in bloom. They bear no petals, but the staminate flowers appear in catkins, each stamen resembling a green string with about a dozen crocheted knots of rusty green fastened along it.

In the shade of the oak copses some tall larkspurs (*Delphinium bicolor*) grow, each flower having five petals separted like the points of a star, each deeper than indigo and what ornithologists at least would call a "hyacinth blue". The leaflets resemble the antlers of a deer.

By the side of the oaks are flowers that resemble clover blooms, with unattractive whitish corollas with purplish keels; they are tidy tips (*Astragalus cibarius*). Nearby are soft, woolly mats adorned with beautiful pink flowers, the sheep pods or lady slippers, which curiously, exactly match in color those beautiful everlasting peas (*Lathyrus utahensis*) intwining themselves about the oak branches.

Over there at the south the orange yellow petals of the western wall flower (*Erysimum asperum*) are showing on rough, pubescent stems, and by them a tiny star flower (*Tellima parviflora*) with quarter inch petals like paper shreds. There also stands the whisk-broom parsley (*Lomatium simplex*) with yellow flowers crowded like crochet-knots.

But there! right at the roadside at the north, growing in the oak-copse, is that most fragrant of all Utah shrubs, the buck or antelope bush with tiny yellow flowers that smell like apple blossoms. Miners lettuce with its elf-like bloom in the center of a leaf is there beside the balsam roots that show big yellow sunflowers everywhere. A large bumble bee, a spurred towhee, a chickadee, a red-shafted flicker, a long-crested jay—such are things awing.

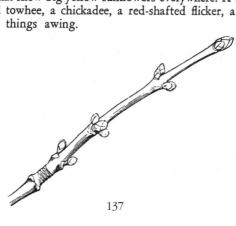

APRIL 29

In going from Parley's canyon over the pass to Emigration canyon, we notice that while the slopes are grassy, shrubs and trees are yet in the budding stage.

About a quarter of a mile from the summit, while yet on the Parley's side, we come to a grassy, south-facing gully where that sweet little bluebell known as *Mertensia brevistyla* is blooming. It is a small plant, four to ten inches high, with narrow, obtuse ended leaves that feel on their upper surfaces as though they needed a shave, and had just had a shave on the lower sides. The dark blue flowers appear in a loose panicle, each flower tube being only about a quarter of an inch long. As we look into a single flower we see that each petal seems to have a tiny blister or bump on it, and neither pistil nor stamens are very apparent. They have no noticeable fragrance.

Near them the trailing barberry is partially in bloom, the unopened flowers appearing like yellow shot bunched on the strong, thorny-edged leaves. Also there the yellow violet is showing its coy petals.

We go over the summit to the Emigration side where in the first oak copse we come upon numerous yellow dogtooth violets or Easter bells. They are extraordinary flowers in that the petals curve backward toward the stem, and the hellebore red anthers stick out nearly an inch from the center. The two leaves are long, pointed and slender, smooth to the touch, and edged with a line of reddish hues.

Then, by their side is blooming that tender little plant known as a Claytonia or Spring beauty (*Claytonia rosea*). It stands not over three inches high, has only two leaves, wedge-shaped and smooth, and a white bell flower only a quarter of an inch long. The inside of the corolla is lined with red, the same color as the anthers. To think that a plant so frail should choose to bloom in the vicinity of retreating snow!

We ramble downward, content that a drear landscape has rewarded with gems of floral beauty never to be forgotten.

Although there are approximately sixty six species and sub-species of wild mammals in the Wasatch mountains and their valleys, most of them are small animals like shrews and mice that have to be trapped to be seen. It is a matter of constant regret to us that sometimes we travel the mountains all day long without seeing any wild mammals other than a spermophile or a chipmunk.

APRIL 30

It is a memorable afternoon on world-renowned Farmington bay. About thirty birds slightly larger than killdeers are flying in a flock from one end of the water to the other not only with a speed excelling that of teals but also with black bellies and white upper sides, a surprisingly handsome plumage when seen as they circle in the bright sun. Instantly we recognize them as either golden or black-bellied plovers; and then, when they alight in the water nearby and their tail coverts can readily be seen to be white, we know they are the aristocrats of the *Charadriidae,* black bellied plovers (*Squatarola squatarola*) in nuptial plumage. Again we remark on the beauty of black and white in birds— the hundred pelicans flying overhead, the black-necked stilts everywhere, the greater scaup ducks of a month ago, and so on. These plovers are so rare a sight that we are loath to leave them. They utter a simple, soft, whistled "wher-et", as they go by us.

With its big head, thick neck, red eyes, black crown and back and creamy white throat, a black-crowned night heron is standing alone in the thick grass twenty yards away, the first we have seen this year. Its two crest plumes hang from its head down its back like white strings. Suddenly it reaches for an edible tid-bit, probably a small frog; at any rate it proceeds to chew as if it had human jaws, the bill opening at each chew. We do not recall having seen any other bird thus chewing its food before swallowing it.

This afternoon the meadows are swarming with three kinds of swallows—one or two northern violet green swallows, a few barn swallows (*Hirundo rustica erythrogaster*) and hundreds of white-bellied or tree swallows (*Iridoprocne bicolor*). The "tsip-prrup" of the tree swallow is a mere token of song.

To our good fortune a Brewster's heron alights on a fence post but a few yards away, and poses undisturbed. Its black bill has a definite downward tilt at the end; and its head sets so closely to its shoulders that it appears to have no neck. Its golden feet show clearly as it stands. Unlike the cormorant which holds its bill at a 45° angle this bird holds its bill about 10° below horizontal. It ignores redwings about it; but snaps occasionally at gnats.

We catch two willets in courtship. The male raises his wings, displaying their inner black and white, and utters " Tuck a a a a tuck a a a a tuck a a a", but the female ignores his efforts and soon they are prodding the mud for food, without thought of breeding ardour.

MAY 1

One spring we frequently visited Farmington bay for the purpose of recording migration dates, especially that of the redwing blackbird. Despite a severe cold winter and a stormy late spring, the male redwings appeared on the creek willows . on February 20th. They sang perfunctorily and while sitting none showed his red epaulets. Day after day there was little change in the male flock, except that it grew more vociferous, on March 19th, for instance, the male chorus being very pronounced with much clucking as well as song. Still only yellowish crescents showed on their wings.

For the next few days the male flock was dispersing, each male selecting his favorite locale, a brook-footed post here, a marsh fence there, or a reeded patch where slow water ran, always apparently a spot where fresh water was near and perches such as willows and wires were either existing or in the making like ungrown rushes.

And then, on March 23rd, a flock of thirty drab little females appeared on the scene, staring curiously about the fen from fence wires and manifesting no interest in the scattered males, who indeed reciprocated their indifference. A male atop a fence post beside the unadorned little ladies treated them as harmless strangers; when the females flew they were in a flock together.

On April 9th the yellow-headed blackbirds appeared, but the redwings were still in status quo—female flock, isolated males. Brewster egrets, coots, marbled godwits, long-billed curlews, white faced glossy ibises, western willets, mallards, avocets, black-necked stilts, bitterns, pintails, and killdeers were their companions.

On April 13th the male redwings' epaulets showed brilliant red in sitting posture; and for the first time the female flock began to disperse. Males began chasing females, and by April 25th no sign of female assemblage remained, for all seemed happily mated or at least won over to definite nidification localities.

Today on the bay, we spend ten minutes trying to catch a brown wandering garter snake (*Thamnophis ordinoides vagrans*), but it eludes us in the pond shore grass and escapes in a hole. It has a protective coloration almost as effective as that of the snowy plover, which when but a few rods away sometimes fades from view against the white alkali mud.

MAY 2

The water birds are nesting on the lea,
Beneath the welcome warmth of cloudless skies;
The waders peck in sweet tranquility,
As overhead the restless curlew cries.

In the springtime changes in nature occur so rapidly that even vigilant eyes and a willing pen feel the stress of recording them. With tulips, lilacs, iris and pansies displaying their beauty about one's home, and with sweet Williams, lady slippers, wall flowers, and balsam roots adorning the hillsides, one seeks the chirming birds of the meadows and reeded sloughs with a feeling of wonder and admiration of it all. Even on our way we stop in astonishment at the beauty of a red bud or Judas tree (*Cercis canadensis*) now in the very height of its glory, with masses of pea-shaped pink blossoms adorning a home lawn. What joy in this and in a double flowering crab tree! But we started for the alkaline ponds.

Notwithstanding diversions we at last arrive at the reeded stretches at the mouth of the Jordan, determined to find a nest or so. There on the ground among the weeds is the nest of a mallard with eight buffy green eggs. As the female quacks away we conclude that incubation has been going on here for several days.

Over there in some bushes is another nest, that of the Brewster heron, with four pale blue eggs. Beautiful bird, the very prize of avian pulchritude, no wonder the fair ladies once almost caused its extermination for its plumes!

We scan the lakeside, listen to the chirm and then espy a nesting meadowlark in her loosely hooded home at the base of a bunch of grass. She flushes as we approach, but after admiring them we leave undisturbed the five white eggs spotted with purple and brown. Economically beneficial bird, not only is it the friend of the farmer but also the loud songstress of the meadowed places.

On our return we find in some creek willows the horse-hair lined nest of the western chipping sparrow (*Spizella passerina arizonae*) with five speckled blue eggs; and nearer the mountains, the nests of a mountain song-sparrow with four greenish white eggs, and that of a Cooper hawk in a tree. Every day is a race with nature, for it is "bounteous May that doth inspire mirth and youth and warm desire".

The truth is, we are entering upon the estival period of bird life, that May and June time of actual nidification and incubation. Man prides himself on harnessing nature with machines and making it do his bidding, but after all his real joy is derived from simplicity without those multiform aids, from his nearness to nature in its untroubled ways.

MAY 3

Flying about the meadow of Farmington bay today is a bank swallow (*Riparia riparia riparia*), readily distinguished by its brown back and dark breast band, the first of its kind we have seen this year.

At a clear grassy slough four small shorebirds are wading and feeding, three of them with their neck stripes of cinnamon and black being among the most attractive of the birds of the bay. They are Wilson phalaropes and the three prettier ones are females! Females indeed, larger apparently than the male and quite his masters. Here is a notable reversal of sexual character; the female is handsomer than the male; in courtship several females pursue one male; the male incubates the eggs of the nest; and the evidence is quite convincing that the female, if able to manage it, has two husbands for each of whom she eggs a nest!

We watch one feed not over ten feet away. She nips insects from the water's surface at the rate of about once each second, making a twist of her body and a step of her foot at each nip. Then, still as near, she stands in the water by a grass clump, tucks her bill back under her wing and goes to sleep. When at last we disturb her she utters a soft hoarse "kweer kweer', as if calling to her companions, and wades away.

A Caspian tern (*Hydroprogne caspia*) flies toward us, showing his black cap, black under primaries and red bill; and, hovering, dives to the water a few yards away. The cry is a strident "cow".

Flying over the lake back and forth above us further on, are a score of Forster's terns. We spend half an hour making certain that their tails match their backs in color, and that the tips of their primaries are lighter than the inner wing—delicate points of discrimination, so near is this bird like the common tern (*Sterna hirundo hirundo*)—; and then, as we peer at them, three black terns (*Chlidonias nigra surinamensis*) come into view. Three tern-arrivals on the same day!

Further on, a Caspian tern, one black tern, and six Forster terns, are standing on a miniature peninsula a hundred yards away in agreeable companionship. The bill of the Caspian looks like a thumb of blood instead of a beak.

A flock of sparrowlike birds fly to the cobbled beach thirty feet beyond, and to our astonishment become indiscernible. They have blackish legs (thus distinguishing them from the least sandpiper), and they are mostly rusty above, whereas the semi-palmated sandpiper is mostly grayish brown on the upper parts—all different birds to identify by sight. Incredible we slowly walk to within ten feet of them—twelve western sandpipers (*Ereunetes mauri*) probing about the algae of the stones. For a quarter of an hour we watch, marveling at their protective coloration; and when we move to eight feet and crunch on the cobbles they fly away with a merry "teet" teet" teet".

MAY 4

On a grassy roadside a mile northwest of the mouth of the Weber river we catch a glimpse of a tall- single-stemmed yellow flower that is so striking we must investigate. It proves to be a groundsel, ragwort or squawweed (*Senecio integerrimus*). It has a single erect stout stem three feet high with numerous dentate leaves about the base, and a short-peduncled terminal head consisting of about a dozen flowers with bright yellow rays and orange centers. It is the solitary flower head on the long, almost leafless stem that attracts one's eyes. This is not a very common flower, as we have seldom noticed it; but there are so many members of the genus *Senecio* that close inspection is necessary for identification.

Ogden canyon is singularly bereft of wild flowers—too many human visitors—; but on the saged hills south of a reservoir we do come upon the wild candytuft or penny-cress (*Thalspi coloradense*), a small ball of white flowers on a slender almost leafless stem seven or eight inches high. In this canyon we find many trees overgrown by the woody branches of that species of virgin's bower that swarms over the bushes with its white plumose achenes in August; it is the *Clematis lingusticifolia,* which so far we have found only in Weber and Ogden canyons, and south of Provo river.

Several of the mustards are in bloom; also service berries, the white flowers of the latter being very noticeable against the rich green leaves of the shrubs. This is a berry of shaded, moist northern sloping gullies.

Far up in the canyons where snow still seeps into the roadways, there is as yet little floral decoration; squirrels are frisking about but even the warblers are not yet singing in the willowed copses. Streams are roily and boisterous; and thus once more nature is in the midst of one of its most important of seasonal changes.

Half way up the canyon in dense clumps along the shaded slopes and streams, that common evergreen known as mountain hedge or mountain lover is showing its tiny dark red blooms, which appear like four-pointed garnets among the leathery leaves.

Often as I listen to the brookside chansonnette of some avian vocalist, perched contentedly on a twig, perhaps a warbler or a thrush, I wonder if the rhythm, the timbre and the resonance of its song might have been affected, or somewhat evolved from the constant purling of the stream over which as a fledgling it first heard the rhapsodic sounds of running water. I have no evidence of it; I cannot make an onomatop of a murmuring brook; nor can I point to a bird whose voice is imitative of the dash, moan, ripple and joy of the stream; but somehow I claim synchronization in the environment of the brook-sung wildland.

MAY 5

As we approached a thickly reeded meadow-pond near the mouth of the Jordan river, and stood for a time listening to western meadowlarks, red-winged blackbirds, killdeers and overflying California gulls, and gazed with deep interest upon a pair of Brewster herons standing in inch-deep pools, there suddenly came from the depths of the dark green rushes not over ten yards away, the guttural, raucous-ending notes, "Oka'zaw", of the yellow-headed blackbird. Every peer with the glasses being unavailing, my companion determined to re-enact childhood memories of this particular slough, and wade after it. As the first bare foot struck the still water, the bird emitted an alarm call, a "chup, chup zwa swa", the first two notes being accented, throated whistles. The bird flushed, and though in the miniature forest of reeds were a nest of the former year and the rushy mound of some muskrats, there was no sign of present incubation.

It alighted but a few yards away, hence we were able to observe the movements of its anxious eyes. Every five seconds or so it emitted a puzzled "kluck". It was resting upon a dry horizontal reed, which as it moved about, we could discern was deliberately chosen in preference to the up-standing green stalks, not only because it made an easier perch but also because it kept the bird hidden about six inches below the tips of the brown-blossomed, green reeds. That explained our inability to see the yellow head in the first place.

Now it sang undisturbed; for we were motionless as pasture posts. "True' true' tra zwa" came its song, the "true, true" being a throaty, fluty whistle. Then later to our surprise, it gave another series of notes, best described as "zolk' zolk' ya razte". Three bobolinks settled into the reed patch, a coot soared down into the little portion of open-water; but the song of the yellow-headed blackbird was obviously the deep, mystic sound of the tadpoled slough.

Today the rough-winged swallows (*Stelgidopterys ruficollis serripennis*) have arrived in a flock and settled *in transitu* upon the creekside wires. Their call is a rasping, tiny squeak, like "pseart".

Since the longest wing feather of the male rough-wing, that is, its outermost primary, has an outer web that is stiffened by tiny, fishhooklike barbs, recurved at the tips, giving a filelike impression to one's finger when drawn along the edge from the base towards the tip, I have often wondered at the function of this novel characteristic. It probably aids the male to cling to the clay mouth of the nest, as the female sets within.

MAY 6

On our way to the reeded places of the Jordan river outlet we find on a cindered, graveled railroad-embankment the blood-red fruits of the sand dock (*Rumex venosus*). We pull one of the plants with its stems of pomegranate-red, and discover that its inflorescence is a panicled raceme, a central stem from which dangle on inch-long, slender threads some forty triple sided pods, each of which has an outer color of Pompeian red and an inner tint of viridine green. The root stems, which to our surprise appear to have no rootlets, are pomegranate purple, slightly more brilliant than the pods. No wonder the children have called this dock the "bleeding heart", for hearts a plenty it has enchained.

We proceed further, and in an alkaline meadow stop to pick a small white rayed, yellow centered flower known as the "wild daisy", which resembles *Erigeron Coulteri,* but that grows in the aspen belt and we feel in its identification the need of a complete revision of the genus. There however nearby is the *Cymoterus longipes* with its dull white seed pods now showing and hanging as if nearly dry. Over the same field is blooming that thin-stemmed, purple-flowered member of the mustard family, known as the "lilac" (*Thelypodium torulosum*), though the one we hold as we write is a single-stemmed plant less than a foot high, with however, a ball of bloom at the top less than an inch in diameter distinctly "lilac" in color. Frail little flower when seen alone, yet in great numbers it hues the fields.

We come to a grassy marsh where the water is only two or three inches deep. There a solitary Brewster heron is standing, with its pretty, ·dissected, filamentose feathers showing delicately at its tail tip. Beside it are two white-faced glossy ibises probing their stout somewhat elongated bills into the grassy mud. We notice that though the birds are friendly, the ibises invariably choose the grassy water, while the egret always stands in the open stretches. They probe; the Brewster egret nips from the surface. Endless are the charms of nature in its intimate ways!

MAY 7

Delightful is the return of the feathered kind; indeed as we rest for awhile at a valley cottage, which is surrounded by majestic black locusts, all nature seems invigorated, filled with ebullient desires and urged by the intense joys of spring. In the foliage of the locusts, which reach eighty feet into the blue of the sky, mourning doves (*Zenaidure macroura marginella*) are cooing *addolorato* their soft love song "who who whoo whoo whoo"; and from the upper branches of those stately trees Arkansas fly catchers (*Tyrannus verticalis*) essay into the air in mimic conflict with shrill cries. Hawk-chasing belligerents, they are truly the tyrants of their domain; yet they live in peace with unobtrusive kindred.

From several of the ancient trees comes the unmistakable "if-if-if-if-if" of red-shafted flickers, while everywhere English sparrows are as incessantly garrulous as ever. Despite his earlier fighting he seems eventually to choose a mate and hold her affection without intrusion upon their intimacies.

Along the creek willows (*Salix exigua*) a pair of yellow warblers (*Dendroica petechia morcomi*) are evidently contemplating a nest, while a score or more Audubon warblers (*Dendroica auduboni memorabilis*) are continually in search of bugs. Unlike the summer yellow warbler, the Audubon does not nest in the valleys, but usually seeks the higher spruces and pines where it twines a nest of pine needles, pine bark, rootlets, hair and feathers. Soon it will be on its way upward where now snow patches fledge its favored haunts of summer. The well known cup-shaped nest of the yellow warbler is, of course, placed in bushes or trees.

In the willows we see actually a hundred or more pallid gold-finches which almost prevent our noticing a tiny lead-colored bush tit (*Psaltriparus minimus plumbeus*) that at first we thought to be a Lucy warbler. Wee bird with wee, thin voice!

A mountain song sparrow, a western vesper sparrow (*Pooecetes gramineus confinis*) all come within our sight and hearing. These are the fields, these are the meadows filled with memories.

Between the roadway and the borrow-ditch a female mallard flushes from the tall dry weeds. There they are—ten buffy green eggs in a down-lined nest somewhat elliptical in shape, well contrived to fit a bird of elongated underside. The surprising feature, however, is that the site is within three feet of vehicles passing perhaps ten times a day.

Redwing males are chasing their mates swiftly and closely today; and the yellow headed blackbirds are in agitated assemblage with many foils and passes at one another. Some sounds like "Quaw, quaw, quaw, ka law" stridently issue from them.

On the graveled roadside about the lake are a score of nests of California gulls. We have at last entered upon the period of eggs and homes.

MAY 8

Undoubtedly the first white men to visit the Wasatch mountains were Father Juan de Escalante and his companions in 1776, for, coming northward from Mexico they descended Spanish Fork canyon, and skirted Utah Lake before returning southward again. Although his diary proves that he gave Spanish names to the principal streams that he traversed on his way, that diary and the names were doomed to languish unknown and unsung until nearly fifty years after the advent of pioneers in 1847, who in the meantime had adopted other permanent names.

Since the Colorado river was an almost insuperable barrier, there was little if any emigration from Mexico to these mountains in early days; but some words of Spanish origin did gradually creep into the ordinary parlance of the Wasatch; thus: lariat (Sp. *la reata*); lasso (Sp. *lazo*); chaps (Sp. *chapparreros,* leather breeches); rodeo (Sp. *rodeo,* a roundup); ranch (Sp. *rancho*); arroyo (Sp. *arroyo,* brook, gully); coyote (Sp. *coyote*); lobo (Sp. *lobo,* wolf) and so on.

Of the Wasatch rivers, Bear came from the many black bears at its head-waters, and Jordan is Biblical; but each of the others derived its name from a particular trapper who cabined along it about 1823; thus: Logan (Ephraim Logan); Ogden (Peter Skene Ogden); Weber (John H. Weber); and Provo (Etienne Provot).

Timpanogos, the highest peak, has its Indian name; and Mt. Nebo comes from the Biblical range from the summit of which Moses saw the Promised Land.

From the number of "Otter" and "Beaver" creeks in the Wasatch mountains, one is persuaded to believe that both of those mammals were numerous here in early days. Today, on Farmington Bay, avocets are assembled on the mud in quarrelsome groups in which male charges male, and females seem to enjoy the courtesies accorded them. Likewise Brewster egrets, forty five of them are for the first time idling together on the water, not in belligerent mood but rather in dreamy contemplation. Their filamentous feathers appear about three inches long.

A pair of Caspian terns sits on a mud island, uttering occasionally a harsh, single-noted "klock", whereas Forster terns in the air screech not unlike night hawks.

More and more we notice the white-faced glossy ibises roaming the grassy meadows with the cowherd; indeed paludicoline, limicoline and pratincoline birds seem almost interchangeable in their habitats at this time of year, when the reeds are not yet grown.

MAY 9

During many visits to the sloughs and ponds of Farmington bay this spring we have awaited the arrival of Wilson phalaropes (*Steganopus tricolor*) to observe their feeding whirls. On May 3rd three handsome females and one demure male were wading in the meadowed fen at the roadside. Having just arrived, they were doubtless tired, since one tucked her bill under her right wing and, standing in the water by a grass-tuft, deliberately went to sleep within eight feet of our delighted eyes. The clear water was placid, the calm afternoon sunny and the gnats bothersome. The other phalaropes were feeding, the usual method being to nip the insect from the water about forty five degrees to the right, then one straight ahead, then one at the left and so on, the time being approximately a second a nip in coordination with the leg movements.

The confiding female before us awoke, and began to feed, first towards us, then away. Her nips at the water were so delicate as not to create a discernible ripple—this side, that side, without either a whirl or flirt of the tail. In half an hour she made no feeding whirl, that is, complete circle.

Not satisfied, we sought them again on May 5th; and after an hour spent watching male avocets try to bill-spear one another and counting a fleet of three hundred white pelicans, we found the phalaropes. Ten yards away six females and two males were feeding and wading in the agreeable company of a score of lesser yellow legs. We began to count feeding nips with whirls, a whirl to us being any movement of the phalarope from straight ahead to straight behind, or a complete circle, but excluding mere side to side movements forward.

The first count was 134 nips without a whirl; then 39, 69, 102 and so on, and still no whirl. Finally one did make a half circle to the rear, and another whirled all around. We selected a female, and counted her nips, which were interrupted only when she chased another female, and once moved out of the way of a yellow leg. Her total count was 239 nips without a whirl. She stopped to bathe, vigorously ducking her head and shaking her wings; and then lapsed into preening, thus stopping our count. We suggest that moving water might change the bird's antics; this water was still. The only sound she makes is a low, guttural "croick".

An old codger today tells us how to grow that edible mushroom known as the oyster shell (*Pleurotus ostreatus*) which from snow to snow we find growing on the stumps of dead Carolina poplar trees. He gets an old apple, maple or poplar short stump, nearly buries it in his yard, inoculates it by shaking on it spores from oyster shells he has gathered, and keeps it fairly moist. He gets oysters weighing nearly half a pound each.

MAY 10

Each day the leafage of the canyons is creeping higher and higher; each week brings forth more and more the dulcet woodnotes of warblers, and the colored array of flowers along the hilly paths. One would indeed have to travel hundreds of miles overland to observe a transition from a summery verdure to an alpine leaflessness and snow such as he may see in an hour in a Wasatch canyon from its mouth to its head.

All along the lower canyon wends the fragrant, white racemes of the choke cherry adorn every lane with floral loveliness; and we determine to make mental notes of the localities for the gathering of cherries in September. In this regard, however, we have noticed that the lower trees generally dropped their fruits too soon, and that the finest cherries have been picked in the higher mountains.

About half way up Big Cottonwood canyon, lupines or quaker bonnets (*Lupinus laxiflorus*) show their delicately tinted blue flowers on a gravelly hillside; and here and there the rather demure bushes of the service berry are displaying their loose blossoms. There in the same vicinity but on a rocky slope, pretty blue-bells (*Mertensia foliosa*) are blooming, a thousand feet higher up the canyon from the enbankment where we caught their pale-blue beauty on the twenty first of April.

There on a damp hillside we notice the greenish white flowers of the black currant (*Ribes viscosissimum*); but near it is blooming one of the sweetest scented shrubs we have come upon this year. It is the mountain red currant (*Ribes cereum*) with half-inch long flower cylinders of pinkish white drooping in threes beneath the very small leaves. We break off a branch and find ourselves for hours afterward admiring the waxy white to pinkish umbel-like flowers. In the distance the bush reminds one of the honeysuckles, as the pinkish tints outdo the tiny leaves. It is sometimes called hereabout "wolf-berry" or "soldier berry".

A little further upward, on a particularly moist slope, the miniature white flowers of the wild candytuft (*Thlaspi glaucum*) are now in full bloom. No wonder the old prospector in yonder cabin enjoys the freshness, the purity and the beauty of his solitary home!

In the upper reaches of Parley's canyon towards the Emigration pass, we see today not only the arrow-leaved balsam root (*Balsamorrhiza sagitata*) but also the cut-leafed kind (*B. macrophylla*) in full bloom. Both have great yellow flowers, but the sticky rich green leaves of the latter, nearly a foot in length, are slashed into lobes. This species likes the rich soil of high valleys, but the arrow-leaved variety blooms on dry hillsides everywhere. Another one (*B. hirsuta*), which is covered with soft gray fine hairs, likes the dry gravelly valleys where it blooms in April, May and June.

To observe a flower intimately, be it large or small, homely or beautiful, is to marvel at the great mystery of life.

MAY 11

In a balsam-scented forest of blister pines (*Abies concolor*) at an altitude of 7350 feet in Big Cottonwood canyon, there is now not only the cool tranquility of snow-spotted hills but also the retarded awakening of deciduous trees and shrubs. Save for the rush of the distant boisterous stream, the buzz of an aggressive blue-bottle fly, and the harsh cries of a solitary long-crested jay, there is little sound or motion to enliven the somnambulant inactivity of the scene.

We spend a few minutes in an effort to record an onomatope of this jay's call. The notes are loud, penetrating, rasping, strident, like "chack! chack! chack!", although once we caught a rapid variation, like "chack-e! chack-e! chack-e!". It appears to be incapable of joyful song.

Oyster-white quaking aspens stand on the slope yonder like naked, slender bones stuck in soiled, dry-leaved encrustation; nevertheless, as we pluck a twig from one of them, we discover that its bark has the tint of ecru, and that a flowered catkin over an inch long, grizzled and browned, is blooming from its tip. A vigorous blowing from our lips easily shatters and dissipates the bloom afar.

Between two quaking aspens an elderberry bush (*Sambucus microbotrys*) grows with three kinds of branches; the dead, ashy gray, half shredded, grandmother stems of three years ago; the dead yet pinkish, whole-barked stalks of two years ago; and the vigorous persimmon-colored grown-ups of the past year, now sprouting lustily with dark green leaves covered by tiny droplets of crystal honey. We taste this nectar of the woods, and envy for a moment the wild-flying bee.

Strewn over a labyrinth of young firs prostrated at the trunk of a large quaking aspen, the stringy, grey branches of a virgin's bower (*Clematis occidentalis*) appear with violet-colored, sharp, four-petaled flowers blooming from apparently dead vines. A wild clematis flowering with its root actually touching a mound of seeping snow!

The mountain hedge now has pin-head buds at the bases of its wedge-shaped evergreen leaves; but there at last we find one in bloom, with four miniature petals of Harvard crimson color, like jewels of garnet at the base of a leaf.

Whether they be living or dead matter no one knows, but viruses reproduce, hence capability of reproduction is not a certain sign of life. Nor do we know the ultimate unit that sustains life. How wondrous it all is, even when we look upon the tiny bloom of a mountain hedge!

MAY 12

In a valley orchard amid a shower of blossoms fluttered by every breeze, one tree holds firmly to its beauty—the winter pear. Like snow-drops gathered fresh from the interspaces of early spring-snow, its flowers are suspended from slender stems, each small blossom resembling the miniature bud of some pure white rose.

Beyond the orchard in a field every grassy flat is dotted by the brilliant yellow blossoms of the dandelion. Nature however adheres firmly to the law of compensation; and, as if to answer our condemnation of a weed, three domestic turkeys tread out before us and enjoy a meal by nipping off the very yellow blooms that we are contemplating. For half an hour we watch them; but along the vigorous green willows at the verge of the sweet smelling meadow many birds are chirping with rapturous song.

Pale goldfinches (*Spinus tristis pallidus*) with their canary-yellow bodies but black crowns, wings and tails, are there singing their lisping "che-we-see" notes as if some sparrow ancestor had married a warbler and given them color as well as melody. Flitting about the same willows, however, are some real warblers, the yellow or summer warbler and that other one of yellow, black, white and bluish gray, the Audubon, which later seeks the sombrous shades of alpine trees as if his ancestor had married a junco. Meadowlarks, redwing blackbirds and killdeers seem to be everywhere; but from a shrub at the laneside we suddenly catch the two prolonged whistled notes of an Oregon white-crowned sparrow (*Zonotrichia leucophrys oriantha*). As we hold the field glasses upon him we notice that not only do black and white stripes run along the top of his head but along his back as well. And there with a big song from a wee bird is a mite of feathered bliss that it takes us minutes to identify; it is a western ruby-crowned kinglet (*Regulus calendula cineraceus*), one of the sweetest midgets of birddom. Its simple call is a lisping "jee-dee"; but its rhapsodic song consists of some twenty notes difficult to describe onomatopoetically.

Then unexpectedly in a clump of grass we come upon a wandering garter snake (*Thamnophis ordinoides vagrans*), which we chase for thirty yards into the water.

The memory of such a place—a willowed lane endeared by cherished associations, personal and general—is like a perenninal flower that recurs with all its beauty to adorn the sacred and almost secret recesses of the heart.

Fortunate is he who in youth can visit many of the natural beauty spots of the world, such as the lakes, mountains and rivers of Switzer-land, Niagara Falls, Bryce canyon, the Colorado river gorge, and so on; for in later years he has but to close his eyes and think to relive those impressive scenes. Again it may be a recurrence of the joy one had upon beholding a halcyon and romantic glade.

MAY 13

As if it had opened only this morning that pretty member of the pulse family, the pink *Hedysarium pabulare* is abloom on the entrance to a canyon, with brilliant flower clusters of rose-purple on stems a foot high. The shape of its leaves readily disclose its relationship to the milk vetches and wild sweet peas; but it stands erect and alone like a bouquet placed in the June grass and among the wilting balsam roots. Such is the quick transition of but a few days, that the blossoms of yesterday are supplanted by the blooms of today; nevertheless the beautiful floral candelabra of the horse chestnut trees (*Aesculus Hippocastanum*) along cultivated paths seem to have held their form and grandeur for a week or so. Perhaps, when they will have gone, the lovely catalpa blossoms will take their place, yet this slow bloomer is just now only getting well into leaf.

Different, indeed, are the birds, flowers and trees of the browned hillsides and dry valleys of the Wasatch mountains from those of the verdant fields of more humid climes, such as, for instance, those of England, which somehow constantly recur to our memory. There in May it is the linnet in the furzebush, the green finch on its mossy nest beside thatched roofs, the chaffinch with a lichen-nest beside hawthorns, or the missel thrush in a showery apple tree. There it is the screaming whimbrel in the sky of night, or the nightingale of moonlight hours. There along country lanes holly clusters about the branches of trees, while the guelder-rose and the rowan show their white blooms; there chestnut trees hold their great waxy flowers. There one hears such birds as the bell-tingling great tit, the starling and the skylark, and sees such trees as the oak, the cypress and the yew. Who, indeed, could forget the triple, mile-long avenues of horse chestnuts in Bushy Park, Hampton Court near London, trees so old that they date from the time of William III, who planted them, and blossoms so extensive and beautiful that "Chestnut Sunday" is almost a holiday, announced that people might see them. Many an hour we have spent beneath those mighty trees, many a day with the beeches of Epping Forest whence came Tennyson's "The Talking Oak" and "Locksley Hall". Nevertheless in the Wasatch there are majestic cumulus clouds in cerulean skies, isolated forests where man has for centuries scarcely trod upon the pine-needle carpets; and above all a wildness and freedom unknown in thickly populated regions. Such after all, are the compensations of life.

MAY 14

Nearly every canyon of these mountains has some lofty cliffs along its course, often with elephantine boulders at their feet. In dry gullies sometimes great naked rocks are strewn, and many gravel pits have vertical faces. These together attract a rather definite mural avifauna.

Two of our bird species are strictly saxicoline or rock-inhabiting. The rock wren (*Salpinctes obsoletus obsoletus*), which often emits its harsh "ka-we, ka-we, ka-we" from the top of some crag and lays its white eggs in rocky niches, really prefers the desolate boulders on the stretches below the canyons; but the canyon wren (*Catherpes Mexicanus consperus*) delights in the steeps and cliffs of the canyons themselves where its strong buglelike song is a moment of rapture to him who hears it in the oak-clad mountains. It is a veritable cascade of delightful notes, often a repetition of "tsee-i", ending with soft vowels, "oo-ee". Unfortunately we seldom come upon it hereabout, but, when we do, it is a pleasant experience.

Other Wasatch birds are saxicoline only in their nesting places. Thus the northern violet green swallow, whose violet back is a memorable glint of birddom, as it flies by, enjoys feeding about pines and oaks, but lays its white eggs often in the crevice of a bluff above them. The cliff swallow (*Petrochelidon pyrrhonota albifrons*) lives on ants and insects but builds its gourd-nest of mud often against a cliff, hence its name; and in this connection it may be said, that the barn swallow constructs its mudcupped nest on the side of cliff or cave when the barns of the valleys are not to its liking. The Say phoebe which in spring charms the verdant hillsides with its sad "phee be", in our experience nests usually beneath bridges, but where these are unavailable it does attach its felted habitation to canyon rocks. The western white throated swift (*Aeronautes saxatalis saxatalis*) is so partial to the higher cliffs and peaks that we do not recall having taken one; but it does glue its nest to a cave or rock and sally forth over pine and fir to snap its insects from the air. By the way, the swifts are more closely related to the humming birds than to the swallows.

153

MAY 15

Where the turbulent silt-laden mountain creek tears beneath un-melted mounds of fir-sheltered snow, the cover of winter yet prevails with its eternal green of conifers, but with it is the olive of leafing aspens. The brook is agitated, swollen, angry, and aerated with foam, forming sandy bottoms in miniature bayous aside the current. Dogwoods show maroon branches; a white butterfly sports in the breezy air; gloomy dens of shade show beneath the steep, fir-shrouded slopes of the canyon-side; but everywhere there is vigor and promise—healthy, all powerful nature awakening from its slumber. The higher the altitude the less the time to bloom and seed, but except on the loftiest peaks, where snow lingers until summer, life flourishes as in the valleys below.

Today on the shrubs of a foothill a male lazuli bunting (*Passerina amoena*) is singing rapturously, his turquoise blue upper parts and cinnamon breast showing clearly in the morning sun, in striking con-trast with his demure brown mate flitting a few feet away. His song is varied, but after many efforts we record it as "Chic chic chic chic cha la cha la te te te te".

There is much activity on our favored retreat, Farmington bay. Mallards are nesting in many roadside tufts of grass, some of the eggs being almost covered with down, and all of the nests being so placed under overhanging weeds that they are unnoticeable even a yard away. The yellow-headed blackbirds are making many squeaky noises, and the male redwings are chasing their mates in speed little short of that of the western willets.

Wilson phalaropes, usually three females to one male, are tame and active. It is interesting to watch them peck bugs from grass blades as well as from the clear water. A pair of black-necked stilts are very handsome with the intense black and white of their plumes; and their pink legs add to their beauty. Seen within a few feet, they convince one of their surprising neatness and dignity.

Tree swallows and northern violet green are together along the valley wires, the former showing steel blue where the latter display green; furthermore, the northern violet green shows a conspicuous white rump patch as it flies. Sweet and graceful birds, they almost touch as they wing their way, although the only note they utter is a weak "tsip", sometimes repeated.

We have come to believe that bird songs are not so much the ex-pression of love as of ebullient well-being and ecstasy; indeed, if it were merely the accompaniment of mating, the house sparrow, which cannot sing a note, would be the most rhapsodic of them all.

MAY 16

If it were our lot to be a water bird, we should choose to be a Canadian goose; this on account of its intelligence, resourcefulness, fidelity, beauty and happy gregarious life; but if we had to be a shore bird we should be a black-necked stilt. Compared with avocets, the stilts wade in fresher water and their feeding habits are daintier; furthermore, being ordinarily unsought by the gunner, they live on placid lagoons in sunny tranquility. Black bellied plovers and killdeers appeal to us very much, but the die is cast—we shall be black-necked stilts if the myths of Plato result in the great transmigration.

With its adornment of black extending along the rear of head and neck, its ebony black bill, white under plumage, and pinkish legs and feet, a stilt is as handsome as a model, standing out among other birds in form and carriage as well as in color and habits. It is an aristocrat, somewhat aloof yet not supercilious. It nips beetle and bug from the surface of water, whereas willets, marbled godwits, long-billed dowitchers and long-billed curlews probe or drill with their beaks into mud, the willets afterward frequently swashing the sticky stuff away. Coots not only paddle in mud but also have cruel social habits and offensive grunts; the voice of the yellow-headed blackbird is unpleasantly strident; pelicans have too much bill for beauty notwithstanding the easy grace of their lofty flight; gulls are greedy and intolerant; bitterns are snakelike; Treganza herons and black-crowned night herons are too lonely; phalaropes are too nearly reversed sexually; and the grebes are too much like fish. We are impressed by the beauty, swiftness and delicacy of the black-bellied plover, and the quiet happiness of western sandpipers; indeed, if it did not act as if in constant apprehension and distress, the killdeer likewise would appeal.

Two hundred Wilson phalaropes are out there in the shallow pond today, some feeding and clucking, many more resting motionless among weeds. Superior adornment of the female is rare in nature.

Such is our good fortune while pondering these matters that a Wilson snipe alights on our post twelve feet away and poses unafraid of our presence. Its eyes are black, its bill long and water-beaded, as if the bird had a running nose; its head is held so close to its body that it appears neckless. It favors us with only an occasional glance; but, when suddenly it espies its mate flying two hundred yards away, it stands up very alert with neck extended and then dashes quickly towards its distant companion.

MAY 17

Following an almost record rainfall for twenty four hours with its subsequent snowfall, flowers are much drooped and broken, mountains are white and bird life is subdued. Parley's canyon shows little of blossom except for balsam roots, larkspurs, phlox and western wall flowers (*Erysimum capitatum*) on the southern exposures.

We listen to the song of a yellow warbler in the roadside maples. It is a simple little lay, which we record as "CHE CHE che ye la la", one of three onomatops we have made of its varied song. As we watch for a time the soft flight of a rough-wing swallow, our attention is drawn to a bird so large and black that the quick impression is of a distant aeroplane soaring into sight over the mountain knolls above us. It is a golden eagle, which with a wing spread of six or seven feet has a right to resemble a plane; furthermore, it soars with wings horizontal, not at an upward angle as does the redheaded turkey vulture. The sheer majesty of the eagle in comparison with lesser raptores wins our admiration. When seen from below it looks as black as a. raven, unless it be an immature bird whose white primaries and tail show to the wondering eye; furthermore it soars more gracefully and longer than does the bald eagle.

Down the canyon, choke cheries are leafing; but along the foot-hills wild sweet Williams show off their pretty clusters, some dark-pine, others nearly white, but all the same species.

We stop to pick an umbrella plant (*Lomatium simplex*), now in full bloom; and there at the road side sits a western chirpping sparrow (*Spizella passerina arizonae*), readily distinguished by its black eye-line white stripes above the eye, rufous cap and grey breast. It rests as if in contemplation; then utters a song that we record as "cha, cha, cha, cha, cha, cha, cha, chee-up". It flies to the ground where phloxes are growing among the tender grass. There also the greenish white flowers of the poison sage or death camas (*Zigadenus paniculatus*) are in bloom.

Whatever the day, whatever the time the mountains respond to the yearnings of hearts weary of artificial life.

It is unfortunate, that Utah's state flower, the sego lily (*Calochortus nuttallii*), with its white or cream-colored bloom, which is adorned with a *patch of purple* "like a candle-flame just above the yellow nectar-gland", and with its delicious bulb, should have as its neighbor on the saged hillsides that dangerous star lily, death camas or poison sego (*Zigadenus paniculatus*). The lethal one, with its white or greenish white flower and *greenish-yellow* glandular spot has a bulb that contains enough albumenoid poison to kill a man.

MAY 18

The western wood pewee (*Contopus richardsonii richardisonii*) is here, the last of migration's mighty throng. It is an interesting little flycatcher with grayish brown back, grayish underparts, very long wings, but no eye-ring. Nests taken here in July usually have three eggs; but, since the bird loves the wild forests, the habitation is little disturbed. We hear it on pine fledged mountain passes, a lonely little voice singing a sort of whistled "pip, pip, pip, pip, pee yee".

Both junipers (*J. utahensis* and *J. scopulorum*) are now in bloom; and the hackberry (*Celtis reticulata*) shows its greenish flowers from limestone cliffs.

We ramble from the mountain to a valley-orchard fringed with tall locusts and brook-grown willows. A dozen or more Rocky Mountain black-headed grosbeaks (*Pheucticus melanocephalus melanocephalus*) are here chasing with loud chatter from tree to tree. Once in awhile a grosbeak will utter an "eek" note. The Paiute Indian name "Uni-gu-eet" is imitative of the grosbeak's song. Bullock orioles (*Icterus bullockii bullockii*) are just as numerous and obstreperous. Robins, Arkansas flycatchers, and mourning doves are in nearly every tree, while, along the willow-row, yellow and Audubon warblers sing beside a beautiful lazuli bunting. In the early morning hours all nature is alive with the rapture of song, but as the sun becomes uncomfortably warm the birds rest from their exultation. Along the willows several green-backed goldfinches (*Spinus psaltria hesperophilus*) are flitting, their olive green backs, yellow breasts, black caps and black and white wings being very noticeable. That is a rare one here.

Every breeze sends showers of apple blossoms fluttering to the ground.

And in the sweet intimacy of the rose-planted yard, a bird with canary yellow body contrasted sharply with its black crown, wings and tail, flits to the fresh trickle of the fish pond; it is a pale goldfinch (*Spinus tristis palidus*). Welcome, finch, to the sanctum we adore.

The song of the goldfinch is not so rapturous or extended as that of some of the other finches hereabout; in fact it could be placed down as a simple "per-chic-o-pee". It is the color of the bird that gives it novelty and charm, for often at first glance it suggests a warbler. A bright yellow bird is not very common either in meadowland or alpine glade.

MAY 19

On the steep slopes of a deep, multi-treed ravine, where oak bushes now spread their full-sized leaves and dangle their withered blossoms, where cottonwoods arise in stalwart might from labryinthine caverns at their brook-moistened feet, a flower of striking scarlet is now displaying its funnelform blooms—the scarlet gilia (*Gilia aggregata*) one of the most solitary and conspicuous of mountain adornments. True, there on the other side of a small gully is a whole bed of Hedysarum (*Hedysarum publare*), but their rose-purple corollas lack the striking showiness of the gilia, which adorns the sandy, sage-brushed declivity where the sagebrush swift (*Sceloporus graciosus graciosus*) scampers with inquisitive jerkiness from one's footfall.

The red false mallow (*Malvastrum coccineum*) with pretty, brick-red flowers, five petaled, is blooming a few rods lower on the dry hillside; and there also is the four petaled, evening primrose (*Oenothera pallida*) with white corollas turning to rose.

Near an oak patch blooms a clump of beggar-ticks (*Lappula Redowskii occidentalis*), by courtesy called "wild forget me nots" but in reality stickseeds with tiny white flowers and prickled nutlets, the burs of annoyance when dry.

This little-visited, secluded ravine has all the charm of idyllic divertisement. Chicadees sing in the oak copses; robins fly about the high cottonwoods; and yellow warblers lend sylvan song to the darksome garniture of the brookside.

The distance between the busy activities of man and the pristine beauties of tranquil nature is often not miles, but rods, often but the ability to alter one's mental attitude towards it all. Indeed, one's love of nature may be such that he may at times not even care to orient himself to the crowds and noises of modern life but, on the contrary, to think of brooks, flowers, birds and trees while all about him are men, pavements and buildings. There is a sort of recreation in the memory of some copsy wood, some trout-darted pool, some scented glade.

Whatever one's vocation, in the busy activities of life, moments of bliss often come to the eyes or ears of him who lives nature, for it takes but a few notes of a wild song, a glance at a blooming vista, to awaken memories that are in a sense the realities of existence.

There is in nature, however, much more than the power to awaken aesthetic joy—it is the final hope of the intellectual that they might discover in it that most important of all things, a solution to the mystery of life. Biochemistry and physics, cytology and genetics, are leading us into strange fields, fields that might encourage the thought of individual sempiternity.

MAY 20

A fretful brooklet, mossy marked and clear;
A flowered glade where busy bees are heard;
Some noble spruces resinous and near—
Ah, there you'll find the broad-tailed humming bird.

Spreading our little table and opening our lounging chairs in a canyon nook, bedecked with gorgeous flowers, we prepare for lunch beside a rill as sweet and limpid as ever could flow through a naturalist's dream. It is a cherished place, enlivened by chicarees, which scamper and scold overhead in the shading pines.

As we enjoy our coffee and sandwiches, a humming bird frequently flies back and forth through the glade making a harsh "chwep" sound. Then one chases another and the sound becomes a high-pitched, insect-like series of notes like "zwee-zup-e-zup-e". We are so interested that we decide to collect the male for preservation as a specimen and for detailed study.

There it lies in the palm of our hand, the most remarkable bird in the world—a humming bird. No other group of birds displays such wondrous variegation of brilliant plumage; no other group has its manner of flight or obtainance of food; furthermore, like the water ouzel, which dives yonder bubbling pool, it belongs only to this hemisphere. It is a male broad-tailed humming bird (*Selasphorus playcerus platycercus*).

As we hold it in hand, we are surprised by the length of its neck, which appears to comprise nearly half of the total vertebrae column; furthermore, the outermost or longest primary of the wing is long and acuminate at the end. Whether this is the contrivance by which it produces that characteristic screech sound we do not know. In our boyhood days we whirled a flattened stick enough to find out that it will make a weird noise in accordance with its shape.

Although innumerable times we have noticed a humming bird perch on a twig or a wire, and on rare occasion, even on the perpendicular surface of a rock, we have never seen one walk; and no wonder, for, although its claws are sharp and curved, its feet and legs are so relatively weak that it can make no progress at all by trying to walk on a flat surface.

To see a humming bird's magnificent display of colors, one must watch the live bird when every movement changes the angle of the sun's rays upon the innumerable facets of its feathers, reflecting and refracting light as if through a prism or the cuts of a diamond. We get some play of color as we turn the bird in hand before the sun. It is mostly bronze-green above but its chin and throat are bright metallic reddish purple, whereas the female's chin and throat are white.

MAY 21

In our rambles today we drift into those delightful meadows at the mouth of Big Cottonwood canyon where milch cows are grazing among flowering choke cherries and hawthornes, and the side hills are adorned with wild sweet Williams and beggar ticks. Dandelions have gone to seed; and every breeze wafts the aerial carriers on their way.

It is a remarkably late season; for at 7350 feet the canyon, where on May 11th we once have enjoyed the virgin's bower in full bloom, the identical plant now is dry with leaves barely sprouting. The mound of snow beside it is three feet deep; but the long-crested jays and robins are therabout, enjoying themselves as if the spring were normal.

We drift downward again, stopping to watch a black-eyed long-tailed chicadee pecking at the flowered catkins of a narrow leaved cotton-wood tree, those catkins that come before the leaves. We know it is a long-tailed because it has no white stripe over its eye. We record it's sweet song as "chic-a-dee-dee".

Further down the canyon on the side of the road in little clumps is blooming the golden corydal (*Corydalis aurea*), a sweet member of the Fumitory family with yellow flowers, the outer petals of which are elongated into a spur half as long as the entire corolla. Capnoides, given by some of the generic name, is from the Greek "smoke-like" in reference to the peculiar smoky odor of some of the species, as in the hedge fumitory. It is reported by some that *C. montanum*, in which the spur is as long as the corolla, is more common than *aurea*, but the reverse is likely the fact.

As we write this in the evening two beetles are buzzing at the window; and when we capture them the wonder is that they have wings beneath the outer shells.

Beneath dried brown grass, tender light green grass begins to show; indeed, one may seldom disturb an upper browned crust of leaves or limbs without finding pale but vigorous young life below. A few weeks of sunshine will change seeping snow to vernal bloom. Nature is like man—it lives that it might have joy, the joy of spring. Every true naturalist is consoled by a serene and imperturbable spirit, a feeling of consonancy with that which ignores the vanities of mankind.

In our peregrinations abroad we came upon greener mountains and meadows than those here, but throughout the world the land of one's birth never loses its primary appeal.

MAY 22

In those extraordinary bird-havens and reed-covered sloughs where the Bear, Weber, and Jordan rivers flow into the Great Salt Lake there are now many nests in the full warmth of incubation; and a ramble about the marshes discloses a variety of bird life unexcelled anywhere else in the world.

There, for instance, floating on a mass of old cat-tails and rubbish, rests the nest of the western grebe with four eggs of bluish white, and, similarly constructed of spare dried reeds, nearby appears the nest of the aggressive black tern with its three brown-mottled eggs. How these terns resent our intrusion, how they scream and dart at our heads! Their note is a shrill, prolonged somewhat metallic "kraick".

Over yonder in the thick grass of the dry ground off shore, is the downy nest of the gadwall, with its dozen creamy eggs; and a little further from the slough, but constructed in the same manner in the heavy grass, the nest of the green-winged teal (*Anas carolinesis*) comes to view, this time with eighteen eggs, a third more than usual. Swiftest of the ducks, this teal speeds overhead at eighty miles an hour or more, and one wonders how even that fastest of birds, the duck hawk, ever catches it.

Turning to the slough and wading through a dense patch of reeds, we suddenly come upon the nest of a black-crowned night heron (*Ncyticorax nycictorax hoactli*), fixed six feet above water and adorned with four bluish green eggs. The flushed bird utters a hoarse "kwock" as we approach.

But come!—over in the salt-grass meadow there bubbles a deep, clear spring fringed with cat-tails. A foot above the water is a shallow nest of reeds and grasses resting on prostrate stocks, the home of the delightful little Virginia rail (*Rallus limicola limicola*), whose nest is built layer on layer above the water. Its ten, light-buff eggs are spotted, especially on the larger end, with cinnamon-brown. The disturbed little lady utters "ca-ca-ca", high-pitched and cackle-like. But stop! over there, deeper in the water is a reed-basket, the nest of the sora rail (*Porzana carolina*) with eighteen eggs literally stacked round on round to the very top. It is deeply fabricated and anchored only to the slenderest grass, which barely keeps it from touching the water. We have always admired the pattern of the egg-arrangement of this pleasing nest. Her voice is more like a repetition of the word "quink", not a "ca" like the other rail.

At the edge of the same reedy spring beneath a willow branch concealed in the dry grass, is the nest of the Wilson snipe, extraordinary bird which in the moonlight and on cloudy days winnows mysteriously in the sky, with a sound somewhat like a rapid "do-do-do-do-do-do" which is made by the air rushing through the tail.

MAY 23

We lunch in a pleasing locale at 7500 feet altitude in Big Cotton-wood canyon where the mountainside is splotched with snow and torrents cascade the gulches. The central stream is honey-yellow in color, overflowing and angry, as if determined to rear and tear. The delightful place is inhabited by three or four pairs of long-crested jays, which winter and summer have learned that human beings there are not greatly to be feared.

These sky-colored birds approach curiously and finally fly to a limb only eight feet from us for pieces of bread, affording us a pleasing opportunity for close study of their mannerisms and voices.

Upon tasting the feast, a male jay hurries with a bit of the food a hundred yards away; but he returns with his mate. They are almost indistinguishable in color; nevertheless a few feet away, the female appears slightly smaller and paler. Alighting on a spruce limb near, she still seems reluctant; so he flies to her, grasps her bill gently with his own, as much as to say, "This is all I'm going to bring you; if you want more it's down there"! At any rate she immediately thereafter flies to the ground, picks up a piece of bread and hastens to the spruce to eat it.

We watch them; in eating the bread they hold it with their feet and peck at it as if it were a nut to be broken.

Then other jays approach, and there is a medley of sound. The loudest is a raspy "chaa, chaa, chaa, chaa, chaa", the "chaa" being repeated usually five times but sometimes as much as ten. This can be heard two hundred yards away. Unlike the male, the female flaps her wings every time she utters the "squaa". Once as she flies to the ground she gives a "qua" sound, then a contended "qumb" as she finds it. Then several of the birds give vent to a long chutter, somewhat like that of squirrels but resembling the clicking of a large fishing reel. One meows like a cat; another issues a throaty "uowl", reminding us of certain expressions of the redwing.

Then there is silence again, the usual habit as they feed.

We ramble in the woods, hoping to get at least one spring flower. The aspens have caterpillar like catkins of green and garnet; and at last we find a solitary wild candytuft (*Thalaspi colorandense*) with its sweet, tiny white blooms.

MAY 24

Blue eyes in human beings are frequently attractive and sometimes very beautiful, but none of the birds that we know is so adorned. During recent years we have habitually used eight power marine field glasses, with the result that we have frequently been able not only to determine the colors of live birds' eyes, but also descry their eyelid movements and often distinguish iris from pupil. A duck-club-house is unexcelled for such study. We have made color notations of specimens observed and checked them with Ridgway's technical descriptions whenever he has mentioned the iris; and we are now prepared to give a resume' of our findings.

The result is surprising—of the 173 birds investigated 155 or 89.6% proved to have eyes of various shades of brown. These browns were distributed as follows: blackish brown, 2; dark brown, 47; brown, 94; light brown, 2; reddish brown, 10.

Of the remaining 18 birds 10 had lemon yellow eyes, 2 orange and 5 red.

Thus we found that all the plovers, snipes, phalaropes, avocets and stilts, terns and gulls visting these parts have brown eyes, except the blacknecked stilt, which has an iris of carmine red, and the ring-billed gull (*Larus delawarensis*) whose eyes are light yellow.

Both the Virginia rail and the sora rail have red eyes, those of the Virginia being the brighter in color. The eyes of the coot are likewise red or reddish brown. We have never taken a sandhill crane.

All of the swans, geese, and ducks taken hereabout have brown eyes, with these notable exceptions: the eyes of the cinnamon teal are orange; those of the shoveler, red head, the scaups, and the hooded merganser, are yellow; the eyes of the wood duck vary from orange to vermillion; the canvas back has red eyes; the eyes of the golden eye are, of course, golden yellow; and the red breasted merganser has eyes of a deep red tone. The oddest coloration of all appears in the rare old squaw whose eyes vary from hazel, straw and carmine, to white, and whose eyelids, even, are white.

It would be interesting if someone would undertake to study the colors of the tongues of birds and mammals, for there must be some surprising variations.

MAY 25

All of the owls we have observed had lemon yellow eyes, and our night hawks have eyes so dark brown as to be almost black. The eyes of our woodpeckers are in the reddish brown category. Our swallows, waxwings, grouse, quail, sage hen, vulture, Swainson hawk, rough-legged hawk, golden eagle, duck hawk, pigeon hawk, sparrow hawk, vireos, shrikes, crows, jays, titmice, nuthatches and wrens have brown eyes of varying hues. Strangely, our goshawk, sharp-shinned hawk, bald eagle, marsh hawk and osprey have yellow eyes, mostly light yellow. The red-eyed vireo does not inhabit these mountains, and we have seen the carmine-eyed phainopepla (*Phainopepla nitens lepida*) only in the southwestern part of Utah, where also occurs the red-eyed cactus wren (*Campylorhynchus brunneicapillus couesi*).

All of our members of the *Icteridae* (meadowlark, blackbirds, orioles) have brown eyes, as do all of the warblers and the *Fringillidae* (grosbeaks, sparrows, finches), except that the eyes of the slate-colored junco (*Junco hyemalis hyemalis*) are claret purple and those of the green-tailed towhee (*Chlorura chlorura*) are cinnamon or vinaceous.

Among the humming birds, swifts, thrushes, larks and flycatchers the brown-eyed rule prevails except that the sage thrasher (*Oreoscoptes montanus*) has lemon yellow eyes. By the way, the hot desert region at the southwest corner of Utah is inhabited by two yellow-eyed birds, Leconte's thrasher (*Toxostoma lancontei lecontei*) and Crissal thrasher (*Toxostoma dorsale coloradense*) the young birds of which actually have whitish eyes.

This resume' does not consider the eagles, hawks, grouse, ducks, geese, ibises, swans, herons, bitterns, grebes and loons, which must await their turn; but enough has been said to show that nature loves eyes of brown.

In reviewing our notes made through many years, we discover that we have recorded very few observations on the color of the eyes of mammals, even when having excellent opportunity to do so; and it is no consolation that other mammalogists, even in their original description of species, have usually neglected to furnish these data, although they have given in detail the colors of the head, including the region *around* the eye.

MAY 26

The verdant mountain slopes of Emigration canyon at 6200 feet are very interesting in floral beauty. Seen from a distance, they look green, for the scrub oaks are in full leafage, while grass and sage abound on the drier hillsides. To closer view, however, flowers appear: the yellow dots are the mule ears (*Wyethia amplexicaulis*) but not so sturdy and high as those of the valleys; and the rose-purple beds of flowers blooming among the sage brushes are the *Hedysarum pabulare*. Here and there a big sunflower or balsam root yet shows its great yellow bloom, but for the most part it has given way to the Wyethia.

There also beside the oaks the wild hyacinth (*Brodilaea Douglasii*) is blooming with half a dozen, podlike, purplish blue flowers on the top of a round, leafless scape or flower stem nearly a foot high. Each flower pod is marked by eight longitudinal stripes of dark blue, but the whole flower has little if any fragrance. Nearby, the wild onion (*Allium acuminatum*) is growing with its blossoms on an equally long, barescape or stem; for both belong to the lily family. The flower of the onion, however, is ecclesiastic purple, bell shaped and, strange to say, with three outer, pointed sepals inclosing three inner smaller petals. We notice no onion smell, though "allium" in Latin means "garlic".

In places the hills display red, white and blue tints, the red being the *Hedysarum,* the blue being the penstemon (*Penstemon cyananthus*) and the white being the little beggar ticks. The penstemons are truly beautiful with their tubular mouth-opening flowers on long round stems adorned by opposite heartshaped leaves. Some of the flowers (*P. brevifolius*) are abbey blue, others (*P. Kingii*) wistaria blue at the mouth and hortense violet at the base.

There also the geranium (*Geranium Fremontii*) is blooming with its open-faced five petalled flowers of dark pink or liseran purple; the nine bark (*Physocarous malvaceus*) with its lovely, sweet-smelling white flowers, the shrub that in autumn will adorn the oak copses and moist hillsides with maroon; and on the gravelly embankments the partridge berry, that sweet smelling member of the honeysuckle family, is abloom with little bells of delicate pink.

Sweet birds sing their chansonettes in the brook-dashed shrubbery or whistle their tender cheeps and lays in the solemn labryinths of lofty pines; the grassy vales and verdured knolls are bedecked with lovely flowers; and the sky is as blue as the vaulted heaven of one's dream—for what more pleasant and inspiring could one ask?

MAY 27

On the grassy edge of an upland field, two beds of beautiful flowers are blooming: one is that winsome member of the mallow family known as the globe or red false mallow (*Sphaeralcea coccinea*) with brick red flowers about half an inch wide, each throated with pallid yellow and pale green; the other is the wild onion (*Allium acuminatum*) with delightful flowers of dark rose purple. Both are much more attractive than the sweet William blooming near them.

A plant that just now fills with gold the wet borrow pits along valley highways is the strawberry buttercup or trailing buttercup (*Ranunculus cymbalaria*). Even though this flower is more or less weed-like in habit, there is no more charming and beautiful blossom. Pick a single flower and see how brilliantly gold and waxy it is. The foliage too is artistically shaped and cut, a dull green contrast to its excitingly vivid golden cups. Small yellow flowers unless unusually shaped or surrounded with complementary green foliage are not so striking as some of the other colors, but when dipped in wax, as is this little butter-cup,—one is reminded of bright freshly churned butter.

Leaving these roadside blooms, we spend an hour on Farmington bay, where nesting is at its height. The black-necked stilts give their "whuck whuck" calls from a distance, fluttering their wings in anger and looking at us menacingly, as they wade and stare at us with their rosy carmine eyes. A pair of avocets "till till till" with their piercing calls; and three fluffy young ones run by them to grass protection. The willets laugh at us with apprehension, as if saying "wek wek wek".

The only new bird we see is a western solitary sandpiper (*Tringa solitaria cinnamomea*). It is a dark bird and almost white below; and, though it looks somewhat like a lesser yellow legs, its legs appear more lead color than yellow. It is alone, but not apprehensive of our presence. It feeds along a brookside and on occasion runs quite rapidly from us, as it utters a plaintive "peep peep".

On our return we notice at the side of the railroad track a tall yellow flower of conspicuous brightness. It turns out to be Dyer's Wood (*Isatis tinctoria*). The flowers are individually infinitesimal but to-gether they hang in panicled racemes like dangled fringes of delicate crochet work. The stems are strong and bare, but the floral top is delightful when examined with the glass.

The truth is, that, with the exception of large flowers, such as the garden dahlias and zinnias, most flowers greatly reward the use of a hand glass, for under it the delicacies of tint and hue, the conformations of anthers and filaments, of stigma, style and ovary, impress one with the unfathomable mystery of life.

MAY 28

Human beings are like the plants and trees of the forested hills and seeping glades. Over there, vigorous baby shoots of the elderberry are coming forth, and tender blades of grass are rising beside trickling rills. Youthful quaking aspens stand about the mountain park, some of them as slender as a baby's arm, most of them bent at the lower trunk by the burdening snow of two winters. Interspersed among them, some aspens with six inch trunks are straight as arrows above the five foot level of winter snow. All of them have the vigorous catkins of maturity. Here and there mighty spruce trees stand with trunks a foot and a half in thickness, trunks scarred and roughened by the perilous hours of a century's storms, by the heedless axe and by the sudden change of dripping water to pressure ice. They are the old men of the woods, still dropping their seeded cones, still harboring the spermophile in runways by their ancient roots, still resisting with non-pliant limbs the swift incursion of gale, but ever growing older, more brittle, more scarred and torn. To them, if they were men, would belong the wisdom of experience in the woodland; to them, the counsel, if such could be, of all the younger things. And then at last there is the graveyard—here a prostrate trunk, wormeaten but yet in form, there a fallen monarch overgrown with grass still holding the sod in the semblance of its form; there again, the gray rotting leaves of many a former year, the immediate transition to mother mold.

Nature is full of strange oddities of shape and behaviour. That wonderful little mushroom known as the stinkhorn (*Phallus impudicus*), for instance, is in the immature stage so similar to an uninteresting puffball that without recognizing it one might kick it aside. Pick one up, cut in in two, and a surprising interior is revealed. The pink "egg-shell" or peridium is lined with a jelly mash; then there are two dark saddle bags destined to form the green mass of the mature cap; then the future stem, and finally the compressed cells. We have the embryonic stage of a mushroom designed to attract flies and to stick its spores upon their legs. Thus an ingenious provision of nature might to the unknowing eye be but another prosaic fungus.

Few scenes are more delightful than the sweet scented alfalfa field of the valley. Busy bees, pretty butterflies, meadowlarks, red winged blackbirds, gulls, varicolored blossoms—these are nearly always present, lending their charm to the ceaseless clatter of the mower, and filling with interest the task of the toiler. Merely to sit resting on a cock of fragrant newly mown hay and to gaze at the mammoth white clouds floating through the deep blue sky, is to enjoy the rarity of undisturbed contemplation. The deepest thoughts of life come to one alone in such a field, alone in an idle boat, alone at the top of lofty mountains, or working in the soil of the good earth.

MAY 29

Venturing to the slippery edge of the waterfall at the confluence of the North and Main forks of City Creek canyon, we flush a water ouzel from a spray-dripped niche. She idles a few feet away, giving a characteristic little bob about once a second. This is neither a teeter nor a nod but a perpendicular movement of the body up and down about an inch, the legs bending or crouching each time. Heretofore we had thought the bird had a nodding or teetering movement forward.

By the way, the water ouzel or dipper belongs to the family *Cinclidae*, Dippers; and being curious to ascertain whether the word dipper refers to this bird's habit of plunging or dipping into the water or to its habit of raising itself up and down with a curtsy or dip, we pause for a moment to see what we can work out. The word *Cinclidae*, as well as the generic name *Cinclus*, has its origin, so far as we can see, not in the Greek word for lattice or opening, nor in the Greek for some bird, as many suppose, but in the Greek word (CINESIS), which, as used by Plato, meant "movement", "motion", and, as used by Lucian, "a dance". Our conclusion, therefore, is that "dipper" refers to the up and down movement, dip or dance of the bird, as, for instance, when it stands on a brookside rock, and not to its habit of taking a dip, or plunging into the water.

Apprehensive of our intrusion, the dipper's mate flies to the rocky edge of the very brink of the fall and utters his protestation by a chatter resembling "ching ching ching ching ching ching", more rapidly than one can count the individual notes, and with a thin, tinkle like sound as if a large fishing reel were clicking. We can hear it distinctly above the roar of the fall.

One of the birds proceeds to peck at some moss, as if finding bugs, and we do not disturb them further.

A ground squirrel (*C. armatus*), seeking crumbs from our canyon table, prefers an imported seeded canteloupe to bread. Another of his kind, male or female we do not know, intrudes upon his domain, and after a few minutes of angry whistling our friend pounces upon it and twirls in a ball of fury. It is soon over, without casualty, and the impudent one scurries from the glade. The call note of this ground squirrel is a short whistle, birdlike, sharp and vibrant.

It is always somewhat difficult to make an onomatop, that is a lettered or syllabic imitation of a bird's song. It is obvious that our alphabet was constructed for human beings who have hard teeth, soft lips, enabling them to distinguish between labials and dentals; but a bird has only a hard beak, without teeth or soft lips, its palate is different and it is not constructed to emit nasals. We humans, by the position of lips and teeth, are able to master more consonants than the bird can; but usually we are able, in making an onomatop, to approximate the voice of the bird. I often give it up, then keep trying.

MAY 30

In the high reaches of Little Cottonwood canyon (7350 feet), where the idyllic creek bounds down between huge blocks of granite, and the brook of a side-gully cascades with such turbulency that in the distance it resembles a sparkling ribbon of snow, leaves are only half grown on cottonwood and aspens; indeed, some of the aspens are yet in the catkin stage.

We sit beside a granite block in a crack of which a ground squirrel (*C. armatus*) has taken refuge to view us warily. The stone is overgrown with a rust-colored lichen, which as we scrape it off brings tiny particles of granite with it. Great cracks split the huge block, leading us to realize that water and freezing temperature are important factors of disintegration but not more so than the patient lichens.

On the way down the canyon we find two delphiniums blooming in a seeping covert at the roadside—*D. bicolor* with white flowers and blue veins, and *D. menziesii* with dark blue corollas. In this same shady nook is blooming the wild spikenard (*Smilacina amplexicaulis*) with lanceolate leaves half a foot long and a terminal panicle of numerous, very small white flowers. "Delphinium" is a Latin reference to a dragon.

In the same place we find a single stemmed plant with sessile leaves and tiny whitish bell shaped flowers; it is a member of the mustard family known as rock cress (*Arabis holbcellii*). There also is a tiny star flower (*Tellima parviflora*) showing its five white petals.

On an oak is a gall made by a gallfly, probably *Plagiotrichus frequens*. This fly in the spring lays its eggs in a young oak-bud, and the resulting legless larvae cause the deforming gall, which is a food and pupal development chamber.

Nature seldom grieves for its dead. It is true that a she-grizzly will with vengeful eyes amble about the body of her slain cub for a day or more, that sometimes a dog will repine and die on the grave of its master, and that a red-tailed hawk, which like most hawks mates for life, has been known after its mate was killed to languish unmated for two years about the old nest, as if broken-hearted, but usually birds and mammals drift away when the body of a stricken companion becomes cold. Bacteria make quick work of a carcass, and even the hard antlers of a deer are soon gnawed away by porcupines and mice seeking their salty flavor. There is no memorial day among the creatures of the wild lands.

MAY 31

In those pleasant mountains between Provo river and American Fork canyon there is just now not only a multiformity of bird life but also a fresh and vigorous display of floral beauty. Even as one leaves the Provo river with its labryinthine willows enlivened by the dulcet notes of warblers, he is, at 5000 feet altitude, apt to see on a dry gravelly roadside a flower of startling redness growing there. It is the scarlet bugler or red penstemon (*Penstemon eatoni*); and as we hold one in hand, after clambering up a rocky slide to get it, we admire the vividness of its small trumpet flowers. It prefers the hottest, driest, barest slopes, as if designed by nature to adorn the forbidding places. We have not noticed it elsewhere in the Wasatch mountains.

Proceeding up Willow Hollow creek, we observe that choke cherries are hanging their blossoms in white, fragrant racemes; and that the "beggar ticks" and hedysarum are likewise in full bloom.

At 6550 feet, in the vicinity of Aspen Grove, we unexpectedly come upon a unique plant—almost literally a leafy post five feet high! It is the American columbo or green gentian (*Frasera speciosa*) with smooth green leaves ten inches long and half as wide, growing in whorls, and with delicate, greenish white or lavender flowers appearing in a leafy thyrse or mixed flower cluster.

A penstemon, this time with lovely dark blue bells (*Penstemon cyananthus*), stands beside the sage bushes at 6600 feet; and a little higher (7100 feet) the blue flowers of the aconite or monkshood (*Aconitum columbianum*) appear in damp places.

At noontime we rest within a forest of pristine aspen trees at an altitude of 7650 feet. The halcyon sky is as blue as a Yale flag; nevertheless there is just enough breeze to keep the aspen leaves atremble, and to imitate the sound of distant falling waters. Some of the aspens are monarchs of their kind, sixty feet tall with white trunks nearly a foot in diameter, and in fact the finest specimens we know in all the Wasatch. A babble-noted brooklet in a glade shows on its bank the footprints of mule deer (*Odocoileus hemionus hemionus*): and, as we examine them, we joyously catch sight of that bushy sister of the Virgins bower, the silky, bushy or swamp clematis (*Clematis hirsutissima*) with its pretty purple bells growing on long stems above the bush. Each flower is over an inch long and nearly as wide, with yellow stamens crowded in the bell. As we descend the American Fork side we come upon the Virgins bower itself, rare and beautiful, drooping and trailing its four sepaled, purple stars, if "stars" we may call them, over shady glades of maples.

While resting beneath a wayside fir, we compare the track of the mule deer with that of the elk in these mountains. The elk's footprint is at least an inch longer and, in walking, an elk steps nearly six inches further at each footfall. One could hardly mistake one for the other. An elk's track is not open in the center, like that of a cow.

JUNE 1

Once in a while we chance upon flowers so rare and either so charming or outstanding that we retain them in memory like sweet ornaments and mementos of our sanctuarii. Thus, for instance, yesterday we felt the joy of discovering the silky Clematis bushes in the seepy glade of an alpine grove of aspens, timid flowers surrounded by the skeletoned whiteness of the tree trunks; and then later of coming upon the wide-eyed purple flowers of the Virgins bower itself coyly creeping over the verdured forest floor; but we did not mention that at 5000 feet altitude down the canyon we suddenly descried a five petalled bright yellow flower actually blooming on a rocky or rather shaly side in the full exposure of a hot afternoon sun. As we clambered after it the entire plant looked rough, thistle-like, indeed like a branched thistle with brilliant yellow stars. There it was, the blazing or evening star (*Mentzelia laevicaulis*), a flower of wondrous beauty on branches with wedge-shaped, saw-edged leaves as rough and hairy as a man's unshaved chin. We gathered the extraordinary plant and noticed that not all of its flowers were open.

When we reached home at night it had opened to display all its brilliant yellow beauty. Seventy five stamens stood up from the center of the flower, like yellow bristles with terminal knobs, and the five petals extended out like a star.

There are four species of Mentzelia in the Wasatch mountains, all members of the Loasaceae or Loasa family: the small-flowered one (*M. dispersa*) occurs on the seeping banks of streams; another (*M. albicaulis*) likes sandy soil; while *M. latifolia* prefers the sandy banks of the mountain foothills, the last named being diurnal. When we think of the evening primroses we must also recall the startling flowers of evening, the mentzelias. Like the red penstemon or scarlet bugler they thrive in rocky, dry, forbidding places; yet after all such is nature's never ending compensation. We forgot to mention where we gathered the Mentzelia, we also found a flower like a yellow coxcomb, in reality called the Prince's plume (*Stanleya pinnata*).

Many boisterous canyon streams, some of them temporarily turbid with sand, are going to waste in the inland lake of brine. In this dry region, where fertile valleys are dependent upon irrigation, it is a shame; hence the time must come when every canyon, large or small, will have its reservoir to hold the run-off of spring. Sweet waters should never reach a dead sea. That is why our summer mountain parks are so pleasant and verdant—they still have the springs, brooks and creeks created by winter's snow.

JUNE 2

At the entrance to Parley's canyon (4850 feet), one of the finest of the penstemons (*Penstmon platyphyllus*) is blooming among the red rocks of the hillside, its lavender-violet corollas making pretty colored patches. This penstemon has a slightly broader leaf than that of *Penstemon leonardi,* which it otherwise resembles very closely.

Nearer the creek but in the same vicinity, a big flower somewhat like a hollyhock is now in bloom; it is the Rose of Sharon (*Sphaeralcea rivularis*), a member of the mallow family with palmalety lobed leaves as much as six inches across and with beautiful cosmos pink flowers nearly two inches in diameter.

Yellow clover (*Medicago officinalis*) blooms on the roadside; the wild rose (*Rosa Woodsii*) shows its pink flowers along the creek; and thistles (*Cirsium undulatum*) with white, woolly stocks and purplish flowers stand conspicuously on the dry places.

Higher up the canyon (5400 feet) the pink flower bells of the partridge berry, sweet member of the honeysuckle family, show now and again among the choke cherries, which themselves are everywhere dangling their white blooms. The blue elderberry is likewise unfolding creamy white, fragrant flowers.

At a slightly higher elevation (5400 feet) one of the finest of the penstemons absorbs our attention: it is the one commonly called blue-bells (*Penstemon cyananthus*). Close examination of its corollas discloses them to be campanula blue, lovely flowers adorning the top of a smooth-leaved stem. There are eight penstemons in these mountains, one red, four blue and three violet-purple, but none, except possibly the scarlet bugler, is more delightful to the eye than *cyananthus,* though it must be admitted that *Eatoni* or the "scarlet bugler", as it is called, adorns the barest, least inviting landscapes.

Pale blue lupines (*Lupinus brevicaulis*) still ornament the hills; and higher up the canyon (5700 feet) wild Fremont geraniums show their pink-purple petals on the creek side; and all the hills are yellowed with sunflowers (*Wyethia amplexicaulis*), mule ears, and little sun-flowers (*Helianthella uniflora*).

It is pleasant to think of immortality, but only if it be in a place where the joyful vigors of life will be continued without disease or pain, where flowers bloom and birds sing, where love and romance prevail, and where ever changing progressive development is the goal. Any heaven that offers man a mere state of ecstatic abstraction seems incongruous as we look upon the reality of nature in spring.

JUNE 3

On the embankment at the very entrance to Lamb's canyon (5900 feet), a little shrub invokes the exclamation "tiny snowball"; but it is that fragrant member of the buckthorn family properly called snow brush (*Ceanothus volutinus*) or mountain lilac, though sometimes quaintly designated as mountain "laurel". At any rate, its flowers are white snowballs about one inch in diameter, so fragrant that for hours after one is plucked it exhales a subtle sweetness. Its subcordate leaves are thick, smooth and leathery, giving the impression that they are evergreen; furthermore, they appear to be lacquered! Remember — varnished leaves.

Further up (6300 feet) this ever coolsome, shaded canyon there is an array of floral beauty. Choke cherries dangle their white blossoms over every turn of the roadway; and the Indian paint brush (*Castilleja angustifolia*) is beginning to show a red head. The blue bells (*Penstemon cyananthus*) are fairly common; but there on a seepy cliff is a dwarf penstemon (*Penstemon brevifolius*) with deep blue corollas and weak slender stems branching from a woody caudex. It is a rare plant and one so favorable to the clefts of rocks that it perhaps is seldom noticed except by those who enthuse over all the penstemons.

A cat breeches (*Hydrophyllum occidentale*) now is in seed, holding out little puffs of green, round as balls not over an inch in diameter, beset with black hairs protruding.

Over yonder in the labyrinth of the willowed creek is a plant that looks like a single-stemmed strawberry two feet high with five petalled yellow flowers ready to bloom. It is a relative of the strawberry, in fact; the cinquefoil (*Potentilla glandulose*). Near it is a *Chaenactis Douglasii* with half inch knobs of orange at the end of a stem about a foot high. The thimble or salmon berry (*Rubus parviflorus*) likewise spreads its large maplelike leaves and shows white flowers over an inch across with yellowish brown centers. Nearby also is the *Chaenactis stevioides* with shredded leaves and small woolly flowers of pinkish white; and close to it stands the wild spikenard three feet high with tiny white flowers in a racemose panicle. Finally in the same delightful glade is blooming the star flower or wild lily of the valley (*Smilacena sessilifolia*) with its minute white stars; and that frail little flower chickweed (*Stellaris jamesiana*) that loves to nestle among the trees of the mountains.

JUNE 4

In Lamb's canyon (6500 feet) the Virgin's bower is climbing with violet blooms beneath trees and over green underbrush, on the north-facing, damper part of a ravine. When Keats wrote of "Virgin's bower, trailing airily" he aptly described it as we see it in our mountains, though he referred to the British climbing shrub *Clematis Vitalba*, sometimes called in Europe "traveller's joy". The sense of exquisite satisfaction at the power of nature thus to decorate its gloomy places that comes over one upon first sight of this purple trailer of the woods is well depicted in the words "traveler's joy".

The first use of the words "Virgin's bower" to describe this plant was probably by John Gerarde, who, in 1597 in "The herball or general historie of plants" wrote "Vpright clamberer or Virgins Bower, is also a kinde of clematis".

Many have thought that the Virgin's bower would be pretty when trailed over lattice work in the back garden; yet, when the attempt at transplanting is made, it is found that unlike the penstemons it does not readily adapt itself to the lower altitudes of the Wasatch valleys, usually over two thousand feet down from its natural habitat. The silky, swamp or bushy clematis prefers even higher ground than the climbing variety; but the white one likes the oak patches of the valley sides lower down.

In admitting exultation over the Virgin's bower, one must not forget that at 6500 feet Lamb's canyon still displays the white blooms of the service berry and the bluebells of the mertensia; but all thought recurs to the Virgin's bower.

> Like elves enbonneted in purple gay
> The Virgins bowers shyly twine the trail;
> In fragile beauty, droop and gently sway
> Through shaded woods of piney hill and dale.

Today every cove below seeping canyon walls, every comb down which water in turbulency descends, is filled with the songs of robin, warbler, ouzel or thrush. The ears are delighted by first one song then another, then one glimpse after another of robins with their mature-sized young, ouzels with their sprayed fledglings, and thrushes with their covert nests between cobwebs and creeping caterpillars but always within sound of the singing brooks. Leafage creeps higher and higher, inviting both nesting and song.

Unlike the spring-fed runnel of a piney glade, the canyon creek or freshet of spring is so laden with grit and debris that it is translucent without being transparent; that is, it so diffuses them as to render rocks and other objects lying along its bottom not clearly visible. It is not limpid or glassy until its turgid madness subsides.

A WASATCH SPRING

JUNE 5

In these day by day rambles we so frequently praise the avian beauties of the high coniferous forests of these mountains that it is interesting to list the birds that one may expect from time to time to find here. By "coniferous forests" we refer to those upper canyon ever-greened places where thrive such trees as the limber pine (*Pinus flexilis*), lodge pole or black pine (*Pinus murrayana*), blue spruce, Engelmann spruce (*Picea engelmanni*), Douglas fir (*Pseudotsuga taxifolia*), white firs or blister balsams (*Abies concolor*) and black balsams (*Abies lasiocarpa*). They comprise most of the sylva of the upper mountains, though not all of them occur throughout the entire range.

In these biotic districts in the course of a year's visitations one may expect to see more or less frequently: the water ouzel (*Cinclus mexicanus unicolor*), the long-tailed chickadee, the Audubon warbler, the gray-ruffed grouse, the Wright's flycatcher (*Empidonax wrightii*), the olive sided flycatcher (*Nuttallornis borealis borealis*), Natalie sapsucker (*Sphyrapicus thyroideus nataliae*), the pine siskin, the red-breasted nuthatch, the black-eared nuthatch, and the Rocky Mountain creeper (*Certhia famillaris montana*). Less often one may come upon those large gray crowlike birds known as Clark nutcrackers (*Nucifraga columbiana*), and Bendire crossbills are usually there when the pine cones appear, singing in joyous flocks, a sort of plaintive but continual "week". The ruby-crowned kinglet (*Corthylio calendula cineraceus*) prefers these forests, and the western tanager (*Piranga ludovicinana*), though oftener seen in the orchards of the valleys, sometimes visits them. The gray-headed junco breeds there, as does the Cassin purple finch.

Ever delightful are these darksome woods, though it takes many a patient and arduous hour for one to glimpse all the feathered inhabitants; nevertheless, some of them are precious rewards of any search.

Everywhere in the first week of June it seems that there is some-thing delightful to smell—the redolent firs of shaded gullies, the antelope brush of canyon sides, the aromatic sage with its new leaves, the sweet-scented fields of ripening alfalfa, and the honeysuckle along the backyard fence. Everywhere the rich chlorophyll of spring is en-couraging the beauty and fragrance of leaf and flower; everywhere bees are gathering pollen; everywhere birds are engaged in the duties of incubation and the rhapsody of song. What a joyous time merely to live! If one have health there should be little need of ethereal dreams.

JUNE 6

Imagine a loud music box which, when thrown into the sky, opens with a run of prestissimo notes and melodies that suddenly penetrate with sweet clarity to the listening ear. Strange thought; yet somehow it describes that ecstasy of bird song, irregular, disconnected, fantastic, that *capriccietto* outburst into the heavens a moment ago by a bobolink in this grassy field. Never can one be startled more exquisitely than by this volley of canorous sounds. Its first hearing from the heavens lingers as a precious bit of memory, truly a "jugful" of notes.

Slightly larger than an English sparrow, the male bobolink, elsewhere called "reedbird" or "ricebird", is black save where his back and breast are marked with whitish ash and his outer primaries margined with yellowish; but his mate is brownish and streaked.

As we watch it now and follow it, a male continually alights on alfalfa stocks, flushing, singing *a capriccio* and settling again, ever watchful of his homely mate broding eggs on her nest.

It surprises one to know that this bird of rapturous roulade unexcelled in the variety and beauty of its melodic outbursts by any other American feathered lyrist, is treated with enmity by the rice-growers of the south, where it is sometimes called "skunk blackbird" in reference to its colors; nevertheless, no matter what its depredations of winter, it proves its economic value among us by eating weevils, grasshoppers, and weed seed. As we ponder them all the plain truth is, not a bird that sings in the fields hereabout does more harm than good; and, when one of them gives the meadows a rhapsody far more intricate and beautiful than that of the kitchen canary, it is welcome indeed.

It is not strange that the delectable love-songs of the bobolink should be heard at their best when two or three males are in ecstatic competition for the affection of some coy, sober female; but such is the way of wooing throughout the world.

One reason why the bobolink is not more frequently noticed hereabout is, that, being related to the meadowlarks and blackbirds, it is pratincoline, occupying fields of grass, alfalfa, or timothy that are not quite wet but close to ponds of running water, fenced fields not readily accessible from roadways.

So explosive, rapid, jumbled and irregular is the exquisite song of the bobolink that, although I have several times attempted it, I have never been able to make a satisfactory onomatope of it, nor do we believe that there is a good one in all ornithological literature. Come to think of it, the same is true of the water ouzel, for, although we have recorded its chatter and remonstrative notes, we have not yet seen an attempt to spell out an imitation of its delightful song.

At Farmington bay at twenty feet a Wilson's snipe in the grass for five minutes straight emits a "chucka chucka chucka chucka chucka" without hesitation and without bill movements. Its throat, however, throbs with the sound. What kind of call is this? At last it flies away. After all is its flight song made by its tail feathers?

JUNE 7

Our locale for the day is historic City Creek canyon, preserved in pristine wildness notwithstanding that its mouth opens upon a great and prosperous city. We start at the famed Eagle Gate at an altitude of 4340 feet with intent to survey the floral beauties of the canyon in this a year when nature's blooms are delayed by cold for several weeks, if not a month.

The evening primrose (*Oenothera caespitosa*) is blooming (4520 feet) along with the wild sweet pea (*Astragalus cibarius*), the mallow (*Sphaeralcea coccinea*) and the big sunflower; and the Hedysarum has its purplish-rose flowers in patches on the mountain side. Here also the greenish blooms of sweet cicely (*Osmorhiza occidentalis*) are showing and beggar ticks, which are to be with us most of the way up the canyon, appear here for the first time, white flowers on foot-high stems.

Robins are singing their evening carols in the creek willows and quail (*L. californica*) are calling on the hillside. The wild pink geranium (*Geranium fremontii*) is blooming (4700 feet) with the white yarrow (*Achillea millefolium*).

At Rock Bridge we stop to view the Sleeping Sailor cliff at the north and further on (4900 feet) we gaze upon the stone elephant in a gully at the south. At this latter place purple wild onions adorn the hill. A chickadee sings its "phee phee be"; and here we find several flowers in bloom: the sego lily, the nine bark with snowy fragrant white blooms, yellow sweet clover, and the pretty red-purple sweet pea or vetchling (*Lathyrus brachycalyx*).

The bluish lupine (*Lupinus argentinus*) with silvery leaves is blooming (4935 feet) along with a very pretty wild hyacinth (*Brodeaea Douglasii*).

Up higher (5250 feet) choke cherries are in unfaded bloom; and at the North Fork (5550 feet) many butterflies are playing about the fountain. Further (5750 feet) where a snowslide has completely roofed the creek a beautiful specimen of *Lathyrus utahensis,* as well as yellow violets adorn the cool, shaded places. The bridge is at the end of the trail.

Arriving at the bridge we denote the end of the travelled road but beyond that a trail bends leading to nooks, yet unexplored by us, and someday not too far off, we must go there in search of nature's enticing by-path secrets.

It has just occurred to us, that in the alkaline ponds of the valley the voices of birds are for the most part either raucous, consisting of various quacks, yawks and zaws, or shrill, involving many piercing, strident calls; but in the mountains the songs are tender, sweet, musical, even spiritual in tone, broken only occasionally by the discordant scream of eagle or hawk. Excepting, perhaps, the meadowlark, our dearest songsters inhabit regions where pure waters lave the mossy stones, and lull our hearts to happiness.

JUNE 8

June is a month of bloom, fragrance, nestlings and baby mammals, the month of nature's proof of the design of procreation and progress. Wherever one goes flowers display their beauty of color and form; valiant birds resist encroachment upon their homes, where fledglings open wide their insatiable mouths; and rodents suckle their tender young in darksome burrows. Like human beings, however, mountain lions give birth to young at all times of the year; but no other mammal or bird hereabout that we recall produces young in the fall. As we have noted, certain birds, such as the crossbills, nest while snow yet burdens the wintered pines; and of course, bears give birth while yet they slumber in January or February; but otherwise spring is the period of reproduction.

In the Wasatch mountains early June finds the mower cutting the fragrant alfalfa of the fields, and often, alas, unintentionally shredding the nest of a wayward turkey as the machine shivers down its swaths. Snakes, especially the Great Basin blow snake or gopher snake (*Pituophia catenifer deserticola*), often succumb to the bewildering noise and slashes of the vibrating knives. Often, as we ourselves have ridden the mowing machine with its ever-shivering blade, we have seen such animals as the mountain weasel (*Mustela frenata nevadensis*) lope away from the approaching knives. (By the way, that word *frenata* in its scientific name is from the Latin *frenum,* a bridle, in allusion to the white chin, lower lips, and sometimes upper lips, which against the brown resemble a bridle). Mammals, snakes and birds hear the sound of the cutting blades but rely on the security of the standing alfalfa until it is too late to flee. One unhappy man we know cut off his own child's arm with the mower, being wholly unaware of the presence of his son in the alfalfa field. Another man whom we knew would jump from his mower, grasp a blow snake by the tail and with a whiplike motion snap off its head; yet he so feared a mouse that his wife habitually cleared the way for him as he entered his granary. Fears cosmopolitan: ailurophobia—of cats; oclophobia—of crowds; keravnophobia—of lightning; kenaphobia—of open spaces; potamophobia—of lakes and large sheets of water; helminthophobia—of worms; erythrophobia—of red color. Why continue the phobias? Most of us are not conscious of fear of any kind; but we all have dislikes, indifferences; nevertheless, the strangest of fears for a woman is androphobia—fear of man; and the most extraordinary fear of man is gymephobia—fear of woman.

Most wild mammals readily detect fear in man; in fact, a mean domestic dog usually subdues its defiance of a man who implicitly has no fear.

JUNE 9

On a warm June afternoon we drive down Weber canyon to its mouth and, having turned to the south over the bridge, glance westward to behold a miniature forest of cacti, that kind known as hedgehog cacti (*Pediocactus simpsoni*). We are so delighted with the yellowish green flowers that we dig up one of the plants, and note that as night falls its blooms close and become pinkish.

The identification of the prickly pears of these mountains, of which there are three genera comprising eight different races, requires at times even a hand glass to distinguish the spines. In all of the cacti the thick green bodies do the work of photosynthesis, and thus take the place of leaves; and while some of them (*O. rhodantha*) have broad red flowers, others (*O. polyacantha*) yellow blooms, and still others (*E. fenderi*) deep purple-violet ones, they are all forbiddingly thorned. When rain falls they drink water like camels, and thus are able to subsist a long time in soil as dry as powder.

A porcupine's quill, being barbed all along its tip, is more torturous than a cactus spine; indeed we have seldom suffered greatly after pulling cactus thorns from our feet.

Not to forget the interesting cacti, of which more anon, as we come upon them, but to illustrate how the day's observation may be further rewarded, we catch a glimpse, as we enter the grounds of Ft. Douglas, of a strange plant that looks like a bundle of green wires with pink flowers at the top. It is the skeleton plant (*Lygodesmia grandiflora*) of the aster family and one of the most difficult flowers to identify in all the Wasatch. Its blosoms look like a garden pink, and a sticky white milk exudes from the plucked stems.

By the way, there are not many spotted flowers in these mountains. The sego lily (*Calochortus nuttallii*) of our hillsides has sepals that are purple-spotted near the base, and the petal has a purple spot, shaped "like a candle flame", above the nectar gland.

In its patterns of coloration of species, nature hereabout sometimes selects spots. Among birds the spots are usually dark brown or black, generally on the under side, such as, those of the American rough-legged hawk, duck hawk, sparrow hawk, red shafted flicker, spotted sandpiper, Audubon hermit thrush and rock wren; but the back of the loon is covered with white spots, and the tips of the secondary wing-feathers of the waxwings appear like drops or spots of red wax.

In mammals we find spots on the fawn of the mule deer, the calf of the wapiti, the kitten of the cougar, and on the bobcat; and on our largest snake, the gopher or blow snake (*Pituophis catenifer deserticola*) as well as on our rattlesnake (*Crotalus confluentus lutosus*) the dark marking along the back are not so much rounded spots as patterned blotches.

Our native trout is thickly spotted, as are many birds' eggs. We think of butterflies—but the subject becomes too complicated for further comment here.

JUNE 10

It is with us the thrill of surprise that we come upon a flower such as occurs today in City Creek canyon (5200 feet) where that fireweed known as *Epilobium paniculatum* adorns the brookside. It stands five feet high with four petalled flowers of a phlox-purple color. Some would call it a willow-herb or silkweed on account of its silky seeds; but such matters not; there it is on its tall, leafy stems, as pretty a member of the evening primrose family as one would see in many a climb.

Hereabout the creek is turbulent, clear as glass, much aerated and moss-verged; but actually growing in its shallows is a member of the figwort family known as the monkey flower (*Mimulus guttatus*)

By the way, as we watch the brook, it appears that most of the whitened bubbles are caused by the falling of water up stream, water that is tripped off its feet by the swift current beneath. In falling, these crested waves catch air, showing white not only as they descend but also as they race down stream in bubble form. A happy go lucky race it is, with solemn moss-grown stones as immovable witnesses.

Cottonwoods eighty feet high are shedding their seeds, which float like single flakes of snow and make some of the underbrushes appear as if a hail storm had just passed over. The trunk of one of the cottonwoods, eighteen inches in diameter, stands over the stream with all its roots on the bank side, somewhat like one's index finger held upright with the palm of the hand touching the water. The vast root system is a rod or more in extent with a maple growing on the soil of its upper side.

The tiny white flowers of the enormously leaved cow-parsnip (*Heracleum lanatum*) are blooming in the thickly verdured places that labyrinth the creek.

The delicious fragrance of the pinkish-flowered dogbane (*Apocynum androsaemifolium*) attracts one's attention a little further down the canyon, reminding us of the partridge bush; and on a rocky ledge a scarlet gilia (*Gilia aggregata*) blooms with leaves so hairy that they appear cob-webbed.

Locusts (*Melanoplus femurrubrum*) are zinging in an endless hissing sound.

Although on many occasions I have watched on ouzel make repeated dives into a bubbling but limpid pool for food, the bird is so timid that I have never been able to observe its eyes as it swam beneath the surface, especially when rising air-pockets, appearing white, distorted the view This I know: that each time a water ouzel rises to the surface and regains its favorite rock, it works its white nictitating membrane to clear its eyes of water and grit. This membrane is not an eyelid, but a thin filament that it can draw across its eyeball. It looks as though it were winking, when it uses it. Over each nostril it has a membraneous operculum or flap, which it apparently closes when it dives.

JUNE 11

Sub-species are sometimes but expressions of the vanities of their originators, a subtle means of personal immortalization. If it were required that all such be authorized by an organization or some such decentralized entity there would be fewer microscopic differentiations. Naturally a scientist cannot be accounted among the great unless his name be appended here and there in the undying renown of print, yet all know that in many, many instances slight geographic variations are the welcome excuse. Strange to say taxonomyphobia and nomenclaphobia are diseases that thrive best among those who should be surfeited with their vanity.

Botanists, ornithologists, mammalogists are particularly afflicted with nomenclaphobia; but after all time relegates much of their work to synonomy and the general result is not harmful. Thus the masked shrew (*Sorex cinereus cinereus*) has been given at least thirteen different scientific names, the little California bat (*Myotis californicus californicus*) at least nine; the Fort Yuma bat (*Myotis yumanensis yumanensis*) at least seven; and so on. In most instances each describer either thought or hoped he had something new.

The proof of evolution depends in all likelihood upon recording the minutiae of forms, but just as one would not maintain that his child belongs to a new subspecies because it has a wart on its ear so there should be some limitation to the recognition of novelty. Nature grades and intergrades with almost infinite variety, otherwise it would be impossible to distinguish instantly any acquaintance from millions of other men.

Perhaps vanity after all is a blessing—the spread of the peacock's tail as well as the exultant rhapsody of a lazuli bunting singing to the blue mountain air may emanate from this buoyant disease.

There is some but not much difference in the songs of our warblers. The Audubon's is a strong repetition of "chwee", and that of the Mac-Gillivray (*Oporornis tolmiei monticola*) has a double connotation, like "cheek-a"; the scarce myrtle's (*Dendroica coronata hooveri*) "wheedle" call. The song of the orange-crowned warbler (*Vermivora celata crestera*) is like "Er-r-r-rtshe-up". One readily learns to detect the song of a warbler, but often it takes a half hour with the glasses to label the little bit of singing joy with a subspecific designation.

JUNE 12

Everytime we happen in the fields upon that rose-blooming plant known as Alsike clover (*Trifolium hybridum*) we are reminded of the fact, that it has been accused in Europe of causing in certain animals what has recenly been called "photosensitization", that is, it really poisons white animals when after eating it they go into strong sunlight. How delicate are the adjustments of nature!

We have, however, in the Wasatch mountains and valleys, other plants capable of causing this strange sensitiveness to light. The spring rabbit bush (*Tetradymia glabrata*), which grows on the dry bench-lands of the artemesia belt, and the spineless horsebrush (*Tetradymia caescens*), which likes the hillsides and dry valleys, both cause the "swellhead" in sheep if they graze upon them too long, but like arsenic the poisoning is slow. There is another plant, the puncture vine (*Tribulus terrestris*), that is said to be capable of this "photosensitization"; but we have had no experience with it. Its horned fruits often adhere to automobile tires; at least such is the report from the Provo region whence it has been introduced.

Even if we humans did eat these photo-dynamic plants it is possible that they would not seriously affect us. Animals do not partake of them unless driven by hunger; in fact, we often see, in the midst of closely cropped pastures, green outstanding clumps that look edible enough, but horses and cows leave them alone. Instinct and taste may decide such refusal; in truth, as we ponder upon the delicious fruits, seeds, and roots we have eaten in the woods and along the valleys, we conclude that taste may often have protected us. That is perhaps why cooking certain fungi and berries may remove the very warning nature has provided. It would require much experimentation to prove our point, and likely the presence of a couple of dogs with which to test our contemplated meals, as did the one-time Sultan of Turkey, when living in constant dread of poison. We shall, however, give the matter some thought hereafter.

The fullness of bird song seems to depend upon di-or tri-syllabic phrases, reiterated sometimes with rhythm but often in mere repetition of musical notes; and, as we survey the ensemble of attainment here-about, somehow we find ourselves repeatedly turning to the ecstatic chansonnette of the lazuli bunting, the sweet capriccio of the bobolink, the roulade of the house finch, the chanson of the song sparrow, the bravura of the bullock oriole, the wildered run of the canyon wren, and the notturno of the Audubon hermit thrush.

JUNE 13

Wherever blooms in mountain glades unfold,
The humming bird enjoys the sweet array;
Wherever pines grow lofty, broad and old,
The chickarees disport in mimic play.

The diversion today is ever-interesting Mill Creek canyon. We set our mileage at zero at the power plant at the mouth, and in anticipation of floral beauty proceed upward. At one mile (5000 feet) *Penstemon leonardi* with its pleasing lilac-colored blooms is conspicuous on the hillsides where also *Hedysarum pabulare* is delightful with its pinkish purple flowers. Sweet Williams are still beautiful and plentiful.

At 5050 feet that interesting member of the sunflower family known as *Chaenactis Douglasii* is showing its pearly white flowers and many toothed leaves. The Rose of Sharon is likewise abloom. Further on (5500 feet) *Penstemon brevifolius, Penstemon cyananthus, Lathyrus utahensis,* the wild raspberry (*Rubus leucodermis*) are all in flower. Here also is the strawberry (*Fragaria bracteata*) which has large white blooms and likes a shaded rich soil, not a meadow as does *F. glauca,* a smaller flowered species.

Further on (6325 feet) the choke cherries are only in bud, the dogwood is half leaved, a blue violet is out; but the ever delightful Virgin's bower is trailing over the damp verdure of the hillsides, showing here and there its sweet purple blooms. It is this flower that has attracted us for the day, this the delightsome end of any trail.

We return to a glade (5710 feet) in the midst of maples, boxelders and Douglas spruces where the atmosphere is not only cool, but chilly in the shade. The brook rushes downward with ceaseless purl like breezes whistling over upper foliage. A bumblebee buzzes softly from nook to cranny; a robin carols as at eventide; a yellow warbler sings from the sweet mazes of the cooling stream. Cabbage and monarch butterflies flutter from sun to shade and back again. A stone in the shade is cold, as if still wintered in memory. In the sunshine, dandelions loose their seeds to every flatus; in the shade, they like the choke cherries are still blooming. The snow at last has disappeared from the evergreened hills, and all nature is engaged in the rapturous work of multiplication and hope.

An exquisite bit of variegated gleam, a vibrant morsel kissing the yawning bloom, a valiant swift and wee protector of its home-domain—such is the humming bird, which in either the garden or the wildered mountain glade wins our affection, admiration and respect as much as any other bird. Although not gifted with the rhapsody of song, it has the sheer independence and bravery to fight its way wherever it might be, whether on the blossomed shores of the lake-wide Amazon or in the alcoves between snow-moistened pines. What a bird!

JUNE 14

In a verdured canyon today an oddly colored flower on the hillsides adjacent to the creek attracts our attention. It is nearly two feet high with a bloom only at the top; and, from its general characteristics, is obviously a gilia; but its funnelform five petalled flowers are in two colors—the older corollas, ochraceous buff to almost white, and the younger ones, antimony yellow. This orange-white combination identifies it as a *Gilia grandiflora,* a flower always hereafter to be associated with Rotary Bridge in City Creek canyon and such well known places. The scarlet gilia, however, still shows its red funnels on an embankment just above the reservoir further down where we have often remarked and admired it.

That interesting member of the evening primrose family, known as *Clarkia rhomboidea,* is now blooming (5500 feet) with its small, phlox-purple, four petalled somewhat facelike flowers almost lost on a much-branched stem a yard high. Each petal has dots of darker purple near its base. One must have an appreciative and discerning eye to catch such miniature beauty by the side of startling plants like the willow herb (*Epilobium paniculatum*) with its large phlox-purple flowers.

In the same neighborhood, where in these sultry June days the coolsome air of the canyon first becomes noticeable, the broad-leafed, lavender-violet penstemon (*Penstemon playtyphyllus*) is still blooming; and, as we hold the pretty corollas in hand, we discover them to vary from light purple to deep vinaceous lavender in shade. Their mouths are agasp, as if resenting their being stricken from their native habitat.

So far as the naturalist can discern every flower and animal lives, strives to bring forth young, and departs. So far as the biologist is able to comprehend, nature takes no more notice of the death of a man than of a squirrel. Yet as one looks into the face of a scarlet gilia and notes the complicated distribution of the specks therein, he wonders if after all everything be in vain. The naturalist, if he be true to his own heart, must hope that a power so marvelously capable in design as that which he sees about himself cannot have failed to provide an ultimate of individual existence.

Everything living seems to have an enemy of some kind. Thus on one of those big yellow mule-ears (*Wyethia amplexicaulis*), now blooming in patches on the dry hillsides, we find a fungous-rust disease (*Puccinia balsamorrhizae*).

JUNE 15

When we see the garden blooming with multi-colored larkspurs it is almost incredible that their leaves are poisonous. The truth is, there are many ornamental plants in our gardens that we should avoid eating or, in the case of some, even handling, among them being oleander, narcissus, the English ivy, foxglove, lilies of the valley, aconite and meadow saffron. Perhaps the most tempting of all to us humans are the beans of the castor bean, that huge annual shrub that to our astonishment in the autumn sometimes reaches a height of eight or nine feet. The mottled beans are so large and pleasing that we have a desire to cook them; yet vomiting and prostration almost immediately follow such an experiment.

We have frequently seen robins and Say phoebes, aye even red-shafted flickers, eat the berries of the Boston ivy; yet the berries as well as the leaves of the English ivy (*Hedera Helix*) are undoubtedly poisonous. Our native larkspurs are almost as harmful to cattle as the loco weeds.

Medicine is made from the leaves of the foxglove of the garden; and they are quite actively poisonous when eaten.

When we think of the many plants about us whose colors we admire, we can only conclude that the safest course is not to eat any but the known vegetables, leaves and berries. We cannot avoid mechanical injury now and again from thorn, bur, awn, or needle, but we can abstain from eating strange things just to taste them. Even the garden toad emits a poison from its skin, when severely mouthed by a dog.

A gauze-covered tumbler held on a stick before an enraged rattle-snake will cause the reptile to strike and discharge a full dose of its venom from its fangs into the glass. This may immediately be swallowed by a human being with no more ill effect than if it were the white of an egg, with which chemically it is indeed allied. Such are the strange ways of poison. The toad's poison does not harm humans.

In the sagebrush of the foothills we succeeded in jabbing a stick upon a lizard's tail; but, just as we thought we had the swift little animal captured, it twisted its body, broke off its tail, scampered away, and left us to observe the wriggling appendage thus discarded. It will grow a new tail, as most of our lizards do in such cases.

With the tail before us, we sit down to discuss regeneration. Are the cells that grow into the new tail guided by an unseen power to take their places to conform to the original pattern, a theory called preformism? This can scarcely be so, when the new tail is sometimes deformed or even forked. Do the cells proceed according to their own capabilities and place themselves as their chemical affinities choose, a theory called epigenesis? Concluding that we are unable to solve the problem, we drift on our less difficult way.

JUNE 16

Pioneer means of livelihood, on the saged shores of the Great Salt Lake seem strange today. Women made their own hats of wheat straw, bleached them with brimstone or dyed them with copperas and oak leaves; but calico bonnets were used for daily wear. The men wore straw hats dyed with the juice of weeds, larkspur or sagebrush. Window panes were light colored pieces of calico, and the cabin roofs were made of bulrushes covered with earth. Wooden pegs took the place of nails, and the trodden earth substituted for floors. Children trampled mud with which to make chimneys; and first rags, then rawhides, were used for doors. A log did for chairs, a sawed log on posts for a table.

Watches being rare, they guessed time by the sun. Houses leaked so badly people often slept under umbrellas, and whitewashed the rain-run walls next day with clay. The use of face-powder was considered wrong; and both curling irons and tooth brushes were unknown. For mirrors the ladies looked into buckets of clear water or even into still bends of limpid brooks.

A "bitch" or "slush light" was made by pouring grease into a tin pan and so placing a wicking in it that it would extend beyond the edge; it was slightly better than a candle, even though smoky. A "button" light consisted of a twisted greasy rag threaded through the eye of a button.

They cut squash into rings, hanging them on a pole to dry, and gathered the encrustations from the lake shore to make saleratus for buttermilk and biscuits. They borrowed buckets of live coals from neighbors when the fires went out; and they had no sugar, no pepper, no liquor. Children were without shoes, some of the youngsters being so hardened they skated barefooted on the ice of winter. Clothes were made of blue denim, bed-ticking or knitted wool.

Threshing was done with a stick; oxen pulled the plows; and the only money used was eggs, cheese, barley or wood. Dancing on an earthen floor was the only amusement, tickets being purchased with squashes or other produce. Girls rode horseback behind their sweethearts. There were no holiday celebrations; and they had few if any books, magazines or newspapers. Ink was made of oak leaves; letters from England were received three or four months after posting. Yet even with sunflower seeds for flour, people were happy and so healthy that doctors were almost unavailable. Anaesthetics were unknown, so if a man's leg was shattered in an accident beyond repair, his neighbors held him while the limb was sawed off. The author's father once assisted in such a terrible ordeal.

JUNE 17

The mountain meadow, margined wide with pines,
Is beautified by willowed brooklets clear;
Rare warblers sing in labyrinthed confines,
And nature's secret ways are very near.

Each of at least three regions of the Wasatch mountains and valley
is an ornithologist's paradise—Bear river Bay, Farmington Bay, and
Parley's Park, the two first for water birds, the last for a veritable
ensemble of pratincoline, oscine and pinicoline forms. What an avifauna
one may see in a day, and study the delights of canyon stream and
mountain pass on the journey!

Parley's Park is an inviting meadowland, let us say eight miles
by four, situated on the head waters of East canyon creek just east of
the summit above Parley's canyon. From its altitude of 6500 feet it
rises through sage lands and conifers to surrounding mountains ten
thousand feet or more in height, and, while pellucid brooks traverse
its rich meadows along willowed lanes, the adjoining hills are fledged
with scrub oaks and, higher up, such *Coniferae* as white pine (*Pinus
flexilis*), lodge pole pine (*Pinus contorta*), white firs (*Abies concolor*),
Englemann spruce, Colorado blue spruce, Douglas fir and Rocky
Mountain juniper (*Juniperus scopulcrum*). Although quaking aspens
adorn the higher gulches and narrow leaved cottonwoods flourish along
the creeks from mountain to meadow, the finding of the Rocky Mountain
juniper leads us to realize that the eastern slopes of the Wasatch have a
flora and fauna enriched by species sometimes uncommon on the west
side.

As we traverse the sagelands surrounding Parley's Park, we notice
a few Brewer sparrows, several mourning doves, a rock wren and some
sage hens, which last are not nearly so plentiful as when we used to
hunt them here.

The actual meadows here, where dairy cattle graze the luxuriant
grass, are to birds not so attractive as the shrubberied brooksides; but,
as we tread through them, we do see a Nevada savannah sparrow and a
lonely vesper sparrow. That bird perched on a bull's back is a cowbird.
We steer clear. While hunting years ago in an open field, we were
menaced by a pawing bull at close quarters, but, armed with a shotgun,
a terrific weapon at a few feet, we stood our ground until rescued
by a dog, sent to bring in the herd for the evening. To intrude upon
America's most dangerous mammal (except for a grizzly) with field
glasses for a weapon is unnecessarily foolish and risky.

As we step to a brookside a Wilson snipe chutters from the sky;
a spotted sandpiper utters a clear "peet-weet", and a belted kingfisher
watches from atop a pooled boulder. We hear the sweet notes of an
olive-backed thrush, sounding like "HAO-HAO-HAO-whee-e-e"; and
then from a labyrinth comes the known song of a catbird, like "twit
twit prit tereet keet".

JUNE 18

Along the willow-fringed brook that drains Parley's Park, we come upon the very bird we had hoped to see—a western redstart (*Setophaga ruticilla tricolors*), a warbler with black upper parts except for salmon-colored markings on wings and tail. There is nothing else like it among our warblers, which usually have yellow and green hues. We listen to its thin, high-pitched song, almost like a toy tin whistle, and record its "cha-see, cha-see-cha—see see".

We flush a short-eared owl, which was hunting meadow mice, and then listen to the beloved song of a lazuli bunting, twigged to face the morning sun. We catch sight of a Macgillivray warbler, which seems to say "sheepa, sheepa, sheepa, sheepa, shee-e-e"; but no more do we see sheep in these luscious meadows. For beauty of song a lazuli bunting makes a warbler seem insignificant indeed.

We catch glimpses of such well-knowns as a red-shafted flicker, a sparrow hawk, a big Swainson hawk, and a red-naped sapsucker.

We ramble by a dairy barn where wide-eyed calves frolic in sweet innocence, and stroll on to oak-garbed foothills. Here is a characteristic bird, a spurred towhee; then a western horned owl, big and sleepy in a tree. It preys upon the Townsend hare and the hoary ruffed grouse (*Bonasa umbellus incanus*)˙ which reside in these parts. It, not the golden eagle, is the king of birddom hereabout.

There is a Wright flycatcher (*Empidonax wrightii*), and from a juniper we flush a black-throated gray warbler (*Dendroica nigrescens*), which coyly sings a "tswe, tswe, tswe, ze ze ze". What a haven for warblers is this Park!

As we climb higher, we frequently rest to look down upon that magnificent dairy herd in the meadows.

A western robin carols; then a Lincoln sparrow sings its sweet, gurgling, and somewhat robinlike song, which with much revision we record as "Twe a tu twa, twee, twee, twee, twa, twa, twa, twr-r-r-r-r-r". With its efforts repeated, we time the song at 18 seconds duration; and conclude that it is far more complicated and musical than that of the warblers. No wonder the singers in house cages are finches (sparrows) not canaries (warblers).

Tomorrow we must go higher—to rocks, banks, aspen groves and coniferous woods.

JUNE 19

We must conclude our faunal survey of Parley's Park by visting the aspen groves, the pine-forested regions and rocky cliffs above the meadows.

The purple martin (*Progne subis subis*) whose entire body is blue-black, once nested here in the holes of dead aspens; but we see several white bellied or tree swallows, with their bluish backs, flying about, also that ever pleasing northern violet-green swallow, which for half an hour at a time courses back and forth over a tumbling brook. Both of these swallows nest in aspen holes. Somehow this violet-green bird, like the mountain blue bird, is to us the sign of pure invigorating, cool mountain air. But we must trudge on through the aspens.

On yonder tree is a Cassin purple finch, a bird we have not seen since last winter when we gazed high into a valley locust tree. The pine siskins hereabout also visit in winter swarms in the valleys westward. The Rocky mountain hairy woodpecker, which we notice here searching for insects about the aspen trunks, is likewise a winter friend in the valley below, because there he grubs the orchard trees. Since the red-naped sapsucker (*Sphyrapicus varius nuchalis*) is common in the aspens of the Wasatch it does not fail us here. Its patterned holes appear on many of the pallid trunks.

As we walk among the pines and other evergreens we are not surprised to see robins, black-headed jays, ruffed grouse, and Audubon hermit thrushes (*Hylocichla guttata auduboni*), as well as water ouzels on the brooks, and mountain chickadees, but we are pleased to discover a western ruby crowned kinglet, that wee bird that once we picked up frozen in a blizzard.

We marvel at the glow-like appearance of a Louisiana tanager, sitting on an evergreen limb. Once, on the other side of the mountain, we watched a pair for hours, the account of which we forwarded to Bent.

We see a gray-headed junco, a red-tailed hawk, some rough-winged swallows flitting before a cliff, and a golden eagle soaring in the fathom-less blue.

We pay tribute to our fellow-ornithologist, C. W. Lockerbie, who in his patient, indefatigable way has discovered in this wondrous park many birds yet to come within our view.

As the setting sun bids us to go home, we feel that one might profitably spend an entire spring and summer in this haven of birds. This locale could well result in the *opus magnus* of some ornithologist.

JUNE 20

Lounging in tranquil ease in a pine-margined glade, we reflect upon the experiences of many years in these interesting mountains and valleys, for the purpose of trying to recapitulate those scenes and things that have most captivated our attention, some of them repeatedly, others on rare occasions.

We think of: lovely mountain bluebirds flitting from post to post in a meadow; a pair of Canadian geese crossing a roadway with stately fidelity; a pair of Canadian geese on a pond with an entourage of goslings behind; a long-crested blue jay of celestial hue flitting alone among the limbs of snow-burdened spruces; a water ouzel teaching her fledgling to dive a turbulent creek for worms; a golden eagle soaring mightily over wooded mountain crests; an azure-colored kingfisher dashing in the glint of the sun from its stream-banked willow to a rainbow trout in the pellucid water below; wapiti silhouetted on a canyonside ridge; a mule deer with her fawn walking towards a mountain brook; a mountain lion running across our pathway a few yards away; the amazing glory of a sunset swathed across the waters of Great Salt Lake; the sight of cumulus clouds on a mountain side *below* us, as we stand at the top of a lofty peak.

Such things make the ensemble of sweet memory. There may not be anything extraordinary about a hundred white gulls settling in turn on the fresh, dark worm-inhabited furrow immediately behind a plow-man; but we watch with pleasure every time we come upon the scene. There may be nothing strange about a long-billed curlew's jabbing its eight inch bill into the mud for larvae, but we cannot resist standing in wonder at it. We think of: a water ouzel's nest, resembling a child's hand muff placed on a mossy cliff within inches of a waterfall; the vibrant wings of a humming bird as it hovers before the funneled flower of a bignonia; the rhythmic sway of a trout's tail withstanding a gentle current in limpid water; the spiritual song of an Audubon hermit thrush when the rising sun first makes lambent the tips of pines; the ineffable depth and blueness of the heavens seen from a mountain top; the trickle of a pure-watered rill through a spruce-margined glade; the wondrous ease of the flight of white pelicans in the afternoon sun; the chutter of a Wilson snipe, made by its feathers, as it dives to earth from a cloudy sky.

> Behold the beauty of a blooming rose;
> Explain the cause of such a lovely flower—
> Perhaps with all that hopeful science knows,
> We yet may comprehend the cosmic power.

A Wasatch Summer

INTRODUCTION

From the northern extremity of Utah the Wasatch mountains extend south over 150 miles, bearing many a peak and many a verdured crystal-brooked canyon on the way. Along their northern portion they. border the Great Salt Lake, with only a narrow strip of fertile valley inter-vening; and along their southern half they skirt the fresh watered Utah Lake and finally empty their pellucid creeks into the long Sevier River, which itself at last flows into another desert-environed salty sea. At the North their eastern slopes drain into rivers that arise in the lofty Uintahs, penetrate them and empty into the Great Salt Lake—the Bear, the Weber and the Provo as the streams are called—; but the eastern declevities of the southern Wasatch plateau drain through dreary wastelands to the mighty Colorado.

The principal canyons detailed in this work are (beginning at the north): Logan, Sardine, Ogden, Weber, Farmington, Ward's, City Creek (at the mouth of which the Utah State Capitol stands), Emigra-tion, Parley's, Mill Creek, Little Cottonwood, Big Cottonwood, American Fork, Provo, Spanish Fork, Payson and Fairview.

Since for many a year the author has had his home on the foothills some four hundred yards east of the mouth of City Creek Canyon, it is from that point that all of his excursions into the wildlands have begun. for within a few minutes to an hour he could from home drive into ten of the canyons named, and easily visit the others in a round trip day's drive, leisurely taken for observation and collection.

It has been his custom to carry with him a barometer for altitude readings, field glasses, a hand glass, and a botanical press; to make notes on the way; and to write the account of each day's trip in the evening after the identification of specimens.

A strange thing about it all is that any one page in the book may have been written as much as twenty years or more before the one preceding or following it, for the excursions have been taken only as leisure time from professional and business duties permitted.

Most of the early trips were taken afoot, either by the author alone or in the company of the renowned botanist, the late Marcus E. Jones, or some visiting naturalist; but in later years, as canyon roads improved, most of the trips were by automobile in the company of the late Louise Atkinson, a competent botanist, whose eyes were remarkably quick to catch sight of anything new or outstanding in flower, feather or fur, as we slowly drove along. She gradually acquired alert and discerning knowledge in ornithology and mammalogy, being a naturalist at heart.

This book is but one of a contemplated series, for, in view of the fact that the manuscript for the entire year is already written, if and when the others are published they will cover in like fashion the autumn, winter and spring of the Wasatch Mountains

The author is grateful to the late Prof. A. O. Garrett, himself an authority on the flora of the Wasatch, for a critical reading of the manuscript, and to R. A. Hart, noted consulting engineer, for technical checking of topographies and careful perusal of the entire work.

The writing of this book has been a delightful diversion from multiform duties, but in a broader sense it is but a token of the love of a naturalist for the beauties and mysteries of the wildwoods.

CLAUDE T. BARNES

JUNE 21

In an embowered nook of City Creek canyon just above the confluence of the North Fork with the main stream an eight-foot waterfall dashes over tawny olive rocks between clumps of birches and alders, making a cool and delightful scene that we call "Nancy's Fall." After the aereated and thus whitened water gushes into the pool below, it takes on a bice green shade, especially upon reaching the calm sides, this being due, no doubt, to some mossy growth or slime beneath the turbulent spill. Here and there are whirlpools of foam; and dead sticks checked from the current lie across mossy boulders.

At the lower edge of the pool is a little rock-island; and on each side of this the water again rushes, but this time in a divided fall, one horseshoe-shaped, the other straight, a true miniature of the great Niagara—miniature, indeed, for the brook is but eight feet wide. Yet, having seen both, one standing over it can easily project his imagination to the magnitude and the overwhelming roar of the suicidal Niagara— "suicidal" because all reality seems there tumbling to its doom, an impression not lessened by the uncanny whirlpool below.

A cool breeze wafts the spray of Nancy's fall into one's face, affording that delicious freshness found only beside rushing waters. A bright afternoon sun shines through the interstices of the cottonwoods, causing the linn now and again to glisten and sparkle as if beset with moving diamonds. A solitary water ouzel flits silently by, unaware of the presence of a motionless human, for otherwise it would chatter with both surprise and alarm.

Seen from above the fall, the speeding waters are clear as crystal, except where ripples appear, up to the very brink of the cascade; but from that downward curving the whole becomes a mass of sparkling white, so quickly does the mingling air give it visibility.

Ever pleasing are the trout-homing, pellucid brooks of the Wasatch mountains, especially where they cascade through rocky defiles or over moss-laden boulders; and ever attendant are the belted kingfisher and the busy ouzel.

JUNE 22

About valley homes robins worm the lawns and on these sultry days sing usually only in the mornings and evenings, but in the cold canyons they feed and carol during all daylight hours. No matter how secluded the mountain glade, if spruces, firs or pines verdure its surrounding steeps, robins delight it with song; indeed, save for them, the trilling warbler and the chattering ouzel, there is in those cool places little else to make song. It is true the brook brawls ceaselessly, and the sun-touched maple tops whisper in every breeze; but otherwise the mountain glen is quiet and motionless. A squirrel whistles with surprise at one's intrusion, as if its domain were sacrosanct.

Among hot dry rocks at the mouth of Parley's canyon penstemons are inlaid patches of color showing clearly from across the South canyonside and beyond where thistles are blooming. Sego lilies (*Calochortus Nuttallii*) adorn the gently sloping hillsides.

In a garden tree we catch an ichneumon fly with a body two inches long and an ovipositor hanging like a thread-snake five inches more. It looks like a tremendous wasp with a five-inch blackish brown whip for a tail. It resembles closely the *Thalessa lunator* of the East except that its long ovipositor is not split as in that species. In laying her eggs this *Thalessa* arches her ovipositor and drills by her side; the egg is thus deposited in the bark-burrow of that harmful tree borer known as pigeon tremex (*Tremex columba*). When her egg hatches, the larva thus produced crawls along the hole until it meets the borer, attaches itself to the borer's body and lives on its juices. This parasitic habit is a beneficial one; but it is not surprising that having inserted her whip-like ovipositor into a hole, this great fly is sometimes unable to extricate herself. Extraordinary are the ways of nature.

In the shade of an oak-copse on the foothills we come upon a delightful bed of wild onions (*Allium acuminatum*), a thousand plants with pretty, light pink flowers. The involucre of two pretty bracts makes a distinct sound as we pin one of the blooms on our lapel.

JUNE 23

The surprise of the day is a milk weed growing in the open fields immediately below the mouth of Mill Creek. It is the isolated clumps of green on the otherwise rather dry slopes that attracted our eyes; and upon investigation, we discover them to be that milkweed known as *Ascelepidora decumbens*. In general appearance it is somewhat like the ordinary milkweed, but as the name *decumbens* suggests, the various stalks do not stand up like the common milkweed (*Ascelpias speciosa*) but spread. We gather some of them for closer examination despite the black ants travelling the intricacies of their stems and blooms. The leaves are somewhat leathery and rough to the touch, also narrow and sharp-pointed. The floral umbel is solitary, and in the distance gives one the impression of glass-green intermixed with dull magenta purple, far different from the purplish corolla of the common milkweed. Each umbel consists of fifty or more individual flowers bunched together as if they were a single snowball of bloom. Each flower, three-fourths of an inch across, has five green petals with five purple hoods. The green calyx is slender and nearly half as long as the corolla.

We know not why this member of the milkweed family so intrigues us; but it is the only *Ascelepidora* in Utah, and its dull magenta purple intermixed with light green delights us. It is found in the desert areas, plains and sloping mountain lowlands of the Corvillea and artemisia belts from Kansas to Nevada and Mexico; but somehow, in all our Wasatch travels we have never come upon it before today.

What rare good luck! Above the oaks at the mouth of Parley's a California cuckoo (*Coccyzus americanus occidentalis*) is singing on a telephone wire not ten yards away. For years we have followed this furtive bird to get sight of him, and there he is, so close we see the twitches of the tail as he gives his loud "Caw caw caw," a call we have often heard at midnight. He flies away swiftly, directly, somewhat like a dove. This is the bird of mystic moonlit nights in the oaken swales.

JUNE 24

When the valleys are almost insufferably warm it is not surprising that the hillsides are so matted with dried June grass (*Bromus tectorum*) that it resembles a carpet several inches thick. In the near distance, however, it has a pinkish tint that on close observation is discovered to be caused by the fragrant dogbane (*Apocynum cannabinum*) *growing* about it.

And there on the roadside (elevation 4500 feet), in the same vicinity, two species of umbrella plants are blooming—one of them small, known as the silver plant (*Eriogonum ovalifolium*) with yellowish flowers that turn reddish purple with age; another, known as the sulphur flower (*Eriogonum umbellatum*) with a long naked stem and a yellowish floral umbel specked with garnet.

Exquisite is the color tint of a thistle (*Cirsium undulatum*), so delicate indeed that it can best be described as pale grayish vinaceous. Unlike the prickled leaves, its silvery stems are as soft as velvet, and the sweet-smelling flowers are as pleasing to the touch as if made of white wool balls with standing threads stuck all over.

Not to be outdone in floral beauty, the common milkweed is standing there with its leafy, stout stems over two feet high, and its fragrant floral umbels of such sweet tinting that, after much comparing, we can describe only as partly pansy purple, partly pale rhodonite pink.

Though for many years we have studied colors, and tried to describe their infinite variety and beauty, having in the course of time considered the views of such men as Anson K. Cross, Martin and Gamble, Luckiesh, Clifford, Church, Cleland, Jacobs, Maerz and Paul, as well as the Royal Horticultural Society, we find ourselves most frequently resorting to the nomenclature of Ridgway, perhaps if for no other reason than that he was not only the author's inspiration to ornithology but also his friend in correspondence. He is the author of the naturalist's color standards, at least so far as American ornithology and mammalogy are concerned. So evanescent are some tints, so mystic some hues, so melancholy some shades, that language must grasp, and cling and fight in its constant effort to describe them on the printed page. The difficulty with Ridgway, however, is that although his nomenclature has became a treasured part of scientific literature, his book, which cannot be exactly duplicated, is practically unobtainable by a new generation of naturalists, especially taxonomists.

JUNE 25

Meandering the willowed shoreline of the upper Weber river, we have our attention suddenly arrested by a shrill buzz overhead, and before we are quite able to orientate the screeching sound we are almost but not quite struck by a furious humming bird in lightning flight towards us. Involuntarily we shield our eyes, and then carefully survey the troublesome spot. There it is, a tiny linchen-made nest scarcely larger than the end joints of two thumbs, placed on a willow limb; and the valiant defender of the wee home is a male broad-tailed hummingbird (*Selasphorus platycercus platycercus*). Despite his pugnacity we peep into his miniature castle, there to discover two white elfin eggs. We desist and withdraw, for why violate anything as neat, secure and beautiful as that masterpiece of avian architecture?

With his gorget of deepest rose, the broad-tailed hummingbird is truly the gem of the mountains, where throughout the summer we often hear his cicadalike clicking in glades where mountain lilacs and spruces grow beside trickling streams. So fond is he of water of crystalline purity that in the course of his buzzing gyrations from flower to flower he sometimes darts to the brook itself, bathes in the shallow water overrunning a stone, and darts away again to dry on a coniferous twig in the sunshine. This we have often observed in Lamb's canyon.

The broad-tailed is the commonest hummer of the Wasatch region; it subsists on the honey and insects found in such beautiful flower blooms as those of the penstemons, and upon ants gathered from seeping tree punctures left by sapsuckers.

The Calliope, that midget even among humming birds, being less than three inches in length and weighing about a tenth of an ounce, does nest in these mountains usually in the pines; but it is not so common as the broadtailed. It is quite easily identified not only by its diminutive size but also by its throat adorned with red stripes on a white background. By the way, the broad-tailed is easily detected by that shrill clicking sound it makes as it flies from place to place.

The black-chinned hummingbird (*Archilochus axelandri*), known by its black throat, breeds throughout the Wasatch, but for some reason is comparatively rare; and the rufous hummingbird, while preferring to nest North of here, is a rather common migrant.

Many a hawk, many a flycatcher has been glad to escape from the homesite of a hummingbird; for, in fighting, this tiny morsel is too alert and agile for any of their ordinary destructive movements.

It is interesting to note that the slender long extensile tongue of a hummingbird is split at the end, and the outer edge of each division is curled inward and upward to form a sort of tube; hence the ability of the bird to sip nectar and gather insects.

JUNE 26

The valley being oppressively warm, we hie ourselves to the shady retreats of Little Cottonwood canyon whose mighty granite steeps have cabin-sized boulders at their lower extremities. Verdured indeed are the hillsides save where the bare granite rises almost perpendicularly from the canyon floor but here and there among scrub oaks, cottonwoods, maples, and quaking aspens granite points stick up along the trails, refusing with their hardness to moulder and conform, and even the brawling creek dashes from sharp-edged rock to sharp-edged rock and around square-shaped corners as if itself had long since given up the struggle to make such hardness soften and round to its will. Nowhere else in these mountains is so clearly displayed the unchangeability, aye the immortality if you will, of rock so hard that only the diamond can cut into its heart. But we come not for stones, but for birds, flowers, trees and the sweet murmurs of the cascaded woods, the things that always give us a priceless euphoria.

At 6100 feet elevation we note that violet colored penstemon known as *Penstemon leonardi* blooming on the roadside embankment, and near by it, the beautiful purple-flowered fireweed. We find thistles, wild onions, lupines and yarrow in bloom; but lacking a shady spot, do not linger to identify either the lupines or the onions. Further up (6650 feet) we come upon another and prettier penstemon (*P. cyananthus*) with large, dark blue corollas; and at 6900 feet the monkey flower shows its lemon-colored blooms. As we rest we can smell the rich fragrance of the mountain lilac whose white flowers inspired the name "snowbush" or even by some, "mountain laurel," but the white flowers of the baneberry (*Actaea argula*) nearby are rather unpleasantly scented. The quaking aspens are dripping specks of honey. As we again look upon the tall cliffs and study them, we are impelled to ask, what in the measure of time is life beside those enduring granite hills? Geologists like Calkins and Boutwell may describe this porphyritic granite as "quartz monozonite made up predominantly of quartz, white plagioclase (*Calcic oligoclase*) and pinkish orthoclase, which forms the phenocrysts"; but the naturalist sees it as the exemplification of eternity beside the brief incident of individual existence.

JUNE 27

On the Parley's side of Emigration-Parleys pass (5965 feet) we stop to listen to the pleasing song of a green-tailed towhee perched on the tip of a scrub oak patch. The bright rufous head cap well identifies the songster whose notes sound like "Klu' klow' klee klee klee klee klee" with the accent strongly on the "Klu klow" and the other syllables very finchlike in character.

As he flushes from our inquisitive approach we glance at the gully hillside before us, where there is a plethora of flowers. In a grassy, sage grown plat not over ten yards across we find in bloom: a scarlet Indian paint brush (*Castilleja angustifolia*); an interesting umbrella plant (*Eriogonum subalpinum*) noticeable for its almost naked flower stalk and the fact that its leaves are green above and white-wooly below; a wild onion (*Allium acuminatum*) with lovely rose-purple flowers; a vetchling or everlasting pea (*Lathyrus leucanthus*) distinguished by its having leaflets that are pointed at each end and leaves with two tendrils each; beautiful specimens of *Hedysarum pabulare;* and a tall yarrow or milfoil (*Achillea millefolium lanulosa*) known for its convex rather than flat corymb.

We go on up the canyon where at 6615 feet we find the mountain lilac in flower and a sweet dark pink rose (*Rosa Woodsii*), the finest we have seen.

Hawks are rather numerous this afternoon, following the rain of the morning, and it is very interesting to watch them soar over the ridges, taking advantage of the updraughts in such a way as seldom to move a wing. What a life of independence and ease—gliders over the mountains!

On our return we again hear the green-tailed towhee; indeed we should here remark that whenever we have described this attractive finch it has been in some cool, tranquil mountain slope where the atmosphere is pure. Its nest made of stems, dry grasses and such material is often lined with horsehair and placed either on the ground or close to it within the shade of oak or sage; for these towhees, like their spurred cousins, delight in the earth, but often arise from their industry there to lend rapture to the upper reaches of their favorite covert.

JUNE 28

So clear is the ordinary Wasatch summer sky that only isolated cumulus clouds are usually floating in it here and there, with great majesty of form and incomparable whiteness against the blue. Being formed by diurnal ascending currents, they have flat bases but domes with protuberances, and are constantly changing into fantastic shapes— now a tremendous castle with projection-like towers and minarets; again a mammoth white locomotive; then, a huge ghostly crocodile with an open mouth; next a ship with upper protrusions like sails; then bulges resembling a hat; and, one by one in turn, a wedding cake, a boat or a fortress, each half a mile long. Seldom is a definite shape retained for more than ten minutes at a time; and there may be no more than three such cloud images in the entire firmament.

Seen in front of the sun, they appear dark with brightened edges, but, observed when the sun is behind one, they are brilliant white with sides brighter than their upper protrusions. With their massiveness, isolation and endless conformations, they ever fascinate us as they drift slowly towards eastern horizons.

Since garden roses have passed the zenith of vernal beauty, we gaze in wonder at a great catalpa tree (*Catalpa bignonioides*) only now in full bloom, with flowers in erect, terminal panicles eight inches long. Each flower, which opens like an iris, is two inches across, mostly white, but with a throat marked by two yellow lines and thickly dotted with tiny specks of maroon.

JUNE 29

As we stop beside a meadow fence and admire a herd of grazing dairy cows, an old codger in overalls and with a shovel in hand willingly engages us in conversation. With his assertion that the flesh of a dairy cow, especially that of a Jersey, is darker and less appetizing than that of a beef-steer off the range, we agree; and, finally, perhaps conclude that his other assertions, that he can tell what an animal has been eating by the flavor of its flesh, has some merit in it likewise.

Undoubtedly some plants other than the poisonous ones do taint the flavor of cows' milk, as every dairyman knows. For instance, that strongly-scented member of the composite family known as the yarrow (*Achillea millefolium*) from which our mothers used to make a tea and which has white blooms even in September, growing on every roadside, can taint the taste of milk. Our wild onion is perhaps more powerful in this regard; for it is maintained by some that a cow need only breathe the effluvium from freshly cut onion tops to pass the odor and flavor on to milk and butter. We like onions and garlic, yet not in this indirect and annoying subtle manner.

Our sage brush, the hedge mustard (*Descurainia pinnatum halictorum*) and the ragweed (*Ambrosia psychrophylla*), which grows in nearly all waste places, are likewise offenders of the milk bottle.

Cows would be very hungry to eat the pointed horsetails of the creeksides (*Equisetum hiemale*), those round, gritty rush-stems that the youngsters pinch and use for whistles; but when they do so they are made sick and their milk is tainted.

Other plants that affect the flavor of cows' milk are the bitter dock (*Rumex obtusifolius*), the cursed crowfoot (*Ranunculus sceleratus multifidus*) and the leaves of the oak brush (*Quercus utahensis*); but perhaps none is more potent than the pulp of sugar beets.

The old codger leaves us to continue his shoveling about a dam in an irrigation stream.

JUNE 30

The shallow cadent brook with its bubbling, whitened rushes, followed by calmer, translucent stretches, all gleamed by the sinking sun save where maples and cottonwoods shadow it with their trunks and delicate foliage, is a thing of life, purity and sparkle, a cooling, animated ribbon beside the high canyon verdure—a ceaseless proof of the immortality of basic nature. The ouzel that dips constantly along the crystal waters of its mossy-stoned shores, the tiger butterfly that flutters about the maple trunks on its leaf-mouldered embankments, the hermit thrush that sings with spiritual loveliness in the tree tops, the robins that carol with vespertine loneliness from the sun-gleaned tips of a lofty conifer—these in the after year will as individuals have faded away, but their descendants will dip, and sing, and flutter, and carol over this enduring stream until another ice age, another inland surging of the sea.

Beauty and variegation somehow seem destined to endure; for they are idyllic and almost omnipresent. Even the brook there is so crystalline that the stones of its bed are a study in multicolor. Some of the round pebbles of the bottom are almost white; some tilleulbuff; some deep olive-buff; some brick red; some old gold; and others either dark neutral gray or vetiver green. Thus they manifest not only a difference of composition—limestone, granite, sandstone and so on—but also a variety of experience and duration in the stream.

The dry rocks ashore are usually either lead color or light gray, but occasionally pale olive buff. Some of them within the bubbling spray are covered with bright reinette green moss; others merely spattered with moss of a yew-green shade.

The water makes a dashing, rumbling sound, the individual gurglings, swishes, splashes and bubble-burstings being distinguishable when thus but inches away; but in the distance of only a rod or so all sounds intermingle in a constant purl.

Caterpillars occasionally drop from above; leaves scintillate in the sun. Yes, there is ever beauty in the variety of canyon sounds.

JULY 1

Many mountain meadows or parks are delightful regions in the upper reaches of brook and stream, some of them being grassy stream-adorned stretches of the Provo, Weber, Ogden and Logan rivers, beautiful not so much on account of surrounding landscapes of varied hills as the sweet purity and freshness of everything that therein grows. These parks are usually surrounded by conifers, quaking aspens and cotton-woods from which often in spring comes the sweet fragrance of the mountain lilacs. There also the mountain hedge shows its evergreen leaves on the wooded slopes. These mountain parks claim their own terrestrial avifauna—birds of the mountain meadows. Often the hill-sides are rich in color—the color of lupines, penstemons, Indian paint brushes, gilias and geraniums—; but the birds, as we have seen in Parley's Park, love the willowed meadows, and there we may find at different times of the year such delights of wing and song as: the white crowned sparrow, which loves the willows of sub-alpine meadows where beside the stream it whistles its doublenote song; the slate-colored sparrow; the western vesper sparrow, which nests in brookside grass scarcely distinguishable from its own streaks and markings; the Lincoln sparrow, which sings in the willows but nests on the ground; and occasionally the green-tailed towhee which utters its mewing call notes from the ground of streamside shrubbery.

Besides these, three species of humming birds favor the mountain meadows: the Calliope, the broad-tailed, and the black-chinned, which build their tiny nests on willow limbs.

Desolate and cold become these snow laden parks in winter, when at night the white-tailed jack rabbits stand like nocturnal ghosts in the very blizzards of the zero hills!

We are now entering upon the serotinal period of birdlife, that July-August time when juveniles flock together and adult birds molt their fine feathers.

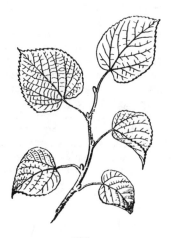

JULY 2

It is a brook-trickled nook at 7,140 feet in Lamb's canyon, a cool place verdured with stinging nettle, wild raspberries, twinberries, false Solomon's seal, and intermittently shaded by Englemann spruces of noble age, huge cones of ancient memory. It is a paradise for flower, tree, shrub and bird, a place that is green, secluded, cool. Robins are all about; indeed, on a spruce branch nearby is a recently-used nest of fibers and mud. A broad-tailed humming bird buzzes about, making a trilling sound with its wings as if it were a miniature spermophile. A red-naped sapsucker stops momentarily at a spruce trunk, then flies to a quaking aspen grove. A spermophile (*Citellus armatus*) nibbles at our feet, and a Utah rock squirrel chatters loudly in the tree tops and then scampers through them over interlacing branches. Once in a while the spermophile whistles in three loud shrill notes like "Ha' ha ha."

Here we find blooming a lively Indian paint brush (*Castilleja lauta*) noteworthy for its lanceolate leaves, glabrous stem, short corolla and crimson bracts; a meadow rue; the clematis or virgin's bower; an everlasting pea (*Lathyrus brachycalyx*); both a white and a pink geranium; and choke cherries just coming into bloom.

Rambling much higher to the verge of a meadow (8050 feet) we find in the very midst of a crystal brook that beautiful white corydal or bleeding heart (*Corydalis brandegei*).

We descend, and discover (6,965 feet) the pale blue languid lady and an ill-smelling, white Jacob's ladder (*Polemonium albiflorum*) forming a pleasing bed on the hillside, with western wall flowers intermingled.

At 6,865 feet an immense dark blue penstemon (*Penstemon cyananthus*) and a lighter one (*P. brevifolius*) are blooming. Here also is a lupine (*L. Laxiflorus*). At 6,800 feet the scarlet gilia shows its conspicuous trumpets—for the moment in the distance we thought it to be *Penstemon eatoni.*

The partridge berry is in flower further down (6,790 feet); and then a little distance more the mountain ash (*Sorbus scopulina*) with its white flowers, and the nine bark with its showy, fragrant white blooms in pretty coryms. The mountain lilac shows hereabout and we soon come upon the loveliest bed of globe mallows or Roses of Sharon that we have ever seen, occupying an acre of burnt-over hillside, each flower being pinkish or white. This alone is worth the venture of the day; for we have followed the trails of the brookside that lead to a lake high in this lovely canyon, whose shores are verged with flowers and grasses, where gushing crystaline water tumbles from steep hillsides as though it were impatient in its venture to life and beauty below.

JULY 3

Even in the fir-adorned reaches of lower City Creek the sunny brookside at midday is warm. Despite the refreshing purity of bubbling water and the coolness of sprayed mossy stones, the stream cannot counteract the beating rays of the summer sun, which dissipates fleeting mists almost as soon as they arise from a foaming pool. Pesky flies disturb one's tranquility, but pleasing tiger butterflies flutter about the open glade, as if the ancient trunks of the lofty cottonwoods were the goals of their playground. A robin occasionally carols desultorily, too languid for aught but perfuntory calls. Scarcely a leaf trembles overhead; only one huge cumulus cloud floats in majestic isolation through the blue. Repose, quietude, mark the midday of the lower canyon; but the cottonwoods exude upon us occasional drops like rain.

We move higher to a place where the canyon brook boils its cold lucent waters over mossy boulders and eddies against embankments staked with horsetail; and there the water ouzel descends from its chattering, stream-guided flight to bill within the stone-held pools for bugs and worms. After making several curtsies while standing atop a spray-drenched stone, it ploughs through a small short-caught pool, and, regaining its stony perch, never even shakes its dripping plumage. Something in the damp mossy sand at the roots of the gritty horsetails attracting its eyes, it for the moment turns backward to peck for grubs, a not uncommon habit in a bird that usually feeds beneath the water. And what a carefree bird it is! Winter or summer, snow or sunshine, it never leaves its beloved stream; for always, even when ice mantles the canyon trail and brookway, some pool remains open beneath a snow-frozen fall. Living in the purest and sweetest surroundings, it is perhaps the happiest bird in all the world. But there comes the query—what is happiness? Should we say: happiness is the enjoyment of a present without worry over an unknown future? What an ineffable word "happiness" is, for to no two people do the identical things constitute joy!

JULY 4

Go with us on a delightful mountain-trip, beginning, let us say, at the mouth of Farmington canyon early in the morning. Barely within the entrance we stop to listen to the sweet song of a lovely bird, a lazuli bunting, perched atop a scrub oak over the creek and faced toward the early sun. He moves his head side to side, showing his turquoise upper parts and black bill, and exultantly facing the morning, sings a sort of "twe twe twe twa twa twa - e - e," leaving out once in a while the "e-e" at the end, which after all is but a terminal rolade; and continues his rhapsody beyond the quarter hour we care to wait. But fifty feet away he disdains us as friends, though in our own minds we are long-tried and long trusted. We know him to be a male, from his brownish breast and sides, and marvel at the exquisite coloring of birddom.

Not to deny but more to vary the feathered beauty of our early soloist, we glance toward the rocky embankment at our side, there to discover the white thistlelike blossoms of the Mexican poppy (*Argemone hispida*) in full bloom. We gather a sample, only to endure prickling the rest of the day. Many of the sweetest things in life are protected by rules, regulations and stings, not the least of which is the *Mentzelia* we saw abloom on the way.

We drive on, ever alert for bird, animal, insect or bloom, noticing as we ascend a species of the evening primrose family (*Gayophytum ramosissum*) that looks so like gysophilia that we call it "baby's breath."

And there at 6,000 feet we remark a sort of frosted appearance on an evergreen, as if someone had tied three inch, stiff, white feather-strings to the end of all of the branches. Strings, indeed; they are the persistent styles of the mountain mahogany (*Cercocarpus ledifolius*), that hard-wooded, leathery leaved evergreen of the Wasatch. We ponder, observe, and tomorrow shall continue our interesting mountain way.

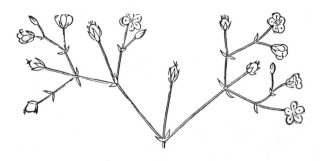

JULY 5

Here we are, the sun yet brightening only the tops of the creekside verdure of Farmington canyon; and, as we arrive at an altitude of 6,100 feet, we notice the fragrant dogbane blooming in the dried grasses of the hills, clarkia blossoming, and the white-topped yarrow showing itself everywhere.

A hundred feet higher along the trail of this diverting canyon we admire again that multi-colored gilia (*Gilia grandiflora*) whose flowers vary from antimony yellow to ochraceous buff; also another gilia (*Gilia linearis*) with delicate, pink, salverform corollas. All along the roadside, especially in the damper places, the giant hyssop (*Agastache urticifolia*) is showing its purplish white blossoms; but this member of the mint family has a strong, unpleasant odor not unlike that of oil of penny royal. The blooms, however, are pretty enough for a flower garden.

The columbine (*Aquilegia flavescens*) shows its pale yellow petals along the creekside at 6,500 feet; and, a ramble higher, we come upon that large flowered wild rose known as *Rosa melina,* which, by the way, is one of the finest that grows in these mountains. Near it is the white geranium (*Geranium richardsonii*), and a species of monkey flower (*Mimulus Lewisii*). Its corollas are a beautiful rosolane purple; and it seems to grow best with its feet actually touching the cold waters of a brook in an aspen grove. That stout, big-leaved plant, taller than one's head, with a panicle of closely intermingled, greenish white little flowers at the top, is a white hellebore (*Veratrum speciosum*), once erroneously thought to be poisonous to cattle and sheep. Some call it "cow cabbage"; at any rate, it has a rather sickening odor when much handled.

Since we are now at the fork of the roads, where aspens grow in profusion and the mountains are decidedly cool and delightful, we choose the right one, which leads higher and higher to a truly alpine region and finally descend by way of Ward's canyon. The multiform beauties of the flowers along its course must await the morrow.

JULY 6

In a region maculated by clusters of firs, groves of aspens and stretches of sage brush—to be exact, on the Farmington-Ward canyon's road at 7,200 feet—our attention is attracted towards the most beautiful columbine we have yet seen. It has enormous, white flowers (*Aquilegia caerulea albiflora*) and to our surprise and joy, it dots not only the verdured but also the dry hillsides everywhere. Even its sepals are white. Not having noticed it elsewhere in the Wasatch mountains, we retain it in sweet memory. We hope someday to find here the Colorado columbine (*Aquilegia caerulea*), the sepals of which are blue.

To our enthusiastic delight, in the same vicinity four kinds of penstemons are in bloom—the pale blue *cyananthus* known as "blue bells"; the deep blue *garretti* on rocky escarpments; the dwarf *brevifolius* in carpets of blue adorning sandy intervals; and the *platphyllus* in delicate tints of lavender violet. Indeed, at 7,700 feet, so dotted are the hills with white yarrow, blue penstemons and red Indian paint brushes that we involuntarily exclaim—red, white and blue, the flag! We could add to these the great pink roses of Sharon and yellow mule ears (*Wyethia amplexicaulis*), for they also are abloom in profusion, some among sage brushes, some on the more verdured slopes. No wonder "a voice was heard upon the high places"; no wonder "is salvation hoped for from the hills"—there the Infinite shows its sweetest flowers, there the deepest blue of skies!

At 8,000 feet two gilias catch our eager attention—one (*Gilia inconspicua*) with flowers of jasper pink; another (*Linanthus harknessii*) with long, slender tubes of barium yellow and white corollas. As a pleasing diversion, we watch a red-naped sapsucker fly over the aspens from dry pine to dry pine, though we know it drills squarish holes in living bark to drink the bleeding sap, or pecks up the ants attracted thereto. Its red crown contrasts its black upper parts.

On the way down (7,500 feet) we come upon the finest Indian paint brush that we have seen. Its Tyrian pink flowers are on longer petioles than those of *C. confusa* growing near—another prize for memory's *sanctum sanctorum*.

In a patch of scrub oaks in Ward canyon (7,000 feet) we come at a turn to a beautiful cluster of purple flea banes or wild daisies (*Erigeron macranthus*). Each flower has over a hundred rays surrounding a center of gold and green. It is sweet and refreshing under the hot summer sun; for joyful indeed are the flowered mountains.

JULY 7

Though the Prophets of old sought the mountains for inspiration and prayer they could take refuge in no such lofty peaks and high grounds as those of the Wasatch, the Uinta or the Rocky mountains. In all that mountain range which extends along the western side of the River Jordan in Palestine, from the gentle slopes of Lebanon in the North to Beer-sheba in the South, the highest summit is Jebel Jermuk, 3,934 feet above the level of the Mediterranean.

The river Jordan over there after which the Wasatch mountain Jordan was named, begins in the Leddan, one of the world's largest springs, and joins a stream called Banias to form the Lake of Huleh, whence it descends rapidly to form the Sea of Galilee, thirteen miles long, and thereafter proceeds amid growths of tamarisk and willows along its course to the Dead Sea. Its resemblance to the Wasatch, beginning at Utah Lake and ending in the Great Salt Lake, is remarkable, though the old world Jordan for part of its length flows through a cleft two hundred feet deep, quite unlike the easy going field level Jordan of these mountains.

Even the lofty peaks of the Wasatch, from Nebo at the South, northward, including the Provo, Timpanogas (highest 11,957 feet), Lone, Clayton, Twin, Ogden, Ben Lomond, and Box Elder, are three times as high as the Biblical mounts, but these in turn seem low beside the King of the Uintas (13,498 feet), and Mount Elbert (14,420), loftiest in Colorado.

If you would find comfort in your grief, inspiration toward your desired accomplishments, tranquility for meditation, zestful pure air for bodily well-being, sparkling waters, and a peace undisturbed save by the spiritual song of the hermit thrush, seek you the mountains, for there the Designer of all seems quite real and near.

Mountains everywhere are to the people relative things, there being perhaps little difference in looking from the shores of the Mediterranean to Mount Ebal (3,077 feet) than from the shores of the Great Salt Lake to the lower ridges of the Wasatch, though actually the latter shores are 4,200 feet higher to begin with. Mountains everywhere mean tranquility, and purity, the very life of man's reverential quest of the Infinite. Perhaps someday there will be an eclaircissement.

JULY 8

Some flowers and trees of the mountains of Palestine resemble those of the Wasatch. The box (*Juniperus Phoenicea*) of Mount Lebanon and the Galilean hills is somewhat like our juniper (*Juniperus Utahensis*); and several thistles and spine-bearing plants are of the same general nature. They have their firs (*Pinus halepensis*) and pines (*Pinus pinea*).

The people of Palestine eat mint (*Mentho sativa*) with their meat just as we decorate our dishes with mint (*M. penardi*) picked from the borders of valley brooks. They are tormented by a stinging nettle (*Urtica pilulifera*) as we by another species, *Urtica breweri*; and their river Jordan likewise has its willows (*Salix octandra*).

Though the Wasatch mountains have their "Mount Nebo", their "river Jordan" and their "Dead Sea", they do not bear such trees as the almond, palm, aloes, myrtle, cypress, fig, olive and pomegranate, nor such plants as the coriander, cummin and mandrake; but several related species of sage brush or wormwood (*Artemisia*) occur in both places.

In the Holy Land several animals exist that are similar to those of the Wasatch; thus: badgers, bats, light brown bears (*Ursus arctos*), rock conies (*Hyrax Syriacus*) like our pikas (*Ochotona princeps Uinta*), deer, jackals, (*Canis aureus*) like our coyotes, "ferrets" like our shrews, as well as foxes, porcupines, field mice and weasels.

In the Jordan valley there in winter may be seen birds that inhabit our own Jordan, such as the gadwall, pintail, teal and shoveller; bitterns, pelicans, cormorants, blue herons, ospreys, sandpipers, vultures, doves, shrikes, ravens, owls, magpies, kingfishers, blue jays, blackbirds, hawks like our Cooper and sharp-shinned, and gold finches all year long. One would over there miss the water ouzel, the hummingbirds, and many of our alpine species such as the Clark nutcracker and the snowy owl.

Palestine and Utah have unique physical characteristics, both combining opposite features: the lowlands and the mountains; the scarcity of the desert and the luxuriance of the high lands; the arable and the pastoral; the dry desert wash and the sparkling brooklets of pine-cooled regions.

Yet the world over people are much the same—living, loving, hating; striving for comfort, glory and wealth, or existing without the pangs of ambition; worshipping the sun, the stars, a great anthropomorphic being or the all-pervading Intelligence of nature; but ever imbuing their despair with hope, ever trying to believe it is not all in vain.

JULY 9

As we linger with luxurious abandon beside a canyon creek so clear that the rocks of its bed show as if mirrored through the silver-flecked waters, we sit in a bower of overhanging alders, maples and willows, where grass grows in rich plenty and currant vines intertwine the grayish trunks of the trees. Robins sing loud roulades among the spruces of the canyonsides and Macgillivray warblers flit about the dry brushwood of the opposite embankment, where noontime shadows give a soft and darksome charm to the fast-running stream.

Here and there summer flies big and black alight upon the limbs. We strike one down and discover it is a large blue bottle (*Calliphora erythrocephala*), the one that destroys the Rocky mountain locust—and annoys ourselves!

A willow-limb, long grown aslant the brook, flicks back and forth as its lower branches catch and recatch the peak of the turbulent waves. Not over twenty feet wide is the restless stream, shallow, swift, and translucent as a window pane; but over it lean the enduring alders like fingers of eternity over the nervous run of the world.

A moth flies by and alights on a pretty yellow flower, and behind it on the hillside grasshoppers stridulate in ceaseless din. So still is the cloudless day that not even the quaking aspen leaves across the vale tremble with accustomed activity; their silvered trunks appear in bright repose. Even a draught or a sweet zephyr will agitate an aspen leaf. Overhead, the sky is blue and unfathomable like a mystic painting possessed of not only color but also ineffable depth.

At eventide dragon flies pursue their swift, voracious ways, grasping in dextrous flight midges, gnats, mosquitoes, flies, wasps and moths. Even when captured and impaled with a pin one will continue to devour insect after insect in ravenous insatiability. Flight models for airplanes, they are honored by imitation; yet on scientific principles, the fat bumble bee cannot fly at all. Nature's stories are ever old, ever new; and her designs by the simple process of conformation to need, protection and propagation are the models on which all progress must build. He who imitates nature but follows the Master builder of us all.

We go home, and there at the fish pond a dragon fly of rusty red evades our every effort to capture it. It is only a guess this time—a ruby spot (*Hesaerina americana*), for such is the appearance of this uncaptured damsel fly.

JULY 10

A reconnaissance of the flora and fauna of Fairview canyon offers attractive diversion for the day; so, leaving Highway 89 at Fairview (altitude 6,033 feet), we proceed eastward up the canyon.

We travel for three or four miles up unflowered terrain; but at 6,780 feet we see groves of firs, find a fireweed (*Epilobium angustifolium*), a wild rose blooming on the hillside, and a short dark-blue penstemon (*P. brevifolius*).

Further along (7,230 feet) our eyes are drawn toward the road embankment where sweet-smelling, pink-flowered antelope or buck brush has won the attention of a score of brown, white-spotted butterflies, which look like Palmer's metal mark (*Lemonias palmeri*), as they flutter beyond our reach.

At 7,380 feet we find blooming on the sidehills and among quaking aspens: the scarlet gilia, blue flax (*Linum lewisii*), white geraniums, those pale, nodding bluebells known as "languid lady" and a fine blue delphinium (*D. bicolor*).

The slopes at 8,000 feet are adorned with flowers, including an orange-colored wall flower (*Erysimum asperum*), a tall phacelia (*Phacelia sericea*) so covered with long stamens and styles that it resembles a purple stick covered with pins, and a penstemon (*Penstemon sepalulus*) with violet-colored bells actually over an inch long.

We next come to a delightful region (8,280 feet) where crystal brooks cascade fir-groved canyonsides, and here find a brilliant red Indian paint brush (*Castillja hispida*) whose leaves look like a tiny three-fingered hand. We listen to the whistles of spermophiles (*Citellus armatus*) and then discover on a dry embankment that shrubby much-branched little cinque-foil or five finger (*Potentilla dasiphora fruticosa*) that has a round, five petalled, hollow flower. We are delighted with its discovery, not having come upon it elsewhere, but no more pleased than in finding all along the slopes further on a flower that resembles a small petal-dropping sunflower but of a pleasing Ta-ming or golden yellow color—it is the sneezeweed (*Helenium hoopesii*) with twenty-five flowers united together lengthwise so as to appear as one flower.

At the fork of the roads (8,530 feet), where thick-trunked quaking aspens adorn a flat that is almost encircled by picturesque lower valleys, we see white columbines (*Aquilegia coerulea*), more delphiniums, robins, mountain blue-birds; and in a pleasant valley further on (8,280 feet) we find a yellow monkey flower (*Mimulus guttatus*).

At the summit (8,580 feet) we observe a little, purple, hairy flower (*Phacelia alpina*); and as the road descends (8,380 feet) we discover a white wild sweetpea (*Lathyrus coriaceus*) growing among the dry embankment rocks.

The hills become unattractive. We decide to return. What a joyful region, reminiscent of the Kaibab!

JULY 11

What an enormous moth! As it spreads before us there it is nearly five inches across! It is a tomato sphinx moth (*Protoparce sexta*), a lovely hawk-moth to look at, with wings of brown and gray irregularly striped with blackish, and with the rear half of its body partly banded with alternate yellow and dark brown. And its tongue is as long as its body! *Mirable visu!*

There are in the United States other moths undoubtedly larger than the tomato sphinx, especially the great Cecropia moth (*Samia cecropia*) of the East, which measures more than six inches wing tip to wing tip; but in the region of these mountains few others can claim to equal the tomato sphinx. Glover's silk-moth (*Samia gloveri*), which inhabits these regions, is one of these.

As we look upon this strange humming bird of the night, it is rather disappointing to realize that its larva feeds on such members of the *Solanaceae* as tomatoes and potatoes; but such is the disappointing truth.

Not many moths of the Wasatch mountains and valleys approach the tomato sphinx in size; there are, however, a few. The Galium sphinx (*Celerio intermedia*) mountain loving species, though not so large, has a striking mark of light yellow on the primary or greater wing, and a wide pinkish band on the secondary wing; the Achemon sphinx (*Pholus achemon*), which has a tremendous fat larva, has lovely pink secondary wings (it likes the Virginia creeper); the western poplar sphinx (*Pachysphinc modesta occidentalis*), which feeds on poplars and willows is almost as large but it is very pale yellow all over except for a broad patch of maroon on the secondary wing; Cerisy's sphinx (*Sphinx cerisyi*), though only about three fourths the size of the tomato sphinx is notable for the fact that on each hind wing is a small yellow ring inside a black spot, very attractive indeed; and the ceanothus silk-moth (*Samia rubra*), though nearly as large, is a pale brown species with a white line running across both fore and hind wings on each of which is a white spot shaped like a tobacco pipe. Its larva feeds on our snow brush or mountain lilacs. That comprises most of our larger moths.

JULY 12

Our locale is a cabined, brook-sung nook at 5,170 feet altitude in Mill Creek canyon. It is the twelfth of July and in the morning delightfully cool, sometimes even uncomfortably cold in comparison with the sultry atmosphere of the sun-scorched valley of the Great Salt Lake below us. Our glade is over-grown with three species of trees: big toothed maple, box elders and Douglas spruces (*Pseudotsuga mucronata*), the last named being scarce at the creekside but thick as a cloak on the upper mountainsides.

Our cabin is in a maple grove, fifty yards from the crystal brook. At daylight a "sip" is heard, repeated over and over, obviously a bird at our kitchen dooryard. The rising sun reveals them—a pair of western flycatchers (*Empidonax difficilis difficilis*) enamored with the very maple that faces the open sunny spot of the cabin yard. With glasses that bring them so close that their black eyes resemble beads we watch them throughout the day.

A copulation takes place, once on a dry twig, once as the female sits on a pointed rock. Her note is a definite "sip", and she upturns her tail usually when she utters it. In the timing of nine times she "sips" on an average once every seven seconds; but once, though sipping, she neglects to twitch her tail for over a minute's duration. The tail movement seems to be a nervous reaction upon a change of position or limb, or in moments of expectancy.

She "sips" even with a fly in her bill, once the fly being held for half an hour while she sips and before she swallows the morsel. She holds it with its head foremost, adjusts it now and again by pressing her bill against the twig, and so far as we can see, almost digests it before final disposition.

The male is quieter than she, but when he does utter a note it is louder, a whistle like "suzzwhip" with a coarser "suzz" character. The notes begin slowly and end with a definite accent on the "whip."

Both prefer dry twigs, and while she is faithful to the rendezvous all day, he forages afar for twenty minutes at a time, announcing his arrival by the loudness of his call.

Once they come together as if mating. They utter a "zwerser zer we", a contented throaty chatter.

216

JULY 13

How lovely the bloom, how singular the habit of the evening primrose! Nine different kinds we have taken in the Wasatch, five of them white, four of them yellow, some in the dry sands of the plains (*Oenothera pallida, O. latifolia, O. marginata*), different ones in moist open places (*O. bookeri, O. strigosa*) and others on sunny slopes of the mountains (*O. subacaulis, O. caespitosa*); but none is more outstanding and delightful than that tall one of chalcedony yellow now blooming at the roadside as we stand in the evening just above the reservoir in City Creek canyon. It is the variety known as *bookeri*, with a stout hairy stem, erect, unbranched, long minutely toothed leaves, and a many flowered spike at the top. Its four big petals make a light lemon-yellow flower more than two inches across, the throat of which is crowded with eight long stamens and a four-cleft stigma of the same delicate tint. Three other flowers, having done their duty, stand wilted and reddish at its foot, for as we have said, it is the habit of this lovely flower to open one at a time to attract the moths to its pollen, and then to close its bloom as another reopens the following evening. It looks so pure and tempting that it is little wonder the moth of evening pauses to give it a kiss.

While we are here about the reservoir we must not fail to mention that growing in the June grass, which is now straw-yellow and as dry as tinder, is a perennial herb with erect branching stems, about a foot high with the sweetest, most fragrant, tiny, bell-shaped, pinkish-white flowers one might see in many a day. Its leaves are smooth like those of the service berry. As we examine one of the wee flower bells, which is not over a quarter of an inch long, we see that the Corinthian pink petals are striped with Persian pink or claret red on the inner side, and that the center of the throat is golden yellow. It is a dogbane (*Apocynum androsaemifolia.*)

"Dogbane" is a name given to various plants said to be poisonous to dogs, principally of the orders *Asclepiadaceae* and *Apocynaceae*. Thus in 1597 Gerarde wrote: "Dog's bane is a deadly and dangerous plant, especially to four footed beasts." Whether dogs even dislike it we have never tested, but as we handle and smell it as we write it is altogether delightful to ourselves.

We have two other dogbanes or Indian hemps in the Wasatch: *A. cannabinum* with greenish white corolla; and *A. hypericifolium* with clasping leaves. They are the joy of the dry mountain slopes and the wet places of the hills.

217

JULY 14

Sweet are the waters and delightful the song of ever-flowing canyon streams, for being in a desert-margined region, the Wasatch mountains quickly parch under summer heat except where deeply laden snow seeps the shaded glades and where brooks trickle down the gullies and dash down the canyons on their way to an inland sea one fourth salt. Along the banks of these higher ever-joyful creeks many shrubs that appeal to birds with their berries grow luxuriantly, such for instance, as the dogwood, elderberry, twinberry, (*Lonicera involucrata*), choke cherry, mountain gooseberry (*Ribes inerme*), and black hawthorn. There also grow birches, aromatic sumac (*Rhus trilobata*), poison ivy (*Toxicodendron rydbergii*), maples, and boxelders.

The canyon shrubbery thus formed has a fairly definite arboreal avifauna. One bird, not however, arboreal, spends its entire life along the waters of these streams; it is the water ouzel often alluded to in these pages. Other birds, delighting in the embankment thickets are: the tiny lead-colored bush tit; the Macgillivray warbler, which likes a dry grass-nest near the ground; the lazuli bunting, which sings a half hour at a time from the tip of a creek willow; the mountain song sparrow, which carols joyously near its nest of tufted grass; the Woodhouse jay, which likes insects as well as acorns and pine nuts; the pugnacious little flycatcher (*Empidonax trailii brewsteri*), which sings a restless, aggressive "pre pe dear" as it catches insects of all kinds; the olive-backed thrush (*Hylocichla usulata almae;* the Audubon hermit thrush, which softly sings its song "oh spero spero! oh rolee rolee"; and the slate-colored sparrow whose nest is seldom more than a yard above ground, but large and made of grass, bark and fibers.

Delightful are the scenes of canyon shrubbery.

JULY 15

Throughout America various substitutes have from time to time been used for tea; thus: the New Jersey tea (*Ceanothus americanus*) of the Revolutionary War; Appalachian tea (*Viburnum cassinoides*); Blue mountain or golden rod tea (*Solidago odora*); wild tea (*Amorpha canescens*); and the tea berry or mountain tea (*Gaultheria procumbens*), to mention only a few.

In the Wasatch mountains the Indians made tea from a species of the joint fir family now known as mountain rush or "Brigham's tea" (*Ephedra nevadensis*). This olive-green branching shrub resembling the horsetail of the creeks, may be seen growing abundantly on the arid hillsides, especially along the southern extremities of these mountains. The Indians called this tea "tutembi"; but they also boiled the mint (*Mentha panardi*), which grows plentifully along the valley brooks, and called the drink derived from it "baugona."

Many a pioneer girl in these mountains gathered the leaves of the wild rose and of sage brush with which her parents made tea. They also boiled spearmint, and for "coffee" used browned barley, or failing that, a slice of burnt toast over which hot water was poured. In the early days real tea, if available at all, cost nearly four dollars a pound, a price far beyond the means of settlers who worked hard merely to appease their hunger.

By the way, we notice today that domestic sparrows (*Passer domesticus*) are greatly bothered by lice. They stand chirping on their favorite perches, shiver their wings, nibble irritating body spots with their bills, and for half an hour at a time endeavor to rid themselves of itches and distress. It is due to the fact that summer and winter they nest in the same niches and holes of houses, for we do not notice that other birds appear to suffer.

Today (1943) is the first time we have seen the English starling in this valley. It is cawing on a telephonewire. It has taken it many a year to reach us from Atlantic shores where it was introduced and where perhaps its numbers are already diminished.

JULY 16

Oh modest thrush within the cadent dell,
Where brooklets gurgle through the tranquil pines,
Where oreads their zephyred stories tell
And wave the spires, the rising sun o'er shines,
You toll the Angelus and greet the morn,
As though an angel blessing earth below;
Your tender tones the fragrant air adorn
And holy chimes the dale of seeping snow.
To think a bird can substitute a choir,
When looms the morn upon a moon-kissed night!
To know one throat can thrum a heavened lyre,
Exalting all the woods with sweet delight,
And make serene the somber morning hush!
Oh whither go you, lovely hermit thrush?

Each naturalist must be ecstatic at times, especially when prompted by something almost spiritual in woodland purity like the Audubon hermit thrush, which nests in the verdured labryinths of the Wasatch and lives unobstrusively with seclusive charm where cool glades provide it insect and berry. Yet even now, late though it seem for wildwood eggs, the Olive-backed thrush is siting on its bulky, moss-twined nest above the clear waters of the Smith and Moorehouse canyon on the upper Weber; but that other modest thrush, the Willow (*Hylocichla fuscesens saliciola*) delighting in the wild rose and boxelder, further down, has ere now trained its fledglings.

In these sultry days, whenever one comes upon a species of snake-weed, such as *Gutierrezia sarothrae*, or *G. microcephala*, which occupy the artemisia belts of the lower canyons, he is apt to notice thereon one or the other of the Wasatch green grasshoppers *Hesperotettix virids* or *H. curtipennis*.

Whenever one sees a mummy grasshopper, clinging in death to a weed, its body is likely filled with the spores of a fungus, for such is the insidious way of nature.

In the high mountain glade, where a forest of darksome firs point heavenward against brilliant white cumuli over the southern horizon, the surrounding quaking aspens shiver listlessly beneath the noonday sun. Wild roses display their pink flowers beside the branch-enshrouded brook; cow parsnips hold high their many handled parasols of white; and white yarrow blooms bedeck the greensward. A tiger butterfly approaches when furiously a black and white one, Weidemeyer's Admiral (*Basilarchia weidemeyeri*) much smaller, drives the big intruder away. Deer flies come ravenously from nowhere; yet all is dry, sultry and still save for the cadence of the fretting water.

JULY 17

Within the entrance of Ogden canyon the silky clematis is draping hillside shrubbery with white blooms, and a little further on the berries of the elderberry are turning green and becoming attractive among maples, boxelders, cottonwoods and firs. There are few flowers except sunflowers and mustards; and we do not even suspect that the end of the ascending trail is to be a floral Arcadia.

At the reservoir we do see golden rods, yarrows, pink geraniums and dogbanes, scarlet gilias and umbrella plants as well as the thimble berry with its white blossoms; but these are all ordinary. Two lazuli buntings playing above the oak brush, cabbage butterflies flitting about, and two Arkansas flycatchers in mimic fray above a power line, win our attention, as does a yellow monkey flower (*Mimulus guttatus*) blooming in the meadow head where yellow warblers and meadowlarks are singing.

We tarry at a village where Northern violet-green swallows course the crystal brook, where pale goldfinches (*Spinus tristis pallidus*) and catbirds sing in the trees and Brewer blackbirds wade the wet meadows. Most pleasing to us is that "little" flycatchers, scarcely larger than warblers, dash about the brookside in noonday play. We used to call them Traill flycatchers. Cliff swallows (*Petrochelidon albifrons hypopolia*) swarm in and out of a wayside barn.

We go higher and come upon fireweeds, common mulleins (*Verbascum thapsus*), more white clematis and *Rudebeckias*; but we are not yet impressed, though at 5900 feet an Indian paint brush (*C. linariaefolia*) is blooming, and we watch a ferruginous rough-leg hawk (*Buteo regalis*) kite with almost motionless wings on gully updraughts above aspen groves.

At twenty eight miles from the mouth of the canyon some beautiful flowers begin to show: the shrubby cinquefoil (*Potentilla dasiphora fruticosa*) in yellow bloom; cream colored umbrella plants (*Erigonum ovalifolium*), the giant hyssop, the dark blue penstemon; golden rods; scarlet gilias; Jacob's ladders and two mallows—one lilac (*Sidalcea oregana*) and one orange red (*Sphaeralcea coccinea*). And there is the discovery of the trip up to now a *Penstemon watsoni!*

We go on and (7,500 feet) find white lupine, blue languid ladies, purple fleabanes, beggar ticks, partridge berries, yarrow, sunflowers (*Wyethia*), a pretty senicio (*S. Uintahensis*) and white columbines.

We go over the summit at 9,006 feet, and just below it find the floral Arcadia of our dreams—a valley of penstemons, paint brushes, larkspurs, and gray sage, a tranquil high valley with mile on mile of undisturbed floral beauty; a garden at the top of the world with waving rolls of pale blue, dark blue and brilliant red, all intensified in color by the shadows of late afternoon, all filled with the redolence of spicy gray sage. Can this be the sanctum we have desired: the sweet retreat from the trials and tribulations of man? Lovely spot—we hope time and time again to tarry there!

JULY 18

Scampering rock squirrels frisking through the canyon shrubbage; a dipping water ouzel pecking about the moss of a brook-sprayed stone; great moving white cumulus clouds like isolated wool-castles in a clear blue sky; solemn weather beaten trunks of ancient cottonwoods with lacy fringes of alder limbs at their feet; copsewoods of nine-bark, aromatic sumac and tender maples; ravenous, dashing deer flies and mild mannered white admirals and tiger butterflies; the ceaseless song of pellucid water over stones of yellow purple and gray—such is a mountain glen on this summer afternoon.

For a hundred years or more yonder lofty long-leaved cottonwood has stood beside this fretting canyon stream, and in that time has grown to be a clump of seven trees upshooting and clustering from the same root system. Its larger trunks are scarred and browned with years of stress and storm, even in places split open or pocked with holes or cavities that are really wells of stagnant sap and decaying nutriment, as if the very heart of the monarch were oozing with tearful age. Yet the leaves of its sun-loving head tremble with the enthusiasm of youthful life.

That strong-flying horse fly or deer fly (*Chrysops*) that has just now bitten our exposed wrist is a female, for in the flies of the family *Tabanidae* to which it belongs only the females have *proboscises* adapted to pierce mammalian skin for blood. This is true also of mosquitos and, in fact, all blood-sucking flies. We keep thinking of Kipling's theory, that the female of any species—human perhaps too!—is more deadly than the male. These deer flies bite without injecting poison; but they are so furious that they look much worse than the more painful mosquito. These flies are seldom found very far from water, which they drink frequently. They deposit their spindle-shaped eggs on leaves, and their larvae, living mostly in water, feed on insects and snails. These flies remind us that in life it is seldom the blusterer, the bombast, the loud-mouthed individual whether man, dog, insect, that does the most harm.

Led by the repeated notes of a mountain chickadee (*Parus gambeli gambeli*), we discover its nest in a quaking aspen, which, twisted by storm, snow and wind, had so cracked as to leave a cozy hole about four inches deep and three inches in diameter. We could easily see five tiny fledglings resting snugly within, but when by means of a pocket mirror we reflected the sun's rays into their domain, they hissed vehemently like a snake, as all the time their mother sat in a nearby tree and often repeated her "chick-a-dee-dee-dee."

JULY 19

Higher and higher creeps the floral display, but in doing so it almost abandons the lowlands to fruit and seed. Thus along the valleys are blooming only such hardened floral soldiers as sunflowers and gum plants, the yellow, wayside weeds sometimes called "arnica".

For the day's locale we select "The Spruces" of Big Cottonwood canyon, where at an altitude of 6700 feet, herbage is growing tall and luxuriantly in the damp interspaces of the ancient evergreens. It is a favorite spot, always livened by the cries of long-crested jays, the dulcet calls of long-tailed chickadees, and the chatterings of Utah rock squirrels; and today it is adorned with floral beauty.

Here and there are thickets of black twinberry, so named because the bluish black berries, which are about a fourth of an inch in diameter, hang as twins, that is, two together on inch long stems, with purple sepals like wings attached above them. They are luscious in appearance but really bitter and unpalatable.

In the shrubwoods are booming those five foot tall fireweeds, willow herbs or silkweeds, as they are variously called (*Epilobium angustifolium*), which have terminal flowers of phlox-purple. We have noticed them at the creekside on the way up the canyon.

And there in the same covert is the monkshood or aconite, growing wandlike four feet high, with racemes of terminal, perfect flowers, each with an upper sepal helmet-shaped and a posterior petal two-hooded. The color is a lithopurple; and as we examine them we can well imagine a tiny face surmounted by a purple hood. Wonderful is botanical nomenclature!

We ramble to a damp place beneath the spruces; and there we find a St. John's wort (*Hypericum Scouleri*) a five-petalled, pretty flower. Its obtuse sepals have marginal black dots, and it is the find of the day.

We come upon a yarrow that has a brownish white convex or rounded top (*Achillea millefolium lanulosa*), unlike the flat-topped yarrow or milfoil of the valleys (*A. Millefolium*). Then as we depart we see among the sage brushes of the dry hillsides many Indian paint brushes (*Castilleja confusa*) with brilliant scarlet flowers. Unadaptable indeed must be he who cannot in the mountains forget for a day the anxieties of life; unobserving he indeed who does not see in the multiformity of nature's ways an underlying relationship and plan that after all indicates a guidance worthy of trust even if beyond comprehension.

JULY 20

As we stop to admire the delicately tinted flower of a thistle (*Cirsium undulatum*) and the better to examine it, clasp its densely bristled foliage, we are for the moment incredulous in our recollection that the rootdigger Indians of this region actually used both the roots and stems of this prickled plant for food. They called it "aiwabok", and doubtless found it edible, after tearing the leaves away and singeing off the bristles.

By the way, since these Indians were called "root-diggers", we may as well divert here upon just what roots they dug for food, especially as most of us like to estimate our own ability to subsist on nature in the raw. Thus the prickly pears which have green bodies so fleshy and thick that, ignoring leaves, they themselves accomplish the work of photosynthesis, have always looked to us as though they would be very tasty when boiled and fried—except for the barbed spines. The Indians speared the fleshy plants with sticks, held them over fires to burn off the needles, placed them over hot ashes in a hole, covered them with more hot embers and, finally with earth. Not so bad served hot—unless with roasted ants for seasoning! They called it "Huvi"; and though they could not store the thick plants, it was evidently a regular summer dish.

They gathered the fibrous roots of the bulrush (*Scirpus validus*), which grows in the shallow waters of lake and pond, eating both roots and lower stem. Indeed, we have it on the authority of Julian H. Steward that the Indians further West "gathered a honeydew exuded by the tule, making balls of it for preservation".

The Indians of this region ate regularly the bulbs of the camas (*Camassia quamash*), which grows in the wet meadows; also the wild onion, which they liked, root and all, and called "gunk". The cancer root, that peculiar plant which is parasitic upon such shrubs as sage brush and entirely destitute of chlorophyll or green coloring, they also found edible. They ate the bulbs of buttercups (*Fritillaria pudica*); and even ground, dried and stored the tobacco root or valerian (*Valeriana edulis*) which trappers insisted was poisonous unless roasted. But the grim winters—there was the regular ordeal that taxed all the ingenuity of the red men who thought not to till and grow.

JULY 21

In the sun-drooped valley orchard of mid-July both calmness and lassitude prevail. The apple leaves are dusty, drowsy and still, wholly unresponsive to passing breaths of air. The big honey locusts (*Gleditsia triacanthos*) that surrounds the tranquil scene, and the tall Lombardy poplars (*Populus dilatata*) that stand like excavation marks at the corners, are animated, however, by the caress of every gentle breeze, the draughts of air being stronger up there; yet, for the most part, they too repose.

The sweet woodnotes, which come from every side, are incessant and clear. English sparrows chirrup continually; yellow warblers "chip", "chip", "chip" with dulcet faintness; a disturbed catbird meows harshly among the raspberries; a robin occasionally rolls its unmistakeable song; a meadowlark, so far away as to be undiscernable, whistles so clearly that every note is distinctly heard; Arkansas fly-catchers chatter and fight about the tallest locusts and the pure-toned mourning dove cooes its soft "ooh who coo! coo!"

And then, when in the evening the garden toad hops innocently into the front yard and the dog both pounces on and mouths it, the dog's discomfiture is due to poison! When handled roughly by such enemies, members of the order *Salientia* not only squirt from the urinary bladder a transparent odorless fluid quite harmless but also emit a poisonous secretion from the skin glands. These glands in the shape of warts and parotoids are much more numerous on the toad than on the smooth-skinned frog. Part of them are slime glands whose purpose is merely to assist respiration, but the others secrete a milky substance that is acidulous in nature and convulsive in effect, acting rather quickly on both the nervous system and the heart of an enemy. If injected into an animal in sufficient quantities it is bound to kill, and that is why the skunks that enter the garden at night roll their toads about the ground before eating them. If a frog is hurt while in the water its poison floats to the surface in a foamy white mass. Yet strangely enough, man is unaffected by the poison of either frog or toad.

JULY 22

Exquisite bits of fluttering color, silent companions of the tranquil places in the mountains, especially in those flowered glades that extend from willowed brooks to shrubberied hills, butterflies are the sweet things that adorn the paradise of any man's hopes and dreams. In the course of many years' observation twenty eight varieties of butterflies have at one time or another held our delighted attention in a single nearby Wasatch canyon. The pretty little red and black Milbert's tortoise shell (*Vanessa milberti*), whose caterpillars feed usually upon that annoying plant, the stinging nettle, and a mourning cloak (*Vanessa antiopa*) both whose caterpillars live on willows in February—they were unseasonable surprises. So each year begins; so the chase goes on.

The brown red and white red Admiral (*Pyrameis atalanta*) appears, though for which navy it is not clear; and then a mottled reddish specimen bordered with black, this one a California tortoise shell (*Vanessa californica*) whose caterpillars feed on our mountain lilac. Then sweet and varied they come: a reddish, black-striped viceroy (*Basilarchia disippus*) imitating in color a bitter relative (*Anosia plexippus*), which the birds ignore; then the white Admiral or Weidemeyer's butterfly (*Basilarchia weidemeyeri*) which is blackish with white bands down its wings, the little pearl crescent (*Phyciodes tharos*) and a West coast lady (*Pyrameis cardui*) with a black band crossing the middle of her primary wing. We have seen thousands of these ladies about apricot trees in April.

Then there are the "angle-wings", such as the zephyr (*Grapta zephyrus*) and the stayr (*Grapta satyrus*), so called because their forewings are deeply excavated; and the "silver spots", such as the Leto-silver spot (*Argynnis leto*), Snyder's fritillary (*Argynnis snyderi*) and Skinner's fritillary (*Argynnis platina*), and the small "hair-streaks", such as the Colorado (*Thecla chrysalus*) and the Texas (*Thecla autolycus*). The orange-margined blue (*Lycaena melissa*) is a sweet memory of one afternoon.

The swallow tail (*Papilio daunus*) and the smaller *Papilio rutulus*, are commoner than the brown *Papilio eurymedon* and the blue blotched Bruce's butterfly (*Papilio brucei*). Just to mention *Pernassius clodius* and the larger *Pernassius smintheus bebri*, the Arizona skipper (*Plestia dorus*), the dusky thanaos (*Thanaos clitus*), the Mexican fritillary (*Euptoieta hegesia*) and the clouded wood-nymph (*Satyrus alope nephele*) is to show in retrospection their beauty in comparison with the common white cabbage butterfly of the valleys. Nevertheless words are inadequate to describe petal patterns on the wing.

JULY 23

As we trudge over a dry rocky hillside on the way to a canyon, we unexpectedly come upon a desert horned lizard (*Phrynsoma platyrhinos*), and soon get the inoffensive "toad" in hand. A pretty little fellow he is, pinkish and brownish gray, about five inches long, and with rudimentary spines about as long as its eyes are wide.

These interesting horned lizards, which are common on the sandy hillsides, are ovoviviporous, producing living young. The little ones are not spiny at first but soon look like the adults and shift for themselves.

Subsisting entirely on insects, the horned lizards catch flies with a dart of the tongue, in the manner of toads, being most active when the sun is brightest. As night approaches they wriggle and scratch until entirely buried in the sand. In captivity they do well in a sand box when supplied with water in a saucer and fed grasshoppers, grubs, crickets, ants and meal worms; nevertheless on the hillsides where we usually find them water is a half mile away. The species that jets blood from its eyelids when teased is found South of Utah, not here.

As we reach the canyon in the drowsy late afternoon, we notice that it is the tree trunks that show brightest in the forested, brook-chattering glade; for the sinking sun peers through the very sideway trees. Flies dashing about likewise reflect the evening light, and appear more conspicuous than at noon. Every movement of squirrels and birds is instantly apparent, even when they are in their labyrinthine coverts; for the sun is like a mighty flashlight illuminating hiding places.

Faint campfire-smoke, deliciously redolent of frying bacon, lingers in grayish fogs about the alders and cottonwoods, then dissipates imperceptively down stream. The aerated, tiny white-caps of the moss-verged brook waft infinitesimal sprays into the cooling atmosphere which bestirs not even a leaf; but little alder branches sometimes dance and sway where their tips actually kiss the rushing upthrusts of the water. There is in all nature the spirit of rich contentment and repose; for where there are ages to live there is no need to hurry.

In Parley's Park we meet an old sheep herder, W. H. Todd. "One July many years ago," he said, "my brother and I herded sheep over those North mountains for Hills brothers. One night a bear killed a sheep, so the next day we drug the carcass a hundred yards from camp and circled it with posts, except for one opening towards which we set a Parker shotgun with a string running to the trigger. We were eating supper when the gun went off. We could tell by the trail of blood and hair that it was the bear, and we followed it through thick timber until dark. The next morning we found it a mile away, shot through the shoulder and dead. It was a big brown grizzly."

JULY 24

Today we tarry on Timpanogos drive, and meander upward from the Provo river side. It is a place of crystal brooks dashing from glacier-flecked mountains, a pine-cloaked region where in tranquility we should choose to dwell. Even to abide there for a summer must prove how inconsequential are the turmoils of man.

At the mouth of the North Fork creek the great mullein (*Verbascum thapsus*) is displaying yellow flowers on stalks five feet high, and, further on at an altitude of one mile rudebeckias or "nigger heads", aconites, and the red-flowered *Penstemon eatoni* attract our attention. There also is the slender leafed *Penstemon leonardi* with its violet blossoms, and wild red raspberries (*Rubus melanolasius*) so plentiful large and delicious that we linger to partake of them. A little higher another plant (*Penstemon platyphyllus*) is showing lavender violet flowers; its leaves are wider than those of *leonardi*.

Higher along the delightful road (6500 feet) we come to the sweet blooms of wild roses, pink geraniums, (*G. fremonti*), flesh colored dog banes, lupines (*Lupinus argentinus*), mountain lilacs and scarlet gilias; and further on, beggar ticks, Jacob's ladder and a larkspur.

In an aspen-verged meadow we find patches of a beautiful mallow (*Sidalaea neomexicana*) whose pink-lilac flowers are cup shaped and marked by a tiny greenish star in the throat. A peculiarity is that its basal leaves are orbicular while those half way up the stock have five to nine clefts, and the upper ones are linear.

Just before we reach the top we descry an Audubon warbler flitting about the aspens in search of insects, and then at the summit we find a rayless goldenrod blooming all over the mountainsides. The swampy clematis there has however gone to seed, resembling enormous dandelion balls but of a gray white color.

We always linger in this neighborhood where venerable aspens grow to mighty size and the tranquility of the place is vaulted by skies of deepest blue.

In descending to a new canyon we are attracted by yellow *Viguiera multiflora* blooms like small sunflowers and by Indian paint brushes (*C. confusa*) on the hills. A Rose of Sharon is in flower beside another mallow (*Sidalcea nervata*).

At a brook that dashes under the roadway we find the twinberry in fruit and see a delicate saxifrage (*S. arguta*) growing almost in the clear water.

Slowly flowers fade from view and we enter the sultry valley.

JULY 25

Surprising indeed are the facts of nature! Having only two weeks ago discovered a western wood pewee sitting on its three eggs in a fibered nest placed on a forest tree near the Weber river, we are surprised that we have just taken yesterday a long-billed dowitcher on its southward flight of migration! The one has been late to arrive, the other early to depart; and the two dates together—July 7th and July 24th—designate, so far as we know, the interim between bird migration movements in the Wasatch mountains.

This long-billed dowitcher, a member of the great order of shore birds and close relative of the snipes and sandpipers, does not breed here, as, for instance, does the chuttering Wilson snipe, the western willet, the spotted sandpiper as well as the long-billed curlew; on the contrary, it seeks the Yukon and other places in Alaska in early May, lays its four eggs in the scratched depression of a moss-covered meadow, feeds the larvae of midges to its fledglings until they are able to take care of themselves, about the first of July, and then flies southward on its way to the winter joys of Cuba, Panama, Ecuador and Columbia.

"Theirs not to reason why" should have been written, not concerning the light brigade but the strange impulse of migration, which, as we see, even in mid-summer makes some birds prepare for sultry weeks of indifference and lassitude, and others for the chills of a far away winter. *Fiat lux!* One fact seems well established—birds and fishes are the leading migrants, though in the sense that migration means a different home in accord with the seasons of the year the word is applicable to seal, turtles, toads and land crabs, if not indeed, to our own mule deer which in the winter often seeks the mildly snowed reaches of the western deserts.

In Lamb's canyon today the twinberry is in fruit where a runnel is shaded by willows, firs, quaking aspens and wild roses. The two black twinberries are supported by garnet wings, and remind one of paratroopers ready to land.

Today is a lucky day: on our return through Emigration canyon we discover (5250 feet) a sunny north hillside covered with blooming clear-eyes or See-brights (*Salvia sclarea*), that big member of the mint family never before taken in the Wasatch. It is a bush up to three feet feet in height, with square stems and long terminal spikes of clustered pink white flowers, the color being furnished by the broad, ovate bracts. Unknown in the West, this European flower must have escaped from cultivation.

JULY 26

From the other side of this maple-verged City Creek canyon brook there is coming a continous cry that resembles somewhat the stridulation of a locust, yet in its lusty character, more like the squeal of a mouse, for it is distinct from the water's purling and prolonged for three or four minutes at a time. Soon the cause appears: a young water ouzel, nearly as large as its mother, hops to a stone on the opposite bank, constantly emitting the crying sound, which, somehow, now resembles the noise of a fighting hummingbird.

The mother ouzel is ahead, wading the stream, diving occasionally into the clear water, and busying herself with the catching of bugs. The young bird cries, watches her, follows her from the edge, flips its wings, and every few moments makes the characteristic bob of the species. Finally the mother bills a worm; and, undoubtedly aware of the fact, the little one begins to agitate its wings violently and to cry greedily for its dinner. The mother ouzel flies to it, places the worm in its mouth, and then jumps to her wading again.

Satisfied for the moment, the young one ducks its head into the water, ceases crying, and temporarily rests; but, becoming apprenhensive over its mother's progress down stream, it soon renews its crying and its following from the shallowed edge. For the most part it keeps where the water is but an inch or so deep and protruding stones are plentiful, though, once in a while, it reluctantly flies a few yards across an inconvenient bend. Away they go down stream with the mother apparently indifferent to the anxiety of the shore-following little one.

An hour passes, and up they come, the mother still wading and leading, the voracious youngster still following and pleading. Save for its slightly lighter color it resembles its mother even in size; yet, truly it is but a babe in the woods.

Proceeding up the canyon, we are surprised to see a yearling mountain lion run from the creek and cross the roadway twenty yards ahead of us. It clambers up the steep cut as we run towards it, hesitates a moment among the maples to look back to us, and then disappears up the steep hillside. It is one of the rarest sights in nature—an unhunted lion in daylight and only a few yards away.

JULY 27

We have often hoped that when we die some understanding friends would place our remains on the limbed bosom of some mighty spruce in that lovely spot known as Wolf Creek Pass, 9,200 feet high, at the head of the South Fork of the Provo river; for its rounded slopes fledged by groves of conifers, its grassy meadows blessed by trickling springs of purest water, and its lofty height favored with the view of distant, white massy clouds below not above the horizon-trees, combine to make this a final dreamland resting place. There the mighty golden eagle soars so near that we can see his eyes. It is, as it has often been before, the day's local.

Its great evergreens, of which some ancient monarchs have trunks three feet in diameter at the bases, have sharp, four-sided needles standing out in all directions, and thus are Engelmann or white spruces. A dozen or more of them point their heads a hundred feet upwards towards the firmament, noble senators of this alpine forum, while all about them are younger citizens awaiting their turn. Here and there is a line of grassy mound, showing where years ago a tree-consul fell to his decay; and, likewise, are those of latter date, still shapen like trunks but prostrate and shelled, their bowels but rotted, orange pulpwood. But in our ecstasy over these soughing forests we must not ignore the occasional Colorado blue spruce, which outstands with deeper color, like a robed princess awaiting her master's call.

We ramble among the grassy interspaces of this alpine Paradise for flowers and berries, and find them blooming luxuriantly—white geraniums (*Geranium richardsonii*), purple fleabanes (*Erigeron macranthus*), dark litho-purple aconites or monkshoods, phlox purple willow herbs or fireweeds, languid ladies or bluebells, lupines (*Lupinus maculatus*), wild spikenards (*Smilacina amplexicaulis*) and white yarrows. In the meadow a knotweed (*Polygonum bistortoides*) is showing its rose-colored spikes and a saxifrage (*Saxifraga arguta*) has white flowers so tiny they resemble baby's breath. A twinberry, beside a blue spruce, has berries black and ripe; jays scream, robins carol, chickadees pule, red-shafted flickers tatoo, and juncos chink. What a haven on sultry days, a place of purity with fledging groves and sweet meadows from which we seem to be looking downward upon a clouded world.

As we meander through the forest glades, treading over many years of fallen verdure, stepping upon a rotting log overgrown with moss and clinging plants, we pause beside a pool fed by trickling rills, and feel an overwhelming fearlike solemnity, as though unseen eyes watched; or an unseen hand would lightly touch our shoulder and a deep voice speak to test our worthiness to enter this sanctum. Words are inadequate to portray this strange yet real association of some great power who has locked within this vast forest the mysteries of nature's eternal way.

JULY 28

Descending from Wolf Creek Pass along the head of the South Fork of the Provo, we notice one of the most peculiar of all flowers. It is a member of the composite family with a head that is a mere brown cone, like a common sunflower with the yellow rays torn away. Yes, there it is, nearly three feet high with ovate, sessile leaves four to eight inches long, and with a brown bodkin at the top of a long scape. It has no rays at all, but the thumb-like head appears under the hand glass to be filled with crowded minute flowers. Some would take it to be anything but the core of a flower. It is the cone flower (*Rudebeckia occidentalis*).

At 8200 feet, we find the red raspberry (*Rubus melanolasius*) growing in the clefts of the rocks, with berries so red and luscious that we linger for half an hour enjoying them. Both the brush and the berries are slightly smaller than the garden berry, but, on account of the wildness of the mountains, even perhaps more delicious to the taste.

A hundred feet lower down we come upon vast patches of groundsel, ragwort or squaw-weed (*Senecio integerrimus*) as it is variously called, with its terminal and lateral yellow heads in full bloom. It also is a member of the Composite family, but its bluish green foliage and yellow flowers adorn the aspen slopes, apparently yet untouched by the sheep herd we left near the summit.

At 7000 feet we come upon service berries not quite ripe, but lower down the choke cherries are so nearly mature that we are constrained to stop and investigate, always with jelly in mind.

Once at the turn of a bend we surprise a woodchuck or golden mantled marmot in the middle of the road just above Stewart's ranch, though armed spermophiles (*Citellus armatus*) are everywhere scampering about as well.

Over the hills a mule deer doe bounds from the roadside, glancing back with a turn of her head each time she goes over a bush. What a thrill to see this agile deer bounce over the dewy sage, whose spicy redolence fills the early morning air. What joy to be so far from the sweltering city to greet the morning sun and watch nature awaken.

Returning after an interesting day we find just below Park City beds of pink cleome, stinkweed or Rocky Mountain bee plant (*Cleome serrulata*) in full bloom. Endless are the ways of nature, endless the things to be seen.

JULY 29

Every naturalist must read Keats with admiration, for the great poet often describes a scene with a word. Alexander Wilson, whose American Ornithology gave him the right to have the period of 1800-1842 designated as the Wilsonian epoch in the historic study of American birds, was an obscure poet on the West bank of the Schuylkill, loving nature in a general way, until he met William Bartram, who had a Botanic Garden nearby, and became accustomed to view things with the trained eyes of the naturalist. The point is: what could Keats have done if he likewise had become a naturalist?

Just now some Keats' lines are appropriate:

"The poetry of earth is never dead:
When all the birds are faint with the hot sun,
And hide in cooling trees, a voice will run
From hedge to hedge about the new-mown mead;
That is the grasshopper's—he takes the lead
In summer luxury—he has never done
With his delights, for when tired out with fun
He rests at ease beneath some pleasant weed."

We call attention particularly to the words, "faint", "hot", "cooling", "ease" and "pleasant". The trouble with most poets is that whether it be a bush tit, wren, thrush, oriole, woodpecker, warbler, or towhee it is to them just a "bird", and curlews or avocets, killdeers, and dowitchers gain only the adjective "water".

Sometimes a poet expresses the yearn of the naturalist. Thus Wm. A. Dunn wrote:

"Amid the clamor of the street
The very fancy often fills
With far-off thoughts; I live again
Among the streams and hills."

But enough of this. During the few days last past house finches have made their presence known by the rather loud chirrups and chips that they utter while sitting on telephone wires and trees. It may be merely their expression of freedom from incubation cares, or their anticipation of autumn.

Delightful is the song of the cricket at the bedroom window. It comes as the shades of evening fall and continues far into the slumbrous night. One would think that the little fellow would tire of filing his wing-covers, but even as we capture him and put him in a bottle he continues to chirrup and stridulate before our delighted eyes.

JULY 30

Fed from slowly melting snow-banks, north-shadowed and hard, white in their setting of gray cliffs and leafy green, the canyon brook issues from seepings and springs high and cold. Seen as a silver thread from lofty ridges, it expands there into a fan of white foam as it dashes down over obstructing boulders; then narrows into a ribbon; then plunges swerving, tearing and hissing over a precipice into a misty cauldron where ouzels nest within its spray. It turns in a placid pool; and, over-running, courses down again by fir and pine, over mossy stones, a thing alive, inspirational and beautiful .With many a twist and wind it enters upon the alpine meadow, where trout gleam in its glassy bends, and warblers enchant its labryinthine willows with dulcet song. It lingers not for the flitting butterfly, for the angel song of hermit thrush, nor for the gorgeous beauty of penstemon, or aconite, virgin's bower or columbine, but slides by the sweet tranquility of it all, down beside rocks again, through groves of spruce, and by rich embankments where elder-berries and hawthorns grow. It marges cottonwoods and alders, flowing so peacefully for a stretch that pebbles of color strew its bed like the beads of wood nymphs scattered there; and then it forms clear pools about lichened boulders too big for it to climb. It reflects the blue plumage of the belted kingfisher standing on a rock peering into its mirrored surface; and ripples to the trout-getting plunge of that dweller among limpid waters. It joins the river of the valley, and though it goes on wider and wider by factory and field its head always remains in the canyon of ice, beauty and summer snow.

All day long we meander the canyon without seeing a mammal larger than a ground squirrel. Gone forever are the grizzly, the wolverene and the wolf; but where are the badgers, the skunks, the white-tailed jack rabbits and the marmots, where the fox, cougar, wood rat and black bear? Yonder is the remnant of an old beaver dam, which once made a pellucid pond. Deer, of course, browse high above our brookside trails. The trapper, the poisoner, the gunner—they have won, but what desolation they have bequeathed!

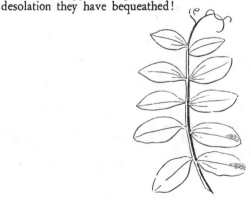

JULY 31

Not always is the introduction of a foreign plant or animal beneficial, as, for instance, the mongoose (*Herpestes mungo*) into Jamaica, and the rabbit into Australia, where even a fence 1,129 miles long, 42 inches high, did not prevent its becoming a serious nuisance all over.

The domestic sparrow, brought to New York in 1860, thereafter overrunning the entire United States, doing much damage to grain fields, now, at last, with the departure of the horse, has come to a beneficial subsistence on weed seeds and weevils. Likewise the starling (*Sturnus vulgaris vulgaris*), introduced into New York in 1890, has required fifty years to arrive at the Wasatch mountains; but here he is with his omnivorous appetite, bustling activity and enmity towards native hole-breeding birds.

Two introduced trees, however, have been an unappreciated blessing in these mountains: the red mulberry (*Morus rubra*) with its luscious dark purple fruit and the white or Chinese mulberry (*M. alba*) with its smaller but equally delicious white berries.

Among the birds that we have noticed eating these mulberries are the following: Batchelder woodpecker, California cuckoo, Arkansas kingbird, Bullock oriole, English sparrow, black headed grosbeak, Western tanager, red-eyed vireo (*Vireo olivaceus*), longtailed chat (*Icteria virens auricollis*), catbird, willow thrush and the robin.

Come to think of it, we have sat for hours beneath a row of mulberry trees, next to willows and great black locusts without once seeing the mourning doves, red-shafted flickers, lazuli buntings, and red-winged blackbirds of those trees manifest the slightest interest in the mulberries. What memories those mulberries bring: Chickens, turkeys, cows, beneath them; the up and down churn handle on the back porch; the milk and green vegetables in the earthen cellar; the old buggy and its equally old horse. Gold could not buy substitutes; honors could not take their place.

Often we have a penchant for empathy, the power to enter into minds, experiences and understanding of birds and mammals and to know just how they regard us humans. Why does a horse mind a child, and even a bull consent to be led by a tot of four?

AUGUST 1

Delighting to hunt over those salt-grass lands on the shores of the Great Salt Lake where willowed streams meander from the mountains over the lowlands, the Swainson hawk (*Buteo swainsoni*) is the summer inhabitant of a region preferred by the sweet-throated meadowlark, the lurking coyote (*Canis latrans lestes*), the nervous jack rabbit. (*L. californicus deserticola*), the sleeping burrowing owl, and the noisy killdeer. Arriving from the southland, aye from the southern continent whence in great flocks it converges over Central America in its migration northward, this beautiful and beneficial hawk reaches us about the tenth of March, ponders awhile in expectancy, and nests a month later, often high in a lonely cottonwood.

What memories these big, rather lazy hawks bring—of wheeling mates descending at times to their nest and feeding their kitten-meowing fledglings; of the little fellows pouncing on grasshoppers and actually flying when only one month old! Easy victim, it soon came to hand—two and one half pounds of hawk, the first specimen of the larger raptors.

When grasshoppers are plentiful, each Swainson devours one or two hundred of those insects a day, but in the meantime it subsists on rabbits, spermophiles, lizards and frogs, seldom if ever molesting farmyard poultry. Our friend, the late John V. Crone, watched this hawk catch insects in the air; others have seen one devour an entire rattlesnake! Such voracity is extraordinary; nevertheless it is not uncommon for one to swallow so many frogs it must either disgorge or choke.

Small birds do not fear the Swainson; at any rate we have seen it wheel above meadowlarks, mourning doves, redwings and Bullock orioles without arousing concern, though, to express fear but enmity towards all hawks, the Arkansas flycatcher sometimes actually rides the Swainson's back as it drives the great bird away.

In October the Swainsons will go South, yet what charm they will have given the lowlands, the saged cow-trails where a barefooted girl once trod.

On Farmington bay a score of Brewster herons today wade a pond in the company of half a dozen pelicans, and Treganza herons here and there point the marshland. On our return we come within twenty feet of a short eared owl (*Asio flammeus flammeus*) sitting on a pasture fence post. Its great yellow eyes with center-spots of black peer at us. It appears neckless with thin stripes on its head; and it finally flies in awkward fashion to grassy ground only to greet us further on from a post. It is a day of showers, hence the activity of this diurnal owl.

AUGUST 2

Of the arboreal avifauna of these mountains of many climes none appears to us more reserved than the birds of the aspen groves, for often we rest among those trembling trees without hearing even the semblance of song. Indeed some of the quaking aspens, like those on the pass of Timpanogos Loop, growing from soil marked by the decaying forms of trees fallen years and years ago, trees from whose dampened bodies mushrooms of inedible kinds flourish—such aspens are solemn, almost funereal, standing as they do over the tombs of the past. Most aspens are not so large as these monarchs; they in fact usually comprise copses of slender whitish-green barked trees growing in well watered sheltered places immediately below perpetual snow. Often ferns carpet their feet, and they are of such cleanly habit that worms and bugs seldom infest them.

There are some birds of such variable range that one may find them in valley and mountain; and naturally they visit the quaking aspens along with other wooded localities. They include: the western robin, which manifests, however, a preference for the evergreen forests, the purple martin, which nests in the holes of trees, and the Wright flycatcher which likes an open burn or valley sagebrush as well as the edge of an aspen grove.

Some birds really prefer the aspen copses. The Hammond flycatcher (*Empidonax hammondii*), the little gray olive bird that makes the thin "sewick" sound often heard about the aspens, frequently builds its fibrous nest on an aspen limb, though cottonwoods, willows, and firs are not entirely ignored for homes. The Rocky Mountain orange-crowned warbler (*Vermivora celata orestera*), which moves like a kinglet and sings like a chirping sparrow, nests on the ground but flits about aspen and pine limbs for worms and insects. The black and white Batchelder woodpecker (*Dryobates pubescens leucurus*), though none too common with us is our only downy and does like to drum the old aspens and lay its five or six white eggs in nest-holes often high above ground. It is in the aspens winter and summer. The red-naped sapsucker (*Sphyrapicus varius nuchalis*), one of the commonest birds of the aspens, noticeable by reason of its black, white, red and yellow colors, inhabits the aspens almost exclusively, for it spends most of its time drilling about the trunks of those tender barked trees, small holes that supply it with sap and attract insects to its liking.

To us few things represent the purity and sweetness of the mountains better than aspen groves.

AUGUST 3

Just before we leave the valley on our way to Mill Creek canyon we stop to examine a much-leaved, yellow flowered plant that, on the wayside, looks like an arnica but turns out to be a golden aster (*Chrysopsis villosa foliosa*), with an oppressed, silky pubescence, and with many small flowers. Some people would, of course, call it a weed, but big, lovely blooms are scarce in the valleys these sultry days and we are thankful for anything that has the vigor to withstand heat and drought. That is why we are so delighted with the exquisite mentzelias with their symmetrical lemon-colored rays, adorning parched and gravelled cliffs and embankments; that is why each morning we greet with pleasure the evening primroses and the scented dogbanes growing where moisture seems entirely to have disappeared.

We ascend Mill Creek to the end of the road where quaking aspens blanket the canyonsides at the North and mighty Engelmann spruces and blister balsams stand in ancient groves at the South. In the grassy or willowed interspaces we find the rayless golden rod (*Chrysothamnus graveolens*) blooming with its orange-yellow flowers born in many heads in a cymose corymb, rounded and beautiful. A baneberry is showing ripe, scarlet berries; and a little shrubby cinquefoil (*Potentilla fruticosa*) is sprinkled with pretty yellow flowers. Here also in bloom are the aconite; the purple aster (*Aster leucanthemifolius*), which smells somewhat like arnica; a pretty aster (*Aster adscendens*) with purplish-white rays; and another, the heath aster (*Aster leucelene*) with white rays. Here among the rocks of a shaded cliff is a delightful little yellow flowered stone crop or orpine with fleshy round leaves.

Being in quest of choke cherries, which are rather scarce in this canyon, we go over into Parley's, thence to Lamb's canyon where not only choke cherries but also service berries are ripe and plentiful, two weeks ahead of time on account of an almost rainless summer. Indeed the entire upper reaches of Parley's is laden with gray ashes and smoking stumps from yesterday's devastating fire. A thoughtless moment can destroy nature's endless exertions of a quarter of a century.

AUGUST 4

Mountain berries are interesting wherever seen, for while all of them are attractive to sight, some are delicious to taste, some merely palatable, some acrid, bitter or pithy, others actually poisonous. Most of them can be identified by their color; so while we feast upon the luscious service berries of this spruce-guarded canyon, let us ponder a moment upon them.

The fruit of the hawthorn (*Crataegus rivularis*) which we saw growing as a thorny-branched shrub a dozen feet high along the creekside of the lower canyon varies from very dark red to black when ripe, and is both mealy and insipid to the taste. Another berry that is blue-black when ripe is the twinberry (*Lonicera involucrata*) but it grows as a shrub less than seven feet high, only in the canyons above 6,000 feet, and its unpalatable berries are in pairs, or "twins", as its name indicates, though one of the two is usually larger than the other. By the way, A. O. Garrett has just called to our attention that this twinberry is said to contain a poisonous soporific in large amounts. The choke cherry while red in the early stages, is the only other berry that turns black when ripe unless we except the black currant and the rare black elderberry. The choke cherry appears as a shrub sometimes fifteen feet high all along the canyons, and its acrid drupes make unexcelled jelly.

Three berries become orange when ripe: the hackberry (*Celtis douglasii*) which likes limestone cliffs and which we find growing in Big Cottonwood canyon, is a bushy shrub ten feet high with leathery leaves and rough bark, having green berries that ripen to orange red, fruit not usually eaten. The mountain ash or Rowan tree, a shrub three to fourteen feet high adorning moist places of the canyons in autumn, has bitter, bright red fruit that is sometimes orange when immature; and our newly found *Crataegus Colorado* in Provo canyon has bright orange berries.

The salmon or thimble berry sometimes called the white flowering raspberry (*Rubus parviflorus*) growing in rich soil of mountain brooks, a shrub less than eight feet high, has red berries too dry and insipid to be palatable; and the elderberry (*Sambucus micrbotyrs*), a low shrub of the mountain above 7,500 feet, has unpleasantly scented bright red berries, not, however, unpalatable.

Blue berries grow, of course, on the delicious elderberry (*Sambucus glauca*) of lower altitudes, and on the trailing barberry (*Berberis repens*) hidden beneath oak patches. The delicious service berries (*Amelanchier alnifolia*) of the dry hillsides are also purplish blue.

Beware of white berries. It is true the dogwood (*Cornus stolonifera*) and the partridge berry (*Symphoricarpos rotundifolius*), sometimes called the "snowberry" or "waxberry" have harmless white berries, but beware of the poisonous white berries of the baneberry (*Actaea arguta*) (sometimes scarlet) and the western poison oak or ivy (*Rhus Rydbergii*).

We know of no poisonous Wasatch berry delicious to the taste.

AUGUST 5

In Big Cottonwood canyon a few rods above a mine-shed roadway overpass, we suddenly come upon the finest rockspirea (*Sericotheca dumosa*) in full bloom that we have ever seen here. Some call it "oceanspray." It is a member of the rose family, a close relative of the ninebark and the raspberries. It is a much branched shrub about a yard high with tiny, double toothed wedge-shaped leaves and with wee flowers that hang in branched panicles several inches long. Under the hand glass each flower—only an eighth of an inch across—displays five petals, some of them jasper or coral pink, some ivory white. In the distance the color effect of the many panicles is a pinkish white spray. Each branch seems to grow out from the old one in such a way as to make the old stub a dead thorn an inch long. We do not know when we have been more delighted than by this find. Nevertheless, as we look about, we see a score or more of them growing on the northern hillside.

We go upward to "The Spruces," where deer flies pester us more than we have ever noticed before, a fact due to the greatly increased number of deer in the mountains the past few years. The pests go right to work on one's skin, even penetrating clothing on the way, and since they are known to carry spotted fever we do not like them.

A Cassin's kingbird (*Tyranus vociferanus*) alights on the tip of a spruce, utters its raspy "queer", and then catching sight of a black-headed jay, chases it into the safe retreat of thick underlimbs. What a tyrant!

The loveliest and largest flower of all the canyons just now is that of the elderberry (*Sambucus glauca*). The same warty-barked bush may have on it not only drupes of near-ripe berries but also cream-colored blooms in clusters as large as a man's hat surmounting the vigorous young shoots. This extraordinary inflorescence subordinates such minor flowers as golden rod, Indian paint brush, willow herb and geranium. Botanically, a berry, with its many sided interior pulpy fruit, scatters its seeds through the pulp when mature, hence the term "berry" could be applied with good reason even to a cucumber.

At night we catch a singing cricket (*Gryllus assimilis*) and examine it with a magnifying glass to find its music box. It consists of a round file on the upper surface of each tegmen or wing cover with a scraper nearby. No wonder there is sound when file goes over membrane. By the way, the ear of this insect is on its front leg!

AUGUST 6

On a drowsy afternoon in August we hie ourselves away to the refreshing banks of City Creek. Even as we near the gurgling water a delightful coolness greets us, similar to the sudden draught of cellar air one sometimes notices coming from barred windows below a hot pavement.

We sit on the moss-grown embankment and peacefully watch blown curls of smoke coil up through the alder leaves. No birds are singing; no breeze is rustling the trees; indeed, there is naught of sound save the soothing, monotonous rush, gurgle and splash of the ever-fretful brook as it dashes, slides, eddies and swerves on its joyful way. Here it whitens with bubbling aeration, as it bounds over stones; there it calms into a placid, almost rippleless level; there again, dashes in a miniature rapid swiftly over rounded rocks; then into tiny whirlpools, level places and—onwards as before.

Near us on a leaf alights a dragon fly, with a thorax and tail as blue as a bit of the sky above (*Aeschna,* very likely *umbrosa*); but for identification it is catching before hanging; then an ominous horsefly buzzes violently about us, reminding us that it can make a bitten skin-spot tender for days. It dashes away up stream.

A butterfly with a mourning border of black on its wings alights on a damp stone and drinks its fill. As we look upon it bee after bee flies to the brookside and drinks from the wet stones just outside the water's ripples.

So pellucid is the water that we hold a piece of newspaper beneath the surface in the hope that we may yet read, but ripples distort the type; so selecting a small pool that has no aerated water and few ripples, we submerge the paper over twelve inches. Presto! We read the print clearly; in fact, the letters seem magnified.

The blue dragon fly hovers over the stream in mid air, motionless save for the vibration of its wings. For five seconds or more at a time it thus holds itself; and then at last it too flies away. We drowse in tranquil lassitude before returning home.

The joy of life consists largely in an absorbing interest in a great variety of things, some large, some infinitesimal, for, if one fail, another is at hand and happiness need have little interruption.

AUGUST 7

Fishing leisurely along the willow-arched bends of East canyon creek, we unexpectedly come within sight of a Great Basin skunk (*Mephitis occidentalis major*) calmly treading about the wet embankment of the opposite shore. Some animals protect themselves with teeth and claws, some with barbed spines, some with poisoned fangs, others in the swiftness of flight, but the skunk stands its ground ready immediately to emit a nauseating odor. We stop; it stops still; and then, convinced of our harmless intentions, it waddles away beneath the willows, showing as it goes its broad white stripe bifurcating near the middle of its back. It lives on crickets, grasshoppers, insects, mice, ground squirrels, eggs, frogs, cottontails and berries, seldom wandering more than half a mile from home, and being active all year round save during the most inclement days of winter.

The rock spotted skunk (*Spilogale gracilis saxatilis*), which is smaller but more agile than the foregoing, prefers rock piles, cliff crevices, hollow logs or deserted burrows for its home; furthermore, it readily climbs trees. Unless in actual peril it is slow to emit its fetid musk; indeed, we have pelted stones for a quarter of an hour into an old rock-stable, where one was hiding, without causing more than an occasional shift to a new place of shelter. A direct hit undoubtedly would have brought results. It can propel its sickening yellow liquid a distance of twelve feet!

The word "skunk", being derived from the Indian names "segankw" or "segongw", has at various times, especially in early literature, been spelled "squinck", "squuncke" or "skunck", and many flowers and plants of abominable odor have been given the unpleasant name. Our skunkberry (*Rhus trilobata*) is one of these, though, strangely it is medicinally known as "fragrant sumac". Even the bobolink, on account of his black and white colors, is sometimes called "skunkbird"; so after all a bad name is worse than no riches. This is usually true in nature; no matter what its name, whether fang, thorn, color or poison, every animal has some attractiveness or even beauty.

AUGUST 8

When at sunset we wade into the waters of the Great Salt Lake for a delightful float under the light of a forthcoming moon, we are impressed by the millions of brine shrimps (*Artemia gracilis*) that crowd the shallow shore in a brown verge. Some of them slip between our toes as if they were flax-seeds. Far out in the water, when we are floating on the briny depths most leisurely, we see them there swimming with their transparent bodies and black eyes as miniatures of life so small that we can study their movements in the cupped-water of our hands.

So high is the salt content of this inland sea, ranging from a concentration of 13%, when its waters are high, to 27% when they are low, and matching in this respect the Dead Sea (23 to 25%) that the existence in it of life at all is a matter of wonder, especially to us who know that to take its water into our nostrils is to suffer partial strangulation; but there they are—the brine shrimps, and the brine flies, which in their larval and pupal stages also swarm the thin-lipped shores.

There was a time when only the shrimp was thought to survive this briny water, which is so heavy, by the way, that it weighs 75 pounds a cubic foot as compared with the 62.5 pounds of fresh water; thus, according to information sent us by Dr. G. M. Relyea, the Scientific American magazine in 1861 states "no living things of any kind exist there" and Dr. David Starr Jordan in 1889 thought only the brine shrimp could live there. Microscopic studies have proved, however, that twenty six species of plants and ten species of animals actually live in the buoyant brine of the lake. Dr. Relyea summarizes the animals as: 7 Protozoans including 3 rhizopods, 3 ciliates, and 1 flagellate; and 3 anthropods consisting of 1 Crustacea (the shrimp) and 2 Insects, comprising 2 species of brine flies; and the plants as: 11 bacillus bacteria, 1 coccus bacterium ,12 species of algae and 2 diatom genera.

In the approaches to Farmington Bay we come upon lark sparrows, savanna sparrows, yellow-headed blackbirds, redwinged blackbirds, Brewer blackbirds, meadow larks, yellow warblers, loggerhead shrikes, sage thrashers, marsh wrens, magpies, swallows (cliff, barn, roughwing, bank and tree), both eastern and western kingbirds, broad-tailed hummingbirds, short-eared owls, mourning doves. In and about the bay itself we see gulls (Franklin, ringbilled and California), Wilson and northern phalaropes, avocets, marbled god-wits, greater and lesser yellow legs, wiliets, spotted sandpipers, coots, pheasants, killdeers, marsh and sparrow hawks, mallards, pintails, redheads, cinnamon teals, gadwalls, Canadian geese, white faced glossy ibis, black crowned night herons, double crested cormorants, pied billed grebes, great blue herons and great flocks of white pelicans. Scores of days we have spent on this bay, winter and summer, never ceasing to marvel at what our glesseas reveal, and there on occasion we have chanced upon fellow ornithologists, such as A. O. Treganza or C. W. Lockerbie.

AUGUST 9

As we sit on a mapled brookside and watch the swift aerial maneuvers of a voracious dragon fly, we admit that no other insect except the butterfly is more beautiful, none more agile and indefatigable on the wing. That it should bear such frightful names as "devil's darning needle", "snake-feeder" and "snake-doctor" is due somewhat to early entomologists themselves, who gave to species such bodeful designations as "viperinus" (viper), "imbuta" (blood-filled), "carnfex" (hangman), and so on. One of our own species has been named "saturata", which in the sense of "gorged" aptly describes the usual condition of this "mosquito hawk", for when captured it will devour flies in incredible numbers.

The adult dragon fly lives but a few weeks, but in that short time there is an ecstatic nuptial flight, an aerial mating, and finally a depositing of eggs on plant stems during which the subdued male is sometimes held a willing prisoner in the vicelike clasp of his mate. In three weeks the spiderlike nymph emerges from the egg, thence lives a voracious life under water for eleven months, devouring even its own kind. At last comes the exquisite moment when it crawls from its cast off skin, shakes its wings in the hot sun, and enters in its turn upon the adult life of a dragon fly.

In our swmiming-hole days it never occurred to us that about the only enemies of the dragon flies, which constantly eluded us, were frogs and swallows; for though these insects would stand for long periods on the tips of half-submerged twigs, they escaped with the swiftness of lightning when exposed to our slow attacks. A gun shooting pepper and salt will bring them down, but unfortunately, usually mutilate them as well; and a net is successful only if used as they fly by rather than towards it.

Of the suborders comprising the Odonata, we have in the Wasatch the following representatives: the club-tail (*Progomphus obscurus*), the stream-dragon (*Ophiogomphus occidentalis*), the common club-tail (*Gomphus intricatus*), the green darner (*Anax junius*), the blue darners (*Aeschna californica* and *A. umbrosa*), the big red skimmers and golden wings (*Libellula saturata, L. comanche, L. quadrimaculata* and *L. composita*), the white tail (*Plathemis subornata*), the blue pirate (*Pachydiplax longipennis*), the ruby spot (*Hetaerina americana*), the argia (*Argia alberta*), the bluets (*Engallagma anna, E. civile* and *E. cyathigerum*), and the fork-tails (*Ishnura barberi, I. cervula,* and *I. utahensis*).

AUGUST 10

Some of the weeds of the wayside have seeds that are slightly poisonous, such as the wild field mustard (*Brassica arvensis*) and the hedge mustard (*Sisymbrium altissimum*). Even the animals refuse the seeds of the cow herb or cow cockle (*Saponaria Vaccaria*), which is a rough herb of the chickweed family, one to three feet high, with pink flowers growing in our dry sandy soils. "Sapo" was a soap used by the Gauls as a pomade for their hair, and strangely, the seeds of this plant when eaten produce a soaplike emulsion in the stomach.

The doorweed (*Polygonum aviculare*) of our waste grounds causes much skin irritation when handled, and is perhaps poisonous if eaten by animals; likewise the seeds of that weed of the waste places known as hare's ear mustard (*Conringia orientalis*) have a mustard oil that is harmful. In fact nearly all mustards (*Brassica*) have distasteful seeds.

There are some plants in the Wasatch mountains and valleys capable of absorbing selenium, one of the rarer elements, from the soil, and causing "blind staggers" or "alkali disease" in animals. These troubles are noticed more in the shale lands of eastern Utah and Wyoming than in the Wasatch mountains; and the principal plants involved are salt-bushes, gumweeds, shad-scales, wild asters and vetches not found in the Wasatch valleys.

We do, however, have several plants with such sharp awns, thorns or spines as to cause irritation and sometimes festering wounds in the eyes and mouths of feeding animals. Our two species of prickly pear (*Opuntia polyacantha*), (*O. fragilis*), which grow on the dry hillsides, have often penetrated even our shoes. How animals unable to extract the spines must suffer is easily imagined when we recall experiences with the porcupine. The bur grass (*Cenchrus tribuloides*) of our lake shores has extremely troublesome bristles; so also the brome grass (*Bromus tectorum*) and the cockle-bur (*Xanthium saccharatum*). After all does not man himself have to choose constantly between the hidden rose and its protecting thorns?

In a field today we learn from a farmer that he never cuts the weeds along his ditches and fences because grasshoppers prefer them and leave his crops for those inviting places. Come to think of it, swarms of hoppers do usually fly before us as we crawl under fences overgrown with tall sweet clover. We learn something new every day; indeed just before reaching home we find in a grocery store, pickled prickly pear! It looks reddish and is eaten like pomegranates.

AUGUST 11

Where chirms the bouldered brook beside the pines
And cooling draughts bestir the spired limbs,
Through darksome glades the pathway intertwines
Below the sound of murmurous forest hymns.

As we sit beside the willowed brook of a canyon-meadow and scan the mountain slopes at the South, which are clustered with tall firs resembling companies of green, giant-soldiers at attention, we have a sense of comfort in the brisk alpine air and a feeling of veneration at the grandeur of ridge and peak; but despite the exaltation of it all we turn to moving things near at hand.

The brook is pretty beneath the overhanging willows; and in an eddy beside a half submerged stone we notice a score or more of those peculiar water-walking insects known as water striders (*Gerris remigis*), which, when we poke a stick at them, skate about on the water with wonderful rapidity and ease. That there really is a skin on water is known to us all, when we often see it stand an eighth of an inch above the edges of a filled tumbler; and it is on this skin that the striders run. These pleasing little fellows are found in all quiet waters, sometimes in veritable swarms. As cold weather approaches, they hide beneath banks under leaves or even under stones below the running water.

Our water boatmen (*Metapodius granulosus*) are rather large bugs capable of remaining under water for a long time, on account of their ability to hold air with the hairs of their bodies. How they remain in mud under water during the winter is hard to understand, unless we jecture that in cold weather their respiration is reduced to a minimum.

The back swimmers (*Notonectidae*) are little bugs that swim upside down in our ponds, feeding on insects which they kill with a sting as virulent as that of the honey bee. They breathe through the pores of their abdomens, thus often remaining a long time under water, and hibernate in the mud of pool bottoms.

Our water scorpions (*Nepa* and *Ranatra*) have swollen fore-legs capable of grasping, like the chiliceres of a scorpion; and tubes attached to the anal end, which hold air brought from the surface of pools. Their eggs are deposited inside the stems of water plants.

Down in the meadows today western flycatchers and ash throated flycatchers are playing about pasture fences. The black crests of the latter are conspicuous as they sit and utter their thin "purits".

AUGUST 12

There is a brook rippled nook in a Wasatch canyon, where thickened balsams stand like soldiers limbed with green; where cottonwoods and oaks cherish the light and sunshine allotted them by the more powerful evergreens; where the gurgling of the water mingles with the cheeps of juncos and the whistles of frisking squirrels. It is a place of fascinating tranquility, not unlike thousands more in these enticing mountains.

It is while we are enjoying such a place today that we notice a pear shaped puff ball (*Lycoperdon pyriforme*) standing in the grass by some quaking aspens. It is dingy white, about two inches high, and with a smooth, papery whitish inner coat. Its inner flesh is white and firm, hence delicious when fried in butter. If we leave it, we know that its flesh will change to yellow, then olive, finally to a powdery mass of globose spores and elastic threads.

When their flesh is white and firm, all of the puff balls are edible—about the only safe rule we know concerning mushrooms. Occasionally one may come upon the giant puff ball (*Calvatia maxima*), as once we did at the pass from American Fork Canyon, balls actually fifteen inches in diameter with thick, cordlike roots; nevertheless, despite their enormous size they are delicious when the inner flesh is white.

A naturalist hesitates to recommend any of the fungi as edible, because it is difficult to describe in words the difference between poisonous and non-poisonous kinds; all the old "silver spoon" safety ideas have been proved unreliable; and good mushrooms when young often become dangerous when old and rotting. No one need fear the puff ball, nor a morel or a coral fungi; but if the common meadow mushroom is the only one you are sure of, never experiment beyond your knowledge. This in life is true; not all that is beautiful is wholesome, for often even in nature beauty is the lure of a hidden death.

In City Creek canyon today we find among dead maple leaves a species of mollusca we have never before taken in the Wasatch. The shell is flat with two thin stripes of black running all around, from which we conclude it to be *Oreohelix strigosa jugalis*. It is in the company of *Oreohelix strigosa depressa carnea;* and beneath a log nearby we find some slugs (*Ariolimas campestris*).

AUGUST 13

Where cattle graze in drying pastures there is little bird activity and even less of floral display; but in those meadows existing between Farmington canyon and the lakeshore are some flowers of striking beauty and some of queer shape and unusual inflorescence.

The golden rod is there with its corymbs of lemon colored flowers which upon growing old become masses of small seeded burs, not stinging to one's fingers but just prickly enough to adhere and scatter to the vast new homesteads of flowerland.

By their side in the damper places is blooming that peculiar plant known as vervain (*Verbena hastata*), a rough perennial four feet high with leafy, four sided stems, and with purplish blue flower spikes at the tip, resembling two score slender greenish worms, two or three inches long, standing straight up, each with a flowered collar below its head. What an odd simile, yet as we hold the flower in hand as we write, the comparison to upstanding worms is emphatically reassured.

Our attention is drawn from the vervains to another unusual plant— a card teasel (*Dipsaeus sylvestris*), standing about two feet high, which has at its top a bristled bur thrice the size of a thumb but protected with six sharp horns five inches long, as if a Texas long-horn had crossed with a bur. They say in England these leaves of the involucres, slender, bristling and up-curving are used for raising a nap on a woolen cloth. Steel tears, but the dried horns of the card teasels break before tearing.

After deliberating upon two surprising plants, we drive on to the mouth of Weber canyon, where we remark a vine with white flowers and akenes like silky bits of down, climbing all over the oak bushes. In the distance the long, climbing stems resemble those of the lovely virgins bower, concerning which we have already expressed our rapture; so upon near approach we are delighted that it is a cousin of the sweet Virgin, in fact a white clematis (*Clematis lingusticifolia*). One must have attentive and appreciative eyes to discern all these things; but how often in spite of automobile engines or the conversation of friends our ears catch the cry of the killdeer, the song of the meadowlark, the soft call of the junco, and even on busy streets, the dulcet notes of a house finch singing at the top of an office building. The eyes, the ears, bring joy to him who heeds.

AUGUST 14

In the meadow near the willows between Silver Lake and Brighton a delightful bed of "butter and eggs" is in full bloom. Silk cinquefoils are all about us, but these butter and eggs are high, lighter, and have several flower-heads from one stalk. We call them "butter and eggs", while others might say "yellow toad flax", "flax weed" or "brideweed"; at any rate they are that member of the figwort family known as *Linaria vulgaris*. Being a kin of the garden snapdragon, each pallid yellow flower opens and shuts in similar fashion; but the chin is bright orange; and there you have your "butter and eggs". Each individual flower has a pointed tail or keel, and the pointed leaves, about one and a quarter inches long, are only about an eighth of an inch wide. How this European immigrant got here we cannot understand, but it is worth the entire trip to see it. Bees may squeeze through the mouth to its nectar, but ants cannot pry apart the lips of that sacred throat—such is the wisdom and the provision of nature!

Flowers were everywhere; but we decide to tarry for an hour at a meadow a mile below (8,300 feet). We notice a lovely monkey flower (*Mimulus Lewisii*) of rose pink just as we enter this meadow, which we find verged with brushy willows (*Salix cordate Watsonii*) and Engelmann or white spruces, some of them a hundred feet high and most of them exuding a sticky, resinous juice. The hillsides at the East and the North are cloaked with quaking aspens.

In the meadow flowers are profuse, among them being: silky cinquefoil (*Potentilla anserina*), shrubby cinquefoil (*Potentilla dasiphora fruiticosa*), pink and white geraniums, fleabanes (*Erigeron tener*), a white aster (*Aster Kingii*), a lavender aster (*Aster adscendens*), a purple aster (*Aster leucanthemifolius*), aconite, yarrow, fireweeds, rudebeckia or cone flowers. Twin berries are ripe everywhere, delicious to the eyes but not to the taste.

In the meadow and damp woods are several species of mushrooms besides the common edible field mushroom and pear-shaped puff balls; for instance: a funnel-shaped member of the genus Lentinus, a leathery, fleshy, ill-smelling specimen; a Chantarelle hygrophorus (*Hygrophorus cantharellus*); and a species of Armillaria.

The hills about the meadow are a glory of flowers, including: dark purple aster, fleabanes, umbrella plants (*Erigonum subalpinum*), golden rod (*Solidago canadensis*) and giant hyssop.

A black butterfly with black-veined white internal spots on both the fore and the hind wings is fluttering about the meadows as we leave this place of lofty tranquility.

AUGUST 15

Trout are like people; for in the middle of the day they prefer quietude and shade. Thus at our leisure in one sweet afternoon we are given opportunity to study them, a diversion much aided by the technical research of Jordan, Vasco M. Tanner and others.

The trout that lie in the creel beside us on the bank of the upper Provo river are the introduced rainbow (*Salmo shasta*), commonly grown in hatcheries but originated along the McCloud river of California. A typical specimen has a bluish back, a red, lateral band along each side (more apparent in the male), and a comparatively small mouth. German brown (*Salmo fario*) and Eastern brook trout (*Salmo fontinalis*) have been introduced into the Wasatch, but the cold, snow-fed waters of this mountainous region are more pleasing to the McCloud river rainbow.

Our native Utah trout (*Salmo Utah*), which are finely and profusely spotted, have been known since the time of Father Escalante (1776), especially in Utah lake where before the introduction there of European carp (*Cyprinus carpio*) they were taken in boatloads not only by Indians, who dried them, but by pioneers as well. Thus it is mentioned on the authority of Yarrow and Henshaw, that in 1864 in one haul of the seine a man took thirty five hundred pounds of these trout from Utah lake; indeed we ourselves can remember that half a century later descendants of the same man regularly marketed them from that same delightful water. Now with carp, catfish and bass imposed upon them there a single individual would be a rarity in a whole day's angling, though once in awhile a few are hooked along the streams and a considerable number yet beautify Bear Lake where the water is so cold that in it drowned bodies seldom arise.

He who fishes not so much to enjoy a tussle with a valiant trout as to experience the tranquility of the woods, the ceaseless murmur of the brook, and the ever-cooling mist of sparkling cascades, gets the most out of this solitary diversion. Philosophy is born in the contemplation of such hours. By the way, we can never forget the trout caught around a willowed bend on the Provo; we could not see; it arose skyward—we had snagged a water ouzel by its toe! Nevertheless ever sweet in our memory are those trout that one by one resisted, dove, jumped, and finally fagged into the seeming restfulness of our creel. Of such memories is that marvelous brain of sylvan-loving man composed.

AUGUST 16

There is a quiet declivity northward sloping from a mountain pass, the sombrous upper expanse of the famed American Fork canyon. It is a dampened place, thicketed with broad-leaved annuals and forested with ancient aspens sixty feet tall, a fern-clad, shade-solemn hillside musty smelling from tree-patriarchs year after year prostrated, ant-eaten and mouldered. Indeed it is a slanting ground so many centuries fed by leaves and snow that underfoot it is like a deepened carpet of spongy decay. On a summer day it is a tranquil trysting place, sweet and secluded, where delphiniums (*Delphinum bicolor*) or "blue larkspurs" wave with the shivering aspen leaves, where strange white-gilled mushrooms (some of them the poisonous fly amanita—*Amanita muscaria*) cling to shelled, rotted logs, and where Hammond flycatchers, almost sole inhabitants of the dank seclusion, give their tender "sewicks" and lovelike calls. Strange, lisping notes of the alluring aspen groves! They prove that no forest is too secluded for some bird, some life to regard it as home. Cicero in his retired years would have adored such a place.

This small Hammond flycatcher, six inches long, grayish olive like the ground, lives especially on the ants that colonize the mouldering trees. Little billed bird, what would the peaceful mountain glade be without its sweet lisp in the fleeting sunshine!

Sitting on the swarded embankment of a meadowed canyon brook, watching northern violet green swallows course up and down the crystal water, we wonder why this swallow seldom seeks the earth for food. Our other swallows sometimes take grasshoppers, spiders, caterpillars, plant lice and leaf bugs; one of them, the barn swallow, even fares at times on a snail, and the tree swallow does not disdain even seeds such as those of the waxberry. We long to see a swallow catch one of those courageous swift-flying tiny airplanes, a dragon fly; for such is not infrequently done.

AUGUST 17

Back in 1882 chewing gum was mentioned as "offering neither savor nor nutriment, only subserving the mechanical process of mastication"; nevertheless, as we casually watch a little feminine visitor to the canyon, we must conclude that there is a psychological abstraction about the chewing that is not altogether either mechanical or masticatory. It represents in truth, the busy employment of an unemployed mind! Africans may chew in substitution for tooth-brushes, yet in Europe before our soldiers chewed in the World War trenches we noticed an almost total absence of idle gum chewing. This divertissement brings us to a consideration of what the Indians of the Wasatch mountains in the pre-pioneer days did for their chewing gum, for strange to say Indian lassies and laddies chewed gum.

Chewing gum is of course the milky juice of the Central American sapodilla (*Sapota Achras*), gathered by the *chiclero* as we might maple syrup, and shipped in blocks (*marquettas*) here to be sweetened and strapped into packages of gum. The Indians hereabout sought the spider milkweed or antelope horns (*Ascelpidora decumbens*), which grows on these dry hillsides and has green flowers with paler margins. It is about the same height as the common milkweed and has pink-purple flowers, but prefers the dry places. Often, indeed, if no other gum was available, they chewed the bark of the lower stems and roots of rabbit brush until a gum formed, and called it "tosamibi", the Indian equivalent of chewing gum.

Ever since childhood we have been accustomed to chewing the gum of the spruce tree (*Picea engelmanni*), which grows in these mountains at high altitudes, and we shall never forget the old prospector who first taught us the gum of the mountains; yet the Indians seem not to have enjoyed its acridity. This, however, we know: whatever was edible; whatever was pleasant in the wilds, the Indians knew, and knew better than we.

We are delighted today when a friend brings us what he calls black gooseberries taken from the mountainside in a canyon. They are covered with bristles and he says the leaves are oily. He hastens to get some branches; there are no spines; the branches are reddish— it is a currant, *Ribes viscosissimum*. It does us a lot of good to see a fellow lawyer thus alert for new things in the wildwoods.

AUGUST 18

The tallest spires of the pines, the projecting cliffs of the canyon sides, the bare, rocky peaks of the higher ridges—these first reflect the morning sun. It is as though everything cheerful, hopeful, faced the East; everything spiritless, discouraged turned towards the gloomy caverns and vales of the West. Nor does afternoon reverse things; for there is awakening, sweetness, freshness, and joy in the morning sun; but only heat, weariness, lassitude, and discomfort in the sun of the western sky.

It is just after the rising sun first glints the highest ledges, that the canyons are most attractive, for at that time robins sing their awakening carols, hermit thrushes sound their clear angelic voices, chickadees tone their delicate notes from the creekside willows, butterflies begin to flutter across the glades, and trout reveal the exquisite rainbows of their sides glinted the better by the undercovert rays.

Most of our larger mammals are active at dusk and dawn. The noon of the day and the noon of the night are rest periods, though, when much hunted, deer browse and graze in the semi darkness of the moon. Even though the mountain lion is a night prowler, travelling along a more or less regular circle a distance of several miles, it seems to prefer moonlight, twilight or daylight for the actual killing of prey. Many instances have been brought to our attention of its attack upon penned sheep and hogs in the darkness of the night, but on such occasions, it of course had opportunity for careful watching and stalking before the final spring. Endowed by nature with the ability to see at night, the eyes of a mountain lion have pupils that are not only vertically linear but also capable of considerable expansion and contraction, whereas the pupils of the eyes of the day-hunting African lion are round; therefore, darkness is little hindrance to the mountain lion. At night, colts, which are one of its favorite foods, lie close to protecting mares; also it is easier to take the deer of its choice in daytime. It lurks on limb or ledge above the water trail.

AUGUST 19

Nearly all of the lower foothills of these mountains are more or less thicketed by scrub oak (*Quercus Gambellii*), and by curl-leaf mountain-mahoganies (*Cercocarpus ledifolius*) immediately above them. Neither of these scraggy trees is usually favored by perennial brooks, so year in and year out they occupy dry slopes where scarcely any other large verdure appears.

Few birds and fewer animals inhabit these foothills, though in the course of years we have in winter found among them the tracks not only of cottontails, coyotes and mountain lions, but also in summer both the armed spermophile and its enemy, the badger (*Taxidea taxus taxus*).

Birds that we have from time to time taken among the oak copses include: the Virginia warbler, the spurred towhee, the Woodhouse jay (*Aphelocoma woodhouseii*), the mountain bluebird, the gray titmouse, (*Parus inornatus ridgwayi*), the plumbeous vireo (*Vireo solitarius plumbeus*), western chipping sparrow (*Spizella passerina arizonae*), the Brewer blackbird, the Wright flycatcher, the Lewis woodpecker (*Asyndemus lewis*), quail (*Lophortyx californica*) and the American or black-billed magpie (*Pica pica hudsonia*). Because these oaken patches are seldom frequented by human beings, who prefer the cool brooks, the magpie likes to build its bushel-big nest there; but seldom does it do so far from water.

So accustomed have we become to the various habitats of birds, mammals, reptiles, flowers and trees, that one has but to mention such words as "slough", "pine forest", "quaking aspens", "cliffs", "meadows", "water falls", "alkali flat", "sage brush", "foothills" to fill our mind's eye with definite living things, most of them known to us by the first sound they utter, the flash of color they show, or the tracks that they leave. It is the way of the naturalist, ever alert for beauty of color, shape or song; ever hopeful that in wide understanding will come greater comprehension of the meaning of it all.

AUGUST 20

While sauntering through an aspen-twinkled glade in the upper reaches of Big Cottonwood canyon, we remark upon the numerous serpentine, mud-ridges that extend like brown ropes of wrist-thickness strewn upon the grass. They are left there by pocket gophers (*T. talpoides wasatchensis*), which in winter knew not how to get rid of the earth from their newly made tunnels save by packing it to the surface of the ground and jamming it against overburdening snow. Each spring as the deep snow melts away these secreted evidences of winter-activity are exposed. Another pocket gopher (*T. t. moorei*) is found in the Wasatch mountains south of the Provo river, leaving the northern Wasatch to *uinta* whose trailings are before us.

The Great Basin pocket mouse (*Perognathus parvus olivaceus*) occurs in these mountains, but, being nocturnal, it is seldom seen, though its little earth mounds about bushes often attract one's attention. It is a little seed-eater, one not known to hibernate.

The Utah kangaroo rat (*Dipodomys ordii utahensis*) inhabits desert places below the foothills of the northern Wasatch, and being neither kangaroo nor rat, it is related closely to the pocket mice. It does have short forelegs, strong hind legs for jumping and a long tail for balancing, hence the name "kangaroo"; but like the pocket mice it stores seeds for winter use and does not hibernate.

An ever-fascinating feature about these mountains is, that every spot a few yards in extent, whether it be a dry scrub-oak hillside, a mossy canyon glen, or a rocky ridge, supports some interesting form of life—ant, fly, butterfly or beetle; worm, mouse or cricket; bird, animal, insect, reptile, tree or flower. Endless are the joys of research with its ever growing coordination of not only the forms of life but also the means of living. They who divert themselves to an investigation of all forms of nature to the end that they may find the meaning of life and the evidence of its eventual perpetuation are of all men most happy, for they are on the very path of eternity.

AUGUST 21

Our locale today is the picturesque region that skirts the east side of lofty Mt. Nebo. Ascending Payson canyon, we notice at first many sunflowers, several great mullein (*V. thapsus*) among the sage and scrub oaks, and, further on, a bee plant (*C. serrulata*) in rose colored bloom beside firs, junipers and dogwoods.

At 5,550 feet we find golden asters (*C. folisa*), scarlet gilias, pink dogbanes, and then, higher, ripe elderberries, purple thistles (*C. undulatum*), and many cabbage butterflies.

At the brook bridge we come upon nine brown and yellow silver spotted butterflies (*Argynnis cornis*) feeding on the flowers of a rabbit bush (*C. graveoens*), and two black and white butterflies (*Gnophaela latipennis*). Here also is a white violet (*V. palustris*), and on a rock near the bridge a Say's mantled ground squirrel (*C. lateralis lateralis*) stands within thirty feet of us for nearly five minutes without moving, as we examine it minutely with the glasses.

At 7300 feet a golden eagle soars overhead, and among quaking aspens we find a yellow monkey flower (*M. guttatus*) and a sheathed Amanitopsis mushroom (*A. vaginata*). Higher, among aspens, we discern a painted boletinus mushroom (*B. pictus*) with yellow sponge tubes instead of gills, a dark red cap, a yellow stem striped with red, and yellow flesh. Near it are several bell-shaped mushrooms (*Mycena haematopoda*). We discover other mushrooms—a large Pluteus, many inky caps, and small puff-balls.

Up higher, on a ridge, the elderberry (*Sambucus microbotrys*) is heavy with drupes of bright cerise red berries, much prettier than those of the blue elderberry below, but with an unpleasant odor.

Among the pines of the summit (9050 feet) we stand for five minutes watching those rare birds, white-throated swifts (*Aeronautes saxatalis*) whose long wings and black spots on white bellies distinguish them from the northern violet green swallow. What a find!

We slowly descend, thinking of wapiti as we look up at the shoulder of Mt. Nebo, and call it a day.

AUGUST 22

On the red sliderock at the north side of the entrance to Parley's canyon is a bed of scarlet flowers so noticeable that we stop to examine them through the field glasses. "Scarlet gilia" we utter; but such they cannot be, for the foliage looks as stiff and forbidding as that of an arnica plant, although the flowers are inch-long trumpets of brilliant red. It is an arduous and somewhat dangerous climb to reach them but "aucun chemin de fleurs ne conduit a la glorie"—we accomplish it. There is our prize, a *Zauschneria Garrettii*, a member of the evening primrose family, and one of the rarest and most beautiful flowers of the Wasatch. We are so delighted that we take it to A. O. Garrett, the botanist for whom it was named, to learn of its history.

One of the joys of writing about these ever-delightful mountains is, that though we traverse them from end to end, from valley to lofty crest, many, many times, we know not what moment we may catch sight of something we have never before seen. Seldom is the surprise a bird or mammal; but frequently an insect, mushroom, snail or flower; and one such is ample reward for an entire day's reconnaissance. There is perhaps no more beautiful flower in the mountains than this *Zauschneria*, with its scarlet fuchsia-like flowers.

We proceed up the canyon where in the higher reaches bright little sunflowers (*Viguiera multiflora*) are everywhere; and a mile below the summit we come upon the finest clumps of yellow-bloomed rabbit brush (*Chrysothamnus lanceolatus*) that we have yet seen. They would look gorgeous in the autumn garden. This one has not the hairy leaves and stems of the rayless goldenrod, the other rabbit brush, which blooms slightly earlier in the year.

We find choke cherries green, red and ripe, discovering that water and sunlight have as much to do with time of ripening as does altitude. Some trees on dry south exposures are dropping their black ripe berries, others a few rods away in damp situations and north slopes are yet green or red. The elderberries likewise manifest striking degrees of ripeness; some are still in bloom with green berries coming; some are green without bloom; some are dark blue with here and there individual clusters, light blue with a bloom. We gather enough choke cherries for jelly and sufficient elderberries for a pie. What joys and memories the meals of winter will bring!

AUGUST 23

Sitting in the maple checkered shade beside a canyon brook and enjoying a pipe of tobacco mixed from the finest of many lands, we drift into the meditative query: a century ago where did the Indians of these mountains—the Timpanogos, the Weber Utes, and the Cumumbahs—get their smoking tobacco? We recall our own boyhood days, when we occasionally stole to the alfalfa fields to smoke the "cedar bark" that we had stripped in papery layers from the fence posts, the Utah cedar or desert juniper (*Juniperus utahensis*); but since that at best was a poor smoke, where did those root-digger Indians procure their tobacco?

A century ago, in the 1840s, trappers frequented the Wasatch mountains, and knew well how to trade real tobacco, beads and "firewater" for the skins of the beaver, the otter, the mountain lion and the wolf; but since the Indians hereabout caught so few animals that they themselves always needed skins for clothing, the trade was insignificant, indeed, almost abandoned in favor of the higher mountains to the North and the East where fur-bearers were more plentiful.

Thus, when they could, the Indians of these regions mixed the tobacco of the traders with the bark of the dogbane (*Apocynum cannabium*), which they called "bahunduwaya". It is a perennial herb with tough fibrous bark; and one of its kind (*A. androsaemifolium*) we have found growing in the broom grass with tiny, bell-blooms of pink as fragrant as honeysuckle.

They often had no tobacco to mix, so they smoked the dried bark of the dogwood (*Cornus stolonifera*), that bright red-barked shrub which grows among the willows of the canyons. This locally is called "Kinnikinnick", a name properly applied to the bearberry which inhabits regions east of us.

Every year, however, the Indians dried the leaves of the tobacco plant (*Nicotiana attenuata*), that slender herb, two feet high, with tapering, long pointed leaves and greenish flowers that grows on our dry sandy places. Thus even the red man was not denied his "smoke". It is said that the Indian chiefs venerated the stem of a peace pipe, not the bowl; at any rate even these digger Indians must have traded for some red bowls made from the fine grained stone (catlinite) found near Big Stone Lake in South Dakota, for that was a stone sacred to American Indians. It is an indurated red clay so extensively used by the Indians that when C. T. Jackson came upon it in 1839 he named it after George Catlin whose drawings of Indians became famous. Throughout the world civilized man prides himself on the exquisiteness of his taste; perhaps the savage knows many contentments to him unknown. If the aim of life is happiness who after all most nearly achieves it—he who drifts furtherest from, or he who clings most closely to nature? One's life is *investigatio rerum naturae*.

AUGUST 24

It is hardly believable that we have in the mountains hereabout a real boa constrictor, yet there it is in a hat box on the front porch, the second for identification in a single year. It is a rubber boa, silver snake, two-headed snake or worm snake (*Charina bottae utahensis*), as it is variously called, taken from the Bonneville shore line only a few hundred rods away.

It is a small snake with a tail as blunt as its head; with a smooth shining body of brown gray or olive above and yellow or white below; and with a head sometimes darker than its other parts.

Being of subterraneous habit, it kills its prey such as mice, worms and lizards, by constriction, as do the great tropical *Boidae*. It manifests no hostility when handled, or we should say "sticked", for despite our love of everything that appeals to the naturalist we have never willingly touched a snake. As we bother it, however, it twists itself into a ball that may be rolled about the porch floor. Often it coils itself in such manner that its tail uptrudes in resemblance to a head, and its head lies alongside as if it were a tail. Such reversal or incongruity of ends must have a food-getting advantage—feint at an opponent with the foot and knock him out with a blow of the fist! In other words there is much yet to learn concerning a reptile so strangely made that casual observation fails to reveal which end is head, which is tail.

This idenification of reptiles often leads to strange incidents; for one bright morning we find on our office desk a perforated shoe box which without any other warning we carefully open only to discover a baby rattlesnake!

The rubber boa leads us to believe there are many strange animals, reptiles, and insects yet to be found in these mountains.

By the way, at the mouth of City Creek canyon today on the west side, we come upon an exotic tree, which appears as though its outer branches were dangling bunches of Japanese light green lanterns two inches long. Such pods, a whole inch through with three red-brown berries inside! It is the Golden Rain or Pride of India tree (*Koelrenteria paniculata*), an imported one grown from seed. Not all the beauties of these mountains originate here.

Among the maples of upper City Creek today we come upon a beautifully colored mushroom—a masked Tricholoma (*Tricholoma personatum bulbosum*) of pale lilac. Although shaped like a common mushroom, its upper surface resembles pale lilac cake-frosting, and its odor is that of rotted leaves. It is edible, but we forego the experiment of eating it.

AUGUST 25

Having touched that stinging nettle just now, we have become convinced that several plants hereabout cause dermatitis or skin inflammation.

The Yellow Lady's Slipper (*Cypripedium parviflorum*), which grows along the streams of the timbered glades of the mountains, a member of the orchid family, about a foot high with a leafy top, has hairy stems that sometimes prickle the hand that grasps them, causing irritation not unlike that induced by poison ivy.

The shade-loving cow parsnip (*Heracleum lanatum*) over there on the canyon creekside, the one that has the largest leaves of any plant in Utah, likewise irritates the skin if the leaves are handled when wet. Fortunately we look at it without desiring to pluck those monstrous leaves. We never did like parsnips (*Pastinaca sativa*), which though cultivated sometimes grows wild in our waste places, for notwithstanding there is little evidence that they actually are poisonous, some people do suffer skin eruptions from handling the flowers and leaves.

About cold springs and on the shores of muddy ponds we often see that stout, coarse, foot-high plant known as the cursed crowfoot (*Ranunculus sceleratus multifida*) which is capable of blistering the skin, and either makes cows sick or taints their milk when they eat it green.

That common weed that prefers irrigation ditches, the yellow dock (*Rumex crispus*) likewise greatly irritates the skins of some people, though we personally seem never to have had ill results as we dug them from the apple orchards.

The alsike clover (*Trifolium hybridum*), which blooms with rose-tinged flowers from May to October in the cultivated fields, and bears serrulate leaflets with sharp-pointed teeth, makes the skin of susceptible individuals smart with pain and inflammation.

Every time we gather elderberries in the mountains we somehow or other run into those stinging nettles (*Urtica holocericea*), which are so densely tomentose that they play havoc with our hands and legs.

The poison ivy (*Toxicodendron rydbergii*) has at one time or other blistered nearly all of us. Our old friend Marcus E. Jones used to prescribe the juice of potatoes or tomatoes, or even soda-water; at any rate he said that an extract from the gum plant or arnica (*Grindelia squarrosa*) is a positive remedy. Perhaps some day we shall test it, though my mentor says a strong solution of soap and water, applied as soon as the poison is discovered, will most effectually prevent the usual annoying blisters.

Some people's skins are irritated by the leaves of such plants as Virgins bower, English ivy, Princess pine, and even by the young stems of asparagus and the lovely flowers of the catalpa. Strange world!

AUGUST 26

Glorious is the end of the Wasatch day. By seven o'clock many delightful tints appear in the canopy of heaven as well as in the hills and valleys below. The mountains of the East are for the most part light cinnamon drab with stretches of rejane green and strips of purple neutral gray. At the South end of the valley there is a more bluish haze, while the mountains of the West show light medici blue in contrast with the neutral grays of the valley floor. The light, neutral gray clouds of the Eastern firmament are interspersed with white ones like those of the neropalin blue of the overhead sky. At the West the clouds are pale ochraceous buff, while those at the Southwest are pale, vinaceous fawn.

Fifteen minutes later the colors generally are much deeper, the mountains of the East becoming neutral gray and the neutral gray clouds of the South being now overhung by others of livid pink and, further West, even of livid and corinthian pinks. Some clouds in the West are even pale, vinaceous lilac, which tint also begins to dapple those of the East.

With the approach of the first gray shadows of twilight, the clouds become almost uniformly neutral gray, excepting some clear white ones in the East and North. There remains a slight tinge of pink in the South. The mountains of the East are now a deep green blue-gray, almost violet plumbeous.

The crickets begin their rhythmic solos; cool wafts of air come from the canyons to the valley; night hawks hunt and cry in the region of flying insects overhead, and another ordinary August day has darkened into night.

Sunsets, with their bright segments along the Western horizon, with their green flashes and their crepuscular rays; sunsets with their cloud irisations and after flows—are common sights in these mountains; yet even all night long in summer there are noctilucent clouds in the sky of this region of atmospheric clarity and purity.

AUGUST 27

Two miles above the Forestry entrance in Farmington canyon we catch sight of a golden rod we have not seen before; it is a *Solidago elongata* with erect panicle branches forming a dense yellow flower thyrse. Most of the golden rods are more or less open, but this is as erect, rounded and dense as a coxcomb.

Further on our attention is arrested by a pair of canyon wrens (*Catherpes mexicanus consperus*) flitting about the rocks of the perilous dugway. A small lizard scampers as we heed it, and then we notice that the yellow sunflower flitting viguiera (*V. multiflora*) and pink dogbanes are plentiful on the steep, mahoganied slopes of the canyon.

The mountain ash is so abundant further up that everywhere on the hillside clusters of its ripening berries appear, but not without fireweeds in silky seed and patches of mountain lilac to keep them company.

We turn towards Mt. Francis, and stop on the very ridge separating Farmington canyon from the Weber valley. Here is a grove of Douglas spruces, and the wind is so strong that with ear to its trunk we can hear one of the bending old monarchs squeak with the strain. The distant islands of Great Salt Lake engross our attention through the glasses; and then we scan the northward interspaces, for it was here once years ago that we so surprised a bear in its wallow that in fleeing it caused willow limbs to flip back into our face.

Here are snow berries in fruit, oak trees with leaves infested with gall, and mountain lilacs in fruit, the clustered capsules resembling black clover leaf rolls. Each has three seeds inside.

We stop—it is a bear across the canyon! A brown bear moving behind a pine! But the glasses say "no" and a black and white Holstein proves it by walking into the glade where grazes her red companion.

We return by the Ward canyon one-way return road. At 7500 feet the hillsides are adorned by lupines and Indian paint brushes. We have our attention excited by a huge pine (*Pinus flexilis*) at the roadside and stop to examine the miniature dry flower cones.

A western red-tailed hawk eyes us from a dead pine limb, then outwings into the swift up-draught, showing clearly his red tail as he soars at ease. At 8750 feet we scan all the valleys below; and at that high point the leaves of Balsamorrhiza are drying to dark red. Sage abounds as well as Indian paint brushes, lupines and yarrow. Then along the ridge red elderberries and red and white baneberries are plentiful with attractive but unwholesome fruit. Give to us the clear air of a mountain ridge, the wild freedom of unfrequented places near the blue of heaven!

AUGUST 28

The world has experienced a war of socialized human groups, groups that fight across thousands of miles of ocean and terrain, but with no more vigor and ruthlessness than do the ants their ant neighbors hundreds of inches away. Men are organized, so are the ants; men have high and low society, so do the ants; men have slaves, so do the ants; men have queens, so do the ants; in fact, what do men possess that the ants do not have, unless, indeed it be a vanity, a superiority-complex that makes them enjoy the error that the world was created for them alone? As we watch a bed of red occidental ants at its graveled mound and its clearing a rod in diameter, we see the intensity of organized activity, and the monstrous strength of insects who, if they were men, would each carry half a ton up a steep acclivity more than a quarter of a mile. Man gloats on his strength, but what if he could carry seven men on his shoulders up a steep mountainside? Sight, hearing, taste and smell—some animal, some insect excels mere man in any or all of these; and some, indeed most, belittle him in comparative physical strength. Men think! Aye, but what do the ants do when they organize communities, assign workers to the care of cocoons, refrain from contact with the individuals of other colonies except in combat, cause plant lice and other insects to do their bidding, indulge in the agricultural pursuit of mushroom-growing, store food, and live together a hundred thousand strong without internal strife? Models indeed would be our cities if the thought of every individual were the best good of the whole community. Place a colony of ants between two window panes not over a quarter of an inch apart, and every act of their complicated life will be revealed to you. Try then to believe that man alone is the elite of living reality; try then to think that a sparrow can fall without in some way affecting the mystic end of all design.

And then, as we leave this pry into antdom, we sit at our cottage door when Hesperus is beckoning to darkness; and three crickets lull our drowsy mood. One is "do", another "ra", and a third "me", for the three have different pitches for their tunes.

As each male chirps with his membranous wing some female holds the ear of her forearm up in rapt attention, for why sing in this world if no lady be listening?

AUGUST 29

Some things in nature seem just now to be at their height of beauty.

Along the dry hillsides, where sunflowers are common and June grass is as inflammable as tinder, golden asters (*Chrysopsis foliosa*) are especially vigorous and pleasing with their bright yellow flowers and leathery hispid leaves curled along the stems.

Wherever a roadway, cut along the old Bonneville shore line, exposes loose, graveled slides, such as those on the East side of the entrance to City Creek canyon, the mentzelias (*Mentzelia laevicaulis*) are a refreshing joy as each morning we ride by them. Being members of the Loasa family, their leaves and stems are covered with barbed hairs, hence the plants are not usually picked for bouquets; but the flowers are truly blazing stars of bloom, all the more attractive because they inhabit rocky slides where little else save sunflowers and evening primroses grow. The five-petalled stars with their seventy five stamens open during the night to greet us in the morning; and then as if knowing our habits, they usually close while we are necessarily away from them, working during the day. In the bright sunlight some of the open petals have a metallic sheen. Many flowers like many men, usually ignored, have qualities worthy of our admiration, if we but take the time to know them well.

On the upper canyon hills a tall, thin stemmed much branched plant (*Viguiera multiflora*) with several flowers on each stem, is now at its best. Each flower has about fifteen lemon yellow petals with an orange center.

As we go along the verdured brooks of the upper canyons to gather service berries (which are beginning to dry), choke cherries, and elderberries (which are not quite ripe) we sometimes catch sight of the orange berries of the mountain ash which hang in clusters and by their very color, peeping through the foliage of other trees, hold the eye in immediate attention. They seem most attractive just now, for although they will turn a bright red later on, they will be in competition with leafy color everywhere whereas now they have the picture much to themselves.

Year by year birds seem scarcer, even in the high mountains; but flowers, especially in such places as Brighton where public opinion frowns on their picking, are as plentiful as ever. Only when we enter upon the domain of vast destructive sheep herds do we come away with a sense of disappointment and sadness.

AUGUST 30

One summer morning there was a mystery in the home—every few minutes something ran along the polished oak floors behind the piano, making clicking sounds like that of a pencil point tapped on a desk. Driving it from its retreat with a cane, we were astonished to behold a black spider, which looked as big as a boy's hand, running next to the wall and making the clicking sounds as the claws of its long leg-tips struck the hard floor. Several times it raced back and forth across the front of the room; but, finally, having wearied and cornered it, we were able to capture it with a large-mouthed fruit jar in which it was unable to climb. What a monster!—a tarantula of the genus *Eurypelma*. It had undoubtedly entered the door, temporarily open the evening before, when sprinkling water had driven it from its accustomed herbage and flowers. One other of similar size we a later year captured in the same manner as it clung to the rough bricks of an outer wall.

These enormous tarantulas are neither vicious nor poisonous; in fact, in all the Wasatch mountains there is only one spider decidedly poisonous—the black widow (*Latrodectus mactans*), which too often we have found about the outer walls, especially where hose taps gave them a fairly dependable supply of water.

Little is known of the habits of tarantulas. They live in natural cavities of ground or tree and emerge in the evening to hunt and capture beetles, their principal food, not by enmeshing the victims in a web but by chasing them down.

Every living thing has an enemy of some kind, and the tarantula has one as startling in size as himself. For instance, one summer afternoon, while we were drenching the shrubs about the house, a tremendously large wasplike creature, five times as large as the ordinary wasp, seemed to have its transparent wings stuck with the water, so we easily took it in hand, finding it to be the black tarantula hawk or tarantula-killer (*Pepsis bognei*). It was a formidable looking wasp, so extraordinary that it was deemed advisable to place it in the permanent collection of the State Agricultural College. Many tarantulas reach such collections, for they are rather terrifying to behold, when first seen, especially if one realize that their relatives further south are known to suck the blood of young birds; but the tarantula hawk is seldom captured. One never knows what interesting form of life is going to show itself in one's very dooryard.

The real tarantula or wolf spider of Southern Europe (*Lycosa tarantula*) is so generally thought to make people want to dance when it bites them that in Spain there is a guild of tarantula players who make money going about to furnish music for tarantula dance victims; but the bite there is in reality no more harmful than that of the Wasatch mosquito. Such, however, is superstition.

AUGUST 31

It is noontide in a secluded glen in Lamb's canyon, 1.6 miles above the entrance from Parley's, an an altitude of 6450 feet. With the brushy mountainside at the East, the shrub-laden flat North and South, and the willowed creek at the West, we are surrounded by verdure. Overhead the sky is a cloudless deep blue, ineffable in its beauty where it meets the rich greenery of the ridge.

Interspersed about the landscape, quaking aspens stand still, then shiver before unnoticeable draughts, the most sensitive of all that lives in the mountains. Nevertheless save for them and half a dozen white firs pointing into the firmament, the upper half of the ridge-slope is mantled with scrub oak thickly leaved.

Near us is a handsome dogwood with most of its leaves green but with a leaf here and there of the color of China rose or wild cherry. Its berries, which hang in clusters of a dozen or more individuals, are oyster white or marguerite yellow in color.

A spring trickles its pellucid water through the grass, and there at its side is a vigorous birch twenty feet high. The bark is covered with white specks, which, when they are wetted and seen under our glass, appear like tiny white lice; but in reality they are lenticels or breathing pores of the shrub itself. What marvels a magnifying glass enlarges for the eyes!

A purple aster blooms at our feet; wild roses show their hips; but we can wait no longer, for all about us service berry bushes are laden and choke cherries are plentiful. We go to work, and without moving more than twenty yards in any direction the two of us pick two gallons of service berries and one gallon of choke cherries in two hours! Service berries for Thanksgiving pies, choke cherries for jelly!

Cabbage butterflies and silver spots are plentiful; and then unexpectedly what looks like a butterfly heavily laden flounders over the little camp site, as though crippled. We capture it, and, of all things!— it is not a butterfly but a moth active in the bright sun. It is mostly yellowish orange, but it has two wavy black bands across each wing, a round black spot on each wing, and six longitudinal black bars at the rear of each wing. It is a Nuttall's sheep moth (*Pseudohazis eglanterina nuttalli*), diurnal in habit, keeping company with species of *Argynnis,* or silver spotted butterflies. Ephemeral thing, it succumbs within a few minutes after we wrap it up without injury, leading us to believe that it was ready to die. Its body is thick and marked with black stripes like those of a bumble bee.

A WASATCH SUMMER

SEPTEMBER 1

A pioneer told us that when she arrived upon the shores of the Great Salt Lake—in 1851, a girl of five—such was the general distress that at once she was taught to flay tall sunflowers with a stick so that their seeds would drop into her apron for the forthcoming winter's bread. Everywhere stretched an unirrigated, inhospitable sageland; and the wonder is, that the Indians of the region, with their primitive methods, survived at all. The red men in winter did on occasion so nearly starve that they ate corpses and as a last extremity, their own children. Selling daughters to more fortunate tribes was a common barter for sustenance.

The Indians, however, had a comprehensive knowledge of what was edible in their vast, rain-infrequented home; and seeds in the fall of the year were always much desired. They knew how to gather seeds of the wheat grass or bunch glass, as we call it (*Agropyron spicatum*) which grows on the Wasatch mountain hillsides; they called it "hugur"; also the seeds of the redtop (*Agrostis vulgaris*), which they named "sihu", and which, by the way, we have noted is frequently eaten by the mourning dove.

When food was scarce the Indians did not disdain the bitter seeds of the common sage, calling it "sawava", nor the seeds of the salt brush (*Atriplex truncata*) or 'kosbadup" to them. They stored the seeds of that arrowleaved balsam root that sometimes is called the "big sunflower" (*Balsamorrihiza sagittata*), which is in yellow array on the Wasatch hills of April and May; they called it "kusiak"; indeed, they gathered the seeds of the milkweed, the big and little sunflowers (*Wyethia* and *Helianthella*), which they called "aku" and the toad rush (*Juncos bufonius*), which they named saip".

They plucked the pipe of the wild rose for storage as "tsiavi", and picked up the acorns of the scrub oaks under the name of "wiya". The choke cherries, which they called "toocawi" they pounded into a mash; then dried and stored it seeds and all.

Lewis and Clark, Fremont, Bancroft, Stansbury, Domenesh, Burton, Chamberlain, Steward and many more attest the accuracy of such things; for hard driven indeed were the Wasatch Indians.

SEPTEMBER 2

Behind the door of an unoccupied cabin over the creek in the lower canyon we have just caught sight of a beautiful black widow spider (*Latrodectus Mactans*)—"beautiful", we says, because her abdomen is as rounded and symmetrical as a marble and she is jet black save for a red spot of hour-glass shape on her under side. Not only that, she is alert, aggressive and strong, a true thoroughbred among spiders. The fact that she is deadly does not detract from her shapeliness and grace any more than the poisoned fangs of a rattlesnake take away the handsome patterns of its back.

Arachnology, the science of the study of spiders, is such an interesting diversion that we seldom can refrain from observing them. Having had considerable experience with the dreaded black widow, both about home and woods, we treat it as a dangerous enemy, especially since one of our friends nearly died from a bite on his lip while asleep in a cabin.

The male black widow, half the size of the female, has four pairs of stripes along the sides of his abdomen; and the reason he is less frequently seen is, that, after breeding, the female lovingly winds her silken threads about him and then—devours him!

This spider prefers to build its coarse web conveniently near fresh water, such as a dripping tap near a wood pile, garage wall or cellar window. It, however, dislikes almost any fly-killing spray, often abandoning a hole saturated with a poisonous liquid. Indeed some sprays so linger on wood that the black widow will not return to it for years.

A bite from this poisonous spider sometimes results in pain within five minutes, and even a week of unconsciousness. It is little wonder that the Indians of California, according to Dr. Merriam, ranked it with the rattlesnake and poisoned their arrow heads with its mashed body. Our friend, mentioned above, was bitten on the lip while sleeping in a miner's cabin and his life was precariously near its end during the ensuing ten days. To know that a grizzly bear is prowling outside our cabin is not so worrisome as to see a black widow spider escape in a hole beside the bed, or to find it nesting, as we have done, on a spare room ceiling!

SEPTEMBER 3

After all we should not too strongly contemn the Wasatch root-digger Indians for eating grasshoppers; for not only did John the Baptist subsist on "locusts" and "wild honey" but also since his time all of the natives of Palestine have regarded the forty species of locusts found there as edible in all the stages of their growth.

When white men first entered the valley of the Great Salt Lake to make their homes, singing "Hosanna to the Lord!" and rumbling their wagons carefully down a rocky canyon, they beheld a parched sageland, brightened by sunflowers, ribboned by willowed creeks, and greened only by an occasional boxelder. Their hearts almost failed them as they too often dodged the coiled rattlesnake, and saw the gaunt jack rabbit scurry with the lizard away from the leathered noise of their foot-treads. Strange sights they came upon; Indians, unafraid of white men whom they regarded as trapper-friends, were seen to be driving "millions of black crickets", which covered the ground, into corrals of sage and grease-wood, there to be burned of their legs and wings and their fat bodies preserved for winter food. Later these same Indians sold their white neighbors flour that only a stray leg or so disclosed to be grasshopper meal. It was the western cricket, not grasshopper, that in later days were devoured by the now almost sacred gulls.

Our common grasshopper (the red leg (*Melanoplus femurrubrum*), is smaller than the American locust, which has a brown body and a longitudinal, yellowish stripe along the back of its head, thorax and wings. The iron clad (*Melanoplus sepretus*), which laid its eggs in the trampled trails of buffaloes was most destructive of all, but it has disappeared from the West save possibly in the Canadian Rockies.

Crickets, grasshoppers, locusts—they were all the same to omniverous Indians. By the way, one may now purchase in specialty food markets not only canned rattlesnake but also cans of toasted grasshoppers!

SEPTEMBER 4

Though three races of the pigeon hawk (*Falco columbarius columbarius*) visit these mountains, they differ little save in the number of white bands crossing their middle tail feathers, yet, strange to say, two other races not so easily recognized have crept into scientific literature. Nevertheless we have always respected the exactitude of a great taxonimist who namd one of them, the late Robert Ridgway, both our friend and ornithological inspiration, the very cause, if you please, of the author's interest in birds. When at the University of Chicago the author first opened that monumental work "North American Birds by Baird, Brewer and Ridgway", and saw depicted therein multiform bird-heads in color, he felt an urge for more, an urge which is yet to be satisfied. Such are the fortuitous circumstances and epochs of one's career.

The hawk that is flying over the low hillsides of City Creek canyon just now is a Richardson "merlin" to us, not "pigeon hawk", as ornithology lately dictates; for as a bird first comes to hand so in memory it remains. At any rate this brownish gray falcon, a foot in length, is a courageous, spirited raptor. Like all the falcons its eyelids are provided with lashes, the better, perhaps to soften the sun; its eyes are directed laterally the easier very likely to pursue its prey; and its claws are sharp, strong and pointed, the firmer to clutch and hold its multiform victims. It breeds northward, but winters South of this region.

Arthur Cleveland Bent once saw a male pigeon hawk drop a mouse to its mate whom the bird had called forth to catch it in the air. Wonderful are such bits of ornithology, serving as they do to prove that affection and solicitude are not characteristics of man alone.

Many a pigeon, dove and robin; many a teal, plover or snipe; many a spider, grasshopper or snake, falls before this agile bird; yet notwithstanding its boldness it is so unsuspicious and domestic that it is an easy target for the gunner.

Feeding on fish, fowl and mammals, man is himself a "hawk" in nature, so who be he to condemn or disdain?

As we traverse fields northward on the lower foothills, farmers are gathering peaches, grapes, onions and tomatoes, cucumbers, cantelopes and melons. It is a busy yet happy time. We stop to talk with one we know and while doing so we incidentally look at Antelope Island in the Great Salt Lake through our field glasses. "For eight years we have been able to walk over to it on dry land," he said. It is true, yet we remember when those intervening miles were covered with briny water.

SEPTEMBER 5

Incredible! but there it is—a *Phallus impudicus* in all its beauty of orange, white and green sticking up from the ground at our very doorstep! It is one of the most interesting of all mushrooms.

This pretty one, known as the stinkhorn, has a pileus of conic shape bearing a jellylike, green mass of spores, a hollow tapering stem and a pinkish volva. It sticks up like a warted thumb. Above the gelatinous green substance of the cap is a yellow-white ring. The offensive odor of the mature fungus is apparently attractive to flies, which carry away on their feet some of the spores mixed with the sticky green jelly.

Only yesterday one of our friends, an enthusiastic mycologist, brought us an immature stinkhorn that he had gathered near a spring of the Big Cottonwood district. It resembles a small pinkish puffball; but when cut in two is extraordinary. Just inside of the pinkish "eggshell" or peridium is a layer of jelly; next appears the layer comprising the future green mass of the cap; then, the future stem; and finally, in the center, the compressed cells. In sectional view each of these are well defined, manifesting the ingenious method of nature to devote a fungus from the very beginning of its existence to the work of making and spreading its own spores. The young stinkhorn is edible, its odor resembling that of a potato; nevertheless, it does not appeal to our fancy.

Of the many species of mushrooms that we have taken in the Wasatch the most beautiful, next to the stinkhorn, is the masked tricholoma (*Tricholoma personatum*). Finding it one twenty second of August in a maple grove near the North Fork of City Creek, we were at once delighted with its delicate, pale lilac color. Its slight fragrance was more that of the rotted maple leaves from which it was growing than of a mushroom. It had no annulus, no volva; and its fibrous stem was bulbous. Its upper surface resembled pale lilac cake-frosting, very attractive among leaves. It is an edible species, not so uncommon as one would think. We have found it also in the high mountains of the upper Provo, growing along a meadow trail by creek willows.

Today high on the brook-sung slopes of Timpanogos where glaciers rest above us, we watch a languorous red-tail hawk drowsing the noon on an aspen limb. It is lonely up there and dry. Nigger heads are plentiful, but *colombos* are parched and brittle. Blue elderberries are common; red ones appear here and there, but the black kind we have not yet found despite its known existence here.

SEPTEMBER 6

Many things in nature are ugly and forbidding to the casual eye but very pleasing on close inspection, especially with a glass, even one of weak magnification. The sides of the dusty roadway ahead of us, are, for instance, matted by Russian thistles (*Salsola pestifer*), a troublesome weed; but a rather attractive maroon hue about them causes us to take one in hand, to discover that it has beauty despite its spines. Its stems are maroon; and on the branches all along are quarter-inch, open-faced flowers of solferina color or hellebore red, some indeed of flaming maple verged with whitish yellow. About each flower are two or more leaves of the shape of a split awl, each hardened at the tip like a sharp needle. It is, of course, a pestiferous weed, introduced from Russia about 1898; for that matter, the lovely Mentzelias with their harsh foliage are perhaps likewise considered a weed for all their romantic awakening at eventide.

A rattlesnake is a repulsive reptile, but not only is the color pattern of its back a work of nature's art but also its fangs with their folded grooves, curved shape and needle points are weapons of symmetry and grace. A skunk is noisome but its pelage beautiful; a fly amanita mushroom is poisonous but it is handsome in coloring; a fungus so offensive to the smell that no one would care to eat it is the stinkhorn, yet the orange top of its cap, encircled by a white ring, fringed below by the rich green of the remainder of its pileus, forms a color combination so pleasing that we contentedly gaze for a long time upon it.

The truth is: there is scarcely an animal, bird, flower, tree, reptile, insect, fungus or snail that is without beauty when closely examined. It may be color, spore, tooth, symmetry or design, but whatever it is, it usually shows clearly its dual purpose of sustenance and propagation. A thing is ugly to us because it interferes with either our welfare or our pleasure, but seldom is it displeasing to sight if wholesome and beneficial. After all perhaps Nature was not designed wholly for mere man.

SEPTEMBER 7

In the mist-laden shade of a balsam bowered nook in an upper canyon at noontide, we sit on leaf-cushioned soil bestrewn with mountain hedge and listen to the sweet melody of the fretting stream. We look upward to a sky of deepened blue, like the blue of Yale, of Napoleon, Rameses, Helvetia, the *bleu de Lyons,* yet a blue possessing in its own quality an ineffable translucency like the depth of a beautiful child's eye. It is richer than the sky of the valley. And, there, behind the lacery of balsam branches, are ephemeral mounds of white, vast clouds floating in the blue. Lovely are the lofty firs whose swaying tips are adorned with rusty cones. They represent the evergreen hope of eternal life-seeds born and reared in sunshine, yet destined to enroot the soil below for hundreds of years to come.

A quarter of a century ago yonder spruce patriarch crashed to the canyon floor, and now, beside the eternal ripples of the pellucid brook, its shattered trunk crumbles in slow decay, yet still showing in its yellowed core the annular rings of its long history. Prostrate across the running water, its once mighty trunk, two feet through, now lies moss-grown and half buried in its aldered soil. Trout inhabit the transparent pool beneath its protruding end, where debris enfoams the head of the miniature cataract below. A water ouzel chatters as it swiftly wings the brook's meander, unmindful, joyous, yet, somehow, the bones of that giant heap make the very home of that insouciant bird.

We move on apace to a fir-charmed brookside, canyoned high, where to the South the chariot-clouded blue harmonizes with ineffable purity into the aspen-clustered ridge. Pyramidal lords of spruce, fir, and pine, taper towards the unfathomable sky. Yonder upshoot several close-tipped balsams, a whole family grown into eleven spires. Fresh, green, vigorous, they are united steeples of cloud-pointing limbs and leaves, hugging one another in the bliss of alpine health, and waving their slender heads in unison with every passing breeze; contented family of canyon-sided evergreens!

At the mouth of the canyon on the alluvial flats, a bush somewhat resembling an oak but with dark red berry clusters arrests our attention. It is a sumac (*Rhus trilobata*), locally known as squawbush, sunkberry, or aromatic sumac. It is a shrub nearly seven feet high, with leaves divided into three leaflets. The dark red drupe is about an inch long, containing about forty closely packed, acid, ill-smelling red berries. This nonpoisonous plant is a cousin of the poison ivy, and it is quite common on the dry hillsides.

SEPTEMBER 8

Wonders never cease! For many years we have regretted that in all our rambles afield we have never once chanced upon a Rocky mountain orange-crown warbler (*Vermivora celata orestera*), notwithstanding that it cannot be considered rare; hence our delight can be imagined when, as we sat here in the lighted study a few minutes ago, in the noontime of a cloudy, windy autumnal day, a male bird of this species flew to the windowpane beneath the porch in a fluttering attempt to enter, and being frustrated by the glass, sat for several minutes on the sash where within inches of him we were able to scrutinize his every feature. Indeed he even turned his own black eyes backward toward the pane when the lids of peach-boiling kettles in the kitchen were replaced and the sound attracted his attention.

Trim little bird, dusky olive green above and greenish yellow below, he stood as if in temporary consternation over the solidity of transparent glass, and then with agile speed flew to the dark recesses of a thick globe locust tree. Obviously he was in migration, but he was so persistent in his endeavors as to enter the house by the back door. There is quite a fluster in expelling him without injury; but it is finally accomplished.

Birds being usually fairly good barometers, he may be contending with two urges—migration and security. Migration takes him into strange environs; security compels him to seek refuge from temporary storm. He is accustomed to the perils of his summer home and avoids them; but in migration he is beset by new dangers every hour—hawk, wind, hail, food scarcity or cold—and is almost bewildered in his effort to escape them. It is little wonder, then that a tender bird sometimes acts strangely, for who knows what his hunger, his fear or his anxiety may be? Who understands why twice a year he must journey not only from mountain to valley, from high brook to low river, but from continent to continent, from temperate zones to tropical ones. When we think of the golden plover (*Pluvialis dominicas*), however,—breeding in the arctic regions and migrating about this time to far away Patagonia—the *raison d' etre* of migration becomes incomprehensible indeed.

The three months, September, October and November, comprise the autumnal period in the cycle of bird life, characterized by movements in mixed flocks, and we may expect many verifications.

SEPTEMBER 9

It is a memorable day in the year 1941; "memorable" because we have the good fortune to discover a tree new to the flora of Utah. As we are driving down Provo canyon (5200 feet) my companion, Louise Atkinson, suddenly exclaims, "A red-berried hawthorn!" We stop to examine the tree, which actually overhangs the roadside; and sure enough, its berries are scarlet and its thorns are four inches long, something unheard of in the Wasatch. (It takes until June 1943 for its status to be determined by Ernest J. Palmer of the Arnold Aboretum, for the genus *Crataegus* is highly critical, and we submit many spring and fall samples. It turns out to be *Crataegus Colorado* Ashe, and heretofore only *C. rivularis*, the common "haw" has been known to Utah's flora. Mr. Palmer says that Ashe, Sargent and other early botanists would likely have called it a new species, since it does not exactly fit into the niche of *C. colorado*. Since the original discovery we have found twenty trees in the same locality; but it surprises us that in the past decade probably a half a million people have driven by within ten feet of our new Crataegus; and we ourselves have been among them.)

Leaving the river where fishermen are casting their lines and chickadees singing, we turn into Willow Creek (5150 feet), the beginning of Timpanogos drive, where an occasional scarlet maple studs the prevailing green. Rabbit brushes, Viguiera and sunflowers yet bloom; but most of the flowers have been trampled by a herd of sheep, which we find nooning in an aspen grove at the summit.

Descending into American Fork canyon, we find (6875 feet) a *Penstemon Eatoni* in full bloom and near it a paint brush (*Castilleja confusa*). Further on, where a turbulent brook emerges from forested hills and crosses the roadway, we come upon ripe red raspberries (*Rubus melanolasius*), strawberries (*Fragaria bracteata*), black currants (*Ribes petiolare*), a cluster of shaggy mane mushrooms (*Coprinus comatus*), and a baneberry (*Actaea arguta*) with hard, round, scarlet, poisonous berries.

Laden with chokecherries, we linger awhile to watch a beautiful long-crested jay, solitary, noisy, among the spruces; and then go on, happy in our discovery of the great-thorned Crataegus.

SEPTEMBER 10

In trudging up Mill Creek canyon above Bountiful today with the Old Prospector in search of mica, we find disused logging trails to be densely overgrown with alders, service berries, squaw bushes, big toothed maples, black willows (*Salix amygdaloides*), black birches (*Betula fontinalis*), and quaking aspens. So labryinthine is the underbrush that our ascent is truly arduous and disheartening, despite the fact that we are both physically as tough as leather. He, however, is my senior by thirty years.

Though the alders are still green, the maples are just beginning to crimson. The broad leaves of the thimble berry, which forms thick vesture along the creek bed, are old gold color, and its red fruit is dry. It is one of the most attractive shrubs of the mountains. Sumac leaves are turning color, and the fire weeds (*Epilobium paniculatum*) have became rich maroon.

Here and there we come upon blue clusters of elderberries. We, however, see no service berries, a fact which my companion assures me means a mild winter.

As we eat our sandwiches beside a trickling stream and recline on dense patches of wood ferns (*Dryopteris linnaeana*), the Old Prospector teaches me something new now concerning birch bark. Peeling a ten inch strip from a nearby tree, he applies a match to one end, which causes the bark to roll on itself until it is as tight as a pencil. He then lights one end, and to my astonishment it burns as perfectly as a candle. It is his custom when alone in the wilds to illuminate his tent at night with these improvised tapers.

When we come to a fine young blister balsam, my friend pricks the blisters with his pocket knife and eats the bitter juice, claiming there is nothing better for kidneys and that in the woods scarcely any other medicine is needed.

We find the mica—muscovite in small sheets marred by garnets and black spots—and leave its bubble of wealth to observe in descending the canyon the habits of gray ruffed grouse and the darting antics of a sharp-shinned hawk.

We like Ruskin's: "The September days were yet long enough for a sunset walk."

SEPTEMBER 11

Among the spruces of Big Cottonwood canyon, in a covert-lane underlighted by the rays of a setting sun, an animal is ambling its slothful way. It is a yellow-haired porcupine, covered with yellowish black-tipped quills; and as we rush towards it and tease it with a staff it turns its head away and switches its tail back and forth with vengeful determination. The quills do not fly like darts, but, being barbed along the pointed ends, they readily stick into anything soft that encounters them, and remain to penetrate and rankle in endless torture of their unwitting victim. As we poke the spiney animal it whines, grunts, squeaks and mews, in fact emits almost every describable sound that one would attribute to a weak old man in distress.

Lethargic cactus of the woods, the porcupine lives an uneventful life, often spending a week at a time in a pine tree, subsisting on tender shoots and buds, being apparently indifferent to snow, rain, or sunshine. Little is known of its marriage relations, save that mating takes place in September or October, the father manifests no interest in the offspring, and the mother constructs a nest-bed in a hollow tree under roots or beneath an overhanging ledge. The young, usually only one, are born in May and, according to Dr. Merriam, are "actually larger and relatively more than thirty times larger than the young of the black bear at birth"; however, a Canadian porcupine observed by Albert R. Shadle and William R. Ploss weighed 12 lbs. 3 oz. just before giving birth to one young, a female weighing 1 lb. 1 oz. If we apply their figures to human beings at the same ratio, a mother weighing 125 lbs. would give birth to a baby weighing 10 lbs. 14 oz. It is interesting, that a newly-born porcupine is covered with quills as much as an inch long.

Sheep herders have reported to us that they have found mountain lions starving because porcupine quills were festering their lips and jaws. From the days of Pliny the porcupine was thought capable of throwing its quills, and in the early literature of England such as this was written: "Porcupins kill lions by darting into their body their quills". The mountain lion really feeds on porcupines, probably slashing them in trees. The fisher, a pine-inhabiting relative of the mink and the weasel found north of here, successfully flips a porcupine on its back and rips its stomach open, without being punished by the twitching quills. Porcupine meat is delicious, as many a hungry trapper can verify.

Porcupine is a word derived apparently from the Latin "porcus", pig, plus "spina", thorn; at any rate, the Old-World porcupines have long, colored quills, and are terrestrial, while our New-World porcupines have short quills and are more or less arboreal.

Despite their damage to the conifers of the Wasatch, animals as interesting and inoffensive as porcupines have their attractive place in the ever joyful ensemble of the woods.

SEPTEMBER 12

An interesting divertissement these coolsome days is to make a botanical reconnaissance of one of our canyons according to a definite locale. We select City Creek, the mouth of which opens upon historic Salt Lake City, a canyon where even at this time of much travel we know not when we may come upon a mountain lion, a deer or an elk in the verdured glades of its side-canyons.

Starting at the junction of Eleventh Avenue and B. Street and proceeding up the canyon towards the cross roads, we see two kinds of rabbit brush (*Chrysothamnus graveolens* and *C. lanceolatus*), a Russian thistle, a member of the Composite family known as *Guiterrezia sarothrae*, a hay fever weed (*Ambrosia psilostachya*), a Mentzelia or evening star (*Mentzelia laevicaulis*) blooming with yellow flowers on the graveled embankment, a salt bush or white sage (*Atriplex canescens*), two kinds of sage brush (*Artemsia tridentata* and *A. Mexicana*), and big toothed maples. On the mountainside we notice the golden rod and the arnica plant, while towards the creek we see: an aster (*A. leucanthemifolius*), birches, a narrow-leaved cottonwood, a wild rose (*Rosa ultramontana*), choke cherries, service berries, and horehound (*Marrubium vulgare*). Sunflowers are common.

At the cross roads we pause, and find these growing about us: the choke cherry, the maple, the scrub oak, the squaw-bush, the dock (*Rumex crispus*), the narrow-leaved cottonwood; willows (*Salix caudata* and *S. exigua*) and the same hay fever weed.

Further on there is a large patch of wild roses (*Rosa ultramontana*), and at Rock Bridge we notice June grass, another willow (*Salix cordata Watsoni*), wild wheat (*Agropyrum Richardsoni*), nettle (*Urtica holosericea*), aster (*Aster Douglassi*), horse tail or scouring rush (*Equisetum hiemale*), Rose of Sharon or mallow, poison ivy, elderberry, dogwood, false Solomon's seal (*Smilacena sessilifolia*), sumac (*Rhus glabra*), which is high on the mountainside just North of Rock Bridge and which in October will display a patch of rich maroon.

Now that we are at Rock Bridge let us rest a moment to note the plants hereabout. The willows here are *Salix caudata,* the maples are big-toothed, while the choke cherries, the birches, the cottonwoods, the wild roses, and the poison ivy are the same species as those already mentioned. Here, however, is a golden rod on each side of the roadway.

Between the Rock Bridge and the Reservoir we find the same plants as at Rock Bridge, and in addition thereto, the mountain hedge (*Pachystima Myrsinites*), our most conspicuous evergreen, here growing in the shade along the further creek bank.

We must return to this spot tomorrow.

SEPTEMBER 13

At the Reservoir in City Creek canyon we see such typical plants as: the birch, narrow-leaved cottonwood, wild rose, milkweed (*Ascelpias speciosa*), dogwood, dogbane, thistle, scarlet gilia, and trailing barberry. We love the trails and verdured by-paths of this delightful region where hour on hour we have sat in camp-chairs and mooded in harmony with the winsome stream.

About one fourth mile above the Reservoir we notice white firs (*Abies concolor*),—the first tall evergreens of the canyon—, dogbane (*Apocynum cannabinum*), flea bane (*Erigeron divergens*), whiskbroom parsley (*Lomatium bicolor*)—the type locality of this species is this very hill.

At the High Line water intake we find these typical plants: the same species of birches, narrow-leaved cottonwoods, dogwood, oak, maples, wild rose, and firs we noticed below, together with: aster (*Aster Douglassi*), False Solomon's seal (*Smilacena sessilifolia*), horse tail, elderberry, and dock (*Rumex crispus*).

Between the High Line and North Fork we come upon cow parsnip (*Hercaleum lanatum*), a coneflower, salmon berry, and more of the same dogbane.

At the North Fork (Alt. 5743), we pause, and see up in the gulch of the South side, another maple (*Acer glabrum*), more white firs along the creek, some red spruces (*Pseudotsuga Douglassii*) on the south mountainsides, and there, also, mountain mahogany. Hereabout we find also: more narrow leaved cottonwoods, box elders, and more of the larger maples we saw below. We find also sage, (*Artemesia tridentata*), sweet clover and hay fever weed (*Ambrosia psilostachya*).

We proceed further to the Rotary bridge and there go down to the Stepping Stone Spring. The typical plants here are: moss (*Hypnum*), alum root (*Heuchera rubescens*), nettle, grass (*Bromus condensatus*), bedstraw (*Galium triflorum*), cow parsnip, cress (*Sisymbrium incisum*), mitre-wort, baneberry, maple (*Acer glabrum*), black birch, angelica, more cottonwoods and a *Brickellia grandiflora*.

This ends a delightful trip in a typical canyon.

SEPTEMBER 14

All vegetation having been washed by a night of copious rain, it is a mild, bright day in mid-September, one of those days that make us wonder whether Spring or Autumn be our chief delight. "Autumn", by the way should ignore the equinox and begin with September.

The shaded portion of the canyon that for the nonce happens to be our locale presents a variegation of mildly blending grays, greens, reds, yellows and browns that for the moment forms a landscape of such pleasing beauty of color that description can only weakly portray it. The maple copsewoods are in some instances carrot red or coral red, again light pinkish cinnamon or even alizarine pink. The foliage of these trees of which there are two species, dwarf maple (*Acer glabrum*) of the higher hills, and shrubby maple (*A. grandidentatum*) of the lower slopes far excels all others in striking polychrome. Cliffs and other bare places are a pale brownish drab.

In the densely shaded gulches where often the cottontails make their secluded homes, choke cherry trees are deep helebore red, often beside fire weeds or willow herbs of dragon's blood red.

All of the foliage of the mountainside shows brownish tints, even through the light greens and the dark greens of the alders, willows, cottonwoods and oaks of the complacent creek.

We reach home, where petunias, chrysanthemums, roses, asters, zinnias, morning glories, marigolds, spectrum red pompons, cosmos and sweet alyssum are in bloom; but most astonishing in regal beauty are the dahlias. We pick five of the magnificent, lordly blooms—one is white; one, a foot in diameter, is Tyrian rose; one a barium yellow; one an amaranth pink; and another, a roods violet, which in tone lies between an amaranth and an aster purple. What a joy in the quiet garden!

Just after sundown the eastern sky is painted with clouds of safrano pink interspersed with others of pale green blue gray; and as the moon arises, like a translucent ball of illuminated silver, it is set before a background of vinaceous gray. Overhead the heavens are campanula blue, clear and incomprehensible; but the western horizon is suffused with primrose yellow and purplish opaline.

Gradually all of the vinaceous hues fade out of the East; and the West, cloudless though it be, becomes golden, then orange chrome, then scarlet, which last brilliant coloring lingers until the stars of night shine bright and clear.

SEPTEMBER 15

The mere mention of hydrocyanic acid or "prussic acid", as it is often called, brings to our minds the thought that a drop of it on the tongue of a dog will instantly kill the animal, and a similar amount beneath the plaster of paris of our butterfly bottle wilts insects with its deadly fumes. That some wild plants are able to produce this lethal substance shocks our notions of the woods; nevertheless, such is the case.

The arrow grass (*Triglochin maritima*), which grows in the wet meadows and alkaline swamps along the Jordan river, possesses this death-dealing poison in either its green or dried leaves, but animals must eat a lethal dose at one time to succumb. It is not cumulative like arsenic. Since man has just discovered that grass contains nearly all the vitamins he had better be sure of his pickings, for like mushrooms all grasses are not edible.

Sudan grass (*Sorghum vulgare*), which we ourselves had thought to plant on the farm, has the same capability of poisoning, though perhaps not in the cured state.

As we loiter in the canyon it surprises us to know that those choke cherries from which we make the most delicious jelly in the autumn, contain this powerful poison in their leaves, especially the young, succulent ones of Spring. Some similar suspicion has been cast on the wilted leaves of the mountain mahogany which is a three-foot shrub of intricate branches, and grows, for instance, in Parley's canyon but not City Creek.

We chatted for an hour with a woman who years ago spent her girlhood in a sage-covered valley and early learned the difference between the edible and non-edible things of the wilds; but she had never heard or even suspected that the choke-cherry leaves might be poisonous. It was not their custom to eat strange, untried leaves, fruits and buds; and the Indians nearby had passed their knowledge from parent to child throughout the ages.

It was not an uncommon sight in our youthful days to see an Indian squaw hunt for lice in the hair of her child's head, and then eat the captured vermin as if they were tid bits; indeed it did not shock us then to glimpse a squaw giving birth to a papoose on the roadside alone and to notice her arrive at camp an hour or so later on horseback with the babe in arms. Despite every hardship, the Indians were a healthy people; healthy, indeed, when occasionally a buck would before our startled eyes drain a bottle of jamaica ginger at one draught—his substitute for "fire water."

As we recline in contemplative mood beneath a balsam, we recall with interest some of the facts we have learned concerning the animal food of these Wasatch aborigines of a century ago. The truth is they ate every living thing they could capture—rabbits, rattlesnakes, spermophiles, snails, lizards, rats, mice, in fact, reptiles, rodents and mammals of all kinds except, possibly, the fetid skunk and the members of the fulsome weasel family.

A stew *a la Ute* was made about as follows: one jack rabbit; cut off all the hair; slit open and press the offal from the entrails; then throw the rabbit, intestines and all, into the boiling pot. Place several red hot embers in an earthen kettle and cast into it one live snake, one live lizard, a hundred live grasshoppers; toss them about until they are nicely roasted, and then empty them all into the boiling pot. Boil until the rabbit is done and then serve with roasted ants instead of pepper and salt.

This is not an exaggeration but a fact attested by such early historians as Bancroft, Farnham, Fremont, Prichard, and Coke. The natives were called "root-diggers", for they were so helpless that they sought lowly foods rather than the larger mammals. It is true that near a meadow spring just East of the mouth of the Jordan river and at other places on the East shoreline of the Great Salt Lake arrow-heads are to this day upturned by the plow; but it is also true that big game was so scarce that these poor Indians had to take roots, seeds and reptiles or starve. They caught ants by placing a fresh hide or a piece of bark over their hill, and brushing the accumulated ants into a bag. Yet perhaps even those Indians knew love and happiness.

Several plants in these mountains bear the common name "Indian", among them being Indian hemp or dogbane (*Apocynum*), Indian lettuce (*Montia*), Indian paint brush, Indian parsnip (*Aulospermum*), Indian potato or turkey peas (*Orogenia linearifolia*) and Indian rice grass (*Oryzopsis hymenoides*). For the moment I do not recall a bird, mammal, reptile or insect hereabout that has the appellation "Indian", although the old squaw duck (*Clangula hyemalis*) is a winter visitor.

SEPTEMBER 17

Surprising indeed are the ways of nature. As we ride over the hills in constant admiration of the reds and yellows that mark the maples, cottonwoods, boxelders, ninebarks, dogwoods and scrub oaks, we pause for a moment to pluck a twig of the yellow-blooming rabbit brush (*Chrysothamnus lanceolatus*) at the roadside. It is not the golden heads of this late flowering bush that attract our attention, however, but the infinitesimal bugs that like threads a twenty fifth of an inch long crawl over our hands from the sharp pointed leaves. Bugs they may be, for some of them under the ten-power hand-glass appear like pale yellow slivers with many legs; others look like long flies, black, active and excited, with a habit of spreading their wings and uplifting their abdomens every few steps. Scorpions we have seen thus up thrust themselves; but these little insects are so small that to the naked eye they are no longer than the periods we herein write in ink.

Beyond the realm of human sight are forms of life most complex and hardy; and beyond the capability of the microscope must be evidences of life equally bewildering in their activity. So far as we can see the tiny speck that calls itself head, body, wings and legs, is just as happy on its rabbit brush blossom as we on a night club floor. Humans who flatter themselves that the world was made for them should peer through the microscope and find their vanities disillusioned.

It is not that we have a predilection for histology as compared, for instance, with the more apparent joys of dendrology, silvicology, ornithology, mycology, nephelology, mammalogy, limnology, and even herpetology—technical words indicative of a study respectively of a special interest in trees, forests, birds, fungi, clouds, animals, ponds, insects and reptiles—but that in our ramble afield we see so much of the minute unknown we hesitate to believe we have even started to comprehend it all.

High among spruces in Lamb's canyon two Wasatch chipmunks climb on our chairs for crumbs, then chase one another over logs, under brush, around tree trunks. Suddenly a big red Wind River mountains chickaree (*Sciurus hudsonicus ventorum*), chattering loudly, approaches and chases the two of them away. In five minutes they are back again. Happily the chickaree goes on, and for half an hour we listen to his penetrating call, which is like a giant fishing reel being wound in the pines.

SEPTEMBER 18

That tiny animal that just darted across the swift waters beside yonder pine is a shrew, not a long-tailed mouse but a shrew, a mountain water-shrew (*Sorex palustris navigator*). The truth is, that, while it has a tail about as long as your little finger and a mouselike body slightly longer, its long-clawed toes are birdlike, its almost indiscernible eyes are apparently useless, and its nose is peculiarly pointed, as if belonging to a mouse without a lower jaw. Furthermore, so difficult is it to distinguish it from others of its genus, color variations being inconsequential, that it is necessary to use a microscope to find identifying characteristics in its teeth and skull. It is no wonder then, that the shrews are the least seen and the least understood of all Wasatch animals, and that among Indians they are thought capable of darting into one's vitals. Far back in 1545 Elyot of England wrote of "a kynde of myse called a shrew, whyche yf it goo ouer a beastes backe, he shall be lame in the chyne."

Mice belong to the order Rodentia and the shrews to the order Insectivora, hence they are no more related to one another than to grizzly bears.

Besides the water shrew over there in the creek, shrews that inhabit these mountains are: the Rocky mountain shrew (*Sorex vagrans monticola*) and the dusky shrew (*Sorex obscurus obscurus*). All of them delight in the verdured, damp, grassy borders of singing streams where they hunt insects and worms along rock-sheltered burrows, and in winter even essay the uncertainties of the open snow. Voracious to an incredible degree, one imprisoned with two others once ate both its companions before dawn. In leafy nests beneath logs two or more litters of from six to ten young are raised by each mature female a year.

Though we tread the stream borders continually it is probably because shrews are mostly nocturnal that we seldom see them. Wondrous imps of mystery and superstition—such are the shrews.

Chatting with the watchman at the reservoir in City Creek, we learn that last February (1942) one morning his wife exclaimed: "What are cows doing across the canyon in the snow?" They were twenty seven wild elk within a mile of a State capitol building! We descend, and ourselves nearly run over a mule deer doe and two fawns.

SEPTEMBER 19

When the coolsome air of fall moderates the summer heat in the sagelands we sometimes ramble there to observe feather, fang and fur. Vast stretches of the upper foothills are covered by sagebrush, either the stunted spiny bud brush (*Artemisia spinescens*) of alkaline plains or the four-foot high sage (*A. gnaphalodes*) of the upper creek banks and graveled slopes.

Not sage alone but also other shrubs inhabit these regions of spines and thorn; for example, among the sagebrush we often find: grease-woods (*Sarcobatus vermiculatus*) from three to nine feet high; rabbit brushes such as *Chrysothamnus graveolens* of the lowlands and *C. lanceolatus* of the foothills; hop sage (*Grayia spinosa*); winter fat or white sage (*Eurotia lanata*), which is a member of the goosefoot family and not related to sagebrush; sweet smelling antelope or buck brush; and salt brush including *Tetradymia glabrata* of the saline deserts and *T. Nuttallii* of the lower hills.

In the sagelands are such mammals as: the valley coyote (*Canis latrans lestes*), the bobcat (*Lynx rufus pallescens*), the painted chipmunk (*Eutamias minimus pictus*), black-tailed pack rabbit (*Lepus californicus deserticola*), and the nuttall cottontail (*Sylvilagus nuttallii grangeri*). There also are such reptiles as the brown-shouldered uta lizard (*Uta stansburiana s tansburiana*); Girard's short-horned toad (*Phrynosoma douglasii ernatissimum*); the whip snake (*Masticophis taeniatus taeniatus*); and the Great Basin rattlesnake (*Crotalus confluentus lutosus*).

These sagebrush areas have their characteristic birds, not birds which casually visit them, of which there are many, but birds that prefer their rather dry and inhospitable labryinths. To such we must give first place to the sage thrasher (*Oroscoptes montanus*), which even at times in moonlight enraptures the dreary places with song. There are, however, others there: the sage sparrow (*Amphispiza belli nevandensis*), which sings with exquisite charm in the Spring but always resembles a bit of gray sage; the little Brewer sparrow whose striped head tips a sage with song, the lark sparrow which purrs with rapture as he raises his head of black and white streaks; the desert horned lark (*Octocoris alpestris leucolaema*) with its tiny horn feathers and pleasant ditty; the Pacific nighthawk (*Chordeiles minor hesperis*), which the Indians called "wyeupahoh"; the sage grouse and the burrowing owl. Verily there is beauty and song in the sagelands.

SEPTEMBER 20

Today our divertissement is Logan canyon, but at the bridge at its very mouth (altitude 4700) we find a multitude of things to interest us. An isolated patch of big-toothed scarlet maples bejewels the mountainside ahead of us; sunflowers are plentiful; a magpie cries and a Utah rock squirrel scampers. On the yellow flowers of a rabbit brush blooming along the creek we find a yellow and brown ambush bug (*Phymata pennsylvanica coloradensis Melin*) which for protective coloration excels anything else we have ever seen. It is only about half an inch long with a flat, round back margined at each side by two brown stripes. What bird could find it amid the yellow blooms? Every once in awhile it tries to fly, and buzzes its wings. It is nature's best example of aggressive simulation.

Upon a rose bush a silky clematis (*Clematis lingusticifolia*) has spread its blooms, which look like two inch balls of tiny white feathers, and on the same plant are the completed seed pods with their two inch balls of wool, which in reality, are the blooms now dry. Tennyson must have seen something like this when he wrote: "Rose, rose, and clematis, Trail and twine and clasp and kiss". We later found this clematis far up in the canyon, often tipping twenty foot trees with its attractive wool packs. But to return to the canyon-mouth.

Here also by the river is blooming a yellow flowered mentzelia (*Mentzelia laevicaulis*) and a burdock (*Arctium Lappa*) with purple flower-burs.

At 4925 feet we see yellow goat's beards (*Tragopogon dubius*) in bloom, likely escaped from cultivation, and further on (5025 feet) a yellow *Viguiera multiflora* appears along with ripe elderberries, and both species of junipers (*J. Utahensis* and *J. scopulorum*) are showing light green berries.

At 5700 feet, we enter upon the quaking aspen groves, with only yarrow in flower; but at 6050 feet all of the hills are covered with golden aspen leaves—a true study in green and gold. At 6350 feet are beautiful groves of lodge-pole or black pine (*Pinus contorta*), some of the long-leafed branches holding flattened gray cones four years old, gray two inch long cones three years old, well shaped brown ones two years old, and little half inch ones only one year old. It is a very interesting tree, sometimes called tamarack and spruce pine.

We continue our way upward to the summit (7500 feet), finding the upper vales dry and bare, as if expecting sweeps of snow soon to drift upon them; but while we note a flock of mountain blue birds, we must reserve for tomorrow an extraordinary experience.

Just as we enter the garden at home, however, we pick from a zinnia a moth that looks like a twig; it is an *Autographa californica;* and we are happy indeed.

SEPTEMBER 21

In Logan canyon, where at an altitude of 7050 feet the hills are fledged with conifers, we unexpectedly catch loud, strident bird notes "squaa", "squaa" reiterated every few seconds, some of the raucous calls coming from large feathered inhabitants three hundred yards away. The glasses reveal that the noisy gray and black birds, almost as big as pigeons but slimmer and stronger, are Clarke nutcrackers (*Nucifraga columbiana*), five of them in the full enjoyment of their locale, each bird answering now and then with a harsh "squaa" the distant call of a companion. Somehow they impress us with the thought that they own this portion of the canyon, and that winter or summer high in the pure air of the mountain it is their haven of plentitude and joy.

Within a few yards of us an ancient, gnarled limber pine (*Pinus flexilis*) stands on a wind exposed knoll, raising its broad open crown on a brown-plated trunk two feet in thickness. Beneath it the ground is strewn with subcylindrical cones five inches long and two inches in diameter.

As we stand listening one of the nutcrackers flies to the tree above us, alighting on the outer end of an upper branch where a cone is suspended. Standing above the cone and working almost upside down, it pecks with its strong, cylindrical, black bill at the base of the cone, clinging the while to the branch with its large toes and sharp, much curved claws. It pecks every two or three seconds, and in its eagerness at times almost tilts over head first, but, without releasing its toe holds, flutters back to position again. Finally after about forty pecks and probes at the pencil-thick stalk of the cone, the cone sags and begins to fall, whereupon the bird clasps the cone with its bill and flies with it to a thick horizontal limb below. Here it takes its time in prying out the quarter inch seeds which it swallows with great satisfaction.

We pick up a cone, a green one weighing about six ounces, and the only one lying about not stripped of its seeds. Beneath each cone scale are two soft-shelled seeds nutritious and tasty.

Another bird alights on a smaller tree, and as we slowly approach, we notice that it is eating directly from the cone without disconnecting it. We are less than ten feet away, and though the bird is aware of us, it pays no attention until our quick movement makes it fly.

What a happy life in a land of plenty—insects in summer, nuts in winter. Yet man claims to find a superior joy!

SEPTEMBER 22

Due perhaps to the intermingling of firs among maples, cotton-woods and oaks, a canyonside this afternoon presents the most delightful polychrome we have ever beheld. As we look upon them the firs are marine green, tinted on the outer edges with silver pine gray. The younger firs are in their entirety a delicate pistachio green. Imagine these pyramids of beauty, if you will, placed here and there on a hillside which has patches of scarlet, flame red, old gold, bitter sweet orange, and ruby, where maples appear.

Some ravines have a garniture of Harvard crimson; some are dappled with spinel red. Solitary trees here and there are bridal rose; others, ember glow, straw color or even the delicate tint of attar of roses. In some places the sumacs and ninebarks form an underblanket of rich maroon beneath single trees of coral pink, French vermillion or Toreador red. Glorious maples! Yet as we admire them we see how livid the scene would be without the softer greens of the firs and the solemn undervesture of the ninebark.

Cumulus clouds white as plucks of wool float tranquilly in the clear blue sky. In vain determination to unveil the mystic beauty of the maples, we pick a single leaf to examine closely its wondrous tints and hues. As we hold it we find that its under side is topaz in one part and light stone in the other. On its upper surface, its veins are rejane green, while here and there it is either inca gold, mustard, ecru, beige, raspberry, or blush rose. One splotch is indeed a deep ruby. It is almost incredible that all these different tints and shades should adorn the upper surface of a single leaf; yet here it is before our very eyes. After all it is like admiring the gown of a solitary little girl who belongs to a great chorus of children—the great and inspiring beauty is in the ensemble.

A Wasatch Autumn

INTRODUCTION

With its maples, nine bark and aspens, sumacs, blue spruces and firs, with its great cumulus clouds floating in the bluest of skies and its glistening cascades tumbling down rocky steeps; with its dry climate, warm days and frosty nights, the Wasatch mountain range is without doubt one of the show places of the world in color in the autumn. Furthermore, the ripened fruits of the valleys, kissed by many a cloudless summer sun, attain a richness of tint and tone not usually seen in humid regions.

This book is the third in a series by the same author. The first was *The Natural History of a Wasatch Summer* (1956); the second, *The Natural History of a Wasatch Spring* (1957). Each is an attempt to give a day by day description of the flora and fauna of the Wasatch mountains as affected by the changing season. These mountains form the north-south backbone of the northern half of the state of Utah in western United States; and they rise from valleys of an altitude of roughly 4000 feet to ridges and peaks as high as 12,000 feet.

As stated before, these pages represent the observations of a naturalist over a period of thirty years or more; and that is why the matter on any particular day may have been written a score of years before or after that of the day preceding or following it. One thing is certain: each page was done on the actual day of its date, often *in situ* on an envelope beside a brook, but more frequently at the end of the day's excursion.

To a naturalist general words like "hawk", "duck", "sparrow", "penstemon" and so forth mean little, for their species are widely different; hence the author has felt compelled to pin point his observations with precise scientific names so that no one can mistake to what bird, mammal or flower he refers.

Early field trips were taken usually alone, when the author was making a collection of the birds and mammals of the region, then later, when the gun had served its purpose, excursions were made with the late eminent botanist, Marcus E. Jones and other naturalists. In later years, with automobile equipped with bontanical presses and many scientific instruments, he had the invaluable assistance of the late Louise Atkinson, who became very efficient in the fields of ornithology, mammalogy and botany and whose alert eyes were quick to discern new species.

SEPTEMBER 23

While yet the valley trees are full-leaved and rich in summer green, it is inviting to realize that the beauty of autumnal color is already gorgeous in the higher mountains. You will recall the Brisingamen, the famous necklace of the goddess Freya, which typified the rich flowers and tints of autumn; hence we must see the reality in nature, not in mythological dream.

That is why, on this bright, cool morning, we find ourselves at a point on the eastern side of Big Mountain somewhat less than a mile below the divide between East canyon and Mountain Dell creek. It is a famous pass on the old emigrant trail.

We look westward towards the summit, and there behold a vista of unusual and exquisite polychrome, a panorama as delightful as we have seen this early in all the Wasatch. It is only a conical hill, up-sloping for a distance of perhaps half a mile before us; but it is the fact that individual trees on it are isolated and alone upon its face, not in groves as is their wont, that so pleases us and makes the necklace real.

In the foreground of the scenic view stand some handsome balsam firs (*A. concolor*) of bice green; and the right side of the mountain cone, even to the top, is clothed by a forest of quaking aspens of pistachio green foliage with trunks that stand dull white and thin, like suspended silver threads bright in the morning sun.

The main part of the necklace—probably three hundred yards wide by two hundred yards high—is marked by a score of maples, each standing alone, a picturesque ensemble, multicolorus and engaging. There is a maple geranium pink, another of rose doree, a third of scarlet and a fourth of spectrum red. The view is outstanding, though small. Over there is a maple of strawberry pink, another of eosine pink, and one more of sulphine yellow.

Descending the western slope, through a canyon pleasingly called "Mountain Dell," we come upon many a maple colored hill; and there at the creekside below us, at the very edge of the old immigration trail, furrowed and clearly discernable after more than a century, stands the reddest maple we have ever seen, a specific tree that year after year causes us to give exclamations of joy.

We coast down Emigration canyon to the valley where all leaves and all landscapes are green, as if oblivious to the glories of the mountains which lower and lower each day are being autumnized with color.

With its rich, irrigated fields and meadowlands grazed by dairy herds; with its willow-ribboned streams and its marshes attracting a great variety of water birds, the valley, especially at harvestime, is ever attractive, ever encouraging; but the high mountains with their purity of air, seclusive, eternal evergreens, their nearness to the unfathomable mystery in the great vault of heaven—they are the places of inspiration and joy.

SEPTEMBER 24

That dark, softly-flying bird, yonder swooping from pole to pole and tall tree to tall tree over the dense scrub-oak copses of the mountain side, is not a crow but a woodpecker, the Lewis (*Asyndesmus lewis*). Furthermore, it is not altogether black, for his upper sides, apparently black in the distance, have a cast of iridescent green; his under sides, a soft rose—as if the tints of a hummingbird adorned the ebony plumage of a crow!

"Acorn bird" they sometimes call him; and well they might, since in the fruiting season of autumn he wedges many an acorn into the fissures of telephone poles, dead cottonwoods and drying pines—tid bits for the stormy, cold days ahead—; yet in truth, throughout the summer he has spent most of his time gliding into the air after passing insects or, hawklike, chasing them with dip and turn over the verdured gullies. Other woodpeckers may tap, in fact bore, as if miniature air-riveters were working in the wildwoods; others may sit peering on a tree trunk, or climb grubby seams, but not he, except on occasion, for in habits he is flycatcher, crow, swallow, and jay, in fact, a woodpecker that even likes fruit-eating at times.

It is not the shade of high coniferous forests or the meadowed lowlands that he adores but the bright intermediate slopes overgrown with scrub-oaks and cottonwoods, home of the imported quail, the mourning dove, the red shafted flicker, the prairie falcon, the Cooper hawk, and the Nuttall cottontail.

Many a Lewis woodpecker endures the snows of a Wasatch winter. Lovely bird! Captain Lewis, he of the rugged adventure from Missouri to Oregon in the days of Jefferson, has in this bird of multicolored sheen a tribute indeed to his western memory.

For diversion we spend the day at Wolf Creek Pass at the Provo river head, so high (9000 feet) that cumulus clouds lie below our spruce grown horizon. For an hour we watch three goshawks kiting with effortless wings as the updraughts hold them; then a great dark golden eagle soars to and fro in the deep blue firmament above us. Clark nutcrackers *"squa squaw"*, and even whistle as they feed on cones; and juncos, chicadees, chipmunks and chickarees are there. We see no maples, but everywhere fir-clad vistas of green appliqued with the pea green, empire yellow or orange buff of aspen groves. Nowhere else that we have seen has nature forgotten the scarlets and browns, and given the Midas touch of color exclusively to the quaking aspen trees. Often indeed, in a distance we see yellow and remark "maples", but on closer observation discover them to be aspens. Wolf Creek Pass, our idealistic necropolis, is too near heaven to be tinted by the scarlets of the maples.

SEPTEMBER 25

Lingering to admire the prepossessing raiment of the south side of City Creek canyon at 5500 feet, we notice that the maples, boxelders, cottonwoods, oak brushes and firs are usually yet a summer-green, though interspersed with outstanding figures of autumnal color. The mantling cap of the south ridge is, for instance, an ochraceous buff; and isolated maples below it are in some instances light viridine green, some flesh ocher, and others a lovely intermingling of the same delightful tints and tones. Spreading below the scrub oaks of the south declivity, a vesture of claret brown indicates the deep, autumnal tone of the nine-bark (*Physocarpus malvaceus*). Nearer to us, vigorous clumps of sage of a light mineral gray upshoot from June grasses still green, but overhead the serene sky is light Windsor blue.

We ride up the canyon to seven thousand feet, where through a glade of choke cherries, rose bushes, boxelders and black balsams a jagged peak of ash-gray limestone looms beneath an afternoon sky of flax flower blue, a sky of darker blue and deeper purity than that seen earlier below. The peak, nevertheless, is not bare, for, below its tooth-side skeletonized and scattered balsams stand like green toothlets set in verdure. No autumnal color adorns the drab escarpment, save one small clump of ninebark of deep persimmon hue.

We descend to Rotary Park, where the shadows of sunset encompass the greenery of the creekbed and part of the spruce covered hills, as eastward we survey the evening landscape. Cliffs of antique bronze and gray loom at the south, cliffs, perpendicular and cracked, yet studded in isolated coves with evergreen trees in solemn assemblage.

At the north the mountain has a roughened backbone of chalk gray, shimmering against the light of a setting sun, a geologic escarpment verdured with firs, maples, and clinging vines.

To the east the translucent beauty of the sky is almost Yale blue; and at the south on yonder sunlit slope is a spruce vesture of Russian green interspersed with dahlia where ninebark holds its somber place.

Long-crested jays (*Cyanocitta stelleri macrolopha*) scold us; a junco chips in the maple shadows; and the willowed brook sweetly babbles its endless song of purity and life. The night has come; and in our minds reposes one more delightful memory. Happiness is the ensemble of joyful incidents past and present.

SEPTEMBER 26

Our locale for this warm cloudless autumn day is Little Cottonwood canyon, in the mouth of which, at the road fork in front of a quarry monument, we set our mileage meter at zero and designate the altitude as 5335 feet. But before proceeding we look about, noting the rabbit brush (*Chrysothmnus lanceolatus*) is in a glory of yellow bloom, an aster (*Aster leucanthemifolius*) is pretty with its deep purple flowers, a least chipmunk (*Eutamias minimus consobrinus*) scampers up the road embankment, a magpie flies overhead and a small lizard too fast for us hides beneath a granite boulder, sharp angled and bare.

The hillsides in the foreground are gorgeous with scarlet and yellow maples, lemon colored quaking aspens and dark green evergreens, but we pay more attention to closer things, observing, for instance, that at 5900 feet the rabbit brushes no longer appear and the yellow sunflowerlike plant, *Viguiera multiflora,* takes their place.

This is a steep, granite-sided canyon with occasional brooks cascading the pine-laden southern heights; grasshoppers stridulate sharply along the way beside us; and, as we stop to catch one of them, we find ourselves beneath a magnificent white fir, which is apparently the predominant tree at this altitude (6550).

Quaking aspens appear further on, and henceforth the upper hills are green and gold, no longer scarlet and yellow. Among the aspens still higher (7450) ferns are growing in a mat a foot deep, some of them being green, most of them already dry and russet gold. And there is a pink dogbane, partly in bloom but mostly in seed.

We stop to gather ripe chokecherries where also a mullein (*Verbascum thapsus*) is standing seven feet tall by the roadway with one flower yet showing; and there, half hidden, as it likes to be, among shrubs and trees, a mountain ash (*Sorbus scopulina*) shows its clusters of shining scarlet red berries. We count one cluster, finding over a hundred round waxlike fruits. To our surprise a penstemon (*P. platyphyllus*) is by it in full lavender-violet bloom.

At a resting nook (7350 feet), we pick golden asters, purple asters and yarrow, see the footprints of a mule deer in an evergreen nook; observe the padded spoor of a mountain lion; shew back flies and black wasps; try to be friendly with a chipmunk—and then we return home. As we enter, there is a man standing with an oyster shell mushroom seven inches in diameter awaiting its identification. A recent suggestion is to cultivate this mushroom on an old stump in your own backyard.

SEPTEMBER 27

Since silvicology is the term we apply to the science of forest trees, silvichromatology should be the science of autumnal colors of forest trees, a study, by the way, that so far as we know has never been undertaken nor mentioned more than casually.

This afternoon, high in Mill Creek canyon where the conifers grow in dark groves, we tarry for a moment and, looking towards the north, behold a sun-kissed mountainside at the height of autumnal loveliness. We seek this extraordinary vista each autumn because it is always inspiring in its beauty. Here and there, sometimes in copses, often as single trees, the maples are brilliant in colorsome rose; some baby rose or tangerine. Other vegetation supplies the greens, the delicate green of the mignonette or the grape. Aspen trunks of new silver or amber white show distinctly; and, over all, great cliffs of oyster white or bare rocks of travertine cap the scene.

For a time we turn our eyes eastward up the darksome canyon where deep groves of pines interfledge with yellow quaking aspens even to a snow-laden peak and a Yale blue sky. All is cold, solemn and foreboding, with no sign of life save the skittish mule deer and the chattering water ouzel.

Half way down the canyon we stop to behold another landscape of striking beauty and color, a vista still at the north, for unlike City Creek and Parley's canyons, this one has its greatest variegation on the northern hills. Here the maples are coral pink or flamingo; other trees, chartreuse yellow; and the general vegetation, artichoke green. The overhanging cliffs are laurel pink.

A long-crested jay calls; a red shafted flicker sounds a lonely autumnal note; a robin utters a perfunctory cry; and a chickadee listlessly "dee dees" as the sinking sun persuades us homeward.

We may talk of those red and yellow pigments, widely distributed in nature, known as lipochromes, of which the commonest is carotin; but what words of man could give due credit to the touch that sets the hills aglow?

Sitting beside the upper Weber river at a place where huge boulders form placid pools beneath the outstretched limbs of spruce and pine, I became interested in the languid manner of a western belted kingfisher, as it stood motionless atop a rock and on occasion plunged to the pellucid water below to grasp a little fish with its strong bill; and then, I reflected how this bird in the desert region southwest of here, when the streams go dry in summer, being averse to leaving its nesting locale, actually plunges to dry earth, not water, for food, and subsists on toads, mice, beetles, snakes, lizards and grasshoppers, diving from a limb down upon them, as is its wont.

SEPTEMBER 28

Late in September some of our muskrats (*Ondatra zibethicus osoyoosensis*) venture forth in partial migration, when, strange to relate, a few individuals not only wander a mile or more from their ponds over grain fields and pastures, but actually attack big mammals like a horse or a man that they unexpectedly encounter on their way. A large muskrat, pacing alone over a stubble field, thus transformed from habitual timidity to pugnacity, is an annoying and belligerent antagonist to meet.

We have strolled along the banks of the Thames and the Ouse rivers in England, the Seine in France, the Rhone, the Po and Tiber, and even along the cliffed shores of the Rhine, without seeing either a muskrat or a sign of one, all of which reminds us that, when the Europeans in America first saw muskrats, oppossums, skunks, turkeys and humming birds, to say nothing of cougars, rattlesnakes, Indian corn and tobacco, they were justified in describing their discovery as the "New World."

On the fresh water sloughs about Great Salt Lake, muskrats build their dome-shaped dwellings of reeds, each house having no entrance except from the water below it; but at Barton's pond, where the willowed shores are fairly steep, they make their homes in the embankments, in which they dig deep water filled runways, usually exposed above for a portion of their course. Barton's pond was a boyhood swimming pool and rendezvous.

Since the period of gestation of muskrats is about twenty one days, it is not surprising that three litters of as many as a dozen young each should be born during the unfrozen season; and when the spring litters start to breed in the fall, great trouble begins, and defeated males retreat to new waters. Nearly all mammals large or small are ill-tempered and pugnacious when thus driven from home.

The flesh of a muskrat is tasty, a fact due to its vegetal origin. Its musk is actually used somewhat in making perfume.

On the Jordan sloughs today we notice five hundred white pelicans at rest on three islets over which a hundred double-crested cormorants (*Phalacrocorax auritus auritus*) are flying. Unlike the graceful pelicans in the sky the cormorants apparently make hard work of flight. Their wing movements are fairly rapid and in marked contrast with those of the slow-flapping Treganza herons, which proceed like enormous butterflies. Hundreds of avocets dotting the water are now drab and unattractive, and snowy plovers sit motionless on the rocks, as if either dreamy or stupid, their black eyes peering listlessly upon the passerby. Brewster herons are dirty white, and most ducks have lost their colors.

SEPTEMBER 29

In the coolsome valley the green leaf is turning to the sere: meadows are straw-colored; and rushes along lane-borrows are not only half yellow but also no longer clutched by joyous red-wings and yellow-headed blackbirds. Cabbages are green, but corn is golden in its shocks; sacked onions dot the fields. Currant bushes along irrigation ditches are shades of garnet and blood; and seeded asparagus resembles green fernery sprinkled with tiny red berries.

We ramble towards the foothills where small patches of poison ivy are livid among the oaks. We examine one cluster: some leaves are primuline yellow at the tips and dragon blood red near their stems; some, entirely Pompeian red; some, coral red; others, brick red, or wholly primuline yellow. The darkest and brightest reds are on leaves most exposed to the sun. We do not touch, but drift up Parleys' canyon.

Above the reservoir some tall oak tree leaves are Van Dyke red but russet-vinaceous on the under sides. This is surprising, for the leaves of the ordinary trees near them are either deep dull yellow green or honey yellow splotched with rust. Usually we do not credit the oak with such beauty as here displayed.

Leaves of the creek willows (*Salix pseudomyrsinites*) are either chromium green or mustard yellow specked with black. The leaves of the squawbush (*Rhus trilobata*) are deep hellebore red or amaranth purple, and the bushes are conspicuous on the hillsides.

Birch leaves are corn color or golden rod yellow; but the alders are still green. The dogwood leaves are veronia purple with light grayish vinaceous under sides. Wild currants are daphne red, and Russian thistles eupatorium purple.

Returning, we seek bowered avenues of color in City Creek canyon. Here some of the maple leaves are Colonial buff, almost ivory yellow, or yellow tinted with Japan rose; others are half chromium green, half old rose; some are entirely eugenia red, and still more, wholly watermelon red, forming lanes of flame along the creek and mottles of scarlet on the mountain sides.

Here and there clusters of dogwood show their wax-yellow velvety leaves on the sunny steep places, often indeed among the dry June grass. The boxelder leaves are wholly chalcedony yellow, and they with the maples and cottonwoods make winding archways of gold, red and green along the cadent brook.

Over the valley, there is a lazy hue. Glorious and tranquil are the sweet trails and vistas of autumn! We miss now the calls of the California cuckoo in one of our favorite oaken glades below the mouth of Webb canyon; it has perhaps already departed for its winter home in South America.

A WASATCH AUTUMN

SEPTEMBER 30

"Autumn", or its equivalent, is a pleasing word in any language or country. Astronomically it is, of course, reckoned as the time between the descending equinox and the winter solstice — September 21 to December 21—but in the Wasatch mountains we sometimes refer to the autumnal period as the whole of September, October and November. Since September usually means the end of heat and December the beginning of snow, our designation of autumn is well founded, far better in fact than the autumn of England, which there popularily includes August, September and October. Having sojourned in that delightful country, where snow is seldom seen, we easily understand why autumn is not there so clearly defined as in either the scorching or freezing Wasatch.

Astronomers retain the ancient Roman computation; but the English associate autumn with appearances about their homes. Thus Chaucer: "Autumpne comeb azeyne heuy of apples"; Shakespeare: "As thunder when the clouds in Autumne cracke"; Walton: "In Autome, when the weeds begin . . . to rot"; Milton: Thir table was . . . from side to side, all autumn pil'd"; Venner: "Autumn fruites"; and Southey: "Wither'd leaves which autumn winds had drifted in."

Dry leaves characterize the autumn of mountains hereabout and apparently the autumn everywhere. Milton's "Thick as Autumnal leaves that strew the Brooks in Vallombrosa" well describes our own scenes of October, though nowhere in England could such gorgeous coloration show as that of our mountains.

So clearly has autumn been everywhere associated with ripeness and maturity that the word itself has even been used as a verb expressive of that thought, as for instance, in "That life's fair spring may autumn into age" from the "Muse in Miniature" of 1771.

After all, the beauty of autumn lies not so much in its delightful coloration, heavy rains, seeded flowers and ripened fruits, as in the gratitude one feels in abundant storage with which to confront the certainty of winter cold. Is happiness more a state of mind than physical comfort?

Excluding the boxelder, which seldom occurs above the 5000 feet artemisia belt, our maples prefer the yellow pine zone, which extends to 9000 feet altitude, and not often do they flourish in the spruce areas above. One has to go into the lofty Uintah mountains to see green hillsides decked exclusively with the pinard yellow of aspen groves.

Truly Janus Quadrifrons, the Greek divinity with four faces, with which to preside over the four seasons, must have saved most of his paints and colors for the forehead of autumn.

OCTOBER 1

Sugar is obtained from a variety of plant juices, chiefly, as we know, from the sugar cane or the sugar beet; and throughout history peoples of the world have enjoyed it in some form. The Arabians call it "sukker"; the Persians "Shakar"; the Dutch "suiker"; the Russians, "cuker"; the Turks, "sukker"; the Bohemians, "sukr"; and the Poles, "sukier". In other words, no matter what the age or the language, sugar has been known. Chaucer wrote: "Yeue hem sugre, hony, breed and milk"; yet, as we sit beneath a cottonwood tree at the mouth of a canyon and survey the fields of sugar beets below, we wonder what plants to the Indians of this region contained what we moderns have come to understand as sucrose, glucose, fructose, lactose, maltose, or the many other substances known as sugar.

Indians, especially those accustomed to a parched, thankless, region, were so resourceful that they found therein not only their chewing gum and tobacco but also their sugar. The coyotes could howl in the utter desolation of it all; but, if rains were normal, Indians here knew where to find and gather the delicacies of subsistence. Nowhere else in America was aboriginal mankind put to the test of such finesse of botanical perception, such reliance on experienced choice. Knowing nothing of sugar beets or cane, they sought the sloughs of the lake shore, where they gathered the common reed (*Phragmites communis*), which in the distance looks like broom-corn; and used its sap as sugar. Indeed, all over the West, such was done with the plentiful reed, for it grows in swamps and at the edges of lakes and streams, and its juice when allowed to dry forms a not unpleasant candy. Its generic name (*Phragmites*) refers to its hedge-like appearance along ditches.

In the mountains, also, they found their sugar; but there it was a tree, the ever-present narrow leaved cottonwood. Peel some of the bark away from the trunk; taste it; and you will realize what the Indians hearabout called sugar.

Vast acreages of tomatoes for canning in Wasatch valleys encouraged us to remark how precarious such a crop may be. A wet cold spring may defer planting until after Memorial Day, and thus start two weeks late. There may be excellent growth during the summer, and then, suddenly, in September, when the vines are laden with luscious red fruits, a three-minute hail may ruin an entire field, for each hailstone causes an irreparable bruise. Then comes the peril of frost, which in a single night can end the story; but, generally, if there be neither frost nor hail before the first of October, all is well.

OCTOBER 2

A fast wind is shoaling crisp leaves across the roadway; and under a stormy sky it is so cold that for the first time this autumn we wear top-coats. The valley trees, yet mostly green, are slowly turning gold; but the mountains appear gorgeous in color below and cold gray along the higher ridges.

Although at the mouth of Parley's canyon, sunflowers, mentzelias and rabbit brush are still in bloom, nevertheless, as we proceed upward and see nothing more of floral beauty save an occasional purple aster or yellow Viguiera, we feel wistfully that the flowers have nearly ended their lovely show.

In this rather sedate mood we traverse leafy vistas of scarlet and yellow, where maples and aspens abound, seeing no more the stubby spermophile at the roadside, hearing no more the dulcet arietta of a brookside warbler, until finally, reaching the summit, we gaze upon the fir-fledged hills at the southeast, a place always capable of filling us with delectation and wonder at the might, grandeur and ineffable mystery of the mountains. The congregated firs there are now grizzled with snow, as if sifted flour had been floated over them by the miller of the gods; indeed such is the sparsity of this first snow that quaking aspens yet show an icy coldness where it enshrouds them. The alpine vale below this lofty assemblage of pines is, however, green and gold with forests of aspens and evergreens; and the north hills are rich with colors of green, gold and burnt umber. So much for the summit; but, even as we descend from it, a solitary long crested jay squawks a parting cry.

We detour for the hour up Lamb's canyon, going even to where mighty spruce trees stand like silent mountain hermits whose hair is turning gray—such is the effect of the first flakings of snow. Elderberries unripened and dry drop from branches; some choke cherries linger on their scantly clothed limbs; and here and there among the verdured labryinths of side canyons and gullies mountain ash berries stand out like bunches of red-wax beads, all the more conspicuous from the fast falling leafage. We hear a chickadee and see a junco, the signs that winter has touched these high reaches of the mountains. How puny is mere man before the invincibility of natural change! It makes one humble as we ponder it in returning along the seepy trail.

> When long subjected to climatic change
> Do hydrogen and carbon spring to life?
> Does evolution in its ageless range
> Itself create the mind with all its strife?

OCTOBER 3

In reconnoitering a mountain for a deer-hunting site, we are persuaded on the way to pause and enjoy the gorgeousness of color of a single vista. Our unromantic horses gratefully cease their plodding, for docility and phlegmatism mark the gelding.

Before us a south-hill panorama ranges from the dull greens of a pine-fringed ridge down through the gold of aspens to the scarlets of maples nearby. There within a stone's throw is one maple of TaMing yellow with darker tints of mirabelle and saffron, and others of light green tipped with troubador red. Verdure-sheltered nine-bark is raisin toned; and the oaks are burnt umber. What colors!

We study mule deer tracks—plain hoof-marks under these firs; hoof-prints there under the aspens; scrapes, touchings and slips here and there; kicked leaves; a nibbled flower; a pine-needled bower beneath a huge evergreen where a deer recently bedded for the night. Yes, there are days a plenty for the hunt, two weeks hence.

At the brookside-lunch opinions are exchanged. Being a browser, the mule deer frequents hillsides and knolls where scrub oak, quaking aspens, and juniper abound, repairing on occasion to brooks for water and retiring at night to the seclusion of a pine-labryinth. Although battles of the rutting season are now raging, deep snows are destined later to bring herds together in amicable association, usually under the surveillance of an old doe.

Hunting methods are discussed—avoid cracking twigs with one's boots and making any noise; walk into the wind; keep near ridges; realize that a brown spot among trees may be not a deer but a man. Then concerning care of the deer after a successful shot—pull its head downhill so that it will bleed thoroughly, for unbled deer meat will not keep; after the bleeding is over turn the head uphill, cut the gullet and windpipe from the jaws, and by pulling them backward over the slit chest and abdomen they can be made to carry out all the intestines in a ball down hill. A trout may be cleaned in the same quick fashion with all the insides coming out on one finger. Fill the carcass with leaves; cover it with branches and tie a handkerchief on it to keep animals away. So the opinions and experiences go on. One of our most miserable occurrences on a deer hunt was sleeping on the crusted snow of a peak and attempting to make palatable coffee with snow melted on a fire.

As we descend, the weather becomes stormy, the atmosphere cold; and just as we reach our garden great snowflakes are falling on the asters, roses, marigolds and chrvsanthemums. Who can predict what nature may do?

OCTOBER 4

Standing on the verge of the dry, saline bottom of a marsh of Farmington bay, we for the moment are diverted by the acajou red or Pompeian red of a small weed growing there. Stooping to examine it, we discover that its scale-leaves are round and fleshy; it is the samphire (*Salicornia rubra*), sometimes called glasswort or pickle weed. "Salicornia" is from the Greek, "salt horn", in obvious reference to its horn-like branches and its saline habitat. "Samphire" is from the French *"l'herbe de Saint Pierre"*, a fleshy ammiaceous herb of Europe (*Crithmum maritimum*), which is sometimes pickled. We have not known of the use of this weed here for pickling, but as we eat one of the leaves we notice it is distinctly salty to the taste, and jecture it might be edible boiled in vinegar. The entire plant is so small it can be almost covered by one's hand; nevertheless, it is about the only color on the margins of the dry marshes.

Proceeding to water-covered sloughs, where literally hundreds of avocets are feeding, scattered about one to each square rod, we remark upon the almost complete absence of the beautiful colors of their spring and summer plumage. Heads, necks, chests and shoulders have lost their light cinnamon and become a drab white. One could be excused for asserting that they are not the same birds.

While observing their friendliness with one another as compared with their sexual belligerency of spring, we descry a Treganza heron standing in the pool; it too has parted with rich bluish hues and become gray. For ten minutes we watch it only a few rods away as it waits almost motionless save for the turns of its eyes and an occasional change of angle of its long neck and snake-like head, a movement so deliberate that jumping minnows before it are not frightened.

No black-necked stilts tread the marshes; but a red-headed duck dives along a deep borrow creek, as if he were a grebe. A few vulgar coots are swimming about, but only a few.

A solitary Brewster's snowy egret (*Leucophoyx thula brewsteri*) flushes before us, it being easily recognized by its yellow feet and black bill. We are accustomed to seeing this egret in these marshes, but we are surprised, indeed, when a few minutes later we come upon a larger common egret (*Casmerodias albus egretta*). As it stands we note that its bill is yellow, and, when it flushes that its legs and feet are black. This is the first time this year we have seen the transient common egret here, though Brewsters have been constant companions of our visits.

We catch sight of an American bittern, some pelicans and killdeers; and on our way homeward observe that asparagus patches are like gold finery beaded with rubies; common sunflowers, rabbit brush, mentzelias and asters are yet in bloom. A meadowlark bobs on a field post, and a red-tailed hawk flies overhead. Furthermore the day is as uncomfortably warm and dry as August.

OCTOBER 5

What an exquisite tapestry of color, a scene fit for the doors of Olympus decorated by Carpo, the Greek Hora of autumn! We stand above Moran flat and gaze with wonder upon the variegated south sides of City Creek canyon. The sky is light Alice blue, flecked here and there by peaceful white clouds; the high mountains at the east are light drab; those to the south at the top, mikado brown where the oak bushes show; and the hills further down, light cinnamon drab where nine-bark is pronounced. Such the horizon-view.

The upper canyon in the foreground to our left is, however, filled with cottonwoods of fluorite green and scattered maples of amber yellow. One maple is an outstanding deep carnelian red!

Directly before us across the canyon are more cottonwoods of fluorite green, intermixed with maples of jasper pink or even Chateny.

Below us at the creekside is one of the strongest color contrasts we have noticed in the wilds: at the left stand half a dozen fir trees of deep andover green; and beside them gleams a large maple tree of antimony yellow tipped with ochraceous salmon! This particular tree is so outstanding in our experience that we have fancied a dryad inhabits it and awaits the return of Vertumnus, god of the seasons, that with her finery she may win him from his beloved Pomona of the valley. The well defined cones of green, the equally well contoured tree of yellow comprise a setting wondrous to behold, truly one of the most picturesque vistas of the autumnal Wasatch.

The firs of the lower hollows appear like scattered pyramids of andover green, though one nearby is artemesia green, a variation due perhaps mostly to the angle of light rays reflected to us. At our very feet are sage bushes of dull grey, oak bushes of vetiver green, and other shrubbery of drab interspersed with Isabella colored leaves.

We shall never forget the beauty of this canyon scene, with its maples of jasper red, coral red and light orange; its oak patches of raw sienna, tan or mignonette green; its fir trees of cedar green; its nine-bark undercoverings of brick red; its cottonwoods of courge green; and its dried grassy interspaces of maize yellow.

Aside from folklore and old wives' tales, that blue cools the blood and calms the storms of fever, there is some truth in the statement, that red irritates some animals and yellow has an aesthetic, almost spiritual appeal. Nature never makes the spectrum clash: it has red, orange, yellow, green, blue and violet to work with; and it contrives, somehow, to keep them thus side by side in that order—an orange between a red and a yellow between a green and a violet, and so on. Man with all his knowledge is a poor imitator of its harmonious tints and shades.

OCTOBER 6

In calling on a banker-farmer, whose attractive home nestles in a canyon glade where springs flow from the oaks to water his sheep-grazed lawns, we pass a fish pond and unexpectedly come upon him shotgun in hand.

"You are a minute late; did you see that hawk I shot at?" he inquired.

"Yes, we saw a Cooper hawk fly away," we replied.

"Well, it's quite a story", he went on pleasantly. "This spring I bought an Indian game cock—you see him over there, red-feathered and upstanding like a penguin. Boy, he's a fighter!"

"All the game cocks are", we agreed.

"He's about a year old", he continued. "All the chickens were out here enjoying themselves when that hawk flew over. I was in the garden just looking around, when I suddenly heard the chickens scurry towards the coop. They all got in somehow—all except one and that was the Indian game cock. He just stood his ground, defiantlike, and watched the hawk's every movement. I could observe it all, and was curious to see what would happen. I had this gun in the garage. The hawk must have realized what he was up against, for instead of coming down with a swoop he flew to the ground right before the game cock".

"He did not strike?" we asked.

"No, he stood before the game cock as if he himself were another rooster. They put their heads down like game cocks and crashed together. They came apart and the hawk tried to circle behind the rooster. The game cock watched and turned, and seemed quicker than the hawk. Time and time again they flew at each other; and then at last the hawk gave up and soared away. I took a shot at him and missed. My hat is off to that game cock".

Then, discussing bravery, we finally concluded that the will to do and conquer is half the battle in the life of a chicken or a man.

Later when about to leave, we noticed a hundred chickens or more feeding on barley spread upon wagon covers. "It's a trick my father taught me", the farmer said. "That barley which I intend to plant has some wheat in it. The chickens will glean out the wheat and I take it away before they start on the barley".

OCTOBER 7

Emigration canyon is now like a paisley shawl that has been washed—gorgeous color patterns are there but faded and commingled. Thus far this autumn we have had no rain and little frost, so the pallid appearance of the once variegated hills is due to a transition unaided by moisture, frost or wind. Chlorophyll descended, leaves dried with beautiful display of their carotene, and then they began to fall—such is the obvious story. Squawbushes and birches are, for instance, now almost bare, as are some of the boxelders near them. Alders, on the other hand, are still green, notwithstanding many of their leaves are so dry they are falling. The catkins of this tree are very long and noticeable.

As we ascend the canyon, roadway locusts stridulate sharply, and, as we linger by the leaf-strewn brookside, crickets are giving the concert we are accustomed to hear in the valley only in the evening. It is now four in the afternoon and quite warm except in those coolsome brook verges.

Cottonwoods are fresh green in color; but the maples are either faded or fallen; and white clover, stripped of leaf and bloom, remains now only dried golden green stalks.

At the very summit of the pass to Parley's canyon a flock of six mountain bluebirds delight us from line-posts. The males are much lighter than usual, the females display little blue—a fading we have noted in both leaf and feather. Autumn for a time may be gorgeous with leaves just as the spring is with feathers; but both approach winter in almost colorless drab.

Flowers are scarce indeed—an occasional blue aster, yellow rabbit bushes, and a thistle yet in purple bloom. Most of the thistles are skeletons of spine and down. June grass on the upper hills is dry and yellow; but elderberries are not only green of leaf but actually in fruit.

Among all the birds hereabout this autumnal washing out of color is to us most noticeable in the avocet. which, as we have previously remarked, in the autumn loses its bright cinnamon of spring.

Although the word "autumn" is of uncertain origin it seems reasonable to suppose that it came from the Latin *auctumnus,* thence from *augeo,* to increase, the allusion being, of course, to the fact that in the fall there is much increase in the number of fruits, seeds and bulbs, and that a single kernel of wheat, for instance, has successfully multiplied itself many, many times. Far back in 1545 Roger Ascham in *Toxophilus* happened to mention "Spring tyme, somer, faule of the winter", and from that Sir Walter Raleigh and Captain John Smith used "fall" for "autumn". Fall is, therefore either a provincialism or Americanism, but, whether we like it or not, it has crept into our language as descriptive of many things, such as, fall plowing, fall wheat, fall term, and so on.

OCTOBER 8

It is as warm as an ordinary first of September, and for forty days we have had little if any rain. This is extraordinary, for the autumnal rainy season starts usually about the first of October, running its course in a week, and then brisk but clear weather lingers until the snows of Thanksgiving time.

Dry, clear autumns like this one interrupt many schedules: trees color early and too soon drop their beautiful leaves; very few ducks appear on valley sloughs where ordinary inclement weather fills them with migration's throngs; deer remain among the higher conifers, and mountain shrubbage is so dry that careless hunters start devastating fires. Strange to say, the mountain ridges are as parched as the lower knolls, and grasshoppers are common everywhere. Gullies ordinarily green no longer sing with trickling rills. Berries have dried and fallen. It would be interesting to know how long the black bear defers its hibernation in seasons of such unusual dryness, clarity and warmth. Doubtless it bides the first storm, subsisting perhaps on late elderberries when its favorite service berries have shrivled and disappeared among the leaves. By the way, here and there in damp, shaded, canyon-nooks we still see elderberries yet in bloom; in fact, each year, we later find snow on some immature clusters of berries.

Phenologists may require the data of many years to determine the precise relationship between dry, warm autumns and such phenomena as migration, fruiting and leaf-coloring; nevertheless, we stili believe that duration of light is the most important factor of all, and that long, dry autumns produce the finest coloration.

We know of no other branches so brittle and weak as those of the elderberry; and if one be not careful in gathering the fruit he is liable to disfigure the tree permanently. Since dried elderberries do not keep so well as choke cherries, Indians hereabout rely more upon the latter, which they crush with the pits, and then squeeze out both seeds and pulp for winter use.

A warm, dry autumn such as this one reminds us that on occasion other countries experience the same thing. One was notable: thus, when Lucius Opimus, consul of Rome in 121 B.C., destroyed a powerful opponent during an autumn of extraordinary heat, the vintage that year was so unusually fine that the people named it Opimian wine in his honor. There are no wineries hereabout, although the foothill slopes of the Wasatch produce excellent grapes.

OCTOBER 9

As we write these words there come to our ears the strains of Canada's favorite song—"The Maple Leaf Forever"; and we are compelled to admit that other regions are gladdened by the autumnal colors of this engaging tree. Of the family *Aceracae,* the maples, there are over a hundred fifty species, with representatives (the *Dipteronia*) even in central Asia. In Canada they have such members as the silver maple (*Acer saccharinum*) the wood of which is used for furniture and the sap somewhat for sugar (it is a big tree, over 100 feet high, with a trunk diameter of four or five feet); the scarlet or water maple (*Acer rubrum*), a similar sized tree with especially beautiful autumnal foliage; the sugar maple (*Acer saccharum*), equal in height to the foregoing, slenderer in trunk, but notable for its maple sugar; the goose-foot maple (*Acer pennsylvanicum*), only a third as tall but with satiny, soft, light brown wood; the mountain maple (*Acer spicatum*) another small one; and the boxelder.

In the Wasatch we have but three maples: the bigtooth maple (*Acer grandidentatum*), which grows along the water courses and with its big leaves is responsible for much canyon color; the Rocky mountain maple (*Acer glabrum*), which thrives along the canyon sides of the aspen, spruce and yellow pine belts and has a three-lobed leaf instead of the five-lobed of the foregoing; and the boxelder. The first is called the "bigtooth maple", the second the "dwarf or Rocky mountain maple", and the third, of course, everywhere the "boxelder". This boxelder, by the way, is the one tree that springs up in almost every garden, responding with unwanted but sturdy shoots wherever irrigation is plentiful and its mother-tree not too far away.

Mountains may display their gorgeous colors, but few of them do so without maples.

One reason why the autumnal landscape of the Wasatch mountains is superior in color to that of even New England states, where maples afford plenty of crimsons, is the presence of a contrasting blue-green pyramid here and there, the famous blue spruce (*Picea pungens*), which, once seen, spoils one when the view is only of ordinary green firs. Furthermore, this spruce grows singly, a delightful exclamation point only here and there, just enough to make the woodland picture complete.

OCTOBER 10

The vesture of the south side of the canyon, at 6000 feet, is one of multiform coloration and beauty. The overbearing raiment is pea green, light yellow and gold, yet beneath it all is the tone of the nine-bark, the deep maroon of the autumn hills. Nevertheless, as if they were coxcombs or baubels upspringing amid the delicacy of autumnal arrayment, maples of striking scarlet and flame outstand in loveliness. As the sun slants over the western hills, its transforms groves of them into a garniture of terra cotta, fading now and again into onion skin pink and Japan rose. Glorious indeed is the apparel of the hills, and, unless we be in a hurry, we seldom fail to linger a moment in almost reverent contemplation of some ravine or nook of extraordinary beauty.

The home-garden is likewise a delight of color, despite a touch of frost. Annual candytuft, cosmos, verbena, sweet alyssum, annual phlox, marigolds, hardy chrysanthemums and asters, continue their floral array. From crocus to chrysanthemum, from frost to frost, snow to snow,—endless and interesting is the joy of it all.

Unlike districts of lower altitude and more humid climate, the Wasatch mountains have very distinct seasons. Mountains and high valleys thus have their advantage that is unless they be too high, for it has recently come to our attention that residents of Colorado are in some places denied the full beauty of the cultivated rose, which cannot endure the hardships of very high altitudes. Vistas of lofty snow clad mountain crests with their pattern of things allegorical and sacred, with their purity of blue heavens, with their high falling cascades, with their evergreens and soaring eagles, must in great measure outweigh such inabilities. The higher the life above the sea the more difficult its conflict with snow and ice, yet more majestic nature's manifestations of mystery and grandeur.

> Betake yourself to limpid lakelets high
> Where pillared pines in mirrored beauty stand;
> Observe the deepened blueness of the sky,
> And wonder whether all its might was planned.

There is a pretty Indian legend, not local, that Kabibonokka dwells in Wabasso (the north); and it is he who paints the autumn leaves yellow and scarlet, he who sends the snow and chokes the rivers with ice; he who drives away the cormorant, gull and heron.

OCTOBER 11

Having seen the Alps only in July, we are not capable of comparing their autumnal colors with those of the Wasatch; nevertheless, in our reading of Ruskin, who thought the Alps the most beautiful mountains in the world, we do not recall his ever having expressed ecstasy over autumnal color there. His joy was rather over the hues of violets, oxalis, mosses, and bell-gentians, the small patches of mountain scenery. Since he saw only Europe we know not what rapture he would have felt in beholding whole hillsides of gorgeous color like those of the Wasatch. We agree that in the Alps many pretty cascades fall, many lofty peaks are mantled with snow, many hillsides are robed with conifers, many lakes are gems of green; and there is likely much autumnal color on the wooded slopes, and along both the Rhine and the Danube.

In our residence in England, autumn was the time of rain, mist and only the rusty shriveled leaf. Poets have adjudged it so: William Blake wrote of "the blood of the grape"; Burns of "yellow Autumn, wreathed with nodding corn"; Carleton of "yellow, mellow, ripened days, Sheltered in a golden coating"; Hood, "The Autumn is old; The sere leaves are flying, He hath gathered up gold, and now he is dying"; Keats of the "Season of mists and mellow fruitfulness"; Pope of "Ye trees that fade, when Autumn heats remove"; Swinburne, of "Cold autumn, wan with wrath of wind and rain" and Thomson of "Autumn, nodding o'er the yellow plain".

It is only among the American poets that autumnal colors in all their intensity appear; Lowell wrote, "what visionary tints the year puts on" and Whittier, "We lack but open eye and ear, to find the Orient's marvels here; The still small voice in autumn's hush, Yon maple wood the burning bush"; and Bryant, "Glorious are the woods in their latest gold and crimson".

If there were in Europe anything comparable with the rich garnets, maroons, yellows, golds, crimsons and flames of the Wasatch mountains in September and October, poets long since would have proclaimed it to the world and such painters as Giotte, Perugino, Angelice, John Bellini and Turner would have immortalized it on canvass.

By the way, we do not know of any native trees hereabout that have purple leaves in the autumn, like the great white ash (*Fraxinus americana*), the tremendous red oak (*Quercus rubra*) and the nearly as tall white oak (*Quercus alba*), all of the eastern half of the United States.

OCTOBER 12

On the salt flats of the mouth of the Jordan a fleshy leaved member of the goosefoot family, likely a salt blite (*Sueda depressa*), gives a brick red color to the desolate scene, and another, a gray molly (*Kochia visita*) with fleshy but sharp pointed leaves, furnishes dashes of pink on the roadside. Cattails are bursting.

A meadowlark on a fence post issues a perfunctory call, not a song. A Treganza heron, three Brewster egrets, rise before us; and then we come to open water where a thousand avocets quietly feed. Only a few coots, some killdeers, and a half dozen lesser yellow legs keep them company. When some of the avocets are resting they stand in a row of from six to twenty individuals, each on one leg.

A solitary ring-billed gull sits in a muddy stretch, but as we approach it flushes readily enough before us. Then to our surprise a male marsh hawk is flying a few feet above the surface of the lake and apparently hunting as he might over a meadow. Nevertheless as we watch him through the glasses for a mile or more never once does he make a dive.

Our attention is next drawn to a flock of a dozen Canadian geese, likewise flying low. We come upon hundreds of wading avocets, see ten eared grebes, and then to our great pleasure and surprise, probably a thousand long-billed dowitchers quietly probing with their extraordinary bills.

On our way homeward, upon entering a canyon in a light shower, two rainbows, parallel the one to the other but about a mile apart, beautify the hills before us, but the thing about them that especially holds our gaze is, that the position of their colors is not the same but exactly opposite. Calling the space between them the inner view, we notice that the red or scarlet shaft of each faces the inner side; the yellows are in the middle, and the bluish green colors are on the outside. One rainbow is fainter than the other, so, after all, one may be but the reflection of the other. Strange phenomena occur through the refraction of light rays.

There is something nostalgic about the words "Indian summer", which in the Wasatch mountains are generally taken to refer to that period of mild clear weather that after the first frosts of autumn usually runs from about the middle of October to the middle of November, for here it refreshes memories of hunts for deer, pheasants and quail over carpets of crisp leaves in an atmosphere chilly enough to make the flannel hunting coat comfortable. No one knows the origin of the words "Indian summer", although some say the Indians used them to describe the short period after autumnal rains and before snows when they moved from summer encampments to winter quarters. To us it is a time of happiness and serenity.

OCTOBER 13

It seems rather strange to us, that our sweet-singing bobolink of spring should this month be regarded as a delicious tid bit in the West Indies, where it is called the "ortalan" or "October-bird". Doubtless many of our smaller migrants are slaughtered in their winter-homes of South America by natives who have little or no regard for their aesthetic or economic value. In the northland birds usually appear in the summer only in isolated pairs, and the swarming seed-eaters of winter, such as juncos, are not regarded as food. Even the ever-hungry Indian natives of the Wasatch seem not to have depended upon birds for food, a habit due solely to the difficulty of catching them. Since bobolinks swarm in thousands upon the wild rice beds of the Atlantic coast states of the south during their spring and fall migrations, there is some justification for their destruction by the farmers of adjoining lands.

There is in truth a perpetual conflict between mankind and wild life, another struggle between hunters and agriculturalists, yet another between those who love beauty and those who see only grazing profit and utility. In these valleys owners of fish hatcheries are in constant war with Treganza herons; many farmers destroy jackrabbits, which make inroads upon their alfalfa and tender grains; and livestock men begrudge the wild deer their forest feed; but aside from the regular destruction of such predators as coyotes, wolves, cougars, bears and lynx there seems to be little interest in animals but those shot as game. The rattlesnake is everywhere killed on sight but only because it is dreaded and its beneficial habits are deemed little compensation for its occasional bite of man.

One aspect of nature is, however, not always apparent to the casual observer—all mammals and birds are more or less prone to fight among themselves, not only during the breeding seasons but also in the daily intimacies and contacts of life. Like people they have their likes and dislikes, their petty jealousies and even hatreds. Some, like the coots, are actually murderous and cruel with one another, but some, like the long crested jay, enjoy the tranquility of solitude.

More and more people are beginning to realize that the character of a man is largely formed by the amount of mother love he received as a baby or young child. Conscience and rules of conduct are the result of environmental factors, chiefly the guidance of the mother. A wild young mammal and a human babe respond to love, just as they acquire viscious habits from the lack of it. Among all mammals, whether whales or men, mice or cougars, the undisturbed mother gives loving care to her young.

OCTOBER 14

Governed by their desire for food and protection, mammals some-times select strange habitats, but none perhaps more unattractive than the high mountain slide-rock chosen by the pika (*Ochotona princeps uinta*), that small rabbitlike, tailless mammal with ratlike ears. Rock conies they are sometimes called, but they like such high regions and such rough slides that we here come upon them chiefly in the Brighton region of the Wasatch. With voices like toy trumpets they live in small colonies, protected by the intricate interspaces of their rocky homes against most dangers. They build bushelsize haystacks of the leaves and tender stems of choke cherries, nettles, currants, snowberries, lupines, aspens, asters, fireweeds, goldenrods, yarrow and ferns, in fact, any edible plant gowing within two or three hundred feet of their caverned runs. Winter may bury their trails with snow, but their haystacks carry them over until another spring. With short legs, padded soles, no external tails, and almost bare, round ratlike ears, it is little wonder that when they first came to the attention of mammalogists in 1769 their Russian representatives were by Pallas allied with the rabbits under the desig-nation *Lepus pusillus*.

In the mountains today our friend "Ed", the watershed patrolman, told us that one spring at the head of the Big Cottonwood canyon he picked up a fawn mule deer so weakened from hunger it made no resistance to capture. Its mother had apparently been killed by a mountain lion. Taking the little fellow to his cabin, Ed held it on his knees while his wife soon revived it with a warm bottle of milk, and thereafter it became a household pet. They named it Billie, and it followed Ed everywhere, into the cabin, if allowed, there to share his sofa, and outside from stake to stake when he was playing horseshoes. When hungry it meowed like a cat, and, as it grew larger, Ed's fox terrier and the deer would chase one another back and forth so long at a time that eventually they would lie down together quite exhausted. If a strange dog approached, Billie would defend his friend from the in-truder. No matter how far Billie strayed from the cabin he would, when called by name, come bounding home with his great ears showing conspicuously at each jump. As autumn approached he stood almost three feet high and his spots had nearly all disappeared; hence, having no accommodations for a pet that size in his city home, when winter came, Ed was compelled to give Billie to a friend in the valley. One night a week later a pack of dogs chased Billie down and soon worried him to death. "I haven't had the heart to shoot a deer since that time", Ed remarked with a tinge of sadness in his voice.

OCTOBER 15

We have just had an interesting surprise. Having sought these scrub-oak hillsides in pursuit of quail at a place immediately north of what since childhood has been to us Beesley's Pond region, a half score of miles south of Weber canyon, we had arrived at the edge of this deep hollow when we noticed two long-eared owls (*Asio otus tuftsi*) sitting in the thick oak brush of the shaded side. One flew silently and gracefully away at our approach, but the other fell to our gun. It is evident that they have been spending their daytime perched on the oak limbs of that densely verdured, secluded and dark side of the ravine. We say "surprise" because this bird, though not uncommon, is so habituated to the vesture of darksome cottonwood glades in the daytime that an ornithologist may go for years without the sight of one.

The specimen that we have before us is in fine plumage: it is a large bird, over a foot long in fact, with long, dark brown ear tufts, mottled gray upper parts, and yellowish under parts marked by blotches of brown and crosses of a darker color. This owl should not be confused with the western horned owl, which is actually half as large again, though the long-eared, as we hold it in hand, is certainly not to be despised in size. Most of the larger hawks hereabout, however, are superior to it both in strength and dimension.

Nesting earlier in these mountains than the black-billed magpie, the long-eared owl is inclined to steal that bird's last year's nest for its own habitation, where its three to eight owlets usually break the shells about the first of May. Nearly all birds accommodate themselves more or less to their environment, hence, if a treeless neighborhood be attractive by reason of its many rodents, a long-eared owl will not hesitate to nest upon the ground.

Though an occasional sparrow may be pounced upon by this interesting owl, its principal fare undoubtedly consists of mice, or, when opportunity offers, shrews, insects, frogs and little snakes. It is a matter of much comment among us through the years, the number of birds that eat snakes.

How unpredictable birds are! When man intrudes upon the nest of a golden eagle the parent birds almost indifferently fly away; when a long-eared owl's nest is endangered it fights like a marine on Wake Island.

As we examine more closely this specimen in hand, we are surprised by its enormous external ear-openings, a feature we have noticed also in the short-eared owl. We cannot explain this charactristic on the theory that an owl needs exceptional hearing ability at night for, while the long-eared is almost exclusively nocturnal, the short-eared is nearly as diurnal as a marsh hawk whose activities are comparable. We believe the tremendous ears are given by nature to both owls because they habitually wait at the side of a mouse or rat burrow for the victim to appear.

OCTOBER 16

On the summit of the mountain, where the warmth of midday belies the frost of night and clear blue skies are reminiscent of summer, there is a dry and leafless nakedness far and wide except where spruces and pines stand attired in changeless green and mountain lilacs spread their slender branches covered with glossy leaves, leaves that are rounded, varnished, velvety and leathery. By the way, this thornless member of the Buckthorn family spreads on the hillside like an umbrella ten feet wide from a single central stock.

Bare are the maples, quaking aspens and oaks, a sight due to an extremely dry summer and autumn. Springs and rills at the wayside are either dry or so seepy that they are bereft of purling song. Jumping from the saddle further on, tethering our faithful horse in a grassy slade beside a trickling brook, we nevertheless unroll our sleeping bag, make a tiny long-sheltered fire, enjoy our bacon fried with eggs and previously boiled potatoes, and prepare to sleep or to lie awake and ponder, as many a time we have done before.

Lying awake at night in a mountain glade, marveling at the clarity of the stars in the firmament, one listens to the soughing of the wind through the hillside pines. Although the sound is pleasing and somewhat undulating, it is after all a noise, as distinguished from a musical tone, for it conveys the sensation of fitful, irregular, confused, and mixed tones, due to the changing movements of air over branches and spaces of infinite variety of contour and size.

One harkens then to the purling of the near-by brooklet as it tumbles down over mossy rocks of various sizes and locations, causing a spurt here, a dash there, or a roaring bound over all in miniature cascades, twists and bends—that too is noise, not tone, which is always uniform, undisturbed and not topsy turvy like a jumble of sounds of limitless variety of wave length. Incredible as it may seem the clear-toned call of the tiny chickadee, *fee bee,* as it prepares for night in the wide sheltering branches of yonder spruce is not only more musical than the purl of water but more penetrating than all the runnel's ensemble of sounds.

The silent touch of frost kisses in the nightime; and on the morrow, as we descend the tangled pathways of the canyon, where wildered cattle stare at the unaccustomed intrusion, no longer do birds carol in the wayside copsewood, nor warblers flit in the willows of the trout-livened stream above which their woven cup rests empty and deserted on its leafless twig. All is bare, chilly and foreboding.

OCTOBER 17

It was in 1942 that a portion of the Wasatch mountains was set aside for the killing of deer exclusively by bow and arrow; and we remember how great was the interest in Emigration canyon, the chosen locality, on that seventeenth of October. Since that time archers have each year been favored with either early dates or special localities; and, so far as we can observe, the bow and arrow is a tremendous weapon at a distance of not more than twenty-five yards, since an arrow has a greater stopping power than a swift bullet and, furthermore, it sometimes goes clear through a deer. It is, of course, useless at great distances; to illustrate, a high powered rifle with a telescope sight has been known to bring down a bighorn at a distance of nearly a mile. We often wonder if the world's distance record for an arrow, 482 yards, made in 1795 in London by a Turk named Mahoud Effendi, has been excelled.

Although we have found flint arrowheads near the mouth of the Jordan river where the savage peoples commonly encamped a century ago, we do not recall ever having seen an Indian with a bow and arrow in our time, nor do we know from exactly what native wood they made their bows. At any rate, east of the Rocky Mountains the finest bow-wood was the osage orange (*Toxylon pomiferum*), a native of the rich soil existing from Nebraska to Texas. The orange-colored wood of this tree was very hard, strong, durable and dense, precisely suited for bow purposes; and doubtless some of the very backward Indians hereabout did acquire some of that wood in trade. In the Wasatch we do not have any native members of the mulberry family, to which the osage belongs, nor does the yew, another superb wood for bows, occur here, although the Utah Indians could likely acquire the yew from their friends in the northwest.

Autumn is the period of fruition rather than melancholy decline. Ever since early spring the birds have striven to rear their broods to the point of physical maturity and habitual independence; they have succeeded and the fledglings have taken their places among the adults, usually in the southlands. Mammals have suckled and protected their young until at last the youngsters, now as big and physically able as their parents, have been driven from the home grounds to fend for themselves in the wide world.

Trees have borne their fruits, cereals have produced their grains; and all that grows in the greenland has blossomed, developed and yielded its seed. It is a time of rejoicing, a universal gratitude for proof of fertility.

OCTOBER 18

Today in our rambles we see both the Uintah or armed spermophile (*Citellus armatus*) and the Utah rock squirrel (*Citellus variegatus utah*), in other words, the "pot gut" as it is locally called, and the "long tailed gray squirrel". We mention it only because the habits of the two animals are so dissimilar as to make us wonder why they are classified under the same genus.

The armed spermophile has a tail of insignificant size, while that of the rock squirrel is nearly three times as long, in fact, long enough to be a blanket for it in slumber; the armed is almost always on the ground while the rock is so agile in trees that we on occasion have difficulty in shaking it down; the armed goes to sleep in late summer, reappearing again in the fall before hiberation, while the rock is active at all times. We have seen it for instance on the snow in March. The first sleeps all winter, the other is awake and active; the armed hibernates and aestivates while the rock stores acorns, pine nuts, choke cherries and other seeds for winter provender.

In somewhat squeamish mood we have mentioned how the Indians of this region ate such delicious morsels as dog meat, rattlesnakes, lizards, crickets and ants, our disgust being apparent in even the mere account of such appetites; yet, *mirabile dictu,* as we write this, we have before us a catalog of gourmet foods advertised for sale at up to three dollars a can, foods that nauseate us beyond those of the Indians. We quote some of the items with accompanying descriptive matter:

"BABY OCTOPUS. Cooked slowly in covered pan with soy sauce seasoning."

"TENDER RATTLESNAKE MEAT. Prime domestic rattlesnake meat ready to eat."

"CHOCOLATE-COVERED ANTS. Toasty—crunchy ants covered with thick, rich milk cholocate."

"YOUNG ROASTED CATERPILLARS. Hand-picked, plump caterpillars roasted to flavorful best."

"FRIED GRASSHOPPERS. Crunchy, munchy, ready to serve."

"FRIED ZAZA INSECTS. An Oriental delicacy, growing in popularity."

"SALTED WHALESKIN. Eskimos love it."

"MEXICAN FRIED AGAVE WORMS. 'Fritos' from south of the border."

"FRIED BUMBLE BEES. Choice of the hive—fully grown. Ready to serve."

"FRIED SILKWORMS IN COCOON. Picked and fried at height of silky goodness."

"FRIED ANTS." We guarantee 2000 in each can . . . and each one fried to crisp goodness."

There you are—may we expect soon to hear that a worm in a can of vegetables, worms in cauliflower, and weevils in flour are but added bits of delicate succulency?

317

OCTOBER 19

When on many a valley and canyon trail we meet happy hunters laden with either ducks or deer, we are constrained to ask ourselves whether, possessing eleven guns, two of which are this hour doing duty under the guidance of friends, we with our scientific rather than lethal equipment really get the highest enjoyment from the outdoors. That we own eleven guns of numerous calibers and bores indicates that we have once enjoyed the kill; yet now our accoutrements consisting of field glasses, barometer, compass, microscope, as well show our predilection towards observation rather than destruction. Being scanty meat-eaters and caring little for the flesh of any wild game except sage hen, we readily decline the invitation to the hunt so far as the appetite is concerned; but the real secret of our unused guns is the fact that a dead animal, fish, or bird tells little about the real meaning of life. A carcass of any kind reveals much of the anatomical similarities and dissimilarities of species but little about the instinct, thought, hope, ambition behind it all.

In that it satisfies his desire to conquer, his zest for adventure, and his yearning for strenuous physical exercise, the young man is as delighted with hunting as the older man is with the greater story the live animal tells. A characteristic of age is a desire to comprehend the meaning of existence. Youth is engrossed with the gladness of life, middle age with its responsibilities; old age with its eventual promise. Some in youth have the cares of the aged; some never grow old; some throughout life take situations as they occur without special worry over the past or the future. True philosophers are from youth troubled with the meaning of existence.

A sudden snow storm, stray shots, men ill clad, inexperienced and unprepared—the result is the usual list of tragedies and toll of death.

It is interesting to note that the grizzly bears of Utah (*Ursus horribilis utahensis*) were mostly brown, not white like the typical northern plains animal, nor grayish like the Montana specimens.

By the way, one of those eleven guns is an inherited old-timer, a carbine type rifle with a tremendous hammer that strikes a pin designed to set off a rim-fire cartridge of about 45-70 caliber. An under lever and simple, strong mechanism uptilts the barrel for the insertion of a cartridge. On a metal side are stamped these words: "Gallagher's Patent July 17, 1860, manufactured by Richardson and Overman, Philadelphia 23541." The old boys, hereabout, had to make one shot count, for, before a grizzly, which was fairly common even in the valleys, there was seldom time for re-loading.

OCTOBER 20

We return from the Jordan sloughs to examine and admire the varieties of ducks strewn upon the club-house floor. Hot coffee and canned salmon sandwiches having satisfied the inner man, we inspect them. For the most part they are mallards with pink feet, green heads and yellow bills, but many are handsome pintails, green winged teals, and shovelers, the last of which have the spatulate bills used to dredge crustacae from alkaline ponds. Gadwalls, with their brownish heads and grayish bodies, are not so common, since they with the greater and lesser scaups and the American golden eyes are expected only with a storm. Though for years we have returned with our share of ducks and geese from the sloughs, it has never been our good fortune to bring home a canvasback, the *piece de resistance* of outdoor gourmets. Mallards and pintails are good, redheads are better, but canvas backs to our reckoning excel them all. The wood duck is a handsomer specimen to look at, if indeed one could desire anything more adorned that a male mallard, a stately pintail, or a greater scaup.

Most hunters, we have noticed, pay little attention to their prey except to distinguish between "butter balls" and mallards, pintails and teal, and snow geese from Canada geese. One hunter, indeed, seemed pleased with the novelty of killing a white-faced glossy ibis, which he curiously laid before us for identification.

The real truth is, that ducks in their fall plumage have somber colors in comparison with their breeding feathers of spring, and that is why some ducks are difficult for the homecoming nimrod to identify.

It is surprising how often on the duck-shooting grounds these late October days we hear the words "butter ball". The reference is of course, to the buffle head (*Bucephala albeola*). (You will recall the celebrated charger of Alexander the Great, which he named *Bucephalos*, meaning "ox-head". The word "buffle" is an obsolete form of "buffalo". In both instances the reference is to the broad head of the duck, which seems big and blunt for a bird of its size). It is a whitish duck, with a dark head and flesh colored feet marked with black toe-nails. It comes here only in the late autumn and winter.

A duck that usually appears about the same time as the buffle head is the American golden eye (*Bucephala clangula americana*), which has a broad head of greenish black, in the male, and brown, in the female; orange colored feet with dusky webs. The Latin word *clangula* means "noise", the reference being to the whistle of this bird's wings very noticeable as it flies overhead.

It is said that many years ago pot hunters, shooting for market on these sloughs, used set four-gauge shot guns.

OCTOBER 21

Where last year's fires burned over the hillsides desolation now prevails. Black, bare limbs uptrude through scant foliage, while once green oak leaves still cling to their stalks, a dismal mummified drab. Here and there new oak shoots bear leaves now turned raw sienna or mars yellow. Each gulch has sheltered on its shaded side some bushes and trees undestroyed by the fire. The wild rose is fast losing its tremulous leaves, but those that remain are xanthine orange. The new rose wood is claret brown; the old stalks neutral gray. Maple leaves that linger are strawberry pink, orange pink or pale yellow orange. The creek bottom is a ribbon or orange or gold. Robins, long-crested jays, magpies and juncos are the only signs of avian life.

We betake ourselves to the orchard and garden, ever sweet with the memory of apples beneath leaves. Here the foliage of the native black currant (*Ribes aureum*), which, by the way, is a golden currant but with berries sometimes black (hence the name, Utah native black currant), consists of leaves of a deep oriental green striped with wine-colored vines, yet some of them are chestnut red with bordering wings of green. Other leaves are purple lake or burnt umber, with tinges of pale vermilion near the stems and along the veins, and still more olive green tipped with gold. Beside the currant stands a gooseberry with leaves of deep cadmium, orange or lemon, all on the same slender branches.

Along cold springs and ditches we find the strawberry buttercup (*Ranunculus cymbalaria*) running freely and vigorously over the ground. This is sometimes called the "alkali buttercup", but, having tried it around our fish pond, we find it too rampant, too possessive of all the ground about it, though, in this respect, not so annoying as the myrtle (*Vinca minor*), which with its creeping stems soon takes root all over the sacred precincts of a small garden.

Since we started this meandering page with the results of a hillside fire, we must not fail to mention that the finest bed of Rose of Sharons we have ever seen bloomed on a knoll that the previous year had been burned to charred blackness; furthermore, we must remark, that, where a fire burns a scrub oak forest to the bare gound and leaves it a dismal hillside of stark limbs and black ashes from which one would think that no tree would ever grow again, ten years later that same hill is a mass of young oak shoots three or four feet high, thrusting their heads upward between the skeletoned trunks of their dead ancestors.

OCTOBER 22

Wherever we ramble in the mountains today red-capped hunters are stalking the elusive mule deer, and showers of crisp yellow leaves are fluttering in all except the evergreen groves. Since quaking aspens are nearly bare, apprehensive and confused mammals quickly descry the movements of enemies; in fact, motionless objects whatever their colors and shapes mean nothing to them unless a strange scent pervades the air. They know every forest sound and, while grazing by the trickle of a brook, jump at the snap of a twig.

One hunter with his buck enlightens us on the art of preserving deer meat in warm weather. Cut a very short slit in the belly, leaving the breast undisturbed; then, after disemboweling, wipe out the interior with clean grass. With two sharpened twigs pin the vent together again to keep out flies, and cover the carcass with leaves and pine boughs as it lies on the cool ground. Only in the freezing night time is it to be removed and hung from a limb.

The mule deer, which has a dark forehead, whitish inner ear and white tail with a black tip, has antlers that branch like two Y's upstanding one above the other, and, although the bucks average about two hundred pounds, extraordinary individuals may weigh as much again. There is one race in these mountains: the Rocky Mountain mule deer (*Odocoileus hemionus hemionus*). By the way, "Odocoileus" is from the Greek "tooth" and "hollowed"; and therefore some authorities say should be spelled "Odontocoileus".

These deer prefer hillsides verdured by sage, scrub oak, quaking aspens and similar shrubs to swampy ground or brookside labryinths; and in flight they bound rather than run. They breed in November and December, congregate in peaceful herds the rest of the winter; and then in early summer the sexes separate, the bucks in little bands nursing their growing antlers in brushless alpine glades and the does protecting their fawns in sweet coverts where hermit thrushes sing.

Man, cougars and wolves are the enemies of these sylvan inhabitants; but blue jays are their unwitting sentinels.

Just as we write this, one of our friends comes in with a buck taken in Mill Creek canyon, weighing 325 pounds dressed. The explanation is easy—this canyon had been closed for years. Usually we glimpse a cougar or so by the side of deer on automobile fenders; this year only one has come to our attention.

OCTOBER 23

If we were asked which of the cultivated flowers gladden us most, we should answer, roses, dahlias and petunias in the order named, and, of all the roses, the exquisitely colored one known as Duquesa de Penaranda. In conversation with leading rosarians from other parts of North America we learn that the roses of the Wasatch mountains have an intensity of color that is the envy of dwellers in lower and more humid climes. The rose is one shrub that demands sunshine, though our wild species are not noticeable for their exceptional beauty. Of all the wild flowers we come upon, few if any are more exquisite in design and tint than the mentzelias, which, however, are prickly inhabitants of bare, rocky acclivities. All this is a matter of fancy, for a score of people will select almost as many different flowers as their first preference.

Animals of desert regions are usually more pallid than those of rainy districts, and birds are apparently more responsive with colors to the breeding season than to climate. This paleness is, for instance, very noticeable in the wood rats, among which the rich buff and ferruginous colors of species in humid climates become light gray in the desert and more arid forms. The gray bushy-tailed wood rat (*Neotoma cinerea acraia*) of the Wasatch was given its original scientific name *Mus cinereus* because it was "the ash-colored rat of Rocky Mountains of Lewis and Clark". All of this leads us to wonder why we have not more frequently mentioned the wood rat. The reason is, that the little animals are chiefly nocturnal and only once in all our meanderings have we come upon their nest. Once on the Weber river in an old cabin we spent several nights in too close contact with these daring and apparently belligerent rats, "belligerent" let us say to the extent that one of the men appeared actually afraid of them. It was ghostly in that old inner cabin-room with its dust-laden piano and night-haunting rats.

These wood rats habitually steal all obtainable manufactured articles of small size for placement on their nests; but when not near the habitation of men, they gather sticks, thorns, bones and leaves with which to build their nests, usually in cliffs, and subsist on bulbs, bark, nuts, seeds and fungi. When a wood rat inhabits a rock crevice or a cellar beneath a boulder it has little need for the protective accumulation of a nest, hence, that may explain why we do not more frequently come upon them. If a female wood rat is capable of having a litter of two young about once a month, we perhaps owe something to owls and ticks. Externally resembling the detestable house rats, they have little to praise, except that they inhabit the wild places.

A woman friend today told us of a locked cabin in the "mountain" district of Parley's canyon which is infested with such defiant rats that they stand up and fight intruding men, juts as a muskrat will on dry land.

OCTOBER 24

A stroll afield reveals many pleasing sights: lofty Lombardy poplars stand like obelisks of gold while their fluttering leaves fall in a continuous shower. So thick and velvety is the carpet of grass and leaves in the orchard that numerous wasted apples are buried; and even beautifully adorned ring necked pheasants hold to their protective grass bunches until one's foot actually flushes them. The male, with his neck of metallic green, his breast of coppery chestnut reflecting metallic purple, and his extremely long tail, is a beautiful sight to behold, exotic indeed, as he flies afield beyond the autumnal leaves.

As everywhere the eyes turn they see the yellows, reds and browns of autumn, one instinctively feels it to be high time to store for winter. Since songsters have nearly all gone, the now somber meadowlarks, flickers and colonies of blackbirds are about the only feathered kind left along the hedge rows and willowed lanes. No more do we hear the exultant songs of spring; nevertheless, after a sultry and languid summer some of the birds, such as the red-shafted flicker, do react to the cool autumnal air with calls reminiscent at least of the ardor of the breeding season.

Having the warblers, humming birds, swallows, night hawks, and fly-catchers in mind, one might suppose that the insect-eaters migrate and the seed-eaters, such as sparrows, the nutcrackers and the crossbills, remain throughout the winter; and in large measure that is true, notwithstanding that worm-eaters like the downy woodpeckers survive the cold and snow. Water birds, of course, must keep themselves south of ice. A say phoebe is a bird no more tender than a valley quail nor a kingbird than a gray-ruffled grouse; yet the former migrate and the latter remain.

It is, therefore, undoubtedly true, that food and food-accessibility are greater migration factors than cold and snow. Likewise with deer, wapiti and smaller mammals, it is scarcity of food rather than heavy snow that often destroys them.

More than any other landscape I love the grandeur and beauty of the mountains. It is true that they have some melancholy phases, such as the scars and piled debris of avalanches, stones and boulders spewed by freshets upon valley floors, and the stillness of the dead in deep untrodden winter now where solemn pines stand like the colonades of a huge sepulcher; but these are rare, transient or but the reflection of mood.

When compared with the flat horizons of plains and lowlands the outlines of mountains are at once break-taking and stupendous. As I behold the Wasatch chain from the valley where this is written the mounts appear like a row of green crocodiles with rugged backs ten to twelve thousand feet high, each with its head behind the tail of the one preceding it where a major canyon cuts through, each furrowed with minor gullies along its side, each touched here and there by a vast solid white cloud just able to surmount its lofty peaks and ridges.

OCTOBER 25

At this time of the year boxelder plant bugs (*Leptocoris trivittatus*) are so common in the vicinity of boxelder trees it is difficult not to squash them under foot. The body of this insect is red, hence, before the wings grow and cover it, the young bug is almost entirely red. The adult, however, is gray marked with red. From an egg laid in the crevice of bark, the young insect emerges and grows with the growth of its wings until they are full-sized, when, of course, further development ceases. They subsist on the sweet sap of such trees as the boxelder or even peaches, plums and apples, which they reach by drilling their beaks through the bark of tender stems. We have found vast assemblages of them hibernating back of window casements of houses near boxelder trees, and even one collection, consisting of hundreds of individuals, in contented repose beneath a garden board. A spray of kerosene is quick death to them, hence with very little effort they may be discouraged from visiting any particular home.

Bats used to winter behind the window frames of a large public building; but, we have not seen a bat hereabout for years. Dragon flies likewise used to be common about the homes in summer evenings, but they too are becoming scarce. Mosquitoes are persistently destroyed by the use of kerosene and other sprays, hence the bats and dragon flies seek other fields.

In bosky coverts beside the huntsman's trail a bevy of deer awaits in breathless fear his passage, yet it is not his desultory eyes that may notice their motionless hides between the leaves but the uncanny perception of his horse, which may snort with surprise at their presence. In the woods, especially in early morning or late afternoon, when the slanting rays of the sun searchlight beneath every coppicing, movement is often suicidal, hence deer sometimes stand in open glades immobile for ten minutes at a time or until unexpected movement explains itself as friend or foe. They far excel phlegmatic man in sense of hearing, sight and smell, except in the differentiation of colors.

How impotent is mere money to one alone on the high ridges! Having once gone into the mountains to deliver a message to one who unexpectedly had moved onward, I spent three days alone with my horse, without food, although I had plenty of money in my purse. With my revolver I unsuccessfully tried to shoot down a dusky blue grouse from a pine limb, and I finally got so hungry that I would gladly have given fifty dollars for a meal. Yet some men spend all their lives in a greedy pursuit of money, to which nature gives no more heed than to the pebbles of the brookside.

OCTOBER 26

At the entrance to Emigration canyon orchard cherry trees still hold their leaves, mostly yellow or green, some the color of light red wine. A large cottonwood by the creek is yellow gold; another nearby, greenish gold; a lonely sunflower and an unattractive mustard are the only flowers at the wayside.

Before entering the canyon we scan the mountainsides, once beautiful in color, now leaden, leafless and drab. Two miles up the canyon (5200 feet), all trees are bare, and drifts of leaves carpet the ground; but further on the leaves of both Lombardy and Carolina poplars are yet golden green upon the limbs.

On our way we remark an occasional hawk and a few magpies; but at the summit between Emigration and Parley's there is naught but stillness and bronze leaves beneath bare limbs. At 5800 feet, where the sage is light green, the grass dry, and the trailing barberry conspicuous in its maroon, a rabbit brush (*C. speciosus*) is still in bloom.

We notice a pair of chickadees busy about the bare oaks, and then a mile further on we spend half an hour watching a fine buck mule deer browsing on the hillside. He is solitary in the very place where usually we find a score or more of both bucks and does. A mile below the reservoir, however, our eyes are attracted to what look like four white rocks on the leafless hillside. Our field glasses reveal that they are four mule deer does in tranquil company, the drab-white color being their buttocks, which are very conspicuous, whereas their bodies elsewhere can hardly be distinguished from the ground.

As we reach home we take from a tomato vine a spider with a body spreading two inches or more. Its body is like a gray shell in the front half but marked with twelve horizontal orange bands (in threes) across the rear half. Its legs have alternate spots of black and orange almost to their tips; and it has two longitudinal light yellow stripes on its under side. It is a female banded garden spider (*Metargiope trifasciata*) the largest we have yet seen. Having a female black widow in captivity in a bottle, we place this spider, five times her size, with her. Presto! in ten seconds the widow bit one of its legs off; then the widow turned with her rear towards it and tapped it with her two hind legs, her method of fighting. In thirty seconds more the widow bit the other on the back. The garden spider within a few seconds drooped, then dropped; its legs began to draw in from the poison. All the time, the widow approached backward, tapping the other like a boxer here and there with her rear legs. It was soon over. What a valiant fighter is that black widow, a ruthless gangster-killer among spiders.

OCTOBER 27

Notwithstanding sumacs are showing orange and scarlet tints, the dry mountainsides are a study in pallid color blending, for, June grass being now a straw gray, there is no longer a sharp definition of hue and tone. Sunflowers here and there have lingered yellow blooms, and boxelders in sheltered nooks are as truly golden as one might anywhere expect to find. Lombardy poplars along valley lanes are still green, as are apricots, globe locusts and weeping willows; but black locusts and Carolina poplars are just turning yellow. Russian olives are gray, but marked with yellow seeds. Leaves of the scrub oak are half green, half rust, often an individual leaf being thus indicative of the seasonal transition.

At Farmington bay, where cattails are bursting throughout the vast expanse of open water, not a bird, not even a coot, is to be seen, for along the embankments are hunters, setting out their decoys, wading or watching for flights that do not come. Ducks are as smart as deer, for the first sound of guns disperses them to hide in seclusion until nightfall.

We can remember when, many years ago, market hunters at the mouth of the Jordan used their great eight-bore guns in pot-shots upon flocks of feeding ducks, and then sold their slaughtered victims upon the open market. We recall later the inauguration of bag limits and then, still later, of having seen the lake shore at the mouth of the Jordan dotted for miles with dead and dying ducks, doomed under the rapid incursion of drainage and agriculture; but at last bird-refuges have appeared to be the answer. Certainly the Great Salt Lake with its innumerable alkaline shoreline sloughs is in the path of one of the greatest of all annual water bird migrations.

The intelligence of man, his ability to form concepts, is apparently but a higher gradation of that manifested in lower animals. What causes the swarms of ducks, after the few early shots of morning, to seek the salty waves of the lake, far from the reach of the hunter, unless it be the application of a species of intelligence to a dangerous situation? Instinct tells them to flee from harm, of course, but it is in their selection of refuges, with correct distances from gun-capability, that must involve some sort of thinking.

As everyone who has visited one of the large parks of the world well knows, live wild animals are often the chief attraction of such places. In large measure the entire Rocky Mountain chain, including minor parallel ranges, is one vast park, seldom permanently occupied except by those who are interested in sheep, cattle, mining or lumber, and, in summer, by thousands of vacationists. It is most regrettable, therefore, that wild life, except deer, is gradually being destroyed by selfish minorities, who account their interests to be superior to the general welfare.

OCTOBER 28

Although this morning, when we arise, snow is falling, it has been a year of almost no autumnal rain, of mountain grasses dry as tinder—then snow! It catches many things unready: tremendous dahlias in full beauty; petunias and marigolds—all stricken under the heavy burden, and chrysanthemums not yet in bloom.

Nature in the wild is fully prepared: the bear seeks its den, the armed spermophile its burrow, the grouse its covert, the quail its spinet, and woodpeckers their dead-tree holes. Some birds, like horned larks, magpies, lesser scaup ducks, pintails, mallards, juncos, chickadees, goshawks, marsh hawks, golden eagles, and snowy owls are resourceful enough to withstand almost any weather, and others, such as the long-crested jay and Clark nutcrackers, have become so accustomed to depend upon spruces and pines that they can actually get food in the darksome woods beneath canopies of snow.

This desert horned lark (*Eremophila alpestris utahensis*), which we have perhaps mentioned only as we came near it upon the dykes of Farmington Bay, is so hardy that it withstands the coldest winters by feeding upon the seeds of weeds, a beneficial habit of many birds that our eminent friend Bent thought over-emphasized in economic importance. Perhaps so; but nature delights in balance and compensation, reproduction fraught with enemies. We do not agree that the work of insectivorous birds is futile, but rather regulatory. It is true that the accomplishment of one bird seems insignificant, but not if its total of a hundred seeds a day or more be distributed in effect throughout the year. Being iconoclasts ourselves, we deplore the destruction of coyotes and mountain lions, notwithstanding the loud outcries of sheep and cattle raisers, for those predators hold deer and rodents in economic balance. It is very doubtful that the destruction of any living thing larger than an insect is of eventual benefit to man.

As one sits waiting for ducks to fly near a reeded blind, and watches the movements of various forms of life about him, he is given to ponder the meaning of it all and to awake from his reverie with the realization that nature cares no more for him than for the muskrat that swims towards yonder rushy mound. The laws of nature are impartial and inexorable. In the coldness of a blizzardy day it would as soon freeze a man as a mouse, and indifferently pelt all living and inanimate things with hail. Bacteria everywhere await them that fall. It takes the vanity out of a man, especially if he had been so anthropocentric as to regard himself and the welfare of human beings as the aim of the entire universe.

OCTOBER 29

When each morning we traverse the lower stretches of City Creek canyon and find nothing in bloom but an occasional sunflower and mentzelia, we turn our eyes upon the hillsides where oaks and maples are bare, where indeed, all foliage has dropped except that of a shrub growing here and there in patches about a rod in diameter. The leaves of this shrub are so colored that in the distance a copse of it looks like a commingling of raspberry red and pyrite yellow. It is about the only coloration left on the drab hills; so, on our way down, we stop to examine a clump in all its glory. Yes, as we thought, it is buck brush, bitter brush, or antelope brush (*Purshia tridentata*), the *tridentata* referring to the fact that each leaf has a three-lobed apex; each leaf, about one inch wide by one and a half inches long, is wedge-shaped; and only the upper surface is tinted, the under side being chamois color. The shrub itself does not grow over six feet high; but aside from its conspicuous position as the last to shed autumnal color, it intrigues us greatly as the delightful shrub of spring with blooms of the delicate scent of apple blossoms.

It is strange that one modest shurb should so please us; but, after all, the mornings are misty, cold and rainy, dried flower stalks, many of them seeded, are everywhere, and we may look through maple groves and willowed labyrinths to the well-defined but once verdure-hidden brook now running sweet and clear below. Birds, aye where are the birds, save those lofty flocks of geese veeing with clarion calls overhead; where are the warblers, thrushes and vireos that once in brookside pathways sang? Nature must change; but wait, all is not in vain—at the very tip of a twig from which we just plucked the bitter brush leaves in all their gorgeous colors are nine buds each about a quarter of an inch long, each showing the tiny scales that envelope the blooms of forthcoming spring! Nature, after all, is but the design for continuous living.

By the way, it is interesting to note that this sweet-scented antelope brush is a member of the *Rosaceae* or rose family. We sometimes forget wide botanical relationships. This rose family, for instance, includes hereabout such differing shrubs as the mountain mahogany, with its long persistent styles; the cliff rose (*Cowania stansburiana*), with its bitter quinine taste; the choke cherry; the nine-bark; the rockspirea (*Sericotheca dumosa*), a surprising bush in Big Cottonwood canyon; wild raspberries and strawberries; service berries, hawthorns; mountain ash and cinque foil.

OCTOBER 30

Now that the upper mountains are veiled in snow one involuntarily queries: whither go the vertebrates and even the insect forms of life? A friend, as we write, relates a strange story: in a mountain north of the Wasatch a road building crew blasted a cliff away and out of a cavern thus exposed rolled a ball of rattlesnakes as tall as a horse. Our friend, A. M. Woodbury, authority on Wasatch reptiles, says that, although he is studying a den of fifteen hundred reptiles, most of which are rattlers, many of which he catches and numbers, he never sees the rattlers hibernate in a ball, though non-venomous kinds do so compactly cling together that individuals are occasionally smothered. This den of his, by the way, is in mountains forty miles west of the Wasatch.

Again, as we write, two reliable friends and witnesses attest to having observed tiny young water snakes, "about a hand full" as one expresses it, flee from danger by running down their mother's mouth; indeed, we are inclined to give credence to this strange phenomenon for the reason that, the mother herself quickly escaping, she need not swallow them. The gastric juices of her stomach would otherwise kill them. This, however, is not stranger than the emission of blood-shots from the Arizona representative of the Wasatch horned lizard, a fact admitted by all competent herpetologists.

Years of experience have taught us not to deny too dogmatically occurrences in nature; for, like the scream of the cougar, some may hear it and testify positively concerning its occurrence while others may remain in doubt. A mere boy, untroubled by the uncertainties of science, may see something of rare and great value; for no matter how one may delve into any subject of appeal to the naturalist he cannot be everywhere, see everything, and lads that ramble in the meadows learn many, many truths.

We recall how, when writing a monograph on the life history of the mountain lion or cougar, we for years refused to believe that on occasion it regularly feeds with impunity on porcupines and actually devours some of the quills from the inner side, until one day, while making a biologic reconnaissance of the Strawberry river country, we came upon an old lion hunter, who forthwith took us to a river-banked grove of firs and showed us several partially devoured porcupine skins on the ground beneath them. Only a cougar, which is plentiful thereabout could have done it, as the fisher does not exist in the Wasatch; furthermore, the old gentleman pointed out some cougar-feces that were actually filled with partially digested porcupine quills.

Likewise we discredited the "womanlike scream" of the cougar until a client, having observed one in the actual process of screaming, signed an affidavit in verification of it.

OCTOBER 31

A few hours travel through a canyon and over a valley below it may be replete with surprises; for, when leaves have mostly fallen and flowers in the main have wilted and dried, one expects little novelty in the drab hills. Nevertheless, at the mouth of City Creek canyon this cold, clear morning we unexpectedly come upon a flock of about two hundred birds, some of them contentedly beaded along a telephone line, others busied among the leaves of a bitter brush copse. They are Cassin purple finches (*Carpodacus cassinii*); and of all things—two hundred of them! *Carpodacus* is Greek for fruit-biting.

The male Cassin finch has a crimson pileum, vinaceous-pink back with markings of brownish gray, rose chest and throat, and white underparts; but the female is olive gray streaked with dusky, a somber bird beside her mate. They are larger birds than house finches, with which the casual observer might confuse them, and are fairly common among the snow laden trees of our valley. We listen to their faint warble, and then their call note, a short "ink".

Going down a valley lane, which is fringed with yellow-leaved willows on reddish stems, we flush a belted kingfisher from a fence-line brook, and watch it as it flies somewhat like a flicker directly southward. This migration urge! Even as we peer after it with the glasses a great flock of geese sounds in the heavens so high we cannot clearly discern its individual members.

As we proceed, a tiny grayish bird alights on a fence wire and allows us to approach within a rod to observe it to our heart's content. It is a ruby-crowned kinglet, less than four inches long, with olive-gray back, two pale wing bars and a short, emarginated tail. We cannot detect its hidden, scarlet-crown patch but we are so close that we can tell when it closes its eyes as if in sleep. A distant locomotive's whistle causes it to tilt its pretty little head away from the sound, the better to catch a meaning. In a few minutes a mate flies from a willow, and our tiny friend goes with a lisping "jee-dee". Happy birds!

Both of our tiny kinglets—the golden-crowned (*Regulus satrapa amoenus*) and the ruby-crowned (*R. calendula cineraceus*)—are permanent residents breeding in the coniferous forests and wintering in valley trees and shrubbery. They are wee birds, more like the blackcap, whitethroat or sedge warbler that we used to see in England than anything else we have here. If you examine one closely you will notice that the maxillary tomium, that is, the cutting edge of the upper jaw, has a notch just back of the tip. The kinglets live on minute insects and aphid eggs.

At a meadow we stop to watch the antics of fourteen meadowlarks assembled in a willow. One sings as lustily as in spring; two more chase over the grassland and return. Obviously autumn incites some of the impulses of early spring.

NOVEMBER 1

In the garden the common raspberry leaves are strikingly variegated and beautiful: their summer color of clear, oriental green still lingers on the leaves nearest the ground, yet some of those that have constantly faced the sun are now Venetian red, fringed only slightly with raw sienna and marked along the veins in light stone. A gorgeous combination! Yet look! there is another leaf; it is raw sienna mixed with old gold. There, on the same bush is one of deep orange, varied along the veins with straw color; and yet another, even from the same branch, a Venetian red, mottled with brown, green and gold. And the stem of each leaf is oxide red! What wealth of color in an unsought, unfrequented, unnoticed, unsung raspberry bush!

Nevertheless, the adjoining strawberry patch is on close inspection almost equally glorious in autumnal color. The summer shades of light Venetian green on the leaves have changed to a vivid, turkey red, intermixed here and there with three-leaved clusters of carmine. The under surface of each leaf is light purple green, a mere tint of the rich, carmine red of the sun-kissed part above.

Over there in the strawberry patch is a three-leaf series of deep Indian red at the extremities and bull frog green near the bases. Gone now are the toads, which in summer were wont to hop from beside the ripe berries of the patch, where their quick-darting tongues had for the day tasted the delicious sweet.

By the way, the common toad of the Wasatch valleys is the Rocky Mountain (*Bufo lentiginosus woodhousei*), while the mountain toad (*Bufo boreas*) inhabits the upper canyons and hills. They have burrowed now into the ground for their winter sleep, and, since they absorb moisture only through their skins, not drinking as do most animals, that place of winter retreat must be damp but not too cold.

It is surprising, that two animals against which all men lift their hands, the coyote and the rattlesnake, year by year somehow manage to survive, even in some cases, near the habitations of mankind. The coyote, of course, becoming more wary as time goes on, avoids the hunter with a gun and the tempting poisoned bait, depending upon live rabbits and rodents for food. The rattler, subsisting on mice, gophers and the like, sticks close to the rocky cliff or sage-covered knoll, and thus usually avoids the paths of human feet.

NOVEMBER 2

In the salubrious climate of this Great Salt Lake side, in a settlement of widely scattered cabins, pioneers lived for years without even knowing a doctor. "No one got sick," was one's simple statement; for contagious diseases were unknown and herbs provided adequate remedies. Some of the medicinal lore of the scarce inhabitants may have been copied from the Indians, but, since they used fewer plants than did the savages, it is more likely that a knowledge of the efficiency of certain genera of plants was a sort of common folk-lore, derived from trappers, travelers, passing botanists and so on. The question arises, however, what did the Indians do for their various ailments?

If an Indian had indigestion he ordinarily drank a tea made from the roots of the common yarrow or from the flowers of any of the umbrella plants (*Erigonum*); but if he merely needed a physic he would drink a liquid made by boiling the whole plant of the bud brush or short sage (*Artemisia spinescens*), or of the whole cliff rose. If these were not available he boiled the ground seed of the Mexican poppy, or the stems and leaves of *Chaenactis stevioides*. Even the boiled root of the common sunflower (*Helianthus*) gave satisfactory relief.

If he had a cold he steamed a whole sage bush, or a complete rabbit brush (*Chrysothamnus graveolens*), and drank the dripping potion. It sounds very much like the drinks given ourselves as children.

For kidney trouble he took what is known as "Mormon tea" or "Brigham's tea" made from the joint fir (*Ephedra nevadensis*), found, however, only on the west side of the Great Salt Lake and thence to the southern extremity of the Wasatch. Sore eyes he rubbed with the juice of the root of the common sage, or put on them a liquid made by boiling an entire snowberry plant (*Symphoricarpos vaccinioides*). Sometimes he burned a willow (*Salix*) and with it applied a sort of ash-poultice to his bothering eyes.

He soothed a swelling by bathing it with the sage tea that he used for a cold, and if he got a bad cut or wound he dug up the first milk weed or sour dock (*Rumex mexicanus*) he could find, washed and mashed the roots, and then put the resultant mixture directly on the wound. It was usually effective, though if he had a bad burn, he was apt to gather the leaves of any of our penstemons, grind them and apply them directly to the afflicted part.

Boiled rabbit brush (*Chrysothamnus graveolens*) afforded a suitable liniment for ordinary rubbing of sore muscles; and for measles he drank this same rabbit brush juice as a tea, or took the bud brush or sage tea; or boiled the gum plant (*Grindelia squarrosa*) and used its juice. Naturally such a disease took a terrible toll in those infrequent periods when it did occur. Julian H. Steward says that to cure venereal disease, introduced by white men, they boiled the root of the aster (*Aster canadensis*), which potion eased urination. No wonder the Indians hated the white men, who brought them only liquor and misery.

NOVEMBER 3

A depressing sight is to revisit a favorite canyon glade and find a few spruces here and there yellowed and dead. All the loveliness of snowladen branches green and healthy nearby does not mitigate the displeasure one feels at this destruction of nature's monarchs, the blissful bowers of carefree days. This drying and dying of the finest of the conifers can be attributed only to some kind of beetle.

The western pine beetle (*Dendroctonus brevicomis*), only a fifth of an inch long, stout, rounded and brownish, attacks the yellow pine by making winding egg-galleries through living and dying bark; and eggs, larvae and adult winter there. It works a continuous round of devastation, and one by one leaves yellow and dry.

In similar fashion the Englemann spruce beetle (*D. englemanni*) slightly larger, makes long curved tunnels, eats the inner bark, girdles each trunk and likewise causes death to these handsome trees.

The stout, dark brown or reddish Douglas fir beetle (*D. pseudotsugae*) is longer, more hairy, and equally destructive with its slightly winding egg-galleries, which branch and rebranch as need demands. The only thing in its favor is, that usually the adults alone winter in the bark, and it prefers felled or injured trees.

All *Dendroctonus* ("killers of trees") beetles, of which the foregoing are but three of nine, are small, and in the early stages of a tree's doom most apparent beneath the bark. Having finished a particular tree and left it a pyramid of rust where once it was green, the adults seek other trees upon which to impose their death-sentence.

It is only meager consolation that some wasp-like insects, predatory beetles, and birds of the woodpecker clan, prey upon these destructive beetles, for in spite of these friends often an entire hillside, which was verduous and beautiful, is sometimes but a vista of yellowed dryness and death.

Forgetful of it all, we ascend to the summit, where stunted maples have strewn their tinted leaves; and we there pluck a branch of the sage (*Artemesia tridentata*). Upshooting from each gray-leaved limb is a stem nearly a foot long with a brown brush of winged seeds. No wonder sheep graze the tips of the succulent sage. Since a sheep tears out flowers and tender grasses roots and all, it is by far the most destructive mammal that roams the mountains, the very cause, if you will, of bare hillsides that permit floods and erosions.

NOVEMBER 4

When hunting through reeded depressions and along wild-grown irrigation ditch banks, we are always impressed with the gorgeous coloration of the male ring-necked pheasant (*Phasianus colchicus torquatus*), as it flushes on painted plumes before us. We can remember the time when neither pheasant nor quail flew about our field verges; but their introduction, especially that of the pheasant, has been so successful that thousands of hunters every year taste their appetizing flesh.

Some pheasants are more extraordinary but perhaps none more beautiful than the ring-necked. Reeves' pheasant (*Syrmaticus reevesi*) of northern China has, for instance, a tail several feet long; Lady Amherst pheasant (*Chrysolophus amherstiae*) is a beauty of blue, grey and red; and the golden pheasant (*C. pictus*) is a handsome bird of gold, red, blue and brown; but the ring-necked has much more complicated color patterns than any of the others. Fortunate, indeed, are we that China has given us such a hardy, useful, and striking addition to our avian fauna. Quail winter-kill seriously, but the climate of these valleys is favorable to the pheasants.

It is said that pheasants quite readily cross with other gallinaceous birds such as the common fowl, the resulting hybrid being called a "pero"; but we have never seen one. Being polygamous, pheasants, like deer, increase despite the annual shooting of perhaps the majority of their male members.

Phasis, a river of ancient Colchis (now Georgia, Transcaucasia) is said to have been the origin of the word "pheasant", which appears in French and Spanish as "faisan" and Italian as "fagiano"; but whatever its name it is a much-sought bird. We remember with pleasing interest the pheasant hunts we have seen in England, where beaters are employed to flush the birds over field hedge rows; but guns are there for the gentry. Here almost every lad knows how to handle a gun; for such is the pioneer spirit of the mountains that individualism and self-reliance still characterize the mountain-dwellers. Very few homes in the autumn fail to have at least one meal of pheasant or venison.

We do not know who started the practice of killing only males as a conservation measure—we first heard of it from Pennsylvania—; but certainly with respect to polygamous animals like pheasants and deer it has had such extraordinary results that occasional open seasons on female deer have become a balancing necessity. Unfortunately the system will not work on the pronghorn (*Antilocapra americana*), which ranges in desert lands close to the Wasatch, for in this mammal both sexes have horns, and it is difficult to distinguish one from the other in the waste lands.

NOVEMBER 5

It is a day devoted to the leaf-colorings of the orchard of our childhood, a place still retaining some of the olden trees and shrubs and many more besides. The artesian well yet trickles its limpid water; and the huge boxelders continue to form a phalanx against the perennial east wind.

In a bridal wreath (*Spiraea prunifolia*) the leaves are changing from oriental green to raw sienna with a wash of purple. Some leaves are dull green in the center bordered with yellow ochre; some purplish red washed with green. Here and there two tiny leaves at the very tip of a series are electric blue above delicately blended with shell pink.

We ponder: here is where a pet pigeon used to fly down to our shoulder; there is where a skunk escaped to an irrigation bridge; and there again is the spot where the sacred bones of the dog "Flossie" lie. Flossie trampled flowers, hence the boyhood heartache from a father's sentence of death upon the vigorous young pet.

Peach leaves are falling in a spiral tremble, far different from the heavy flutter of those of the catalpa; but they vary from green to pale light stone or bright venetian red, or from oxide red above to pale green below.

Every step of ground we once weeded time and time again.

Most of the native blue currant leaves have fallen; but those that remain are green veined with wine, chestnut red bordered with green, or purple lake, stem and all. One, indeed is burnt umber tinged with vermillion along the veins and stem; and another, olive green, tipped with sienna and gold. Simple everyday things.

Here is a gooseberry with dark green, deep cadmium, orange and lemon, all in the same foliage. One leaf is green tipped but marked inward with pale vermilion and gold; one is mottled with terre verte and burnt sienna.

Having come upon color here we must adjourn until tomorrow, for, of all things! we are to sleep tonight in the room of boyhood days—the old homestead where we milked cows, stored pumpkins, shocked corn, dug beets and potatoes; and often in the late afternoon stood in wonder at the gorgeous sunset over the distant "Dead Sea."

NOVEMBER 6

We are dissuading sentiment about this old home garden and its colored leaves; but look!

The apricot tree is comparatively prosaic, since most of its leaves are dull Saxon green mottled with patches of rust; and the French prune is lusterless in its dappled burnt umber, emerald green and gold. Likewise the leaves of the apple are raw umber spotted with green, though a younger tree presents leaves of gold veined with yellow; but here at last is a tree of wonderment in color—the crab apple. One leaf is a flaring cadmium yellow, blotched in a decayed portion with vandyke brown, and richly marked along its veins with deep vermilion. Another leaf is vivid brown madder, almost alizarin crimson throughout stem and all; and the under surface a yellow ochre wash. One more leaf is a blend of deep vermilion and gold. Only the raspberries and the snowball compare with this tree.

Most of the leaves of the winter pear are dark India red, almost purple lake, blending with brown. Around the edges are tinges of green; and hanging pears harmonize with the leaves.

There is the spot where the rabbit hutches stood.

Here is a young cherry whose cream colored leaves are flecked with green; another, with leaves dried to a vandyke brown; but a third cherry is beautiful—some leaves raw sienna, some Indian red on the edges, then greenish and pale vermilion towards the middle.

The enormous leaves of the grape are crisp and brown; but those of the chrysanthemums are either green or damson brown. Rose leaves are gorgeous;—some claret, some bronze green; others blotched with alizarin crimson, emerald green, and brown madder; still others, brilliant carmine interblended with raw umber and marked with pale cadmium along the veins. One series is more highly colored on the undersides—green above but rich purple lakes and carmine below.

The leaves of the snowball are supreme—deep Tuscan red almost purple brown, or oxide red with green and yellow veins, or even red, gold and brown.

Lilac leaves of olive green and rust; English ivy leaves green and soft like rubber; green weeping willow leaves turning to gold; and dark green leaves of the snowberry with clusters of snow-white berries —but why go on. Who does not long to see once more the orchard and garden of the old home?

NOVEMBER 7

Crisp yellow leaves carpet every canyon, glen, and swirl lightly with each whiff of passing mountain air. High upon the hillsides among the upper rocks zephyrs from below unite to form a breeze which flings pebbles with stinging force. Clouds float together with distant views, gradually obscuring the landscape with graceful curves of mist; and then at last drops of rain here and there fall, to be followed presently by blinding sleet and snow. Within half an hour every twig, every trail, is covered with quiet and glistening snow, thus transforming the pleasant mild November morning into an afternoon of winter cold.

Wintry weather, numberless smoking hearths, fill the atmosphere of evening with fog; then the moon shines through the haze with an obscured outline, and only the brightest stars penetrate the smoky mist. Leave the crowded streets and trudge again up the mountainside; for there the real pellucid nature of the heavens appears. The humid covering over the city then becomes repellant, and, but for the cold of the lonely hillsides, one would linger in their sweet limpidity.

We trudge to the very crest of the mountain, where a veil of snow is seeping under the warmth of a cloudless sun. Nothing much to see; sweet clover, dried and yellowed; rabbit bushes with parched blooms; and a magpie squawking vociferously in an oaken copse.

We descend a few hundred feet; and here, beside the leaf cluttered brook, rose bushes have young shoots of garnet red. Surveying the canyon, we notice that the birches have new catkins, and the haws make patches of rich garnet.

On our way we come upon the automobile-killed bodies of a white-tailed jack rabbit (*Lepus townsendii townsendii*), a porcupine, and a great basin skunk (*Mephitis occidentalis major*). The intensity of focused light is the confusion of death to many a mammal of the night.

Our thoughts drift towards the slumberers and the hibernators among wild mammals, the slumberers being the ones that indulge in a restless long sleep with not much change of body temperature, and the hibernators being those whose bodies go as stiff as a board, whose hearts scarcely beat and whose temperature is cold. Carnivorous animals like bears, badgers, raccoons and skunks are mere slumberers; the real hibernators are seed-eaters like ground squirrels and marmots.

NOVEMBER 8

Sitting before a log fire at sundown, when snow is gently falling outside, we meditate upon the superlatives of nature as we have observed them throughout many a year in these mountains and valleys of varied life-zones and forms. It is a fascinating pursuit, for, to ascertain which is most this or most that involves reflection upon several hundred species of birds, mammals and other animals.

We begin, for instance, by asking: what is the most beautiful bird of this region? and, before answering, we ponder over the lovely roseate spoonbill whose accidental appearance here we recorded, and then consider the handsome male mallard, the tender blue bird, and the lazuli bunting until at last we almost involuntarily exclaim, "there it is, the Bohemian waxwing", with its body of silken fawn and tertials decorated with red wax-like appendages. Since boyhood days, when we stood in the snow-burdened apple orchards of Februarys and watched these lovely birds but a few feet away from our wondering eyes, they have been to us not only the acme of avian pulchritude but to a large extent the very *raison d'etre* of our deep interest in ornithology.

The most loathsome bird is the western turkey vulture, although the vulgarest is the coot, not only for the sounds it makes but also for its uncouth ways. So we go on.

Of the birds, the cruelest is the marsh hawk, as it sometimes devours the breast of a victim before attempting to kill it; the swiftest is the duck hawk; the most voracious, the double-crested cormorant; the finest singer, the house finch; the saddest noted, Say's phoebe; the most spiritual in tone, the Audubon hermit thrush; the most graceful fliers, white pelicans; the most apprehensive, the avocet; the wisest, the female Canadian goose that leads the flock; the deepest voiced, the American bittern; the daintiest, the black necked stilt; and the most furtive, the California cuckoo.

The beauty and tranquility of the trout-laden river, where the western belted kingfisher dives for its prey, leads us to regard that bird as the most picturesque of all. Birds most faithful to their mates are the large hawks; the cowbird is the laziest of the feathered tribe, as it lays its eggs in the nest of another species; the most libidinous is the English sparrow; the most weird at night, the great horned owl; the mildest mannered, the Bohemian waxwing; and the friendliest to man, the mountain chickadee. The most useful birds are the meadow lark and the Swainson hawk.

Of the mammals the wolf is most faithful to its mate, as it is also the most untameable; the mountain lion is the most stealthy, and, at night the most horrifying with its scream; the most truculent, a migrating muskrat on dry land; the most indifferent, a porcupine; the sleepiest, a ground squirrel (*Citèllus armatus*) which not only hibernates in winter but also aestivates in summer, that is, sleeps a month in the late summer.

NOVEMBER 9

Eager to find some wild flower still in bloom we climb the crisp-leaved by-paths of City Creek canyon. A common sunflower soon wins our eyes by its bright yellow rays; but, not satisfied, meandering onward through a bare-limbed grove, we at last notice there on the roadside above the rock bridge—an aster (*Aster canescens*), conspicuous in its beauty of violet rays. It is only a foot high; and its linear, older leaves have occasional rigid teeth on their margins, teeth which flip back with a dry pin-point snap as we touch them with a finger. Each flower has about a dozen violet-colored rays; but the disk flowers in the center are gold and lemon yellow. Each flower-head looks as though it must have borne several sets of purple rays during the season; and some have already gone to seed. Each seed is like a tiny black-headed dart with white hairs behind, the whole being only a quarter of an inch long. Having found what we hope is not the last flower of the year, other asters, such as *leucanthemifolius*, being perhaps even later, we ramble further up the canyon.

White clover is still blooming; horsetail or scouring rush is green at the brookside (how clear, pure and cold the gently flowing water); trailing barberry leaves are most attractive in color; and mountain hedge clumps the wooded slopes. Plucking a branch of this hedge, we notice that the maroon limbs support leathery green leaves, over half an inch long and a quarter wide; and that at the base of the leaves clustered red buds are so small that we examine them with the hand glass. They are the forerunners of those wee red flowers we discern in May. Why can't all flowers have leaves that withstand winter snow as do the mountain hedge, the barberry, and the cold-defying pines?

At Rotary bridge we examine the beautiful evergreens; they are balsam firs or black balsams with thin, gray bark, sharp-tipped leaves between one and two inches long, circular leaf scars and pyramidal shape. With a hand-lens we examine one green tip; and there in all its forthcoming glory is a miniature yellow cone not over a sixteenth of an inch long.

We see a chickadee, a long-crested jay, a junco; and there, right before us, the mountain lilac is still showing shining green leaves. We pick up an *Oreohelix*, a snail; we notice two golden insects flying, insects that we must identify; yet we started for a flower in bloom.

Wherever we go in the central portion of the Wasatch mountains we come upon shallow blasted holes made by prospectors in years gone by; but we seldom find any at either the northern or southern extremities.

NOVEMBER 10

Hardy indeed is a plant that can bloom in the cold of a Wasatch November, yet our notes of many years prove that more than a score may at one time or another qualify in that category. It is true that some of them have escaped from cultivation, many of them are mere weeds, and most of them are unattractive, but they bloom.

Our list includes: chickweed with the white petals frequently seen in lawns; pepper grass (*Lepidium virginicum*) with white blooms in moist places; shepherd's purse (*Capsella bursa pastoris*), a white flowered weed; hedge mustard (*Sisymbrium officinale*), a yellow-petaled weed; black mustard (*Brassica nigra*) with bright yellow flowers on roadsides; white clover (*Trifolium repens*) with white or rose-tinted blooms along streams; red clover (*Trifolium pratense*) with pink or red flowers; alfalfa (*Medicago sativa*) with its well-known purple blooms; black medick or none-such (*Medicago lupulina*), sometimes called "wild yellow clover"; white sweet clover (*Melilotus alba*); milk vetch (*Astragalus utahensis*), often called "lady slipper" or "wild sweetpea"; filaree; mallow or cheeses (*Malva rotundifolia*) having whitish or bluish flowers with pink veins; phlox or wild sweet William; plaintain or rib grass (*Plantago lanceolata*); dandelion; sow thistle (*Sonchus asper*) with yellow flowers; chicory (*Cichorium itybus*); pine apple weed (*Matricaria suaveolens*); gum plant; aster (*Aster adscendens*) and the common sunflower.

Weary of this recapitulation of our notes, we hie ourselves to the very end of the roadway in City Creek canyon. Hornet nests in scrub oak trees are as conspicuous as magpie homes; there is a spicy fragrance from carpets of maple leaves; and many trees are donning their winter-gray woolens. Moss is growing up the trunks of some cottonwoods, some alders and even maples; but this only in damp, shaded canyon curves. How red the roots of the brookside! How mottled the hillsides with snow!

While sitting on a rock beside the mossy stream, we behold on the other side of the narrow canyon a blue spruce so fine, outstanding and lovely, so commanding in its picturesque isolation that we inevitably ponder

> Many a pine tree stands on a hill alone,
> And holds with sturdy limbs its 'lotted ground;
> Many a man could well himself enthrone,
> If faith and courage in his heart abound.

NOVEMBER 11

Whenever we visit the mouth of the Jordan during the half frozen days of November, it is usually our good fortune to see a flock of snow geese. Being of pure white plumage, excepting their black wing-tips and rusty-orange stained heads, they are easily distinguished from all other geese hereabout. If the marshes remain open, as they sometimes do in mild winters, these geese may decline to migrate further southward at all.

To see a flock of snow geese veeing high above the sloughs and uttering their shrill call notes, and then later, when they alight, to watch them feed in joyous comradeship upon the grassy fields near their swimming waters; to listen to their conversational sounds and to realize that after all they are perhaps one mighty family led by some great, great grandmother of many years experience—to do this is to understand that in nature ways of happiness are comparable with those of the highest civilization.

The Hutchins goose (*Branta canadensis hutchinsi*), which resembles a small Canadian goose, but nests further north, seldom visits our marshes. The black brant (*Branta nigricans*), the white fronted goose (*Anser albifrons frontalis*) and the blue goose (*Chen caerulescens*) are all rare here.

Although usually preferring the far north for a nesting ground, stray pairs of Canadian geese (*Branta canadensis moffitti*) do breed in our sloughs; indeed a few of them on Farmington bay have been our unafraid companions since early spring, true exemplars of connubial bliss. We have watched pair after pair swim about with convoys of youngsters in June. They disappear southward in the severest weather, but usually begin to come back in February. Once several hundred of these geese alighted on a stubble field almost within the confines of our native village on the shores of Great Salt Lake; we remember how many men hastened forth with rifles to shoot them and how watchful guards on the outskirts of the gabbling horde gave such quick warning that without loss of a bird the noisy throng honked its way over the horizon.

For sociability and mutual solicitude geese are the paragons of birddom; indeed in their ability to post sentinels, sense danger, and follow recognized leaders, they make us wonder if after all man alone can form concepts.

> Philosophers have probed the mind in vain
> To ascertain the whither and the why,
> For all they've found within the strange domain
> Is but conjecture guessing at the sky.

NOVEMBER 12

Snow gradually appears lower and lower along canyon roadways, resulting in sleek impassable places, and compelling us to mount saddle horses to reach upper by-paths. Here and there along the chill brook, spray forms huge chunks of ice on overhanging branches, which sway with their burdens as if affected by waves. Although it looks very cold in those darksome underbanks and shaded brook-niches, we know that such noisy secluded receses are perhaps the favorite home of the timid cottontail. As mountain chickadees are very active about the maples of cold canyon glades, for several minutes we watch one pecking vigorously into the tip of a broken horsetail; and upon examining the stalk we discover that it is black and rotted at that point, and likely filled with some insect-nutriment. There is a lemon tint on the bodies of these confiding and useful birds, more than we have noticed at other times of the year.

As several contented red shafted flickers fly about the canyon trees, we discover that the holes of two of them are in dead cottonwoods at the brookside. A few juncos here and there complete the ornithological picture.

It is not, as might be supposed, that such is our love of nature that only the population of a zoological garden would satisfy us, but, that we deplore the growing scarcity of birds throughout these mountains. Often indeed, even in summer, one may traverse many a mile of wooded beauty without seeing any wild mammal or bird. The cause is complicated, diverse, yet none too complimentary to man's understanding of the advantage of a balance in nature or to his use of poison to kill wild animals.

Man is largely to blame. A "buck law" which forbids the killing of does restores the deer in great numbers; the making of ponds and lakes over areas once unwisely drained increases the duck population to plentitude again; the permitted shooting of only rooster pheasants gives every weeded ditch bank its family of ring-necks. It has taken many years for America to learn the art of conservation of game; now they must study the far more important art of the preservation of soil, oil and minerals. Perhaps we could learn something from the Chinaman who has good crops on the tiny farm that his ancestors cultivated for forty centuries before him. Thus we are told that the agriculture of China supports five persons to every two acres, that in the basin of the lower Yang-tze river, for instance, they grow cereals in winter and rice, tea and cotton in summer—four crops a year! They have canal mud and river silt, but for fertilizer they depend in the main on green manure and legumes in crop rotation. They even pulverize ashes and mix them with organic matter, but they use little of chemical commercial fertilizers. A matter that shocks us, however, is that in their quest for more arable land and green manure they have cut down almost every tree in North China and not many pines, chestnuts, palms, maples and camphor woods remain in the agricultural heart of the lower Yang-tze.

NOVEMBER 13

When only an inch of snow has fallen, the mountains with their bare shrubs and leafless trees look neither white nor brown but a pallid gray like that of snow swept from a dusty porch. Hills of sandstone flecked with snow become a delicate safrano pink; and it looks cold and lonely up there in the dark but congregated pines.

Here and there in sheltered recesses of the gloomy canyon brookside maple trees stand, so protected from wind and storm that they are still in their glory of colored leaves; but such examples are usually small, not over ten feet high, frail like the midgets of the world. Conspicuous now for their colors are the richly gowned green firs, the slender but intensely red dogwoods, the reddening birches, the green brook-snug horsetails, the mountain hedge, the trailing barberry leaves of many hues, and the wild rose bushes, not entirely denuded of their reddish foliage.

It is not that we are so delighted with colors as to let them engross our attention, but, in truth, that animal life is so scarce in the Wasatch in November that one is driven to an admiration of tint and tone. It is probably the deadest month of the year: trees are leafless; song birds have gone and there is not enough snow to reveal the tracks of animals that roam the half frozen pathways. Snow is the greatest foot-printer known, revealing tales of tragedies, jaunts and prowls; and, since most mammals are more wary than birds, few activities are disclosed in the November woods.

The canyon brook is but a miniature of its raging self of spring, but it is so pellucid and cold that one feels he might find in it the very elixir of life. Heretofore dropping leaves have cluttered its movements, but that is all over now—leaves destined not to float but to moulder into soil form a fringe half a foot deep on the shore lines, often within a hand span of the running water. They can never make the journey to the water unless a gale perchance sweep them into it before the snow deepens. Their destiny is to form mountain soil, not to drift into the distant valley or the inland sea of preserving brine.

Mountain soil, the rich black loam of the lower foothills, made by scrub oak leaves dropped by thousands of autumns, is much sought by flower-gardeners, who excavate beside the trees wherever permitted to do so. The soils of the canyon creeksides are just as rich and desirable, although rotted for the most part from maple leaves, but rock strata are usually so near the surface that it is impractical to dig more than a few buckets-ful.

NOVEMBER 14

On the saline flats of Farmington bay the most conspicuous color is a single stemmed dock about two feet high with each leaf now a mass of about a hundred winged, heart-shaped seeds. The entire plant, which is burnt lake or claret brown, stands like an exclamation point on the dry-grassed shores of the springtime ponds.

There are several species of dock or sorrel in the Wasatch. Introduced from Europe and found about settlements, especially along irrigation ditches are the sheep sorrel (*Rumex acetosella*), a slender plant less than a foot high; the patience dock (*Rumex patientia*), two or three feet high, a weed of waste places; the yellow or curled dock (*Rumex crispus*) with smooth, erect stem two feet high; and the bitter dock (*Rumex obtusifolius*) with rough stem two feet long and membranous leaves.

The western dock (*Rumex occidentalis*) with smooth stout purple-tinged stems two to three feet high grows in the artemesia or sage brush belts of meadows and canyons. The Mexican dock (*Rumex mexicanus*), nearly two feet high, prefers mountain meadows; and *Rumex subalpinus* reaches even high places near spruces and aspens. The golden dock (*Rumex persicarioides*), a much-branched dock less than two feet high, likes the wet borders of lakes in the valleys and mountains. *Rumex maritimus athrix* chooses the fringes of saline ponds where it is often associated with that peculiar burro or pickle weed (*Allenrolfea occidentalis*), a fleshy member of the goosefoot family that has heretofore won our attention. The veined dock (*Rumex venosus*) is the pretty one with rose-colored valves that we have found growing along railroad tracks.

Drifting back from Farmington bay, having seen a hundred or more avocets and coots and a score of killdeers contentedly feeding, we pass a large flock of redwing blackbirds in some tall black willows and listen to them singing as vociferously as in spring.

NOVEMBER 15

The ways of nature are sometimes not only subtle but surprising. Just what causes certain mammals such as the weasel and birds like the white tailed ptarmigan (*Lagopus leucurus altipetens*) to turn white in winter? We mention the southern white-tailed ptarmigan because it delights in mountain peaks upwards of ten thousand feet, and should do well on Timpanogos as well as on the higher slopes of the Rockies at the east. It does not occur here. Why, then, do they turn white in winter? The answer, so far as the willow ptarmigan (*Lagopus lagopus*) in captivity is concerned has been given by Per Host (Auk,59:3). Extensive experiments conducted in Norway established the fact, that individual birds could be changed from dark to white or from white to dark, not in accordance with temperature, but in response to the hours of *light* they were allowed in their cages per day. This is a surprising discovery, one that we should like to see applied to mammals, which, we had thought, took on their luxuriant winter pelages solely as a result of increasing cold. Similar experiments could be applied to plants, a control hawthorn by one either denied the normal or given more than the normal light. However, "chlorophyll is life."

We speak of a "late spring", an "early spring" believing that either cold or warmth is responsible, perhaps not realizing that we mean less light, or more light. Yet in the wet spring of 1944 blooms were nearly a month behind time.

A thousand years could a naturalist ponder the ways of nature, and honestly say: "I do not know". Furthermore, nature is capable of giving almost anyone little thrills of joy. To one it might be the squeak of hard snow under foot or the sight of the first bluebird of spring; to another, the gorgeous autumnal coloring of a protected glade or the trail of a white-footed mouse in deep snow. Some are pleased by the view of a fine contented dairy herd in a meadow verged by high trees; others look with wonder upon a sunset over the Great Salt Lake. Such things are almost infinite in variety; but when you see a man reach down with his bare hand to feel rich loam and exclaim "Good old earth!" you will know that he is one of nature's favored children.

When in the moonlight we look at the darksome mountains and gaze upon the stars of the unfathomable firmament we ask ourselves: can it be that the universe, the earth, the canyon cliffs, the trees, aye even our own brains consist of exactly the same material — atoms composed of protons, electrons and neutrons that differ only in the number and arrangement of the particles? Is death but the cessation of activity in materials organized in one way? Ultimately in what does man differ from the stone?

NOVEMBER 16

Very early this November morning the upper Weber river is a scene of almost fantastic beauty: an inch of snow having just fallen, leaving the mountainsides freckled with snow and uncovered sage bushes, fields are white, but the course of the river is marked by huge cottonwoods delicately veiled in smoky white, as if unreal. The airy lace, which envelops them, is indeed ephemeral, for the warm sun of noon will dissipate it into steam.

Herds of cattle and some horses nibble about the sparsely stubbled fields, many of them seeking the partial cover of hawthorn groves growing along the river. Since their frosted coats are thick, they are apparently content.

Black-billed magpies (*Pica pica hudsonia*) fly about us with such even grace that, with their tails sticking out straight behind, they seem to be models from which great airplanes have been made, especially those called "flying fortresses".

A covey of quail scampers before us and then, as we reach once more the valley of the Great Salt Lake, two thousand feet lower in altitude, there in a big willow a hundred redwings are congregated, some of them singing despite the snow. We shall watch this place at the meadowed roadside, a vicinity so damp that its nocturnal fogs make it a notorious deathtrap for transcontinental speedsters. Fog indeed often characterizes the lofty Wasatch passes of the winter night, those dreary flats where mountain white-tailed hares stand like white muffs with reflecting beads for eyes.

There is something about November that we like: winds blow; snow falls intermittently; and it is just cold enough to invoke the home-loving spirit of man or beast. The lesson is, that nature is ruthless upon lack of preparation. Such birds as magpies and juncos are adapted to winter-rigors; but quail, tender, family-loving valley quail, are not indigenous here—they must fight snow unknown to their heritage, and cold entirely strange to their native habitat of California. Ring-necked pheasants, originating in China and other wintry places, survive the rigors of it all.

So expert are both quail and pheasants in the art of hiding among the thick dry weeds of irrigation embankments or in shrubbery that they lie still when the hunter all but brushes them as he tramps on by, but at the near sniff of a dog they flush in wild confusion, At that, a ring-necked pheasant is not nearly so difficult a shot as a quail.

A quail should be eaten the day after it is killed, and when the head and neck are removed and the wings clipped, it may be trussed easily. We know of nothing finer than the breasts on toast.

NOVEMBER 17

Numerous species of birds and animals hurry to the rescue of one of their number under attack, and, especially if it be young, cuddle and protect it until it is out of danger; they will even aid the crippled and the blind; but, so far as we know, they usually not only have little sympathy for sickness but actually sometimes take it as the excuse for cruelties and expulsion. Domestic chickens disdain a sick member and peck the comb of an injured one.

Elephants and geese aid their wounded companion to escape; but we have no record of their attitude toward sickness.

Many instances could be cited of the sympathetic consideration of the blind. Captain Stansbury found an old male pelican in the Great Salt Lake that was totally blind but fat and healthy, the obvious beneficiary of the kindness of his companions.

Though extremely solicitous of the safety of one of her brood in danger or some sort of predicament, the ordinary hen will stroll away from a chick too sick to chirp its remonstrance or to follow. Often indeed this is the only means of discerning that a chick is ill.

Sick wild animals and birds habitually isolate themselves in secluded nooks such as dense thickets, closely grown reed patches, and so on, where, reasonably free from danger, they calmly await the issue of life or death. Coyotes and wolves are ever alert to find such individuals and to take immediate advantage of the situation; in fact these intelligent predators are not only able to detect sickness when they see it but also to understand the difference between a man with and without a gun.

Though one may come upon innumerable illustrations of parental protection, the attitude of the adult bird or mammal towards sickness can be ascertained only by a great number of observers having in mind the recording of the fortuitous circumstances in the rare times when they occur.

The question arises: to what extent do the lower animals practice the ethical principles that had been thought to be peculiar to mankind? Why does a dolphin swim beneath a wounded companion and thus keep the stricken one above water until it can proceed on its own accord, if not as a result of a spirit of magnanimity? A lower mammal is not prompted by conscience to do such things. Is there an inspired conscience, or is moral conduct the result of experience only? We often ponder.

Throughout the world the rules of conduct, especially with respect to sexual relations, are so varied, inconsistent and incongruous that one wonders if after all conscience is but a matter of geography.

NOVEMBER 18

Some animals once fairly common in these mountains such as the grizzly, the otter, the wolf, the wolverine and the fox are now either extinct or rare. As the buffalo (*Bison bison*) in pre-Caucasian times ranged in most of the valleys of the Wasatch and even into the Humboldt river country of Nevada, remains taken from the caves north of the Great Salt Lake have proved that it was at one time even abundant there. That the climate is suitable is established by the fact that a few head placed on Antelope Island in Great Salt Lake over half a century ago have so increased without any assistance whatever that their numbers have to be depleted every few years, and this in feeding competition with herds of domestic sheep. Old Indians have reported that about the year 1820 there was a snowfall four feet deep in the Great Salt Lake district, a snow so deep that all the buffaloes were in one winter exterminated by it. That such a thing was possible we do not doubt, when we recall that we ourselves in the winter of 1916-17 walked on the snow over the top wire of valley fences, and for weeks roads were impassable. It is natural to suppose that bison would at such a time crowd into every available cave, and, becoming weaker and weaker, gradually starve.

It is not improbable that the horse had much to do with the extermination of the bison in the Wasatch. Investigations by such men as Steward and Wissler convince us that the horse reached the Ute Indians about the year 1730 from the Spaniards who introduced it to the region south of them; and that it did not arrive among the Blackfeet of Idaho until about twenty years later. With the horse as an aid, hunting the bison readily became a slaughter, for even the riflemen of the plains relied upon it to bring them to the very sides of their fleeing quarry. The root-digger Indians here were customarily so hard pressed for food that horses if available were used to the limit; but the red men were such a despised race with little to trade but their daughters, that horses never apparently became very numerous among them. Certainly the white trappers found them to be hungry and degraded, subsisting not on the meat of the hunt but on grasshoppers, roots, rabbits, snakes and other similar foods.

NOVEMBER 19

Deep snow is both a boon and a torment to wild life, a boon because it makes the inner spaces of spruces and firs almost as warm and habitable as stables, a torment because it buries grasses, nuts, seeds and other foods. When it freezes on its upper surface it is a distressing vexation indeed; for few birds can penetrate its glazed crust, and deer break through it in wearisome floundering, sometimes in their help-lessness being preyed upon by the golden eagle.

In these mountains perpetual snow occurs only on the north side of peaks rising to a height of ten thousand feet or more, such as Timpanogos (11,957); the equivalent of one thousand feet at the Arctic circle and seventeen thousand feet at the equator. Indeed, save for isolated and constantly shaded gulches, the Wasatch mountains are flowered in summer everywhere save in the timberless regions; and even there we find such plants as whitlow grass (*Draba uncinalis*), umbrella plant (*Erigonum neglectum*), a phacelia (*Phacelia alpina*) and an ivesia (*Ivesia utahensis*). Since we are unaware of any driveway in these mountains that traverses a region of ten thousand feet altitude, our chances of giving more than occasional study to these lofty but inspiring regions are quite remote.

Snow sometimes comes in great quantity in the silence of a night. This morning, for instance, it is over a foot deep in the valley, the valley where yesterday dahlias, marigolds, clematis, chrysanthemums, aye, even roses, seemed to enjoy a gentle rain.

Snow brings us such visitors as the western golden crowned kinglet, the northern shrike, the Bohemian waxwing, the Arctic towhee, the Montana junco, the pink-sided junco, the western tree sparrow (*Spizella arborea ochracea*), the gray-crowned leucosticte, the rare Merrill song sparrow (*Melospiza melodia merrilli*), the western evening grosbeak, the snowy owl, the lesser snow goose, the American golden eye and the red-breasted merganser; aye, even the uncommon snow bunting (*Pletrophenax nivalis nivalis*).

Few physical aspects distinguish the hardy bird from the tender one; nature seems willing to put an overcoat on all alike; but in the ability to find food birds and animals vary as do man. A black bear is as well coated to withstand cold as is a mountain lion, yet in deep snow one thrives, the other hibernates to prevent starvation.

Thousands of different snow prisms have been photographed; yet as they fall there outside the window they all have fluffiness, gentleness and charm.

NOVEMBER 20

Attracting wild birds with natural foods involves plenty of ground, though even the zinnias, sunflowers and asters of the small garden will furnish many a seedmeal if left where they bloomed. Our junipers, pines, birches, alder, boxelder, and mountain ash, all have seeds or nuts that the birds enjoy; but there is truly the problem of room in limited gardens.

Many shrubs and trees produce delicious berries that the birds like: elderberry, sumac, dogwood, hawthorn, trailing barberry, hackberry, Virginia creeper, and snowberry, for example, are all winter birdhavens.

The mulberry tree is the most attractive of all to summer birds, but quite useless in winter; for this reason one must plant a juniper, pyracanthus, mountain ash, Russian olive, or creeper, even a Boston ivy, to win feathered visitors when snow lies deep and cold. The fruit of the mountain ash is bitter, that of the twinberry unpalatable, and that of the baneberry even poisonous; but birds select by instinct as well as experience.

Bohemian waxwings so prefer frozen apples left on an orchard tree that one may be almost certain of their visitation in February if he possess such an attraction for them. Juncos like patches of dried weeds; chickadees peck about the winter maples; evening grosbeaks live for days in a single boxelder tree; and Lewis woodpeckers eat their stored acorns. Quail quickly respond to wheat scattered on the snow, while robins, flickers, English sparrows, house finches, kinglets, and Say phoebes seek the window box containing suet, raisins, wheat, peanuts, celery tips, lettuce leaves and so on. The truth is, a hungry bird in winter, whether it be by habit, granivorous, frugivorous or carnivorous, picine, passerine, pinicoline or oscine, gladly accepts almost anything edible you have to offer, especially if you enjoy its confidence.

English sparrows are naturally granivorous (seed-eaters); but necessity has made them pantophagous (all kinds of food); in fact as often as not nowadays one sees them both about the garbage can and in a busy swarm nipping the tender shoots of the winter lawn or pecking out the seeds of weeds.

Long-continued snow may even drive those dwellers of the high mountains, the Clark nutcrackers, down the canyons to your dooryard pine tree in the valley. Birds in distress are like people—they find food, but sojourn where they are wanted.

As we write, word arrives that two duck hunters lost in the blinding snow at the mouth of the Jordan saved their lives last night by huddling in the scant shelter of a muskrat home upstanding among the reeds.

NOVEMBER 21

Mill Creek canyon has always seemed to us comparatively steep and narrow, in fact, so bereft of mountain meadows and glades as to lack much interesting fauna and flora. We are aware that such is the stratigraphy of the Wasatch mountains that they are for variety almost unexcelled in all other America, offering as they do examples of every period and era except the Silurian; we are equally delighted with the pre-Cambrian formations and post-carboniferous intrusives of Little Cottonwood canyon; but in Mill Creek we discover no such variety of geologic history—merely carboniferous cliffs, mountainsides and boulders. Such things are almost beyond the ken of the naturalist; but when the demonstration is so unmistakable and clear he can but notice and ponder.

What we started to say, notwithstanding our geologic apostrophe, is, that this is a *narrow* canyon, so narrow that the Indians of this region once habitually drove deer and antelopes down it to the narrow defile at its mouth.

Without horses or guns the Indians of the Wasatch had to catch wild mammals by trap or strategy. They held almost festival rabbit drives at the north end of Great Salt Lake, where they formed great Vs of sage brush, and drove the bunnies to their club-armed squaws.

Likewise, many suckers ("pahgar") and speckled trout "mpahger") were taken on Utah lake; and on the Bear river, where the suckers were called "auwok" and the trout "tsapankw". Deer were driven over cliffs wherever suitable topography prevailed; antelopes were hunted along the Bear river flats; and squaws habitually turned water into gopher holes to force those rodents into their nets.

The canyon is misty today. A cloud is merely vapor of water which an already saturated atmosphere cannot absorb, hence the vapor passes into the state of small vesicles, assuming a definite shape and having movement. Mist, though not much different from a cloud, is on the other hand motionless and really the transformation of the vapor of water from the visible to the invisible. It consists of small opaque bodies of water the molecules of which are grouped in the form of hollow spherules; and they do not scintillate in light as do drops of water. All of these wonders are apparent with the aid of magnifying glasses. However, seldom are we troubled for long with mist and fog.

> Expect a storm, but calmly rest awhile—
> 'Tis seldom clouds remain within this sky—;
> And so in life there often comes a smile
> When our foreboding told of but a sigh.

NOVEMBER 22

November days are often as tranquil and balmy as those of early September. As we ramble over the fields, yellowed with dry grass, we frequently come upon beautifully formed cattails (*Typha latifolia*), the dense cylindrical terminal spikes of which are not only the color of chamois but also actually almost indistinguishable in texture from it as we touch them. The stems are raw sienna color, very tough and strong. Some of the spikes are bursting and casting into every breeze their tiny parachutes, about seventeen silky white hairs a quarter of an inch long from the uniting point of which dangles on a quarter-inch yellowish stem a yellow seed scarcely longer than the width of a pen point and with a brownish tail a quarter of an inch long. One cattail must contain a hundred thousand or so of these almost infinitesimal seed parachutes, thus assuring the propagation of this plant wherever suitable marshy water abounds. If any thing more efficient for its purpose grows hereabout, we do not recall it at the moment.

Existing all over North America except in the extreme north, the broad leaved cattail has acquired many names, such as: Great-reed mace, cat-o'-nine-tail, marsh beetle, marsh pestle, cat-tail flag, flax-tail, blackamoor, black-cap, bulls-egg, bubrush, watertorch, and candlewick. Locally we have not heard any other name than cat-tail; and though we have been favored with much information concerning the pioneer life of this region, we have never heard of the use of the cat-tail as a candlewick. Perhaps pioneers did not realize that it is equal to any wicking they might have had. Nor did they tell of the use of these airy parachutes to fill their pillows, notwithstanding that nothing more soft and downy could be imagined. Duck and chicken feathers apparently were the reliance for the downy bed, which, to tell the truth, was more often made of straw. We are wondering if a myriad of these wee parachutes would not under the compression of a pillow resent their crowding and sog down into stubborn solidity.

We watch a solitary duck hunter wade toward a reeded island of Farmington bay, where for thirty days now no water bird of any kind has dared to venture; and we wonder if this duck-hunting business, especially on a clear warm day, is not after all a psychological relief and diversion, from let us say, children. Then, again, every man likes to feel, now and again, that he is a wild, indomitable character, ready to face death, or whatnot to test his mettle. It matters little, that in the Wasatch there is little danger—man's instinct is to face danger and overcome, to conquer even though but psychologically. The most dangerous of all are automobiles; but man loves to feel that in the woods he is close to that indescribable thing, danger. The most dangerous mammal is the bull in his own barnyard; the most deadly of all animals is the black widow spider in his own cellar.

NOVEMBER 23

Upon observing a medium-sized cougar brought in by a hunter today, we are prompted to make some comparisons of it with the African lion and leopard. We have before us two photographs, made at our request at equal distances; one of the skull of the largest cougar killed by Theodore Roosevelt in Colorado, the other of the skull of his largest African lion. The African specimen has enormous comparative strength and size. His Colorado cougar (*Felis hippolestes*) weighed 227 pounds and measured 8 feet in a straight line from the nose tip to the end of the tail vertebrae of the unskinned animal.

N. Hollister reports that the largest African lion (*Felis leo nyanzae*) in the U. S. National Museum measured approximately 9 feet 8½ inches; and that Col. Roosevelt and his son Kermit killed males of this species weighing 410 pounds and 412 pounds respectively. "Both of these animals were thin". Our conclusion is, that, even with its comparatively longer tail, the cougar averages about a foot and a half less in total length than the African lion, which is, furthermore, almost double its weight. A cougar can bring down a grown horse; an African lion, a mature buffalo; so there is little difference in weight between their heaviest victims.

The largest African leopard (*Felis pardus suahelica*) in the U. S. National Museum is likewise reported by Mr. Hollister to have a total length of 2160 mm, (approximately seven feet tip to tip). In his "African Game Trails" Roosevelt gives the weight of an old female leopard he encountered as 126 pounds. Every leopard he killed charged and recharged with such courage and ferocity that he was compelled to marvel that an animal very little more than half the size of a cougar should be incomparably more harmful. All of our reading of the experiences of such great African hunters as Selous and Carl Akeley convinces us that the African mammals most dangerous to man are the lion, elephant, buffalo, rhinoceros and leopard, and that few agree on which is the most formidable. Probably the most men have been killed by the lion and the leopard, in that order, though this is merely our own conclusion from extensive reading.

The cougar destroys wapiti and horses far greater in weight than the monkeys and such other animals that constitute the leopard's fare; furthermore, the cougar manifests almost incredible strength in carrying its victims. Why before man it should be a coward and the leopard a very devil of ferocity, is difficult to understand; nevertheless, for diabolical brutality nothing we know of could equal our wolverine, which is about the size of a bull dog.

NOVEMBER 24

During autumn and winter there are many more signs of life on the marshes of the valleys than in the snow-laden mountains. In the canyons one sees chickadees, long-crested jays, juncos, and occasionally the tracks of deer, coyotes, mountain lions and mice, seldom anything more, but in the meadows and frozen sloughs aquatic migrants as well as resident hawks and owls always attract the eyes. Excepting deer and rodents, wild mammals have become so scarce that often we go an entire season without remarking any one of them, notwithstanding that we usualy trudge the paths of every large canyon. To illustrate: though the type specimen of the western red fox (*Vulpes fulva macroura*) was taken by Baird in 1852 on the foothills above Salt Lake City, and though a kit fox (*Vulpes velox velox*) was trapped several years ago at the mouth of the Jordan, it would be a lucky day indeed for us to come upon any fox at all, whether in valley or hill. The badger used to be common; now it has almost disappeared. No animals can long survive guns, traps, and poison; and the disconcerting phase about it all is that even some competent mammalogists fail to see the wisdom of a balance in nature. The grizzly has gone, and, fools that we are, we are gradually exterminating the black bear.

We have known many woodsmen in our time, men who slept in sheep wagons or beside the stolid burro, men who brought back the hides of grizzly, wolf or cougar, men who had read the Bible through many times in their loneliness; but they are no more. Gone are most of the larger predators; and the habitations of herders have the comforts of summer encampments. Where are the martens, the minks and the wolverines; where are the foxes and the wolves? Where are the bobcats and the lynxes—all of them animals that in early days made conversation in ranch house and village? But the tiny forms of life—worm, insect, fungi—increase almost beyond every control, for their enemies have departed.

It is often difficult, however, to understand just what factors determine the well-being of a given species. Consider for a moment that outstanding kingbird that we have always known as the Arkansas flycatcher (*Tyranus verticalis*), often called the "western" though that common name is more applicable to *Empidomax difficilis difficilis*. (By the way, why cannot ornithologists leave alone those common names that are often more parmanent than the scientific ones?) This Arkansas flycatcher for no apparent reason is gradually extending eastward; indeed where fifty years ago it was a rare straggler along the Atlantic coast it is now not uncommon. We have always understood this bird was so named because it was taken on the headwaters of the Arkansas river in the mountains of Colorado by Long's Expedition in 1823, and the name has no reference to the state.

NOVEMBER 25

Like a finger extending south from a great northern biogeographic palm, the Wasatch mountain range with its lofty altitudes and low temperatures, when compared with the valleys and basin lowlands, affords an extended habitat for some northern avian and mammalian forms, which otherwise, would not venture near the region of parched desert, greasewood and spine.

Thus in writing of the wolverine (*Gulo luscus*) some mammalogists scarcely mention the occurrence of this weird and large mustelid south of Canada, yet we have records of its having been seen on Mt. Baldy, Piute county; Boulder mountain, Garfield county; and, even a year or so ago, on Henrys mountain, southern Utah.

The marten (*Martes caurina origenes*) is likewise a mustelid of the great northern wooded region, yet it does inhabit the high coniferous forests of the Wasatch as well, and apparently is increasing in number.

The Canada lynx (*Lynx canadensis canadensis*) is, as its name implies, an inhabitant of the cold Canadian forests, yet it does occur sparingly throughout the Wasatch. At one time it was not uncommon, as many as half a hundred being killed for bounty in one year; but it is rarely seen now. By the way, that word "lynx" comes from the Greek *lygx*, meaning lynx, but the allusion is likely to its bright eyes, from the Greek *lyxnos,* lamp. One must not overlook the Greek word *leyeeo,* to look, as the animal not only appears to stare but also can see well at night.

The snowshoe rabbit (*Lepus americanus bairdii*), which occurs throughout Canada and the frozen north does inhabit the high coniferous forests of the entire Wasatch.

One thinks of the northern flying squirrel (*Glaucomys sabrinus lucifugus*) as likewise a mammal of the algid north, yet specimens have been taken from one end of the Wasatch to the other.

In like manner some birds would not be in Utah if it were not for the Wasatch and Uintah mountains, which offer a continuation of the coniferous woods and high altitudes to which they are accustomed in the north. The alpine three-toed woodpecker (*Picoides tridactylus dorsalis*), for instance, which we have found at 8,000 feet at the top of Farmington canyon, chooses only the high pine forests that only lofty mountains can bestow.

Clark's nutcracker (*Nucifraga columbiana*) a bird that has the bill of a crow and the soft gray body of a pigeon, resides in the high mountains from British Columbia to New Mexico; and we ourselves have observed it from Logan canyon southward to Marysvale, always in the higher pines.

If in some incredulous scheme of transmigration we should have to become a bird, we might hope to be a nutcracker—it is carefree, it lives on pine nuts, and inhabits high altitudes, places of pure cold air, far above the smoke, din and avarice of man.

NOVEMBER 26

Many years ago before Thanksgiving day it was the custom in the villages of these valleys, to hold turkey-shoots in anticipation of that festive occasion; but none could have been more interesting than that just described to us by a codger of the time. Being smarter than most of the other boys of the town, and having an English friend who had stored several bottles of homemade red currant or "bunch" wine, he ·purchased a score of turkeys, a lot of the wine, and, having advertised, went to an open field to put on the contest. While stationing the turkeys behind their embankments so that only their heads showed, he liberally passed the wine around; and having indulged in much preliminary measurements and so forth, finally gave the order to shoot at ten cents a try. By ʰthat time the contestants were half groggy frᵒᵐ the wine, cheerful, hopeful, and uncertain in their aim, and, furthermore, becoming more shaky as the shooting continued. The result was that turkeys which had cost him six cents a pound fell to the bullets at an average of thirty cents a pound, which, above the wine, gave him fifty dollars profit for the day.

Wild turkeys did not occur in these mountains; hence at Thanksgiving the residents usually relied upon chickens, beef and pork, though not infrequently rabbits, venison, bear meat, and grouse appeared on the holiday board. These together with dried corn, potatoes, dried fruits and pumpkin were the edibles available ·in that canless age. The pumpkins had in the fall usually been cut into rings and dried on a pole, for in the earliest days flies were unknown. The truth is, first settlers were so scattered and poor that the only holiday they observed for many years was the Fourth of July, which came at a convenient time for assemblage at a bowery and for outside games.

In Thanksgiving there is such deeper significance than the mere physical enjoyment of a plethora of foods that one is impelled to express gratitude for the privilege of living without pain too much to endure.

> No ailment long withholds the heart from joy,
> For peace and love reside within the mind:
> The body may with many aches annoy,
> But sweetest thoughts will always solace find.

NOVEMBER 27

With grateful hearts for health, happiness, and the bounties of life we partake of a turkey dinner, and with a comfort enhanced by softly falling snow seen through the windows, we seat ourselves before the hearth, merrily flaring with a sweet-scented balsam-log. Our little group includes a naturalist, poet, botanist, banker, lawyer, business man; old timers and young timers—men, women, children, all contented friends.

The very plentitude of good food, mild wines, fragrant tobaccos, nuts and sweetmeats, many of them from distant lands, the choicest, indeed, of every country and clime, induces the oldtimers to cogitate on the contrast between now and the days of yore, between the days of television and the days of the candle.

One, glancing at the shining oak floors, observed: "I can remember when we used skim milk for floor wax"; and that caused the memories to be spoken in an apparently endless chain.

"Yes, and I can recall when we had straw for padding under the carpets", replied another.

"And straw bed-ticks", put in one of the ladies.

"My mother used to send me to the sloughs at the mouth of the Jordan for cat tails ;we filled the pillows with the down", said another lady, who was born when Theodore Roosevelt was President.

One of the older women venturerd the observation that when she was a girl she would moisten red crepe paper and rub it on her cheeks as a rouge, and that corn starch was the only face powder she knew at that time.

One of the men spoke up: "The first tooth brush I ever saw was a piece of cloth sprinkled with salt and soda".

"Well, I used mutton tallow to water-proof my boots", put in the naturalist.

"We made soap out of grease and lye—I can remember cutting it into blocks for my mother", said the poet.

"And we made caps and gloves from muskrat pelts", observed one of the men.

So the conversation went on, it appearing that in the days of yore oak leaves were used as a dye for tanning; chewing gum came from squaw berry; sage tea was brushed on the hair to darken it; egg was rubbed in the hair for dandruff: arnica blossom in alcohol made a medicine for sores, and sage tea was a physic.

The general conclusion is that there is always a way if the heart is happy.

The query arises: has America already entered the decadent period of plentitude? Is our luxury, the highest standard of living ever known, slowly taking us down mentally, physically and morally? We look at yonder snow-bound hill, where ski jumps are made, and ask why do Europeans hold the records? The answer comes—they walk where we ride, and their muscles respond.

NOVEMBER 28

The old botanist, noteworthy for his researches on several genera, is always welcome, especially when it is cold outdoors but cosy and comfortable before the balsam-logged hearth. His beliefs are latitudinarian, his knowledge encyclopaedic; his home life, that of an erudite man with leisure to devote to his vocation.

Just for the fun of it we pursue the meanings of scientific botanical names. "Oenothera", designating the evening primrose, is from the Greek "wine-scenting", since the roots were once used for that purpose. "Cornus", the dogwood, is from the Greek "horn" because of the toughness of its wood.

"Asclepias", the milkweed, is dedicated to Aesculapius, the Roman god of medicine. The morning glory's name "Convolvulus" means in Latin, "roll together", and "Phlox"' the wild Sweet William' means "flame" in Greek. Our puccons or Indian paints of the borage family get their designation, "Lithosperum', from the Greek "stone-seed" on account of their hard nutlets.

The mint family's "Teucrium" is from the Trojan king "Teucer", mentioned by Plutarch in his account of Alcibiades. "Agastache", the giant hyssop, means many spikes.

Our beautiful "penstemon" is Greek meaning "five stamens"; "mimulus", the monkey flower, is Latin, a diminutive actor.

"Collinsia" or blue-eyed Mary is named from Zaccheus Collins, botanist of Philadelphia (1764-1831) just as Castilleja, the Indian paint brush, is in honor of a Spanish botanist, Castillejo. Lonicera, the honeysuckle likewise commemorates the name of Adam Lonitzer, a German botanist (1528-1586). While we are on proper names, we may as well mention that the "cone flower", (*Rudbeckia*) are named in honor of Claus Rudbeck, a Swedish botanist (1630-1702); and the sage brush (*Artemesia*) commemorates Artemisia, wife of Mausolus.

We rest awhile, poke the logs, and then go on.

"Galium" of the bed-straws is Greek for "milk" because one of this species was used for curdling. Cichorium (Chicory) is Arabic for "blue-sailors"; Chrysopsis (golden aster) means in Greek "looks golden".

"Solidago" of the golden rod is "To make whole (Gr); "aster", a star (Gr); "erigeron", very old (Gr), because this daisy has an early hoary pappus.

"Senecio" of the squaw weeds is Latin ("senex") for old man, and "Cirsium" of the thistles is so named because the thistles were once used for swollen veins.

Men have ambition to be this and to be that, but one thing never fails in its tranquil sweetness—the storehouse of a mind rich with garnered facts—; for even when the body fails to perform as once it did such a mind exemplifies the youthfulness of eternity.

NOVEMBER 29

On Lost Creek, a tributary of the Weber, we today come upon a dam constructed by that most energetic and ingenious of wild mammals, the beaver (*Castor canadensis frondator*), properly called the Sonoran or broad-tailed beaver. Having seen the fresh workings of this interesting animal on Goosebery Creek and about the headwaters of the Logan, Weber and Provo rivers, we conclude that like the bison under the encouragement of protection it has passed the crisis of near extermination.

Though beavers sometimes cut down conifers, especially lodge pole pines, quaking aspens are their principal food in these mountains. No aspen is too big for them to fell; indeed the chips they strew are at least equal in size to those cut by a man with a dull axe.

The function of the beaver's broad tail is still in doubt. It is not a trowel for plastering mud on a dam; and it is not the instrument of propulsion when the animal is swimming, notwithstanding that it may occasionally steer the way or assist in turning. Not only are the beaver's hind feet webbed but also the second hind toe is double, and thus the hind feet need no assistance when the animal is swimming. The tail does, however, aid in making the loud flop-signal of danger, and in providing support during cutting operations. An old trapper named Henry Lambert told Edward R. Warren that a pet young beaver used to sit with its tail under and in front of it, and thus used it as a table on which to place its food. Since beavers are nocturnal and much of their activity is either in their lodges and caverns or beneath the water's surface, observation of them in action is difficult; but their dams and canals are alone sufficient to mark them as mammals blessed with the spark of intelligence. Their companions are watersnakes, trout, and frogs; their enemies, coyotes, mountain lions, and lynxes; but their clear watered ponds are usually places of sylvan beauty where juncos chip in winter and warblers sing in summer.

The old prospector told us that once, being impelled by hunger to eat a beaver, he was surprised that its flesh tasted like pork. Certainly this rodent's food—water lily roots, bark, leaves and berries—is clean enough, but most trappers agree that the flesh of the porcupine, which subsists on tender shoots and leaves, is superior. Some woodsmen hereabout prefer the mountain lion to either; so there is no accounting for differences in men's tastes.

NOVEMBER 30

In the quietude of night, a deep snow having fallen, the morning is a surprise of whiteness and winter; in fact, it is all so solemn and impressive that it inspires reverence for the night that so easily brought it to us. We marvel that the vast blanket of snow, which later may tear away even habitations with its floods, can descend with such fluttering gentleness that the hush of darkness is not disturbed for sensitive ears. One stands with awe in the silence of a tomb, and there is something of the same mysterious and almost uncanny power in the hush of a morning heavily clad with fresh snow.

We spend the afternoon in traversing that oak-verdured region extending for five or six miles south of the canyon mouth of the Weber river, a region filled with the sweet memories of romance and adventure, a vicinity still more or less wild despite the constant passage of vehicles along a paved highway. We detour through a by-road, one of those farm-lanes infrequently used. Before us flushes a male ring-necked pheasant, which our eyes caught hopping before it rose. One of its legs is broken, perhaps healed and permanently lamed, for it flutters its wings rapidly as it alights among the distant trees. Perhaps a month ago one leg was almost shot away during that daytime of apprehension among pheasants known by hunters as the "open season". Hardy bird, it seems better adapted to survive than any other game importation! We often wonder what would happen if some elephants from lofty Mount Kenya in Africa were transported to this region. Do we want an exotic fauna?

We wait but a few minutes, when a mountain blue bird several times flies from a field post to the roadway and back again, its black bill, blue upper parts and gray undersides being as pronounced as unmistakable. Remarkable bird! We recall having taken it here once in February.

A magpie flies by. Its white belly and wing patches are as conspicuous as ever but its black parts are of extraordinary beauty; its crown is glossed with bronzy green; its back is bluish green; its wing coverts are metallic green. One of us with binoculars, one without, catch these hues; and we deeply admire this handsome bird.

As if it were an avian criminal the magpie is accounted stealthy, elusive, wily and cruel; yet why should we condemn a bird for being resourceful and smart; why censure it for the ability to withstand hot summer suns and freezing blizzards; why look down upon it because it devours everything from carrion to young birds and even pecks at the sore backs of cattle? Should not any animal that manifests great survival capability win our admiration rather than our scorn? To keep his place in nature man does not hesitate to kill and eat other animals of his choice. Why should not a bird do likewise?

360

DECEMBER 1

As winter's white robe mantles peak, ridge and canyon the scarcity of animal life becomes apparent in the trackless pathway. Over there beneath that hillside boulder is the den of a golden mantled marmot that in summer whistled at our approach, a rather rare sight for us in the Wasatch. His burrow is deep, probably fifteen feet or more, choked with snow and dry grass behind which he sleeps in almost lifeless torpidity. The period of hibernation is unknown, though October through February apparently approximates it, notwithstanding that restless individuals may be about in both November and February. Weather, of course, has some influence upon all hibernation but food and the pangs of hunger may alter many schedules. A dry fall may make grass, tender leaves and soft seeds very scarce, as it has this autumn, and thus an animal such as a marmot may not accumulate its ordinary pre-hiberation fat; bad weather and natural drowsiness gradually force it into winter sleep; but it may feel an untimely urge for food again and reappear before its habitual time. All this, however, is conjecture, as we have naught but occasional unexpected winter appearances to substantiate our conclusion.

The desert harvest mouse (*Reithrodontomys megalotis megalotis*), which inhabits ditch banks and slough borders west of the Wasatch acclivities, apparently does not hibernate at all, as it subsists on weed seeds and grain and shows no evidence of autumnal fattening. Very often in the mountains in winter we come upon the snow-trail of a deer mouse (*Peromyscus maniculatus rufinus*) but these little fellows must be nocturnal, as we never see them during the day. The pocket gopher (*Thomomys talpoides wasatchensis*) is busy all winter, for as soon as the snow melts away its earthen burrows are exposed like black ropes, the evidence of winter activity above ground, from root to root, but beneath the snow.

It gives one a creepy feeling to discover that a cougar is following one's trail in the snow. Fortunately for the nerves the presence of the lurking animal is usually unknown to the walker in the hills, but it may appear with startling realization if his downward path by a different route chance to intercept his upward footprints. Even though one understand thoroughly the cowardly nature of the brute those big saucerlike pads are fearful and uncanny.

How deathly silent the snow-mounded woodlands seem! But listen! Over there is the soft gurgle of the ice-marged creek, still bounding down its rocky canyon way; and there, at the pool of a linn, a water ouzel is singing its sweet chansonette as if the mossy embankment were bedecked with the dog-toothed violets of spring. What a bird—to utter a tender capriccietto from a floating cake of ice!

DECEMBER 2

Many years' observations of bird life in these mountains of several life-zones prove to us that nearly a hundred species from time to time occur here in the very midst of winter, some of them resident like the grouse, quail and ring-necked pheasant, some of them migrants from places more burdened with snow.

Among the winter-water birds we may mention the not uncommon whistling swan, Canada goose, mallard, baldpate, pintail, green-winged teal, redhead, canvasback, lesser scaup duck, American golden eye, hooded merganser, Virginia rail and Wilson snipe, as either usually or occasionally inhabiting the winter sloughs, while the ring-billed gull may ordinarily be keeping them company. Some of these we have mentioned in November; many of them like the canvasback as actually breeding here.

Among the winter-hawks we should include the Eastern goshawk, the sharp-shinned, Cooper's, the sparrow, the western red-tailed, and the marsh; and among the owls, the barn, the great basin screech owl, the Montana horned, the western burrowing, the short-eared, the snowy and long-eared. If the Western goshawk occurs here it has thus far successfully avoided us.

Of the woodpecker family the red-shafted, Lewis, Rocky mountain hairy, Rocky mountain downy, and the rare alpine three-toed of high altitudes are present throughout the year, though one may go many a season without seeing some of them.

Likewise we may depend any day upon sighting the magpie, the desert horned lark, the raven, Clark's nutcracker, the long-tailed and the mountain chickadee, the gray titmouse (*Parus inornatus ridgwayi*) and the water ousel—it all depends upon where we are, among the high conifers where snow is deep, or out in the duck-sloughs where blizzards blow.

Robins, mountain blue birds, meadow-larks, redwings and Brewer blackbirds, are here usually despite the deepest snow; indeed, as we write this, we have just returned from a sheep-feeding ranch on the Jordan river a mile or so from its mouth, where a flock of a thousand Brewer and redwing blackbirds were enjoying themselves in and about the corrals.

Every winter we see Western evening grosbeaks in snow-flecked boxelder trees and Bohemian wax-wings in sweet-mannered flocks of lovely color. Likewise the gray crowned rosy finch or leucosticte (*Leucosticte tephrocotis tephrocotis*) swarms among snow-blown foothill weeds, being more common than the Hepburn (*Leucosticte tephrocotis littoralis*) or the black rosy finch (*Leucosticte atrata*) with which it associates. Northern pine siskins, Shufeldt's and gray headed juncos, Bendire's crossbills, pale goldfinches, and mountain song sparrows— sweet indeed are our memories of these winter birds, some rare, some plentiful, all interesting and pleasing.

DECEMBER 3

A soft, exquisite song in December! It is almost incredible, yet there is the bird, perched on a juniper and undeterred by the vast snow of the whitened foothills. It is a gray-bodied bird, two inches longer, we should say, than a mountain bluebird; a bird with a white eye-ring and white tail-sides; even with some buffy on its wings; a bird with the pose of a Say's phoebe or even a sage thrasher—it is a Townsend's solitaire (*Myadestes townsendi townsendi*), perhaps the sweetest of visitors with the winter snow. We have records of its occurrence here from November to April, though we are fully aware that it merely descends from high to low, as it were; for its breeding locale is the chill peak of the lofty mountain range.

We have long been interested in this demure but delightful bird, not only on account of its dulcet "pink" note and exquisite song of winter but also the ornithological difficulties that have attended it. When we first became acquainted with it in a Wasatch canyon, it was classified as one of the *Ampelidae* or chatterers, close relative of the waxwings; but even then its relationship to the thrushes was strongly indicated. Now it is, indeed, one of the *Turdidae,* cousin of the robin, the hermit thrush and the bluebird; but it nests in altitudes above those of these mountains and favors us with its presence only in winter. Its song is rapid and warbled; but the extraordinary thing about it, as we see it today, is, that there is a song at all on these bleak and snow-mounded hills.

We should like to read a thesis on why some birds deliberately choose high altitudes for their homes. We ourselves love the clarity of atmosphere, the loneliness, aye the feeling of the nearness of diety, of higher altitudes; we cherish the utter disregard of monetary consideration in the sweet proximity of a mountain-crested pine; but what of the birds? The answer is, of course, neither philosophic nor sentimental; it is—the higher the altitude the fewer the enemies. Food may be plentiful below; but enemies lurk there too. Our admiration is greatest for those birds that endure the blizzard-hissed peaks and darksome conifers of winter.

> Where lofty peaks abide in heavens blue,
> And clouds as well as forests lie below,
> The birds and mammals thereabout are few,
> For only brave ones cope with wind and snow.

DECEMBER 4

In comfort and warmth one finds December in these mountains a joyful experience, for what matters it if the wind whistles with blizzardly sting through burdened conifers and at noon water drips from icicles several feet long—when the hearth is aglow and food is plentiful?

To many people December has always been forbidding. In 1573 Tusser wrote

"O dirtie December
For Christmas remember".

Wraxall mentioned it as "cold and piercing"; and in a letter to Mrs. Dunlop, Burns complained, "I am in a complete Decemberish humour, gloomy, sullen, stupid". Sterne wrote: "In the many bleak and Decemberly nights of a seven years widowhood".

If one have health, happiness, and comfort, December, or any other month as far as that is concerned, is a matter of mood. If one be joyous the long-crested jay is a bit of heaven flying about the pines; if he be depressed, it is a squawking member of the crow family. So it is throughout life—external things reflect our will to be happy or miserable.

December, however, has much appeal to the aesthetic eye: hoar frost, for instance, the most beautiful form of crystallization, appears on misty mornings when the temperature is below freezing; and it adorns twigs, branches and grass with a delicate lace of icy dew, giving the landscape an aspect of both severity and melancholy. This exquisite embroidery is quickly dissipated by the warm rays of the late morning sun.

On Farmington bay it is as calm and warm as a day in September. notwithstanding that the distant atmosphere is hazy. Dry grass is sea foam yellow, almost white; and great docks in the sloughs are columns of maroon. We see marsh hawks, Brewer blackbirds, killdeers, gulls and lesser scaup ducks, nothing more, except a gas-bubbled hole with standing water the color of old blood. We decide upon the mountains.

As we descend Parley's canyon in the late afternoon we are entranced by the western sky, which is grey except for a stratum of burnished gold. This marvelous layer of color is vivid behind the canyon walls, which are maculated with snow and oak patches. What a wondrous sight down a canyon—a grey western sky ribboned with glowing gold!

Do I sublimate nature until it becomes an apotheosis, or do I recognize it to be reality entirely removed from the carnalty, avarice, dissension, and epicurism of man? There can be no greatness in a crowd.

DECEMBER 5

Many of the greatest men in history have found happiness in secluded woods and brook-sung places of pastoral beauty. If winter drove them away they longed for return in spring.

Virgil, greatest of Latin poets, was never quite contented away from his country home near Nola in Italy. The Roman poet Horace, whom Virgil loved, so yearned for a place in the country that he penned an imaginary picture of it:

"My prayers with this I used to charge—
A piece of land not very large,
Wherein there should a garden be,
A clear spring flowing ceaselessly,
And where, to crown the whole, there should
A patch be found of growing wood".

The prayers of Horace were answered when his friend Maecenas presented him with just such a place. It consisted of woodland, meadows and arable land thirty miles from Rome, his "Sabine farm", where to this day a sweet spring flows as copiously as when Horace described it. When kept away from his beloved farm he longed for it, as witness his words:

"When, when shall I the country see,
Its woodlands green—oh, when be free . . .

Both Virgil and Horace were bachelors, a fact that we mention not in disparagement of marriage, for on his country estate Sir Walter Scott wrote his novels almost literally with children on his knee, but to show that the woods have their appeal whether or not one be alone. For sheer loneliness Thoreau's Walden Pond must be highly considered, unless we accord first prize to my poet-friend, the late Alfred Lambourne, who, in utter solitude actually for a year homesteaded that deserted rock in the Great Salt Lake known as Gunnison Island and there wrote "Pictures of an Inland Sea".

But to animadvert to our theme: That amazing master of rhetoric, Marcus Tullius Cicero, apparently did his best work in the quietude of the country, at least as far as his philosophic essays are concerned.

To appreciate the wildwoods in all their mystery and beauty one must disassociate himself from thought of either personal ambition or aggrandizement, and strive for the unfoldment of truth; for such portions of it as are there revealed to him make him conjecture on the cause of it all. Be it winter or summer, autumn or spring, in the mountains or on the plains, every square yard of them shows some form of life that the genius of ages has yearned to comprehend.

If you would be happy learn to depend upon the joys of your own cultivated mind, rich in its store of knowledge and eager always to fathom new mysteries of nature and life. People sometimes fail you, and often thwart your cherished ambitions; but, if your happiness is never anchored to them, they cannot hurt you, whatever they do.

DECEMBER 6

A blizzard makes the path from this isolated cabin door to the yet gurgling brook a pleasant adventure. It is stinging, frigid, sweeping, hissing. The word "blizzard" is onomatopoetic, in fact an American's description of the sounds—the blasts, blusters and zeeing tings.

Somehow we delight in winter-camping, for notwithstanding their vesture of snow the firs and spruces under it are actually as green as the sheltered mountain hedge along the brook-borders. The trailing barberry has color—wine, brown, red, green—but it snugg'es beneath snow and awaits the surprise of one's trail-making foot to reveal its freshness and beauty. There it is beside the blizzard swept trailway, reminder of Christmas holly, a lesson in resistance, vigor and fortitude. We have never feared solitude, for it affords a grand opportunity for one's mind to express its deepest capabilities.

Winter here is always an adventure of climatic change, for it makes no compromise with summer, no attempt to intermingle with spring. Its flora and fauna must either accommodate themselves to temperatures of one hundred to zero or abandon the struggle in migration or death. It welcomes the hardy feathers of the algid north.

We like a blizzard despite its sting, its cold, its solemn warning of stillness and death; we like it because it challenges our stamina and leads and drives towards a sleep as treacherous as mild. Resistance is nature's insignia of perfection, whether it be from heat, thirst, starvation or cold. The trees withstand it; the birds avoid it, the animals sleep beneath its snow, yet ever are there hardy ones to whom the blizzard is but a daily experience—the juncos who eat seeds within its blasts; the great white owls which skim its snow waves in hungry eagerness; and the cougar which pads over its crusted surfaces to claw and fang a spruce-gladed deer.

Nature is not only heartless but indifferent; it establishes rules and quickly destroys those who disobey them. It starts man and bug on a course of living, with an injunction against disobedience, a warning native and instinctive against poison, disease and climatic change; but it also says woe to him who heeds not.

What bothers us at times is, that in all this intricate arrangement of nature man seems not to be higher in its regard than the wee chickadee calling on the seeded maple of yonder wayside. I do not like a godless fortuity, yet in the yearning of my heart I am compelled to wonder.

DECEMBER 7

Scant is the raiment of snow: weeds protrude in ragged nakedness; and branches stick out leafless and rimy. Snuggling sparrows fluff in interspaces of the backyard creeper and beneath the nooky eaves, as the day closes with the lustrous tints of chalcedony.

One of the most inspiring sights of a Wasatch winter is the clear sky of night after a day of purifying snow. Its diaphaneity is at once fathomless and incomprehensible, and in it the ordinary opalescence becomes a soft violaceous blue, a blue solemn and infinite. The high mounds of clouds, peak-overhanging, possess a radiant, incomparable whitness; the stars stud the heavens with an argentine glow; and the moon, ordinarily aureate, gleams like a ball of phosphorescent silver. All the former smoke, soot, and atmospheric dirt, now lie beneath the earth's covering of snow, as if a celestial broom had cleansed the firmament of an unwelcome defilement.

It is always so in the declining days of the year, when only juncos and an occasional magpie show themselves where scrub oak trees are bare and male willows display their reddish color.

But look! We come to another day and tarry for the afternoon in the vicinity of the Jordan, at a ranch where sheep, horses and cattle are fed. There a swarm of blackbirds chatter about the meadowed stackyard. Our estimate is a thousand Brewer and a thousand red-wings, congregated not exactly together but at least in proximity. First a hundred Brewers arise from the very groundside of the sheep; and then, as if expecting us to shoot when really we only honk, a thousand red-wings arise from the adjoining weed-land. Nearby is a strawstack, a wheat field, in fact all around are those willowed and meadowed environments these members of the crow family enjoy. Some of the Brewers are chasing as if in the erotic enthusiasm of spring. The answer is: wherever in the animal kingdom there is food and comfort, there also is joy.

This is not a land of continuous cold like the frozen stretches of Alaska and Canada, but one of freeze and thaw; in other words, no matter how bleak and frigid the night, usually, if clear, the next day is so warm that icicles drip and fall, barnyard manure piles steam, sparrows fight in mimic fray, and tender blades of grass uptrude beside the melting snow in front of the rocky garden wall.

DECEMBER 8

It is interesting to note, that in the preparation of his profound work, "Index Generum Mammalium", T. S. Palmer found that the generic names of mammals have been derived mostly from the Greek (70%), a considerable number from native names (23%), but few from the Latin (5%) and even fewer (2%) from modern languages. This proportion does not obtain here, for of the 55 generic names in the writer's work on Utah mammals, 33 are from the Greek, 19 from the Latin, 2 from modern languages, and only one from native names.

Science necessarily has a universal nomenclature of its own, hence, for instance, the words *Antilocapra americana americana* are readily understood by the Chinese, Russian, or German mammalogists to refer to our prong-horn. The spelling is the same, the pronunciation the same, no matter what the language of a particular scientist may be.

Some of the generic names of Wasatch mammals speak for themselves; thus, for example, in the scientific designation of the red fox, *Vulpes fulva macroura* the genus *Vulpes* is readily seen to be the Latin word for "fox"; but the derivation of some other generic terms cannot be ascertained in any dictionary, and we are compelled to search in such works as those of Palmer, Trouessart's "Catalogus Mammalium", Waterhouse's "Index Zoologicus" and so on. To illustrate, take the word *Citellus* in *Citellus armatus*, the Wasatch "pot-gut" or armed spermophile; only in Palmer may we find that it is derived from the specific name of the type *Arctomys citellus*, Linnaeus, from Eurasia, which is the Latin name of the ziesel. Webster's calls it "new Latin" and the great Oxford is silent on it.

The genus *"Sorex"*, comprising our shrews, is derived from the Latin word *"sorex"* meaning a "shrew-mouse", as used by Pliny, the Roman naturalist of the time of Christ; likewise *"Euarctos"*, once the generic name for our black bear comes from the Greek word for "typical" plus "bear", while *Ursus*, which is now the generic name of all of our bears, except the polar, is derived from the Latin "ursus" meaning bear.

We have at least five genera of bats in these mountains. How did they get their names? *"Myotis"* of the little brown bats comes from the Greek words "mouse" and "ear", in reference to the large ears; *"Lasionycteris"*, the generic name of the silver haired bat is derived from the Greek words "hairy" and "bat"; *"Eptesicus"*, naming the big brown bat, is from the Greek "fly" plus "house"—house-flier—; *"Nycteris,"* describing the hoary bat, is simply the Greek word "bat"; and *"Corynorhinus"* designating the western big-eared bat, springs from the Greek words "club" plus "nose", referring to the club-shaped enlargment of the ridge between the eye and the nostril.

We must pursue this fascinating subject further by the hearth on the eve of tomorrow.

DECEMBER 9

Continuing our observations on the origins of the generic names of Utah mammals, we find that *"Lutra"*, describing the otter, comes from the Latin word *"lutra"* meaning otter; so also *"Martes"*, from the Latin for "marten"; *"Mustela"*, from the Latin for "weasel"; *"Felis"* of the mountain lion, from the Latin for "cat"; *"Canis"* of the coyotes and wolf, from the Latin for "dog"; and *"Marmota"* of the woodchuck from the Latin "marmot". Others are not so easy.

The generic name of the raccoon, *"Procyon"*, springs from two Greek words meaning "before" and "dog", while *"Bassariscus"*, naming the ring-tail, is the Greek word for "fox" with a diminutive suffix. *"Gulo"*, applied to the wolverine, is Latin for "glutton", in reference to the insatiable appetite of this animal; *"Mephitis"* (the skunk) is Latin for "foul smell"; the spotted skunk is given the generic name *"Spilogale"* from the Greek "spot" and "weasel".

"Taxidea", the generic name of the badger, on the other hand, is derived merely from the Greek "form", because it resembles the common form of badger in Europe. The gray fox's *"Urocyon"* consists of the Greek words "tail" and "dog", while *"Lynx"*, describing our wild cats and lynx, comes from the Greek word "lynx" which in turn is formed from the Greek "lamp", in reference to the bright eyes of these felines.

The word *"spermophilus"* is Greek for "seed" and "loving", and we see it often used. Thus once the rock squirrel's *"Otospermophilus"* means in Greek "ear" plus "seed" plus "loving", while the chestnut tailed spermophile's *"Callospermophilus"* merely prefixes the Greek word for "beautiful" to the "seed-loving". So also with the white-tailed spermophile's *"Ammospermophilus"* where the Greek word for "sand" is prefixed to "seed-loving", in reference to the sandy color of the pelage and the desert habitat of the animal. All of these squirrels are now listed under *Citellus*, which indicates that scientific nomenclature is almost constantly changing, a thing least desired by original taxonomists.

"Cynomys" (prairie dogs found east of the Wasatch) is interesting in that it is derived from the Greek words "dog" and "mouse", referring to the fact that these animals bark and sit like dogs but eat roots and grass like mice. *"Eutamias"* (chipmunks) is Greek for "typical" and "steward" in allusion to the storage habits of the munks. *"Sciurus"* of the chickarees, however, means literally in Greek "shade-tailed" in reference to the animal's tail when it sits. *"Glaucomys"* of the flying squirrels means "silvery" in Greek.

The embers of the hearth are dying, so we must await another evening to continue.

369

DECEMBER 10

Some mammalian generic names have very sensible derivations. Thus *"Thomomys"* of the pocket gophers consists of the Greek word for "heap" added to "mouse", in recognition of the earth heaps of the rodents' burrows. The kangaroo rats have the generic name *"Dipodomys"*, which in Greek means "two-footed mouse", in reference to the appareance of the animal as having only two feet. *"Perognathus"* (the pocket mice) is from the Greek "pouch" plus "jaw" referring to the extended cheek pouches. In similar fashion, *"Onychomys"* (grasshopper mice) is Greek "claw" plus "mouse", describing the long fossorial claws; *"Reithrodonotomys"* (harvest mice) consists of three Greek words: "channel", "tooth" "mouse", while *"Peromyscus"* (white footed mice) means in Greek: "pouch" and "little mouse" in reference to the small cheek pouches.

"Castor" (the beavers) in Latin means "beaver", just as *"Mus"* (house mouse) is Greek for "house mouse;" *"Lepus"* (jack rabbit) is Latin for "hare"; *"Cervus"* (elk) is Latin for deer or "stag"; *"Alces"* (moose) is Greek for "elk"; *"Ovis"* (mountain sheep) is Latin for "sheep"; and *"Bison"* (buffalo) is Latin for "wild ox". Such generic names are easy to understand.

"Neotoma", designating the wood rats, is, however, more difficult; it consists of the Greek words "new" and "to cut", in reference to the teeth, a new genus or rodents; the Greek word *"Microtus"* (the voles) consisting of "small" plus "ear" gives little indication of the animal intended; and we get even less from *"Lagurus"*, (pigmy vole) since in Greek it means "hare" plus "tail", from the rabbitlike tail of the little animal.

"Rattus" (black rat) from the Latin word meaning "rat" is self-explanatory; and the Greek word *"Erethizon"* (the porcupine) meaning "to irritate" is clear enough when we understand what the quills do.

The wonder is that mammalogists were able to apply distinct, and often picturesque, names to all the genera of mammals; but in most cases they did. Take the cottontail, for instance; it was given the generic designation of *"Sylvilagus"* which is a very pretty combination of the Greek words "wood" and "rabbit". The *"Odocoileus"* of the mule deer, which by the way should doubtless be spelled *"Odontocoileus"*, is the Greek word "tooth" plus "hollowed". The *"Antilocapra"* of the antelope comes from the Latin words "antelope" and "goat"—goat-antelope.

The two generic names of Utah mammals that are derived from other than Greek or Latin are *"Ochotona"* (pika), which is the Mongol word for pika, and *"Ondatra"* (muskrat) which is an Indian name for the muskrat, probably in the language of a Canadian tribe.

If you will put a new log on the hearth we shall divert to other subjects.

DECEMBER 11

Old and romantic, the apple trees of the orchard not only revive sweetest memories of zeeing waxwings and carefree hearts but also surprise us now with their weather-resisting inhabitants. We may kick the snow from the leaves and find fallen apples there hidden yet well preserved. It is a delightful experience, to tread the paths of those early years, when juncos seemed flitting and intimate, and chickadees astonished us at their indifference to cold. What is it that makes one bird really enjoy a blizzard and another perish in it? Not feathers and their number, perhaps, for even warblers seem as adequately gowned as kinglets, and a canyon wren as a chickadee. The answer, very likely, is food—the kind and abundance of food.

Even as we look upon that old tree whose apples we have always maintained are of such nutty sweetness as to constitute a sport worthy of the widest heralding, we are agreeably surprised by the presence of a Rocky Mountain hairy woodpecker (*Dendrocopos villosus monticola*) upon it. Pretty, white-breasted bird, one of the largest of the hairy kind, it has the habit of only vertical migration — from the mountainous regions of pine to the lowlands of boxelders and domesticated fruit.

There it goes to work now, not upward as one might expect but downward on the trunk of the old apple tree, tapping here and tapping there with its bill as it descends. Perhaps a certain sound, too faint for our less keen ears, indicates grub or no grub; and, if the intonation be just right, off the chip goes to expose the tender morsel esconsced there. Nature always provides a way!

On our return we detour for an hour or so along the dykes of Farmington bay. The road is pock-marked with pan-sized holes made by the travel of duck hunters. A score of the men are hidden in brown-weeded retreats; even on this cold day a hundred ducks are far out in the water, appearing black and white as they fly. They are too distant for us to be sure until we approach near enough to catch sight of a white spot between bill and eye when we exclaim "American golden-eye" (*Bucephala clangula americana*). Just then we got our reward—nine whistling swan (*Cyngus columbianus*) are contentedly feeding or sleeping far out there beyond shot or shell. What a sight! They look almost as large as pelicans; but their long graceful necks and black bills reveal their identity. This hour is truly a memory-gem.

DECEMBER 12

The American raven (*Corvux corax sinuatus*), a black bird as large again as the common crow, delights in desolate cliff-margined valleys where the juniper grows. We do not recall having seen it where water is plentiful, where deciduous trees are common, or where homes of men are numerous, except once in a rime-fogged meadow in zero weather.

Ravens are self-reliant, seclusive, resourceful, hardy, gregarious, and wary; but without much cause they are also somewhat repulsive to man, a condition due a little bit to Poe's "Raven" but much more to their obscene habit of subsisting on carrion. Rabbits killed by highway automobiles are especially pleasing to them, as they also are to to magpies; but dead sheep, horses, in fact, any decomposing carcasses appeal to them. Crickets, worms, grasshoppers, even an occasional spermophile, may enter into their fare; but they are so suspicious of the presence of man, and so unattractive to him, that intimate studies of their habits are seldom undertaken. To some extent the same is true of all the crows, jays and magpies, since they are all hoarse-voiced, wary and independent birds with inedible flesh and few pleasing habits. The jays are, of course, the most attractive members of the clan.

In making their nests, ravens select those inaccessible mountain cliffs upon which they habitually rely for protection, and lay their half dozen pea green eggs in a stick-laced mass lined with such soft material as wool, cattlehair, bark and moss.

We seldom see the crow (*Corvus brachyrhynchos hesperis*) in these valleys except in late autumn and winter. It is larger than the Brewer blackbird, smaller than the raven, but equally black. A few times we have watched crows in the meadows at the mouth of the Bear river, but, certainly, they are not so common in summer as the raven.

If it were possible we should like to get into the heart of a blackbird, a crow or a raven, to ascertain why they select their respective places of abode—the first, the paludal pasture; the next, the grassy plain, and the last, the wild juniper regions where scarcely fruit or flesh relieves the environment of starvation.

DECEMBER 13

It is a mere mite of a bird, prostrated and frozen on the snow, a western ruby crowned kinglet *Regulus calendula cineraceus*, a tiny fluff of gray with a ruby on its crown, a hardy inhabitant of the spruces and pines caught by storm on its way to southern Utah or even to distant Guatemala. Though its bill is notched at the tip, and the claws of its toes are sharp, long and curved, they seem inadequate to substantiate the name *Regulus*, given this genus by Cuvier in 1799 in his "Lecons d'anatomie comparee". *"Regulus"* means "petty king"; indeed a kinglet. That it is a miniature of birddom is apparent from its length of slightly less than four inches (its relative, the goldcrest (*Regulus cristatus*) is the smallest bird of England, being only three and a half inches long and weighing but five grams). Our own western marsh wren (*Telmatodytes palustris plesius*), and black-eared pygmy nuthatch (*Sitta pygmaea melanotis*) are about the same size; but our western golden crowned kinglet (*Regulus satrapa olivaceus*) is actually no greater in length than our black-chinned hummingbird (*Archilochus alexandri*). The smallest bird of the Wasatch mountains is the calliope hummingbird (*Stellula calliope*)—two and three quarter inches from tip of bill to tip of tail!

But to return to the kinglets. In Plutarch's "Moralia" praise is given the Spartans for fining their king, Archidamus, because he had married a woman of short stature and thus proposed to supply them not with kings but *kinglets*. Being forest-insect eaters content with the species of food that they find in the tranquil shelter of great conifers, the kinglets often brave Wasatch snows, but they are not little kings in disposition even if raptorial in their claw-construction. These sharp little toes are used to hold the bird to the rough bark of pines while it examines cracks and interstices for lice and other tidbits.

The western golden crowned kinglet is not an uncommon winter resident in these foothills and valleys, but like its cousin it is always a woodland sprite, a tender, useful feathered mite of the snow-robed evergreens. We marvel, not how strangely but how well science has applied its names.

In the afternoon we seek the gas bubbled hole filed with what looks like old blood, a cavity of the mud-laden Farmington bay slough. We cast a roped bucket into those gruesome waters; we fill a gallon jug— it is a bucket of water chemically colored like a bucket of blood. The explanation is that once a gas well was drilled there, and the abandoned iron pipe tinctured the water.

DECEMBER 14

Every time we come upon a mountain lion's (*Felix concolor hippolestes*) footprints in soft snow we involuntarily begin to reflect upon the astonishing number of names by which this elusive animal has been known in North America. "Cougar", "panther", and "puma" are fairly common, despite the fact that to many even those names refer to three different animals; and in the West, where "mountain lion" and "cougar" are commonly used, "panther" is not heard at all. To these, however, we may add the following names given to this great cat in various parts of the country: "catamount", "wildcat", "American lion", "California lion", "silver lion", "mountain devil", "mountain demon", "mountain tiger" (its young does have spots), "mountain cat", "purple panther", "tiger", "lion", "deer tiger", "deer-killer", "pampas-cat", "Mexican lion", "Indian devil", "red tiger", "bender" (among Pennsylvania Germans), "brown tiger", "poltroon tiger", "sneak-cat", "mountain screamer", "Rocky mountain lion", "black puma", "kingcat", "varmint" and "catomountain".

We have assembled seventeen names by which it is known in South America, and twenty two, among the North American Indians.

The word "puma", the native Peruvian appellation for this many-named animal, appeared in English writings as early as 1783; it is the name generally used by scientists. "Cougar", a word derived from the French "couguar", is an adaptation made by Buffon from the native Brazilian name "cuguacuarana".

Since this animal is in no sense comparable in size, courage and ferocity with the lion of Africa or the tiger of India, it is best to stick by its real names, "puma" and "cougar". The smaller panther or leopard of India or Africa is one of the most dangerous mammals in the world.

One cold winter night many years ago a cougar entered a sheep pen a few miles from home and jumped over the eight foot board fence with a grown ewe in its jaws. The feat was the talk of the village next day.

So elusive is this great cat, so nocturnal when near the camps or habitations of man, that in all our rambles in the mountains we have only once come upon one, wild and unpursued, in the daytime; but it was but a few yards away. Merely to tree the mountain lion with hounds and then to shoot it down, is, as we have long since concluded, an experience almost bereft of information concerning its habits, which must be learned chiefly from the lonely sheepherder.

DECEMBER 15

One of the fairly common Wasatch mammals is the Rocky mountain marten (*Martes caurina origenes*), a wood-brown member of the weasel family, about two feet long, a close relative of the mink, weasel, wolverine, fisher and otter, but, unlike the weasel and the mink in that it inhabits the remotest part of the coniferous forests, avoiding, if possible, the very sight or trace of man. We have had several brought to our attention from the Brighton region, where they were evidently subsisting on those inhabitants of high rock slides, the pikas; but they are much more frequently seen along the head waters of the Provo river and in the Uinta mountains generally.

Though martens belong to a blood-thirsty tribe and are able equally to chase a squirrel from pine limb to pine limb to its doom, or to follow by scent a rabbit to a similar certain end, they are not so liable to kill wantonly and beyond their needs as are the weasels.

They favor the fallen pine, the rocky ledge and the hollow tree, in any of which they may make nests of leaves, moss and grass, and bring forth their helpless half dozen young in April or May. In winter their broad, well-furred feet permit them to pursue rabbits in even the deepest snow, and, being inhabitants of the lonely, high snow-feathered wilderness, they have but few enemies, except perhaps an occasional venturesome horned owl, which in killing may itself be destroyed by unlocking fangs.

The fur of a marten is not only longer than that of a mink but also the tail is fuller, hence these animals are eagerly sought by those trappers who appreciate the value of such a prize. Not only that, but if one care to go into the high country, where among the conifers such animals as pikas, mice, wood rats, pine squirrels, and chipmunks abound, he may find the marten an easy prey to his trap, baited perhaps with a rodent or a grouse feather.

Some day fur-growers will master the needs of these seclusive forest dwellers, and, if so, marten furs may take their place among the obtainable luxuries of the world.

It is surprising how snug an animal's den may be under the wide-spreading limbs of a spruce heavily laden and a quarter buried by snow, and how the billows and mounds of outside snow over hill and dale become encrusted so that in the moonlight the marten may lope in hunting ease;—aye, it is interesting how the forbidding places of the world have many refuges of comfort if we but knew them.

DECEMBER 16

When at noontime a warming sun melts the thinning snow from a patch of lawn, hungry domestic sparrows swarm upon the tender grass and somehow find a meal from what they once disdained. Adaptable man-loving birds, blessed by a Biblical promise of immortality, they resist the southward avian urge of fall and winter, and wherever human beings dwell in temperate regions fight valiantly to share their food. Beggars and tramps that they are, they have fortitude, self-reliance, resourcefulness and an unswerving hope. Like Schubert they are ugly, miserably poor and uninteresting, but unlike him, who at thirteen gave us Leichen fantasie they have not an even unrecognized power of song. Such is the law of compensation, that even the despised among men may possess characteristics worthy of praise.

Up in the mountains the rutting season of madness, battling and desire being over now, mule deer are forgetting their differences and gathering in peaceful herds consisting of males, females and fawns, all willing to browse under the protective watchfulness of the general assemblage. We do not observe that the deer post sentinels as do the Canada geese, and omnipresent magpies, but we often notice that an old doe or buck seems more alert than the others to strange sounds.

Two red shafted flickers fly to the house fence before us. They are dirty and sooty, as if having spent cold nights near chimneys and dusty holes; and though apparently well, they excite our curiosity concerning where they find edible things. The berry of the Boston ivy, the discarded bit of the garbage pail, the succulent morsel from fish pond and sun-dripped wall. Is this the answer?

Black and dreary is the railroad flag stop in winter. With no shelter one nearly perishes with the chilling wind, and features of nature otherwise attractive are worthy of but a shivering place. No birds flit in the weeded and snow-beaten wayside, and the brook that ordinarily trickles along the field-border is a frozen channel of icy silence.

The hair of horses, all but abandoned in the snow-crusted fields, stands out like pins coated with rime, and the hungry animals walk along the wire fences hoping for bales of hay that too seldom arrive. Once in a decade a sub-zero blizzard comes so severe that it freezes a horse or a cow while yet the animal stands; and the morning light reveals the victim as a ghostlike block of ice on legs with eyes like balls of glass! Ugh! We never want to see that again.

DECEMBER 17

That handsome little falcon, the sparrow hawk (*Falco sparverius sparverius*), is resident in these mountains. Many of them endure the winters of our valleys, especially where they can loiter about the corrals and granaries of the farmers and take a regular toll of English sparrows, which habitually congregate there. Thus it is interesting in snow-drowned winter to observe a hundred sparrows chirping vociferously and gleaning bits from a sunny poultry and cattle yard.; to see them flee in terror and death-like silence as a sparrow hawk plummets from apparently nowhere with the swiftness of lightning down upon one of their number, tearing open the victim's skull with the naillike impact of its strong bill, and flying off with the trembling body, all with appalling precision and speed.

Nevertheless, despite its erroneous name (it is more closely related to the kestrel than to the European sparrow-hawk), it eats sparrows and other birds chiefly when snow cloaks the landscape, and depends on grasshoppers, crickets, small snakes and lizards most of the other time.

Not only is the female sparrow hawk larger than the male but she is also more belligerent and daring. Even when the two are fledglings in a nest, at which time the sexes may be distinguished by the colors of their plumages, the little female fights an intruder while the male cowers in a far corner. Nesting, by the way, occurs here from about May first to July first, as weather and other factors may determine, and the site may vary from an old flicker hole to a magpie's deserted nest.

Courageous enough to fight the ruthless sharp-shinned hawk, playful enough to dash in fun about an apprehensive red-shafted flicker, beautiful enough in form of body and color markings of plumage to win the admiration of all observers of the raptors, the sparrow hawk is a delight to the farmer, a charming visitor on the parapets of tall buildings, a favorite of ornithologists, and a beneficial inhabitant of the woods. Its plumage is as soft as down; its colors as pretty as a flower; and its ways as jaunty as a schoolgirl skipping on her way home.

> Throughout this world of multiform desire
> An animal may kill or live on seed.
> This one is mild, the other full of fire,
> And no one knows why thus it was decreed.

DECEMBER 18

After many years experience as montivagants (they who wander on the mountains), we have concluded, that among the rarest and most diabolical of wild mammals known to us is the wolverine (*Gulo luscus*), that peculiar glutton which on account of its size, posture and chestnut side-stripes is not inaptly called a "skunk-bear", as if indeed it were a hybrid of those two animals, whereas in truth it is related more closely to the minks, otters and weasels. No wild inhabitant of the snowlands is more fieldish when cornered, none more uncanny in its molestation of traps and the destruction of bait We know that it has occasionally been taken in the higher Wasatch, infrequently it is true and not nearly so often as in the lofty Uintas, which provide its favorite environs of unvisited timber. Brigham Spencer took one on the Aquarius Plateau and Lynn Williams saw one on White mountain, both at the southern extremity of the Wasatch; they are friends who gave us details. A century ago it was common in the Wasatch.

When an animal weighing not over thirty five to forty pounds is so vicious, uncompromising and devilish in encounter as to cause one of our friends, noted for his hunting of big game, to exclaim that he would rather meet a grizzly than a wolverine, we must admit this mammal's unrelenting prowess; and when a trapper is so annoyed by its mysterious cleverness in springing traps and stealing bait that he abandons his line as if the place were bewitched, we must acknowledge intelligence far superior to that of the usual animal ken.

We have no desire to glorify the wolverine, rather, to impress the facts of its weird capability and personality. Indians of the far north regard its pelt as the greatest prize of all, perhaps not without some superstitious belief in the efficacy of its possession, for otherwise their sacrifice to get it cannot be explained; but we of the southern extremity of its range know little of such happenings.

Wolverines pair in March, build a caverned nest of dried leaves, and in either May or June give birth to from two to five young. The adults are great travellers, ranging over territory fifty miles or more across. They gnaw through cabin logs a foot in diameter, even though their jaws bleed; and take everything they can carry away to their caches, where they befoul them with their fetid glandular secretions. Even a black bear hesitates to tackle a wolverine in possession of a desired meal; indeed, a wolverine has been known to kill a black bear by springing from a tree down upon the bear's neck and fastening its fangs into the victim's vertebrae.

One must not only visit among, but sojourn in the high coniferous forests even to glimpse the strange visitors there; but when he has the patience to do so he has the feeling of being close to primality, the thought that a pristine cave man may after all emerge with hairy strength from yonder labyrinthined cavern.

DECEMBER 19

The approach of death is not unlike the tightening grip of hoary winter, yet elderly people with whom we have conversed on the subject have anticipated it with a resignation amounting almost to insouciance. If well, they have seemed not to care about the mere accumulation of years; indeed, they have argued with good reason that the dangers of modern life no longer make age especially indicative of the approaching end. Many of them retain their good nature and long cherished ambitions until the very last; and, in this respect, there is only this difference between youth and age—youth plans for the future; age often relives only the past. Age also has this happy characteristic—it believes its ways of life from childhood up have been the best, indeed, indubitiably superior to those of modern days. Age disdains change and stubbornly prefers the warped old chair to the new one.

Nature expresses itself in many ways; among trees, such as the conifers, the aged monarch retains its supremacy until the very parchment of its leaves, and even long after death its tall dry skeleton sometimes overwhelms its younger neighbors. Only when a terrific breeze at last prostrates its trunk to the ground do moisture, mold and worms give it the ignominy of disintegration. Many such a king have we sat upon, and noted ant bed or grass clump where once was mighty branch.

Among mammals the aged male is often cast into solitude; but the female, as among the geese, if often revered for her wisdom. Apparently young mammals never cease to regard the aged male as potential competition. For instance solitary old bison bulls, ill-tempered and remorseful, usually outskirting the main herd, fight alone such predatory enemies as pester them, until their toughened hides are torn and they themselves at last succumb.

Eskimos desert their aged ancestors far out on the frozen ice, to endure a slow but peaceful death; but this action is prompted by lack of food, not by sex. Among other humans the old folks of the orient are much pampered and revered, a duty of treatment devolving especially upon the eldest son.

Death even among elderly people is never quite comprehended until it actually is about to occur; and perhaps, after all that is the better way.

DECEMBER 20

Scores of times we have participated in organized rabbit-hunts on the sagelands about the Great Salt Lake, often with only three or four friends, sometimes with three or four hundred hunters accommodated by an entire railway train. It has even been our good fortune to be "high man" on one occasion, and to see a railway express car half filled with frozen and meaty "jacks". Since the line, consisting of hunters and farmers' bob-sleighs, is often several miles long, a lucky hunter is he who through the topography of the ground chances to be where the rabbits attempt to funnel through; at least such was our experience on the day of the score.

Though these desert jack rabbits (*Lepus californicus deserticola*) are very destructive to farm crops and we therefore have no compunction over killing them for distribution to those who enjoy them as food, it is often rather pitiful to hear the squeal of a wounded jack upon the approach of the hunter. It is the animal's expression of helplessness and despair; for one chased to its death by a coyote within fifty yards of us once uttered no sound as it dodged back and forth. Without wound there is always hope.

During recent years we have been wary about handling jack rabbits; for, like sage hens, coyotes and other inhabitants of the sagelands, they are sometimes carriers of the dreaded tularemia caused by a microorganism (*Pasteurella tularensis*).

Since the divided upper lip, long ears and hind legs of a jack rabbit mark it as a true hare, the word "hare" is seldom heard in these mountains. Common parlance uses the term "jack rabbit" or "cottontail". The cottontail is however a true rabbit. It is generally agreed among mammalogists that rabbits burrow in the ground and bring forth naked blind young, while hares use some kind of surface form and have young with eyes open and with thick coverings of fur.

In these mountains above eight thousand feet we sometimes are fortunate enough to glimpse the Rocky Mountain snowshoe rabbit (*Lepus bairdii bairdii*), which is noted for the extraordinary size of its feet. Nature steps in and gives feet of astonishing size to this rabbit's chief enemy, the Canada lynx; so here again the law of balance and compensation prevails. Nature always provides some enemy of everything that walks, crawls, swims or flies.

The snowshoe is an unsociable, seclusive rabbit, fond of dense mountain labyrinths and accustomed to feed more in the light of the moon than the sun. When snow is mounded high and all the evergreens are heavily laden with white, aye, when every twig is laced with enduring rime, it manages somehow to nip a willow bud or find some blades of dry grass beneath the limbed canopies that enrivon its home.

DECEMBER 21

As we walk by the now frozen marshes and see neither of those common waders, the avocet or the black-necked stilt, we are prompted to recollect the dignified appearance of this latter bird as we have seen it standing on its long legs in shallow alkaline water. Though it belongs to the family *Recurvirostridae* it has a straight, slender, only slightly upturned bill, whereas the bill of the avocet is distinctly recurved, the only bill strongly so directed among birds hereabout.

What we started to observe, however, is that the black-necked stilt is here sometimes called an "elder", a novel epithet that takes us to a description of its appearance. It is a bird about fifteen inches long with extravagantly extended stilt-like legs of rose pink tint. Its long pointed bill is black but its forehead, under half of neck and entire lower plumage are immaculate white. Yet note this: its hindleg, hindneck, back scapulars and wings are uniform black with only a slight greenish blue gloss. This contrast gives it a rather solemn and dignified appearance; and, since it is the custom of some missionaries and elders to wear white shirts and black Prince Albert coats, the name "elder" is understandable. In many places in the United States the bird is called "the lawyer" in obvious recognition of the dignity of that profession, especially of judges who don the black mantle when in court, a vanity not much indulged in this country except by the Supreme Court and by some state courts who do not realize that garb can add nothing to brilliancy of intellect and the administration of justice.

The avocet is sometimes erroneously called "the lawyer bird"; but its cinnamon coloration suggests neither a lawyer, priest nor nun. "Bluelegs" is more apt for it; at any rate, whenever we watch the two birds feeding side by side we fancy the avocet sweeps slightly with its recurved bill whereas the stilt nips, points and takes with the delicate precision required of the legal profession.

As winter draws nigh the dreary and frozen wastes of Farmington bay seem strange without the piercing, almost hysteric cry of the avocet. It is little wonder that the European counterparts of these apprehensive waders are sometimes in Scotland called "yelpers", for such is the wide adaptability of words descriptive of the wildwoods.

Plant Synonomy

<table>
<tr><td>OLD</td><td>NEW</td></tr>
</table>

OLD	NEW
Blister Pine	White Fir, *Abies concolor*
Black Pine	Lodgepole Pine, *Pinus contorta*
Niggerheads	Western Coneflowers, *rudbeckia occidentalis*
Red Pine	Douglas Fir, *Pseudotsuga menziesii*
Utah White Oak	Gambel Oak, Scrub Oak, *Quercus gambellii*
Acer interium	*Acer negundo*, Water Ash, Box Elder
Artemisia gnaphilodes	*Artemisia ludoviciana*, Louisianna Wormwood, Ludwig's Sage
Berberis aquifolium	*Mahonia aquifolium*, Shrubby Oregon Grape
Berberis repens	*Mahonia repens*, Creeping Oregon Grape
Brodiaea douglasi	*Triteleia grandiflora*, Wild Blue Hyacinth
Claytonia rosea	*Claytonia lanceolata*, Spring Beauty
Delphinium bicolor	
D. menziesii	*D. nuttallianum*, Nelson Larkspur
Draba raptans micrantha	*Draba reptans micrantha*, Dwarf draba
Echinocereus fendleri	*E. ???*, Purple Torch Hedgehog Cactus
Epilobium paniculatum	*Epilobium brachycarpum*, Autumn Willowherb
Equisetum hiemale	*Equisetum hyemale*, Common Scouring Rush
Erysimum capitatum	*Erysimum asperum*, Western Wallflower
Fragaria bracteata	*Fragaria vesca*, Wild Strawberry
F. glauca	*F. virginiana*, Mountain Stawberry

Geranium fremontii	*Geranium viscossissimum*, Sticky Geranium
Hedysarum pubulare	*Hedysarum boreale*, Northern Sweetvetch
Lappula redowskii	
occidentalis	*Lappula ???*, Western Stickseed
Lathyrus utahensis	*Lathyrus pauciflorus*, Utah Sweetpea
Lithospermum	
angustifolium	*Lithospermum*
Lomatium simplex	*Lomatium scabrum*, Rough Lomatium
Lupinuslaxiflorus	*Lupinus caudatus*, Spurred Lupine
Malvastrum coccineum	*Sphaeralcea coccinea*, Common Globemallow
Mertensia albicaulis	*Mertensia ???*
M. dispersa	*M. ???*
M. foliosa	*M. ???*
M. latifolia	*M. ???*
Pinus murrayana	*Pinus contorta*, Lodgepole Pine
Pseudotsuga taxifolia	*Pseudotsuga menziesii*, Douglas Fir
Radicula nasturtium-	
aquaticum	*Nasturtium officinale*, Water Cress
Sambucus glauca	*Sambucus caerulea*, Blue Elderberry
Salix caudata	
Smilacina amplexicaulis	*Smilacina racemosa*, False Solomon-Seal
S. sessilifolia	*S. stellata*, Wild Lily of the Valley
Tellima parviflora	*Lithophragma parviflora*, Smallflower Woodlandstar
Thlaspi coloradense	*Thlaspi montanum*, Wild Candytuft, Penny-Cress
T. glaucum	*T. montanum*, Wild Candy Tuft, Penny-Cress
Thelypodium torulosum	*Thelypodiopsis saggitata*, Thelypodiopsis
Viola palustris	*Viola canadensis*, Canadian Violet
Viola venosa	*Viola purpurea*, Yellow Violet

About the Author

CLAUDE T. BARNES

lawyer, business man, mammalogist, ornithologist, poet, biographer, essayist, philosopher.

Born, Kaysville, Utah; son of John R. and Emily Stewart Barnes. Married Annie Elizabeth Knowlton, dec'd.; children: Stuart K. Barnes (see WHO'S WHO), Kathleen, dec'd. (Mrs. Eugene M. Zuckert, see WHO'S WHO).

Educated, University of Utah, University of Chicago, University of Michigan. Member of the Utah Bar, the Bar of the Supreme Court of the U. S., and Federal bars. Defense attorney in world-famous polygamy cases of 1944.

Speaker for Republican National Committee, 1938-44. Declined Rep. designation of nomination for United States Senator from Utah in 1944.

Long time President of John R. Barnes Co. (farming), Barnes Realty Co. (real estate); and director Barnes Banking Co. and Kaysville Canning Corp.

Charter member American Society of Mammalogists; charter mem. Society for the Study of Evolution; hon. life mem. Am. Ornithologists' Union; first President Utah Audubon Soc.; fellow Zoological Soc. of London; fellow Philosophical Soc. of England; hon. fellow Eugene Field Soc.

Some of his books:

Mammals of Utah (for Univ. of Utah)
Utah Mammals (for Univ. of Utah)
The Wending Year (poetry)
The Grim Years (biography)
Toward the Eternal (biography)
The Duration of Mind (philosophy)
Some Arts of Living (essays)
The Natural History of a Wasatch Spring
The Natural History of a Wasatch Summer
The Natural History of a Wasatch Autumn